RHODA:
Her First Ninety Years

RHODA:
Her First Ninety Years

෴

A Memoir

by

Rhoda Curtis

ISBN 1-4196-6607-X

Book Design and Layout by Deo Arellano
Cover Painting by Aaron Stell
Back Cover Photo by Karen

Printed in the U.S.A.

Published by BookSurge
www.booksurge.com

DEDICATION

⟶

To my ancestors;
To my immediate and extended family;
To Ric, Remi, Ade, and Aba;
To my Support Group, members of which range far and wide;
To my teachers and mentors;
To my students, from whom I have learned so much.

TABLE OF CONTENTS

∽

Introduction and Acknowledgments

"A woman born in the Year of the Horse is difficult to ride."
(A Chinese Proverb)

A S A WOMAN BORN IN THE YEAR OF THE HORSE, 1918, looking back over more than eight decades of a life filled with six career changes, three marriages and divorces, many grand adventures, shot through entirely with streaks of independence and risk-taking, I wondered whether that Chinese proverb had some application to me. I used to think it was silly and sexist; now I think it's amusing.

Having kept many journals, beginning in my early teens, I found those writings, plus notes on small pieces of paper tucked away in odd places, valuable resource material. I started assembling that material in 2000, and want to thank Cathy Miller, a writing instructor at UC Berkeley, now at San Jose State University, and a founding member of Wild Writing Women, for prodding me to get started. Judith Barrington and a couple of weeks at the Flight of the Mind retreat in Oregon pushed me further, and writing classes with Monza Naff sent me into outer space. Thanks to all of you, including everyone in the Redwood Writers Group, Jennifer Privateer, Laura Zulch-Hays, and everyone else who read the manuscript as it developed.

I'm glad I followed the advice I gave to the students in my own classes: Writing is rewriting, as long as it takes, and as many versions as necessary. I hope you find reading this memoir as engaging and enlightening as I found in writing it.

— Rhoda Curtis

Pa   Ma

My Siblings (6 years before I was born):
Back row: Jeanne, Irene, Sara;
Front row: Fay, Al

Chapter One:
From Braila to Chicago

⌒

GROWING UP IN A FAMILY where I was the youngest (and unwanted child) with four older siblings meant that I learned early the art of single-minded manipulation. My sister Fay, nine and a half years older than I, told me that Ma didn't want any of her children except Sara, the eldest in our family, but that information did nothing to change my feelings of rejection as I was growing up.

I could see for myself that Ma was a passionate woman, and it must have been hard for her to say "no" to my father. My sister Sara was nineteen when I was born, Jeanne was fifteen (there had been another sister, Irene, who had died at the age of fourteen), Al was twelve, and Fay was nine. Pa was affectionate and loving, especially toward me. I'd sit on the edge of the claw-footed tub in the bathroom while he soaped his face, sharpened his straightedge razor on his leather strop, and carefully shaved around his magnificent red handlebar mustache. I inhaled deeply the bay rum with which he patted his face, and whipped a towel around to cool it after he was finished. He'd wax his mustache and glance down at me, crinkling up his blue eyes in a conspiratorial smile. He always hummed or sang during this process, and I loved to share that time with him.

My father also warmed my long underwear on the radiator in the dining room, so that when I came out of the bathroom on a cold winter morning, I would be able to step into warm and cozy long johns. Those are things that hang on in my memory, and warm me as I remember them.

Many stories circulated around the family about how my parents got together, and I recently acquired a ceramic pitcher from my sister Fay, which she had been hanging onto for seventy years. Thinking about that pitcher, I've created a story about how things might have happened between my mother and my father. It's a matter of piecing together stories I heard, combined with my own memories of their life together while I was growing up.

Bucharest, Romania, 1869, was called the "Paris of the Balkans." My father, who was born in Bucharest that year, used to say, "When it rains in Paris, people in Bucharest put up their umbrellas." Bucharest was a thriving metropolitan city, a center of commerce, art, literature, and elegant salons where French was the language of choice. My father, Mayer Kurtzbond, and his family were working-class Jews, and he grew up under moderately tolerant laws. Laws against Jews in Romania went back and forth between moderate tolerance and aggressively restrictive. The years between 1869 and 1895 were moderately tolerant.

During those years Jews had an accepted, limited place as merchants and shopkeepers; Jewish boys were allowed to learn a trade. The laws of Romania allowed one Jewish boy in each ghetto to compete for acceptance to the local *gymnasium* (high school), provided the parents could afford the fees, and the child could pass the entrance exam. Apparently my grandparents had the money, because my father competed and won. After graduating from the *gymnasium*, my father became a tinsmith, and grew up to be a handsome redhead with a mind of his own. He had a lush handlebar mustache, and he loved to dance, sing, and tell stories. I don't know how he did it, but he managed to avoid marriage with several eligible young women his parents tried to match him up with. By 1897, when Mayer was twenty-eight, he was a sought-after bachelor. That year he went to Braila to attend the wedding of a cousin, and that's where he met Ruth Hoffman.

Ruth Esther Hoffman, my mother, was born in Braila, a small shetl on the outskirts of Bucharest in 1879. Ruth Esther was the fourth daughter of an impoverished widow, and her village was hardscrabble poor. Mayer's eye fell on the slim, dark-eyed, dark-haired beautiful sister of the bride and invited her to dance a polka. Mayer's parents looked on in alarm as their handsome son danced with no one else but Ruth Esther Hoffman, who was nineteen and obviously had no dowry. She worked as a dressmaker in the town.

In 1898 and 1899 anti-Semitic agitation against the Jews intensified, and all opportunities to work disappeared. It became against the law to employ Jews as carpenters, construction workers, cobblers, and tinsmiths. Jews began to leave Romania. A group of Jews from Braila who joined the Fusgeyers (those who travel on foot) were unemployed craftsmen who became traveling actors, singers, performers. They decided to walk across Europe and get onto a ship for any country that would accept them—Australia, Canada or America. They traveled from small town to small town, putting on performances, earning their living as they went. When you don't have any money, you walk, and that's what those Jews from Braila did.

However, Mayer's brother Irving had enough money to get to Marseilles in 1897, and from there he made it to Minneapolis by the time Ruth and Mayer married in 1898, in a simple ceremony. They went to Vienna on their honeymoon and that is where they bought the ceramic pitcher I still have. That pitcher, passed down to me from Fay, is decorated with elaborate carvings of roses, in gold, around the lip of the pitcher, and faded letters spell out "Souvenir d'Wien 1898" encircled by more carved pink roses on a vine.

After the wedding, Mayer's parents made room for the newlyweds in their house in Bucharest, where Ruth became the unpaid domestic servant and chafed under her mother-in-law's orders. My sister Sara was born in March, 1899, and Ruth began a campaign to get out of Romania. From all the stories I heard about my parents' lives in Romania, I can imagine their voices, my mother's insistent and persistent, my father's patient and conciliatory.

"Mayer, can't we go to America? Irving and Sophie live in Minneapolis. We get letters from Irving all the time. I'll die if I have to live like this much longer. Please, Mayer, try."

Mayer, anxious to placate his new bride, responded, "Tell you what I'll do. When I go to Marseilles next week, I'll talk to the union men there, and find out about ships going to America."

The Socialist union my father belonged to at the end of the nineteenth century was one of the few worker organizations that admitted Jews. It was built on the model of fifteenth century guilds, and my father was a tinsmith, a sheet metal worker in today's designation, who also made pots and pans. He was a talented organizer and a respected member of the union. My father was also a good talker.

When Mayer returned to Bucharest, he was in a triumphant mood. He had lined up a job and a place for them to stay in Marseilles. Ruth, thrilled, offered to get work as a seamstress in a dressmaking shop. Mayer told her that he had put their names on a list, and that all they had to do was to wait for a place on a ship going to Canada. My uncle Irving had sent them a letter, advising them to come to Ontario, from which it would be easier for them to come across the U.S./Canadian border. Better than New York, he said.

Mayer told his mother and father that he had a better job in Marseilles than in Bucharest, feeling sure they would agree to let my parents go. He didn't say anything about going to America. In all the stories my parents told about leaving Romania, they were never specific about the leaving. What I do know is that my mother packed her silver candlesticks, her crocheted table cover, and the souvenir pitcher she had bought on her honeymoon in Vienna. At the end of two weeks, they were ready, and moved to Marseilles in August 1899, with Sara. Five months later, in January 1900, they made it onto a freighter bound for Montreal. They traveled in steerage, and Mayer was seasick most of the time, but Ruth managed to find a place for them to sleep near the steps leading to the deck, so that every time the hatch was opened, there was a breath of fresh air for them. Sara was ten months old, and quickly captivated one of the stewards, who slipped them leftovers from the crew's mess.

My father told us the story of Irving meeting them in the immigration shed at the U.S./Canadian border. "My brother Irving said to me, 'Listen, Mayer, you have to change your name.' I said to him, 'Why? I like our name.' He gave me some cockamamie story about our name, Kurtzbond being too long, and how he changed his name to Curshan. Well, I didn't like Curshan, and I told him so! Irving got upset with me, told me not to hold up the line, there were lots of people like us with bundles and baskets waiting to get through. So I pointed to a Curtiss candy bar sign, and said, 'That's my name.'"

Every time my father told me that story, I laughed. The immigration officer left off the final "s"—but that was how I ended up with a last name like Curtis rather than Kurtzbond. That story has given me a sense of belonging with every other immigrant who's had to change his name in order to get past an immigration officer gatekeeper.

My father, mother, and sister Sara moved to Minneapolis, where they lived with Aunt Sophie and Uncle Irving. The Curshans' white, wooden frame house was part of a neighborhood of similar houses, evenly spaced, with sloping green lawns in front, neatly tended yards in the back. No fences, the houses had front and back porches, the back ones screened to protect against summer bugs. A pleasant, middle-class neighborhood, it had a quiet settledness about it.

Irving was a prosperous pharmacist, and both Irving and Sophie, as members of their local Orthodox synagogue, had become respectable members of their new neighborhood. My sister Irene was born in April, 1901, and Sophie, childless, adored her.

My mother was restless, wanting a place of her own. Her pattern was to nag and nag, always wanting my father to "move up." Just as she had pursued her campaign to get them out of Romania, Ruth began to talk about "opportunities" in America.

"Look at Irving," she said. "He's got a business, he's got a house, why can't we find some place for us to live by ourselves? Isn't there a union in Minneapolis? Ask Irving, Mayer, find out." I heard this kind of prodding many times during my childhood. My mother kept a close eye on the finances, demanding that my father turn over his weekly checks so that she could budget the income. She didn't trust my singing, cheerful father to be as careful with money as she was.

One evening, my father asked his brother if he had any connections to the local workers' union. Uncle Irving recoiled in horror. He was a druggist, and was not interested in politics. He felt his younger brother was a radical, and thought that all unions were full of communists. My father, an ardent supporter of the union that helped bring him and his family to America, realized that Minneapolis was not the place for him. According to my mother, Mayer went down to Industrial Workers of the World headquarters in St.

Paul, and found out that the steel mills in Gary, Indiana were hiring. So my parents moved to Gary.

Finding work as a sheet metal worker, my father rose to the position of foreman within a year. Since they now had two children, my mother tried to get my father to give up organizing. My mother used to interrupt the story at this point, saying, "I told him he didn't have to be such a big shot, he was already making good money, he could give it up. Think about me and the children, I used to say to him."

At this point, my father looked at my mother. He addressed her by his pet name for her: "Ruchella, you still don't know anything about it. I had to go, I couldn't let them down. Besides, you don't know how big corporations cheat the workers. They try to break the unions, hire new guys, and then they tell everybody business is bad and they have to lay off workers. Then they lay off only the union workers. The workers have to strike." My mother shrugged.

My father continued, "When I went to the meeting, we were told that the bosses had already hired strikebreakers, to break the union. The leaders warned us that the goons would probably come after us, and especially they warned me. All the men decided to strike. When the meeting was over, four of my best friends came over to where I was sitting and we planned what to do. They said to me, 'Listen Mayer, go home, pack up, and be ready to go any time. There's a train for Chicago every three hours. We'll park a car in the alley, and get you to the train station. Just be ready.' I have to tell you I was worried. I came home, and I told your mother that we had to move. I knew she wouldn't like it." My mother nodded, her mouth a tight line, remembering. "I told her we would probably go to Chicago."

My father continued, "There was a strike call Friday. Three of the guys came over on Saturday and we barricaded the front door. One guy parked his car in the alley, and we all sat in the dark house waiting, just waiting. Saturday night the vigilantes came after us. When we heard the pounding on the front door, we picked up the children and ran out the back door. Our union friends barricaded the front door, while we piled into the waiting car in the alley, and raced to the train station."

I was eleven years old, listening raptly to my beloved father.

"Were you scared?"

"Of course," my father sighed. "I didn't think this would happen in America."

"And then what happened?"

"When we got to Chicago, we went immediately to a union 'safe' house on the west side." At that point, my mother came back into the dining room. "What a dump!" she said. "Three families crowded into a small flat. I pushed Mayer into finding a flat we could afford. He finally found one on Polk Street, near Kedzie Avenue, also on the west side. That's where Jeanne, Al and Fay were born."

My brother told me about living on Polk Street. It was a Jewish neighborhood, a ghetto without walls. My brother Al told me that he often ran through a hail of stones, sometimes cutting through back alleys, leaping over fences. My brother and sisters, Al, Jeanne, and Fay were born between 1901 and 1909, and everything I have learned about Ruth Esther Hoffman Curtis tells me that she resented every pregnancy except the first one, Sara.

My mother always said she wanted some kind of independence, a small shop of her own, a dressmaking or alteration shop, but there was never enough money to put a down payment on a location. Sometimes I saw her pick up the small engraved ceramic pitcher they had bought in Vienna in 1898, contemplate it, and then put it down. Perhaps she was wondering how she had ended up with five children, struggling to make ends meet, resentful that the charming man she married was not such a "good provider." On the other hand, she might also have thought that she could push him to provide a life similar to Sophie's.

My father was a strong union man, and never saw himself as an entrepreneur. But on one of his trips to the union hall, he met a roofer named Kaplan, and Kaplan persuaded my father to go into business with him. There was very little work for tinsmiths or metal workers in Chicago at that time, and so, against his will, my father became an independent contractor in the roofing business. Kaplan, his partner, owned the truck. Tinsmithing and metalworking are relatively clean jobs; roofing is not. My father had to adjust to being a businessman, plus doing a dirty job he hated. However, he stuck with it, continued to vote the Socialist ticket, made wine, sang lustily at family celebrations, and in general was as optimistic as Ruth was pessimistic. For my father the cup was always half-full, for Ruth it was half-empty.

When Ruth complained about the small amount of money Mayer brought home every week, my father would shrug, and respond that it was better than nothing. "Be grateful for small favors," he would say.

I remember how my father insisted on making wine. Every autumn, beginning in September, my mother and father sat in the kitchen of our second-floor flat with a large tin tub wedged between their knees. There they sat, hour after hour, squeezing black Michigan Concord grapes by hand. They squeezed the grapes through cheesecloth, and the flat was full of the smell of fermenting grapes, clouds of gnats everywhere. My father relished the process, singing lustily as he squeezed. My mother approached the task grimly, as if she did just because she had to. Pouring the juice through a funnel into gallon jugs, my father then carried the jugs down the back steps into the cellar, three flights down. It was a long, arduous process. Once in the cellar, my father transferred the juice into three barrels, one which would become strong wine for the men, another one milder for the women, and one, sweet, for the children. That was the wine we drank on Friday nights, and on festival days like Rosh Hashanah and Passover. My father and his buddies made frequent trips to the basement to sample the wine, to decide on the right time to put it into bottles.

I don't think my mother expected to have any more children after my sister Irene died, in 1916. Irene died of peritonitis, which set in after a burst appendix. My parents, leery of hospitals, had waited too long before getting her there. I'm told that Ruth wept and beat her breast, and that she was appalled when she found herself pregnant again, this time with me.

Aunt Sophie, trying to console Ruth, told her that I was the child waiting to take Irene's place. My earliest memories tell me that my mother was not impressed. I have memories of being almost smothered by clean clothes in a laundry basket, being told I was a difficult child, throwing my glass bottles of milk out of my crib, wanting the breast instead. By 1918, the year of my birth, we had moved to 1647 Millard Avenue, a mixed ethnic neighborhood, Polish Catholics and East European Jews, all immigrants.

Sara (at 19) with Rhoda (1918)

1647 Millard Avenue, Chicago

Pa and Ma in front of house on Millard

Rhoda at Four

Chapter Two:

Early Years

M Y SISTERS AND I REGARDED AL WITH MIXED ENVY and anger because we saw him as the privileged one in the family. My mother saw to it that Al got the best cuts of meat. Al's underwear and handkerchiefs were ironed for him by me, the youngest, who inherited the chore from Fay as soon as I was old enough to hold the iron and not drop it. But Al saw himself as a discriminated-against minority of one, since he never had a bedroom of his own, and had to sleep on the dining room couch or on a screened-in back porch.

Al was very disappointed that my mother had not produced another boy. He was twelve when I was born, and he was fully prepared for the new baby to be a boy. He had already bought a baseball mitt for his new brother. I was told that when Al answered the phone at seven a.m. on February 21, 1918, and found out Ma had had a girl, he slammed down the phone and didn't pass the information on to anyone at home. It was only when Pa got home later that day that my sisters found out they had a baby sister.

Al was partially successful in turning me into a tomboy, at least between the ages of eight and eleven. All of the kids on Millard Avenue went to the same elementary school, Delano, which was within walking distance of our homes. The Jewish kids didn't mix with the Polish Catholics and we all stayed on our sides of the school playground. We did our fighting in the street. My father told me that Jews fought with words, not with fists or fingernails, but sometimes I got into the fracas anyway. I found they were fun, in a way. The frequent group fights followed a set pattern.

"Hey, you kike! You Christ killer! What're you having for supper?"

"Who're you calling a kike? You dirty Polack! Go wash your neck!"

That would do it. It didn't matter who started it, boy or girl. Soon the hair-pulling and stone-throwing began. Boys beat each other with bare fists; girls scratched and screamed. Parents or elder siblings would arrive, pulling us apart, beating and cuffing us. They would drag us home, scolding us. My mother would pinch my arm as she pulled me along, moaning about why I couldn't be "a good girl like Jeanne."

The street would quiet down until the next fight. On quiet summer nights, the street was also the playground, but, at seven years old, I was seldom allowed to play there at night. One hot summer night, I was sent to my small bedroom off the living room at seven-thirty. This was a vastly unfair time to go to bed, when it was still light outside and the voices of my friends playing under the streetlight just opposite taunted me with their chanting happiness.

All the windows in the flat were open on this particular hot night to catch whatever breeze interrupted the smothering humidity. My bedroom window opened onto slanting red tiles, with a drainpipe anchoring the right-hand side of the roof. I kneeled on the floor in front of the open window, my elbows resting on the sill, just a few inches from the roof, watching the activity across the street, consumed with envy. Suddenly I saw my parents, my sisters Sara, Jeanne, and Fay, and my brother Al troop out of the house and amble up the block. They were going to visit a neighbor whose father had died recently. My mother was carrying the family's offering, a chocolate frosted sponge cake.

They were gone! Quickly, I shucked my pajamas, put on pants and a shirt, stepped through the open window onto the sloping roof. Moving cautiously to the right, I grabbed onto the drainpipe and shinnied down to the street. My friends Irving, Harry, Bessie, and Tillie greeted me happily.

"Hey, Rhoda! You made it! We were just going to play 'Living Statues.'"

"Okay! Let's go! Are you first, Harry?" I jumped up and down.

Harry leaned on the lamppost, his back to us, covering his eyes with his hand. He began to count, "one, two, three—"As he counted we ran off in all directions, trying to get out of sight before he said, "Ten!" Then we froze in as many funny positions as we could, and Harry looked at us carefully to see if any of us moved at all. If he saw anyone moving even the smallest bit, that person was out. Then he turned around again, and we ran and hid. The game was for Harry to try to find anyone he could, and then race that person to the lamppost. If Harry got there first, he was still in the game, but if one of us got there before him, Harry was out and we started over again. After that we played "Kick the Can."

We were in the middle of "Kick the Can," our version of soccer, when Irving shouted, "Hey, Rhoda! Here come your folks around the corner! Better go back!"

I scrambled up the brick steps to the porch, grabbed hold of the pipe, but my hands kept slipping. Irving and Harry ran up the steps; Harry bent over and Irving boosted me onto Harry's back. I clutched the eave and pulled myself onto the roof. Scrambling through the open window, I ducked into bed with my clothes on, pulling the light cover over my head, closing my eyes, while trying to slow down my heavy breathing.

I heard Fay come into our room briefly and then go out again. I knew I would have a few minutes while she spent some time with the rest of the family gossiping about who was at the Beckers' that night. That gave me enough time to get out of my clothes, throw them in the closet, slip on my pajamas, get back into bed, and turn my face to the wall.

Fay and I shared the space we called a bedroom, although it was really just an alcove, curtained off from the living room by a heavy blue velvet drape. The bed took up almost all of the space, making it necessary to move sideways to get to the small closet behind the bed.

Our flat was a long, "railroad car" style, with a living room facing the street. The living room led to a long hall which passed the entry door and proceeded down to the dining room, from which a kitchen on the left led to a screened-in back porch. Two bedrooms on the left and a single bathroom on the right opened off the hall. My parents had the larger of the two bedrooms; Jeanne and Sara shared the other one. Al slept on a couch in the dining room, keeping his clothes in a hall closet. Mornings were shouting bedlam. With only one bathroom for seven people, Al was the only one to get the bathroom all to himself. There was much pounding on the door and shouts of "What are you doing in there? Your ten minutes were up five minutes ago!" I remember hopping up and down the hall with crossed legs to try to keep from peeing in my pants.

One of my chores was to dust the living room furniture, and this became my favorite playacting time. Using the blue velvet drapes separating my sleeping alcove from the living room, I pretended they were the curtains of a stage. I would come through the drapes, close them dramatically behind me, and bow deeply to the adoring crowd beyond the footlights. One morning, when I had just finished speaking the final lines in Shaw's Pygmalion, and was taking Eliza Doolittle's bows, I heard my mother's voice, "Rhoda, what are you doing?"

I quickly grabbed my dust cloth and began to dust the piano keys vigorously, making as much noise as I could. I wondered how she knew I was off in my dreamworld. Finishing the piano, I flicked the cloth rapidly over the books on the shelves, skimmed lightly over the Victrola and the radio, opened the window, and shook the cloth down over the porch onto the street.

"I'm finished dusting the living room!" I called. "Now can I go read?"

"Bring me the cloth and come to the kitchen," was her response. "You can peel the potatoes."

Shuffling to the kitchen, I put the cloth under the sink and sat down heavily at the table, dragging the chair noisily across the linoleum.

"Go wash your hands." My mother's back was turned; she seemed to have eyes in the back of her head. I shoved my chair back and stomped to the bathroom.

"You walk like an elephant! No one would believe you're only eight years old! Lift up your feet!"

I wondered if she would ever say anything to me that wasn't scolding. I wondered if she ever saw me. I felt invisible, although I knew I was not. Looking at myself in the mirror, I felt great pity for the image that looked back at me: reddish brown hair cut short, bangs across my forehead, a long skinny neck, small brown eyes. I remember sticking out my tongue and tossing my head back in a defiant gesture. I wiped my rinsed hands on a towel and stomped back to the kitchen.

My mother turned around from the sink and fixed me with a baleful look. "Did you use soap? Let me see." I held my hands out, palms up. She turned them over. "Hmm. All right. Sit down. Start peeling." She put two bowls in front of me and went out.

I sat at the kitchen table, letting my eyes wander to the screened-in porch at the rear of the flat. That's where Al used to sleep. At twenty years old, Al was going to law school at night, and working during the day. I knew how he always complained about not having a real bedroom, but I didn't care. I thought he was mean. He was always bossing me around, acting like a big shot. I dug viciously at the potatoes, digging out the "eyes"; wondering why they were called eyes; they didn't look like eyes to me. I thought about how I had to iron Al's shorts and handkerchiefs and how I hated that job. Then I remembered one night last winter when Al came whooping into the house from the back porch, yelling about a big fat rat that was sitting on his chest when he woke up at three in the morning. How he had to sleep on a couch in the dining room after that. I felt sort of sorry for him, but I still didn't think that made it all right for him to push me around.

My brother Al was a small, skinny man with bow legs, a long hooked nose, small brown eyes, curly hair, and a mischievous grin hovering around his mouth. His expression seemed to say, "Ha, ha, ha, I know something you don't know, and I'm not going to tell you." He was a great storyteller, and he could recite "The Shooting of Dan McGrew" so effectively it made chills run up and down my spine. I could hear the below-zero wind whistling around the cabin every time he recited that poem.

Chapter Three:
Early Influences

⤳

ALL OF MY SIBLINGS AND PARENTS, too, were small people. When I was fifteen, I was the tallest in the family, having grown four inches in one summer. Sara, the eldest, was not necessarily the most influential. That role went to Jeanne, who was considered the family beauty. She was slim, and carried herself as if she were six feet tall. She had dark brown hair, expressive brown eyes that looked at you sadly, and she seldom smiled. She wrote poetry, and was working on a novel, which we all called GAN—*the Great American Novel*. She had an aloof dignity that made her Al's ally. Jeanne and Al really loved each other, and often danced together with joy and grace.

Sara's passion was dance, just as Jeanne's was poetry and the novel. Sara took me to see Isadora Duncan when I was six years old; she had studied modern dance, and she kept encouraging me to "stand tall, like a dancer." She also took me to see Mary Wigman, Harald Kreutzberg, and Ruth St. Denis, all of them great dancers. Sara had auburn hair, like mine, and an open face and manner that said, "Talk to me, I'll listen." People did talk to her. Everywhere she went, people would talk to her. If she were on a bus or a boat on any extended trip, she would come home with the life stories of people who sat down next to her and unburdened themselves. I remember her as gentle and accessible. I remember Jeanne as tough and unapproachable. Jeanne had a mean streak, and often made fun of Sara. She claimed that Sara talked in her sleep, and would regale the family at dinner with things that Sara supposedly said. There was no way Sara could deny it, of course. Jeanne seemed to be smugly sure of herself, but I found out later this was a cover for a basic sense of insecurity.

Fay, the closest sister to me, considered herself my mentor. She took me to Symphony Hall to hear Frederick Stock, to the Goodman Theater, to the Art Institute. She encouraged me to read, insisted I get a library card when I was five, and cheered when I took out my first library book without pictures when I was ten. Fay encouraged me to use my imagination, and was always asking me to visualize different scenes when we were listening to music, or walking home from an excursion. I remember one extremely cold day when we were walking home from the El (an elevated train in Chicago) coming back from downtown. I was shivering and my teeth were chattering.

"Take a deep breath," she said. "Imagine you are walking across a desert. It's hot, it's very, very, very hot. The sun is beating down on your head, and you're sweating. Do you feel warmer now?" She said this with great confidence.

"Noooo," I chattered. "I'm still cold."

"Well, take more deep breaths. We'll be home soon." When her efforts at hypnosis failed, she always reverted to a pragmatic approach.

Fay was the smallest in the family, and considered the most delicate. She had been a tomboy as a child, seeking her older brother's approval, but when I was growing up, I was only conscious of her extreme femininity. She had large breasts, maturing early, and Al teased her about her "boobs." She was almost eighteen when I was nine, and she was attending Normal School (a two-year Teachers' College) at that time. When she was taking psychology courses at school, she would try out all the experiments on me. I didn't mind, it was fun, and it meant that very close attention was being paid to me. Fay was dating her future husband when she was eighteen, and she kept talking about how wonderful sex was, especially if you were in love. Sex was beautiful, she said, and I believed her. I never could figure out why dirty jokes were funny.

Fay loved drama, and we would often act out scenes from plays we had seen or read. That pattern helped me get through sixth grade. My sixth grade teacher was a strict disciplinarian; I was eleven years old and moving into a rebellious state that would last a long time. That teacher and I were on a collision course from the first day of the term.

Mrs. Parsons had a unique way of enforcing proper deportment in class. She had posted on the back blackboard a grid with every child's name on it, along with a graph running along the top line, with the number one hundred at the top. For every infraction, such as talking at the wrong time, throwing a spitball, giggling, dipping the ends of girls' braids into inkwells, the miscreants would have to go to the blackboard and take a certain number of points off their beginning score. A perfect score would be between ninety and one hundred and very few children achieved that. A normal score would be around seventy-five. I usually came home with minus fifty, sixty, or even seventy, if it was a particularly bad month. Then my parents would be called for a conference.

One of the bad months occurred in March 1929. Fay had given me a pencil with four little dice on top of it. I loved that pencil. On a day in the second week of March, Mrs. Parsons gave us a written assignment to do at our desks, and then left the room when she saw we were all writing busily and silently. I was sitting in the last seat of the first row. Since students were arranged alphabetically by last names, Curtis sometimes ended up in the last seat of the first row, or the first seat in the second row. My deportment scores were always higher when I landed in the first seat in the second row.

I had finished my assignment, and was fiddling around with the dice on the end of my pencil. Suddenly the boy across the aisle reached over and grabbed my treasure.

"Hey! Wait a minute!" I reached out and grabbed his wrist. The dice fell to the floor. We both scrambled to pick them up and were scuffling on the floor when Mrs. Parsons came back.

"Rhoda Curtis! Henry Wandruski! Come here this minute!"

I grabbed the dice and stood up. Henry glared at me. We walked to the front of the room.

"He took my pencil—"

"Stop! I don't want to hear any excuses! Rhoda, go to the board and take twenty-five points off your score. Henry, you do the same. And if there's any more fighting between you two, I will ask your parents to come for a conference."

It was a familiar scolding, and this time I gave up all efforts to conform.

"The heck with it," I thought. "I can't win." Following my natural impulses, I joined a few fights and rubberband spitball contests, and went home at the end of the month with a deportment score of minus eighty-five, a record for me.

Luckily, Mrs. Parsons became ill, and we had a substitute teacher for the rest of the semester. Miss Hill, the substitute, loved plays, and I got to perform in two of our productions. One of them was an excerpt from *Little Women*. I got the role of Jo. I loved Jo. She was the literary one of the March sisters, and I remember reciting Jo's lines, "I can't get over my disappointment in not being a boy" with such passion that Miss Hill enlarged my part. We performed the play in front of other sixth grade classes, going from room to room in our costumes. I swelled with the applause, grinning until I thought my face would crack.

Miss Hill allowed me to help direct too. Again I identified with Jo. She was always the one pushing her sisters around when they rehearsed their own home theatricals. Jo directed Amy, "Do it this way; clasp your hands like this, and stagger around the room—" I was in heaven. The deportment score became irrelevant. I was finally somebody important, even if only at school. At home, I knew I could never catch up to my sisters, that I would always be the "kid sister" off to one side, there and not there.

My sisters were kind and took an active interest in what they called my "development," but they made it very clear that I really didn't belong in their magic circle. Sara and Jeanne had gone to Yellowstone Park in their Dodge touring car the previous year, and I dreamed of hiding in the backseat so I could go with them.

Our family was still doing well in 1928 and 1929, that is, up until October of that year. My brother Al had graduated from law school by that time and was working in a law office; my father brought in a little money; Jeanne and Sara were executive secretaries, so the family was in good shape.

A friend in Jeanne's office had suggested that they get together and rent a cabin at the Dunes near Gary, Indiana. Since the land was owned jointly by the Standard Oil Company and the Gary Steel Mills, it was not possible to buy land there. However, it was possible to build cabins on the beach or on the solid hills above. Jeanne's friend, Thelma, Sara, and Jeanne contracted for a lease on a cottage called "The Firm," and it was at the top of a long flight of uneven wooden steps above the beach. I had listened to all sorts of stories about the fun at the Dunes, and longed to go there, to belong to their group. I got my chance the summer of 1929.

Sara bought me a pair of hiking boots and a small knapsack, and we set out on a Saturday morning for the Indiana Dunes. I felt very grown up. We took the Illinois Central train to a stop called "Wilson," about an hour from Chicago. Once there, we had a choice. We could either hike through the woods to the beach, and then hike up the beach to the cabin, or we could take the "beach buggy," an open truck with heavy tires that could navigate on the sand. Jeanne said the beach buggy was for sissies or old people like Ma and Pa, looking at me as she made this pronouncement.

The beach buggy, also known as "the truck," was an important part of life at the Dunes. Not only did the truck meet passengers at the train, and ferry them to their cabins, it was an extension of the small grocery store located at the point where the woods met the beach. The owners of the store stocked canned goods and a few perishables like milk, butter, a few vegetables, and ice cream. It was possible for people to place orders at the store for deliveries the next day.

Needless to say, we hiked. We hiked through the woods to the beach, then up the beach to the steps leading to the cottage. My knapsack, even though loaded with light items, got heavier and heavier as I slogged through the sand, my new boots rubbing blisters on my heels. If I faltered, Jeanne called me a sissy and told me to keep moving. As soon as we got to the cabin, my sisters hurried to take off their clothes and get into their bathing suits. All I wanted to do was rest, but I got into my suit as well. We ran quickly down the rickety steps, across the hot sand, and blissfully into the cold waters of Lake Michigan. That water was heavenly, and the moment was sheer bliss. I floated on my back and stared happily at the feathery clouds above me.

It turned out that my sisters didn't like the rickety steps any better than I did, and they soon found another cabin for rent right on the beach. That was the one I remember best. This cabin had wooden shutters that were propped open with long poles, and it was screened in on all four sides. For warmth in the winter, there was a small wood-burning stove at one end, with the stovepipe poking through a hole in the roof, a sink with a hand-pump for water, a two-burner kerosene stove for cooking. The owner of the cabin had dug a hole in the sand below the kitchen area and had built a trapdoor covering the hole. There was a bucket into which my sisters would load the butter, meat, and other perishables. Then they would lower the bucket into the hole with a rope. Everything kept remarkably cool in that hole, which they called the cellar.

1931, graduation from Delano Grammar School

1932: The Four Sisters (Rhoda, Sara, Fay, Jeanne)

Chapter Four:

The Dunes and Singing to the Moon

⌒

I DIDN'T GET TO GO TO THE DUNES as often as Sara and Jeanne—they went every weekend, but in the summer of 1930, when I was twelve, I went to Fox River Lake with my mother and my sister Fay. It was July, the city was hot, sticky, and dirty, with our second-floor flat hemmed in by other red-brick two-story buildings on our block. My mother, suffering from migraine headaches and psoriasis, was wiped out by the heat. She decided to take my sister Fay, twenty-one, and me, twelve, to a summer cottage at Lake Forest, Illinois, loaned to us by a friend.

The cottage was located on a small lake, with a wooden dock extending into the water. I noticed with delight that there was a rowboat tied up to the dock. My friend Bessie and her parents had a cottage directly across the lake. Bessie and I had already talked over plans to get together during the two weeks I was going to be there.

The first few days at the cottage were marked by the usual clashes between my sister, my mother, and me over what they considered my reluctance to do my chores exactly at the time they wanted them done. I wanted to sit and read on the rickety porch swing; they wanted me to wash the kitchen floor or the windows or some dumb thing. I was told repeatedly that I was not to take the boat out without special permission. I knew how to row; I had been rowing in the Douglas Park lagoon hundreds of times, I told them, but they consistently refused.

On one particular afternoon, there had been a spectacular thunderstorm in the morning and the wind had whipped up the lake into high menacing waves. Fay had gone off to the small town nearby to pick up supplies, and I, bored, stood on the dock, looking at the water. There was the rowboat, bobbing crazily at the end of its rope; the waves, slapping at the dock, splashed up on the wooden planks. The wind whistled in my hair, whispering in my ears, challenging me to "take the boat, take the boat!" I stood there, looking over the grey lake, remembering the oft-repeated admonition to *never take the boat out without permission!* Suddenly I turned, dashed up the path to the cabin, jumped over the creaking second step and into the room where the oars to the boat rested against the wall. Glancing into the bedroom, I could see my mother, on her back, a cloth over her eyes, breathing rhythmically in a peaceful sleep.

I shouldered the oars, tiptoed out of the house, and closed the screen door with a gentle pop. I walked down to the shore with a rising sense of elation as I stepped into the rocking boat and fit the oars into their locks. Pulling away from the dock, using all the strength in my thin arms, I leaned way back, feeling the oars slicing into the waves. At times I would rise slightly from my seat, my sandalled feet gripping the floor of the boat, a sense of power surging through me. It was late afternoon, and the wind was abating somewhat as I beached the boat on the opposite shore.

"Hi, Bessie," I called. "I'm here to play awhile!"

Bessie and her mother came out onto the porch.

"Does your mother know you're here?" asked Mrs. Cleveland.

"My mother's taking a nap," I said, not meeting Mrs. Cleveland's anxious eye. "It's only five o'clock, I can stay awhile."

I quickly ran off to play with Bessie. Later, at dinner, Mrs. Cleveland said, "I think I hear your mother calling you, Rhoda."

"Oh, no, that's just the wind," I said, "and besides, my mother isn't strong enough to call that loudly."

After dinner, Bessie and I went back to our fantasy play.

"Okay," I said, "I'm your older sister, and you must do everything I say."

"Why?" asked Bessie.

"Because I'm older, that's why."

"Oh."

"Girls!" came the voice of Bessie's mother. "It's nine o'clock, Rhoda, time for you to go home. The moon is up, and the lake is calm. Time to go."

The full moon shone on a glassily quiet lake. I got into the boat in high spirits, and rowed confidently back across the lake. Singing all the way, I was full of an exalted joy, feeling strong and free. "I am one with the universe," I sang. "Oh, moon, I am part of you and you are part of me."

The oars bit smoothly into the calm water, and I glided easily to the dock. I walked up the path, whistling happily, right into pandemonium. Neighbors stood there with flashlights, lanterns, and coiled swaths of nets with all the lights in the cottage blazing, and my mother in an armchair, with a cloth over her eyes. Angry faces turned toward me.

"Where have you been?" screamed Fay, rushing toward me. "What did you do?"

I leaned the oars against the wall and said, quietly, "I rowed across the lake to visit Bessie."

"Didn't you hear me calling you? How dare you take the boat without permission!"

The neighbors left, shaking their heads about "kids these days." I sank to the floor. That was the end of my vacation. The next day I was packed off in disgrace, back to the sweltering city by train. I was sad, but nothing could take away from me the sense of power I felt rowing against the wind and the waves, singing to the moon.

Chapter Five:

Depression Years

~

T HE STOCK MARKET CRASH IN OCTOBER 1929, had been a shock to the American economy, and the full impact hit our family in the spring of 1930. Jeanne worked for an insurance company and Sara for a broker on LaSalle Street. Al was a junior partner in his law firm, and still getting a salary, and Fay was employed as a kindergarten teacher in the Chicago Public Schools. The talk around the dinner table was about the stock market, stories in the paper about the bread lines, and about former big shots selling apples on the street. My father, a staunch Socialist, had nothing but scorn for Herbert Hoover, and none of us believed that "prosperity was right around the corner."

By March 1930, Jeanne and Sara were the only ones left in their respective offices, and Al's senior partner was having trouble paying the rent. There was a traumatic week in March which has left an indelible mark on my memory. Fay came home after school one day with a doomsday expression on her face. "The city of Chicago is broke," she said. "We've just been notified that we will be paid in scrip, not cash." (Scrip in those days was the equivalent of food stamps today.)

"Scrip? What can we buy with scrip?" My mother's voice was an agonized cry. "Can we pay the rent with scrip? Oy, vey." She clutched her head as if she felt another migraine headache coming on.

"Ma, we can buy food with scrip, and maybe clothing in some places. We can offer scrip to the landlord and hope for the best." Fay tried to reassure her without success.

"Clothes I can sew, but potatoes I can't grow in concrete. Soup I can make from carrots and onions, but not from stones."

Fay went into the kitchen to get a glass of milk. I saw her take the bottle out of the icebox, look at it, put it back, and pour herself a glass of water instead. I marked that in my brain. Check what's left before you eat it or drink it.

When Sara came home a couple of days later, she walked into the dining room with a heavy step. "The office is pretty empty. The only ones left are Mr. Howard and me. That's all. I didn't dare ask if I would get a paycheck this Friday. Today's only Monday." She sat down at the table, her shoulders sagged, and her whole body crumpled. As she cupped her face in her hands, she stared off into space.

The door slammed. My brother Al came in, threw his briefcase on the table, and said, "Court adjourned early today. Rumor is there's no money to pay the court clerks. God knows what's going to happen. Anybody listen to the news yet?" Nobody said anything.

I don't know how we got through that week, because the next day, when Jeanne came home, her face was pale, and she looked as if she'd seen a ghost. She sat down without saying anything. My sister Fay got up and brought her a glass of water. Jeanne took a sip. "Mr. Sloan tried to kill himself," she said. "When I came in this morning, I saw him half out the window, just his legs sticking out. I grabbed him and tried to pull him back in, but he kept pushing with his hands. I screamed, 'Help!' but there was no one else in the office. Finally I grabbed the belt of his pants and leaned on his legs, and he finally relaxed and let me pull him back into the room." She put her head down on the table. "I couldn't believe what was happening. It felt like a nightmare. We sat there on the floor, and Mr. Sloan began to cry. I couldn't believe it. Here he was, a man like Sloan, crying like a baby. I didn't know what to do, I just sat there. Finally I got up and closed the window. He said to me, 'Why did you do that?' 'What?' I answered. 'Close the window?' 'You know what I mean. Why did you save me? I'm ruined. Ruined!' What could I say? All I could think of was would there be any money for the payroll?"

"Gevalt!" my mother exclaimed, "How would killing himself solve anything? Goyische kopf!" (Gentile head!) She made a disgusted face.

My father came dragging in at that point. He walked over to where my mother was sitting, sat down, and put his hand over hers. She looked at him with an "oy, what more can happen?" expression.

"Hymie went off with the truck and all the tools. He's gone, the truck's gone, everything's finished. Kaput." Pa was wearing his work overalls under his work jacket, and his face and hands were grimy with tar. His step was heavy, his eyes were glued to his feet.

Oh, boy. Now we really were in a spot. I knew my mother had been suspicious of Hymie since Pa had gone into business with him. Curtis & Kaplan, Roofers, it was. Ma blamed Hymie for being careless, for allowing my father to fall off the roof they were working on, even though Pa kept telling her it was not Hymie's fault. Now Hymie had gone off with Pa's only chance of making a living.

But Ma didn't say anything. She just gave Pa a look that would shrivel a plant, got up and went to their bedroom, and came back with her bankbook. "Sara, Jeanne, Al, Fay, get your bankbooks. We have to see what we've got." This was when "money in the bank" was the mantra recited as protection against calamity, before the bank failures of 1933.

When all the bankbooks were lined up in front of her, she said to Al, "All right, add it up." Looking at Fay, she said, "Yes, we have to count the money you've saved for your wedding, too." Fay burst into tears and ran out of the room. I watched Al. I didn't know then that Al would reserve out some of his money, wouldn't count it all, and that he would gamble it later on the stock market, even though all the signs of the times shrieked warnings. He was one of those who made risky investments, hoping to make up his losses. I wouldn't know until three years later that he had lost the money he promised he had put aside for my college education.

After Al counted up the money, he gave Ma the total. She looked at it, and announced that we had enough for four months, that is, four months' rent. She looked around the table. I was twelve and I wondered if I would have to drop out of school the way Sara and Jeanne had had to do when they were teenagers. That was when Pa had fallen off a roof, before I was born. I knew Al had worked in a grocery store while going to law school at night, and Fay had gone to Teachers' College for two years, which was a big concession. But I wanted to finish high school and go to a regular university, not to night school.

"If we can use scrip for food, I think we can hold out for a few months, take care of the rent and the electricity," my mother said. "Al, what kind of business is coming in for Ward & Curtis?"

"We have a few personal injury cases, I don't know exactly. I'll talk to Ward tomorrow. Molly will stick with us, no matter what."

It was as if Pa was the man who wasn't there. Jeanne started to cry. Sara began drumming her fingers on the table. Ma's glance slid over me, and I shrank down in my chair, for the first time not wanting to be noticed, not wanting to be told I couldn't go back to school.

"I think Fisher & Marcus are solvent for the time being," Sara said. "I think the office will still be open tomorrow. I'm the head secretary and I know where all the important papers are. I think I'll still have a paycheck. Fisher & Marcus are stockbrokers, and the market isn't dead yet."

Jeanne sat up, wiped her face, and blew her nose. "I made sure Mr. Sloan went home. I called him a taxi, anyway. I hope he went home. I locked up the office. I still have the key; I'll go in tomorrow and see what happens. Mr. Sloan is a one-man insurance broker; I don't know what his reserves really are. He sure doesn't think he has any." The air in the dining room was thick with an unquiet silence.

I figured I'd better do my homework and stood up.

"Where are you going?" Ma nailed me. "Better go in the kitchen and start fixing the vegetables for dinner." Ma stood up and handed the bankbooks back to Al, Jeanne, and Sara. She gave Fay's bankbook to Jeanne. "Here, give this to Fay. The wedding isn't for a few months yet. We'll see." A pause, then, "We'll manage," she said.

Our family made it through the depression years; Fay had her wedding in 1930; I graduated from high school, and worked my way through college. We all managed in our own ways to survive, but we were scarred by those years, haunted by the fear of poverty. Mr. Sloan didn't make it. The Chicago police fished his body out of the Chicago River at the Wacker Drive Pier.

Marshall High School

Yearbook page (1935)
Marshall News Staff

Rhoda & Arnie (1936)

Chapter Six:
High School and the Awakening

IN THE SUMMER OF 1931, my mother decided that we needed to move to a neighborhood closer to the only high school on the west side, John Marshall High, since I would be ready to enroll in the fall. I didn't know anything about those plans, and I was happy in my own private world. Fay was married; I was even more isolated from my older siblings.

I spent most of the time playing in our backyard. I had created a sandbox by stealing sand from a construction site down the street. Our yard, a small square of dead grass and dirt, surrounded by a concrete walk, was no different from other duplexes on the block. Every evening, after dinner, I went to the construction site. The owners of a neighboring duplex were adding a porch to the downstairs flat, and there was a big pile of sand in the back as well as gravel and other stuff. I hung around until all the workers were gone, filled up my pail, came home, emptied the pail, went back, and filled it up again. I did this for several evenings until I had a pile of sand that covered most of the small square of dead grass and dirt.

I built sand castles, forts, and trenches, and in my imagined life I was alternately an imprisoned princess in a castle or a besieged guardian of a kingdom. Some of the structures were quite fantastic, with turrets and balconies, even drawbridges. I shared my sand with no one.

The summer came to an end, and one day I heard my parents talking about an impending move. I didn't want to go anywhere. *Move? Where? Why?*

What would happen to my sand? I began accumulating cardboard shoeboxes in which to transport my beloved sand. The day came to leave, and I showed my mother my packed shoeboxes.

"What? Are you *meshuga*? (crazy) I should pay to move that dirty sand? Forget it! Go upstairs and bring down the boxes from your room! *Shnel!* Hurry up!"

Everything was packed; the flat was empty. Still I lingered.

"What are you waiting for? If you don't hurry up, you'll have to take the streetcar, and it's two transfers. Come on, get in the car." She was getting madder by the minute.

I hung back. "I have to go to the toilet!" I yelled. "I'll take the streetcar!"

My mother shrugged and got into the car. The van and my parents drove off. I ran into the backyard, picked up three of my shoeboxes, and nearly fell down. Boy, were they heavy! Deciding to carry two at least, I set off down the street, staggering under the weight of two sand-filled shoeboxes. I intended to come back later for the rest of the sand.

I made it on and off the first streetcar and onto the second. As I stepped off the second streetcar, on the corner of our block, the bottom of the bottom box gave way, and all the sand spilled out at my feet. I gazed mournfully at my spilled dreams, then slowly opened the other box and let the sand pour out. I kicked it with my foot, and walked down the street of my new home, lost, spilled out like my sand. I walked with my head down, ignoring the kids playing kickball in the street, wondering what I was going to have to do to fit in.

The name Curtis was neutral enough for us to pass in our new WASP neighborhood. The important thing was to speak English without an accent and behave like gentiles. This was how we would become "true Americans." We would fight anti-Semitism by the conservative way we dressed, eliminating extravagant hand and head gestures when we talked, cultivating a flat, mid-western, nasal way of talking, with clear enunciation of our consonant endings. We aimed to be identified as "Chicagoans," not Jews.

I knew all this in a subconscious way, and it didn't make the move from Millard to Van Buren any easier. Van Buren Street, in the Garfield Park area of Chicago, was still the west side, but, according to my elder siblings, it was a definite improvement over the lower west side, near Twelfth Street and Douglas Park, where we used to live. The new place was a different kind of challenge. I would have to be careful, move cautiously for a while, check out who was in, who was out. In time, I learned to ignore the ingenious puns on my first name, like: "Hey, roadapples, whatcha doin' today?" It took me a while to figure out that "roadapples" meant horse shit. The kids in this neighborhood were certainly different.

Our new neighbors were Irish Catholic, and one of them was a girl my age, named Cynthia. I tried to be as much like Cynthia as possible. She was a kind girl, with long blond hair, green eyes, a heart-shaped face, and a confident air. She went to ballet school, and whatever Cynthia did, I wanted to do. I pestered my sisters and my mother to let me go to ballet school also. My sister Sara decided she could afford it, and paid the fees. Cynthia and I took the El to the school on Michigan Avenue every Saturday morning, and I managed to become part of the neighborhood under her protection. Cynthia and her brothers were leaders on the block—her brothers were football players and she was sought for every street game she would deign to play. Being accepted by my new friend was an automatic pass.

Without my mother's knowledge, I went to church with Cynthia on Sunday mornings, and longed to be Catholic, so that I could bask in the warm glow of the candles and the incense and the beautiful music. Our Orthodox Romanian synagogue was full of men, young and old, rocking back and forth, chanting in a mysterious way on the first floor; the women, relegated to a separate area upstairs, followed the service between their gossiping. I found the separation of men and women upsetting. Compared to the ordered ritual of the Catholic service, without understanding the Latin, my adolescent mind rejected the individual chanting in the synagogue as strange and foreign. I didn't want to be strange and foreign. I wanted to belong.

Cynthia introduced me to Albert Guy, a friend of her brother's, who lived one block away. Albert was Scotch-Irish, Protestant, but Cynthia's family tolerated Protestants. My mother tolerated no boys for me except Jewish boys, which narrowed the field considerably.

Cynthia would go to a Catholic high school in the fall, and Marshall High, my school, was about a mile away, across the Garfield Park golf course.

Albert (who wanted to be called "Guy") would also be a freshman at Marshall in the fall. Guy played the saxophone, was a runner, a brilliant mathematician, and very shy. He had weak eyes and wore thick glasses. But he was the first boy who ever wrote a poem just for me:

REFLECTIONS IN THE RAIN

In shining mirror street and puddles small
Is found a lifelike counterpart of trees,
Of lamps and towers. Down through a maze of seas
Diminutive beings pass, and fall
To toss and whirl in cataracts: a pall
In life—in miniature a travesty.
When heaven's fiery spark is struck we see
A moment's glamour and then a sombre all.
From rain and all the rainy days that pass
We learn, if we have eyes to see and mind
To understand, of transient joy and pain,
All minor things. The greatest truth, alas,
Slips through our fingers and we seek to bind
The fates and check the fall of falling rain.

I was in awe of his intelligence and knowledge. My mother forbade the friendship; after all, he wasn't Jewish, but that didn't mean we couldn't walk to high school together, across the golf course in all weather. Albert insisted on carrying my books even on the coldest days; he never wore gloves. I remember his red, chapped hands. I don't know why I never bought him a pair of gloves; I always meant to.

We worked on the third page of the Marshall News together. He was editor; I was co-editor. That meant we spent long hours after school putting out our prize-winning newspaper. I always considered Guy a friend and confidant; I don't think I ever realized how deeply he cared for me. Looking at the nubile, rounded girls in my class, I couldn't imagine how anyone would think my thin chest, long neck, and skinny body were attractive. I always managed to start a discussion about Spinoza or Galileo or Einstein whenever Guy moved close to me or put his face next to mine as we proofread copy for the paper. I missed the signals that would have told me how he felt.

Guy and I also worked together on a project for our Civics class. We decided to research the source and purity of water that the Chicago Water Department delivered to residents of Chicago. We went to the Filtering Plant, interviewed various people in the pumping departments, and discovered some fascinating things about the ways in which the water was thoroughly, and not so thoroughly, purified. We never bothered to clear our report with the Water Department; that never occurred to us. We simply turned it in to our teacher, who checked it for grammatical errors, and then passed it.

"This is a very good report, Rhoda, Albert," Mrs. Harding said. "I don't find a single mistake. You must have worked very hard on it. Congratulations."

We smiled modestly and took our report to a radio station in Chicago connected with the *Chicago Daily News,* call letters WMAQ, and they were delighted with it.

However, City Hall was not so delighted; what an uproar! We had revealed certain aspects of the water purification process that were not what City Hall wanted reported. We were unprepared for the reaction to our report. Apparently, in our innocence, we didn't realize that even though we were high school students, City Hall viewed us as whistle-blowers or, as investigative journalists were called, "muckrakers." Sadly, the result was that our report became the last public broadcast open to high school students in Chicago.

During my final two years of high school, 1934 and 1935, I seldom came home before five p.m. My mother greeted me with variations on the same complaint every day, "What do you do at school? How come you never get home in time to do anything but set the table?" And sometimes she would add, "Fay always managed to do chores at home and keep up with her homework too!"

Muttering something about being busy with important things, I usually managed to escape to my room. One day I emerged with a carefully thought-out statement. "Look, Ma, I'm an editor on the paper. That's important. I have to help set the paper in type. I'm learning a lot. Also, I'm in the Drama Club. I have to rehearse and help build the sets."

She didn't really accept my excuses. With her mouth set, she fixed me with a steady glare, and I stared back, keeping my face as expressionless as I could. I knew, and she probably knew, too, that my afterschool activities were designed to keep me away from home as much as possible. *What was there for me at home on Van Buren Street? Hanging around the kitchen, listening to my mother complain about my father, her headaches, how incompetent I was?* No, the only place I had any sense of belonging, any sense of importance, was in the afterschool activities of Marshall High School.

In the summer of 1934, when I was sixteen, I experienced a sudden and sharp pain in my right side. Sara, remembering Irene's death from peritonitis caused by a burst appendix, sounded the alarm, and Al agreed to take me to our family doctor, Dr. Abrams. We sat in the waiting room, and Al went into the doctor's office to consult with Dr. Abrams. When he came out, he said to me, "You can go in now. It's all for the best. You'll thank me for this later." I thought this was a curious remark, but simply shrugged.

Up on the table, in the doctor's operating room, I felt a sharp stab in my vagina, and the probing fingers of Dr. Abrams. He straightened up and removed his bloody glove.

"You can get dressed," he said to me as he left the room.

We sat in his office, and he said to Al, "The appendix is definitely enlarged. It should come out immediately. I'll call the hospital and reserve a room."

Neither one of them spoke directly to me. Al took me to Michael Reese Hospital; we didn't talk at all on the way. Once there, I was taken directly to a room. Al went home and sent my sister Fay back with a small suitcase containing a toothbrush and a nightgown.

When Fay arrived, I asked her to sit down, and she sat on the bed. All of my sister's talking about sex had not prepared me for what had happened in Dr. Abrams's office.

"I want to ask you something, Fay. Something happened at the doctor's office. Dr. Abrams stuck something up my vagina, and I felt a sharp stab. Then he put his fingers up me and pushed on my stomach. It hurt, and I hollered. After that, he took off his bloody glove and told me to get dressed. Al and I sat in his office and he told Al I should come here right away. Now, what did he do that made me bleed?"

Fay looked out the window. "Do you know what a hymen is?"

"No," I replied. "What is it?"

She sighed. "Didn't they teach you anything in your biology courses?" Then, as if quoting from a textbook, she told me that a hymen was a thin mucous membrane that partially closes the opening to the vagina. She said that maybe Dr. Abrams needed to make sure I really had appendicitis.

I thought about that, and then I asked her, "Why did Al say that I would thank him for this later?"

Fay gave me a long look. "I don't know," she said. "I can't explain it." She stood up. "I'll be back tomorrow after school. Goodnight."

After the surgery, I was pretty groggy and didn't even know that Fay and my mother had both come that afternoon. The third day was a different story. Since Michael Reese was a teaching hospital, every day four or five young male interns made rounds with a supervising physician. The young interns took turns probing me and then exchanged knowing looks, smirking and rolling their eyes. That night I rang for the nurse, who was young and friendly.

"What's up?" She greeted me. "Can't you sleep?" She plumped up my pillow. "It hurts a lot," I said. "But I wanted to talk to you about something else. Why do the interns smirk and look at me in such a funny way when they poke me? Some of them stick their fingers up me. Do they have to do that?"

Norma straightened up sharply. "I'll be right back." When she returned, she said, "The notes your doctor left state that he broke your hymen to verify the diagnosis."

"What does that mean?" I wanted to know.

Norma said, "If your hymen's broken, it usually means you're not a virgin."

I thought about that. "Do you mean that if someone feels around inside of me, that person can tell if I have a hymen or not, and then... ? Wow."

"If the person fiddling around with you knows anything about physiology, yes," she responded, "but that is not acceptable behavior in this hospital. I'll leave a note for the supervising physician and make sure it stops. Now take this pill."

I fell into a troubled sleep. Ten days later, ten pounds lighter, I left the hospital. When I got home, my mother and sister were worried about how thin I had become. They decided I should go to the Dunes to recuperate. We had kept up the rent on the cabin at the Dunes, and since school was out, it was decided that Fay would go with me. The plan included Fay's husband Henry, who came out on weekends with supplies for our larder.

I remembered the Dunes of Indiana as the magical place I had first visited with my sisters when I was eleven. I was happy to go back there, and be able to spend the whole summer. The Dunes was a place of constantly changing landscape. Lake Michigan roared across the shore, gobbling up huge chunks of sand, flinging them up to create small cliffs. Then the forest crept back, encroaching upon the sand with grass, small scrub, blueberry bushes, and tiny wildflowers. We never knew, from week to week, how much beach we would find.

The Abrams family had a cottage near ours. Irving the doctor didn't come often, but his younger brother, David, a medical student, was always at the beach when I was there. I was flattered that David, twenty, considered me a friend.

One moonlit night, after a bonfire, David and I went for a walk. He had a blanket and suggested that we climb a small cliff to a secluded patch of sand. We lay on our backs, enraptured by the star-filled sky, lying peacefully without words. I felt his hand on my thin chest, under my T-shirt, and I didn't resist when he pulled it off. He quickly shucked his shorts and mine, and we lay close together. I had never been stroked before; I felt self-conscious about my skinny body, but David's hands were reassuring. He probed me gently, and his fingers were not at all like his brother Irving's!

Ooooo, I gasped in surprise as his penis slid into me. I'd never felt anything like *this* before! I grabbed his arms and hung on. When he withdrew, he stared at me.

"Oh, I'm so sorry. I thought, after I felt inside you, you were... but the way you reacted... gee, I'm sorry."

His voice trailed off. I didn't know what to say, conscious only of sand in my crotch. We got up, dressed, and walked back up the beach. It was late, the moon had set; he kissed me tenderly and walked off.

I burned all over, feeling a fire along my groin. Exploding inside, I shivered as my hands stroked my tiny, trembling breasts. I felt alive in a way that was deliciously, deliriously new.

When I got back to our cabin, I grabbed a towel and said to my sister

Fay, who was reading by the kerosene lamp on the table, "I'm going for a swim. I won't be long." I had to get that sand out of my crotch. I ran down to the water, just a hundred yards from the cabin, exulting in the squish of the soft cool sand between my toes. At the edge of the water, I yelped as the cold water of Lake Michigan hit my naked body. What a glorious feeling! I floated on my back, gazing up at the stars, stretching my arms to embrace the universe.

After my swim, I wrapped myself in the towel, and glowing all over, ran happily back to the cabin. I slipped on my pajamas, and crawled into my cot.

"Good night, Fay," I said, and pulled the covers over my head. I hugged myself, hanging on to my new sensations.

That fall, back at school, I didn't sleep well. I turned and tossed, ending the night tangled up in the bedsheets. My mother noticed the dark circles under my eyes and insisted that I go to see Dr. Abrams.

"What's the matter?" he asked as he entered the examining room. "Your mother says you're not sleeping well. Do you have bad dreams?" He thumped my back. Then he looked at me, taking the stethoscope out of his ears. "Your blood pressure is normal. You're a little anemic, and you're thin for your height. Are you eating enough? I don't see anything really wrong. The incision has healed well. Is there anything else?"

How could I tell him I kept dreaming of that night on the beach with his younger brother? How I kept reliving that moment when David entered me, and of how I felt myself burning all over? I took a deep breath and said, "I have sexual fantasies." I swallowed. "I feel like I'm burning up."

Dr. Abrams stood up and regarded me pityingly. "My dear," he said. "Your feelings are very common for a girl your age. I suggest you take a cold shower whenever you get any of those feelings. You'll be fine." He walked out of the room, and I sat on the examining table for a minute, clenching and unclenching my hands.

Shortly after that visit, I invited one of my friends, Bea Harmer, to sleep over. I now had a room of my own since my sister Fay had gotten married. Bea was about my height, but had a much better figure. She had *real* breasts, not "falsies," and she had developed a mysterious air about her that attracted boys. I figured it must have had something to do with her summer in Paris.

She had gone to Paris that summer to live with her sister and brother-in-law, a journalist, and she came back with a different walk, a kind of languid slouch. She had let her hair grow long and pinned it up in a French twist. She tilted her head a bit while looking off in the distance with a small, secret smile as if she knew something special. All she had to do was walk into a room and sit down and every boy in the room was next to her in a minute as if she were a magnet and they were iron filings. I was determined to discover her secret.

That night, when Bea slept over, we spent most of the night talking. We were both sixteen, but Bea seemed older, more sophisticated. I told her about what had happened at the Dunes during the summer she was in Paris, and how tormented I felt. I also told her about my humiliating experience with Dr. Abrams.

"Oh, heck," she said. "Do you have any carrots?"

I sat up in bed and looked at her as if she'd gone out of her mind. "Carrots? What for? I'm not hungry."

Bea laughed. "Just go get a couple of carrots, and I'll show you what I mean. It has nothing to do with eating."

I got up, went to the kitchen, and brought back two carrots, which I had carefully washed. "Okay. Now what?"

Bea said, "Watch," and proceeded to show me how to masturbate.

Following her instructions, I was suddenly transported back to the moonlit beach at the Indiana Dunes, reliving that glorious moment with David. *Wheeee! I was off to new sensations, and all on my own, too!*

Bea grinned at me and I grinned back. "Thanks, Bea."

"Don't mention it," she said. We both sighed and drifted off to sleep.

The awakening of my sexuality was so pleasurable, so exciting and thrilling, that I found myself aware of everything around me in a more intense way. I looked at boys differently, but I also began looking at paintings and sculpture differently too. I saw erotic shapes in the curves of Jean (Hans) Arp's and Jacob Epstein's sculpture. Epstein's massive depiction of "Adam and Eve" (two figures clasped together, melded into one) was my idea of what a really beautiful sexual experience was all about.

Chapter Seven:
The Nathanson Group and Power

I WAS A SENIOR IN 1935, and that year I began to go out with older boys, pretending to be eighteen. I wore my long hair parted in the middle, pulled back into a bun, and secretly practiced smoking in front of my bedroom mirror. I decided to drink Manhattans or champagne cocktails on a date, as I had seen my older sisters do. I started to wear "alsies" in my brassiere, yet felt terrified that when I wore a bathing suit to the beach, the boy I went with would find out that I really didn't have any breasts after all! I didn't know exactly who I was, and kept trying different personae on for size. I thought of Bea as a cosmopolitan "woman of the world," a "bohemian," and I wanted to be like her. I wasn't quite sure what a "bohemian" was—some sort of artist, I thought, sophisticated, of course.

There was a moody poet in my English class named Richard Modell. He had dark hair, wore glasses, and was always quoting some obscure poet or other. He had a soulful look and seemed sad. I wanted to nurture him. He seemed to be mesmerized by a gorgeous red-haired girl whom I considered an uninformed dunderhead. Outside our classroom I heard Richard talking to her about a group he belonged to.

"We read different poets and philosophers," he said, "and then we discuss their ideas."

"How boring!" the red-haired girl remarked. "Sounds just like school!" She laughed and walked away.

I wanted to kick her. I walked over to Richard and said, "Who runs this group you belong to? Can anyone join?"

He looked at me as if he were seeing me for the first time. "Are you interested? You have to be invited by someone who is also a member."

"Yes," I said. "I'm interested. I like to read poetry, and I write stories and plays. Also, you know, I'm co-editor of the third page of our paper, and I'm a pretty good critic too." I was determined to impress Richard.

"Well," he said, "we meet on Friday nights at the home of Mr. Nathanson, Leybusch's father. You know Leybusch, don't you? He sits by the window and doesn't talk much."

"Yes, I know him only because he's in our class, but I've never really talked to him."

"Tell you what," Richard said, "I'll come over to your house Friday night and we can take the streetcar to Nathanson's house. Bring something you've written."

I couldn't believe my luck. Richard told me a little about the Nathansons on the way to their house. He said that Mrs. Nathanson had been a practicing physician in Russia, but she worked as a low-paid aide in a Chicago clinic because she didn't have a license to practice in the United States. Mr. Nathanson, according to Richard, was an intellectual, a philosopher.

"Where does Mr. Nathanson work?" I asked.

"He doesn't," said Richard, dismissively. "He studies."

"Ah," I thought. I remembered hearing my mother rant about "talky men who do nothing but study and act important while their wives and children support them." But I also thought about how my father spoke of those men with respect and longing. I remembered my father telling me how they studied Torah and discussed with each other the fine points of Talmudic teaching.

As if reading my mind, Richard said, "Mr. Nathanson is a secular as well as a religious scholar. You'll see; he selects readings from Spinoza, Kant, Hegel, Thomas Mann, and sometimes from Nietzsche for us to discuss."

I was getting more and more anxious as Richard talked. Would I be accepted? Would I be considered intellectual enough?

That first evening was an eye-opener. The Nathanson living room was small, stuffed with upholstered furniture, the backs of the chairs and couch covered with handmade lace antimacassars. Nathanson, a large man with a florid face, sat in a huge rocker, a floor lamp with a fringed shade by his side, with an end table for his pipe and book. He smiled benignly as he surveyed us. He looked like a happy Buddha.

Nine of us sat around on assorted dining room chairs and a small sofa, five women and four men. Sima was working as a stenographer in downtown Chicago; Selma was studying art at the Chicago Art Institute, as was Annette. Bernice was going to Teachers' College. Philip was in law school and Harry was studying accounting. Richard, Leybusch, and I were the only high school students. We were all first generation children of immigrant Jews, and we all considered ourselves political activists.

At that first meeting, Nathanson read an excerpt from Goethe's Faust, and directed the discussion around the concept of selling one's soul. Nathanson was a good moderator, and didn't tolerate flippant or superficial remarks. At one point, Philip spoke up, saying, "Everyone has a price, Mr. Nathanson, and I think that was Goethe's point."

"No!" Nathanson said, sharply. "That is the superficial point! The real point is that to sell one's soul means that one is doomed to hell forever. No price is acceptable! There is no excuse for even considering the possibility that because everyone is doing it that makes it all right for you to do it too!"

Philip opened his mouth, but closed it quickly after a sharp look from Nathanson. Happily, just then it was time for a break. Mrs. Nathanson served pastries and her famous boiled coffee. It was the strongest coffee I have ever drunk. She put eggshells in the bottom of a porcelain pot, then put in coffee grounds and water and boiled the mixture until it became thick. With plenty of sugar, this was a hefty drink. After coffee, rejuvenated, we began the rest of the session. This was the time when members of the group read their own work: poetry, stories, essays. I was invited to read some of my own writing. I read the first act of a play I was writing, called "Footfalls," about a blind girl listening for familiar footsteps but hearing strange ones instead. I planned to send the play to a mystery program broadcast at midnight by Station WGN in Chicago. After the reading, I went to the kitchen, where I waited while the group voted on whether or not I would be invited to join. I remember my forcedly cheerful conversation with Mrs. Nathanson.

"What was your life like in Russia?" I asked, trying to interview her.

"It was not like here," she said, ducking my question. "There I had a profession. I had respect." She closed her mouth firmly. "Excuse me," she said, turning her back. "I have to finish washing up."

That was the end of the interview. I wondered what a practiced journalist would do. Richard came in and said I should come back to the living room. With my palms sweating, I looked around the room. Smiles and nods greeted me. I had to sit down quickly before my knees gave out. I felt exhilarated and sophisticated. Being accepted by this group meant more to me than winning a top grade on a high school exam!

The discussion about Spinoza was a turning point in my own thinking about religion. The bishop who denounced Spinoza in the seventeenth century as "that insane and evil man, who deserves to be covered with chains and whipped with a rod" echoed the actions of the Jewish community of Amsterdam, which excommunicated him. However, I found that I agreed completely with Spinoza, who believed that man's soul and body were inextricably tied and were subject to natural laws. I liked the idea that Spinoza's God helps those who help themselves, and this belief has stayed with me. If that meant that I was an agnostic, or even an atheist, that was fine with me.

Friday evenings became the high point of the week for me. I felt superior to the rest of my schoolmates, because I was part of an elite, exclusive circle. I respected both Mr. and Mrs. Nathanson, but couldn't get over the feeling that Mrs. Nathanson was somehow the important one of that couple. She worked, she held the family together, and she provided the amenities that made the evenings so comfortable. Nathanson was like a rabbi—a learned teacher. I expected him to be erudite, but I wanted him to be more inclusive of Mrs. Nathanson. I judged him harshly, believing that he should be working somehow, bringing money into their joint household. Nevertheless, I worked harder on projects for the Nathanson Group than I did on schoolwork. The Nathanson Group provided another escape valve from my bossy siblings and my elderly parents.

Coming home after midnight, following a Friday night meeting with the

Nathanson Group, I usually found my brother Al waiting up for me. At sixteen, my anger and humiliation stiffened my backbone. Why did he feel he had to wait up for me? He always lectured me about getting the right amount of sleep ("an hour before midnight is worth two hours after midnight") and so on. I insisted that I could always sleep in on Saturday morning. Considering himself my guardian, Al shrugged off my defense. I didn't elect Al to watch over me, and resented his assumption of power. "I'm sixteen, I know how to take care of myself. You keep treating me like a baby."

"Yes," said Al, in his lawyerly voice. "You have just revealed your immaturity by your specious argument." He lifted his shoulders inside his smoking jacket in disdain, and knocked out his pipe into the special ashtray beside him. His gesture dismissed me.

Four years earlier, when I was a freshman in high school, Al told me that he had invested money in the stock market for my college education. He advised me to enroll in the college prep classes at school, and I trusted him. Even though I knew that I was expected to "support the family," as Sara, Jeanne, and Al were doing, I was determined to go to a four-year university, not a two-year teaching college, as Fay had done. Although I was on the "college track," my mother insisted that I take shorthand and typing. "Just in case," she said.

One evening in March 1935, in the final semester of my senior year, sitting at our dining room table, preparing for scholarship exams for the University of Chicago, my brother Al came over to me and sat down. The dining room was a mellow place to study, the oblong oak table lit by a hanging lamp that cast a soft glow over the entire room, still full of that night's pungent supper smells.

Sensing tentativeness in his manner, I put my books aside, on the alert.

"I have something to tell you," he said.

"What is it?" I said.

"Do you remember the money I told you I had put aside for your college education?"

"Yes," I said, feeling my stomach drop.

"Well, I lost it. I had to use it to cover margin for another stock I invested in."

Parts of dinner rose in my throat. I swallowed hard.

"You lost it?" My voice rising, I gripped the edge of the table. "You gambled with the money you promised me for school, and you lost it?!"

"Yes, I'm sorry." He shrugged, unapologetic, simply stating a fact. We were alone in the house during this conversation. The flat was quiet.

I took a deep breath, stood up, and walked out of the room. I went to the bathroom, locked the door, and vomited. Then I washed my face again and again with cold water. Before I walked out, I looked in the mirror and said to my reflection, "Damn! I'll find a way to go to college full-time, anyway!" A sense of power rose from the anger in me, and I decided not to bother trying for a scholarship at the University of Chicago. I wouldn't be able to pay the fees or buy books without a supplemental income, and I wouldn't be able to keep up my grades at that university if I had to work. The standards at the University of Chicago were high, and competition was tough.

Okay. A job, after all, not college right away. No point telling my friends that I would be working for a year. I would tell them I was going to Northwestern rather than the University of Chicago. I knew I would be able to maintain a high enough grade average for a scholarship at Northwestern while working part-time. Oddly enough, I sensed that I was now free of my brother. In a strange way, I felt liberated.

I left the bathroom, walked carefully back to the dining room, picked up my books, gave my brother a withering look, and went to my room. I closed the door quietly, resisting the impulse to slam it, and fell across the bed, shaking.

As luck would have it, my brother invited a friend of the family, George Becker, to dinner one evening about two weeks after my graduation from high school. George was a real estate appraiser who worked for Al's senior partner, Max, in Al's law firm. George and Al were the same age, but George always treated me as if I were grown-up. We kidded around a lot, and George acted as if my opinions were worth listening to.

"Hey, George," I said after dinner. "How about hiring me to type your appraisals? I'm looking for a job."

"You are? How come you're not going to the university? I thought it was all settled?" George looked puzzled.

"Oh, the money disappeared," I said airily, not looking at my brother. "I need to find a job, and you know we're still in a depression."

"Boy, do I know it! And I'm just starting out. I can't afford a full-time typist. How about asking Max—he's the senior partner, after all, to hire you as a secretary/typist. I could pay part of your salary, and we'd all be happy."

I looked at Al, whose face was almost purple with repressed rage.

"No! That would be nepotism!" Al spluttered. George and I looked at him in astonishment.

"Nepotism? Al, why is it nepotism to help your own sister get a job in your law office? I can't figure you out."

"My brother is pretty mysterious sometimes," I said to George. "Maybe *you* could talk to Max, then Al could pretend he didn't know anything about it." Keeping my face still, I didn't show my inner glee. Al got up abruptly and went to the kitchen to get a drink of water. I looked at George and shrugged, my palms up.

George called me the next day and told me that the "skids were greased." I guessed that the time was right for me to call Max Ward, the senior partner. I made an appointment for an interview, which I didn't mention to my brother. All went well, and I was hired. Max told me that the job involved running the switchboard, taking dictation, doing the filing, and typing George's appraisals. My mother's advice echoed in my head. She was right. Learning how to take dictation and type paid off. I earned ten dollars per week for a forty-five-hour week, which included three hours on Saturday. Wow! Suddenly, I had power. I was free! I had my own money—after I gave my mother my share of room and board, and skimped on lunch, I had a little left over for anything I wanted to buy—a scarf, a blouse, a book.

My mother's frustration suddenly became clear to me, and I remembered how she had wanted a business of her own, either dressmaking or a small shop. She hated being dependent, powerless, and her hidden yearning had become part of my personality without my realizing it. I also finally understood that money of one's own was the key to personal freedom. Virginia Woolf, the author of *A Room of One's Own*, had money; what she wanted was a room of her own. At seventeen, with my sister Fay already married, I had my own room. Sara had gone to Cuba to work for the government; Jeanne and her husband Arthur Quadow had gone to Palestine; Al had his own room and I had mine. Now I had my own money.

The law office job was empowering in other ways. Molly, the red-haired, Irish, bossy executive secretary, educated me in navigating the business world. Not very tall, she was solid, and every gesture she made was full of authority. Her eyes sparkled with humor, as if harboring a secret joke. Molly, direct, straightforward, never minced words.

"First thing you do when you get a job in an office, anywhere, is get control of the files. Low-level jobs always include filing. You take a look at the files, and declare them to be in extremely disorderly condition. Offer to reorganize them. Your boss will love you for that. Of course, once you reorganize the files, no one (other than you) will be able to find anything, and you will quickly become indispensable!" She stopped, looked me in the eye and said, "Don't try it here though. I've already done it." *What marvelous advice! I never forgot what she told me; tried it in several jobs, and it always worked.*

I worked in that law office for a year, never losing sight of my original goal. Fay and Sara knew it, and in June of 1936, Fay offered me a proposition. She said she had contacted Sara and Al and that they had each agreed to put up one thousand dollars to get me through the first year at Northwestern, if I would agree to go the rest of the way by myself. Fay said she hadn't contacted Jeanne and Arthur because she knew they didn't have any money. She said she and Henry had had to "lean on" Al, but that he finally agreed. She asked me if I thought I could get a scholarship and make it on my own. Full of confidence and optimism, of course I said yes, and immediately filed an application for the fall semester.

I was full of exuberance that summer of 1936, and when I met a tall handsome man at a party, I tried out some of the techniques I had seen Bea use. They worked, and Arnie invited me to go to a concert at Grant Park, on Michigan Avenue. Arnie was built like an athlete and carried himself with an easy grace. He had short curly hair, blue eyes, and a smile that lit up his whole face. He also had a way of looking at me as if I were the only person on the planet. I had trouble breathing normally in his vicinity.

As we were walking to the El after the concert, he told me that he and his family were nudists, and that they often went to a special nudists' camp outside of Chicago, but located on Lake Michigan. Would I like to go some weekend? Well! Would I! It didn't take long to make up my mind.

"When are you going?"

"Actually, we're going this weekend. Day after tomorrow. Do you really want to go? We don't wear any clothes at all, you know. All kinds of people come—it's a family camp. We're Swedish, but there are lots of Germans and Latvians too, who come. I could pick you up early Saturday morning."

I thought quickly. "Would we stay overnight? I'm not sure I could arrange that. It would get complicated."

Arnie looked disappointed. "We usually stay the whole weekend," he said, and paused. "I guess I could bring you home Saturday night, and then go back to camp early Sunday morning. That's if you really want to come."

"Of course I'll come," I said. "I just have to figure out what to tell my mother so she'll say 'yes.' When you come to pick me up Saturday morning, I'll tell you how long I can stay."

The camp, at a place called "Michigan Shores," was beautiful. Hidden in a grove of trees, there were individual rustic cabins with screened sides, a large communal building with a fireplace, a large kitchen, and bookshelves filled with books and magazines. There was also an outdoor picnic area with a large cooking pit and iron grills set up for barbecuing. The indoor communal dining area was for fall and winter get-togethers. I gathered that this dedicated group of nudists met year-round.

Our first stop was a disrobing area, with lockers. Arnie and his family methodically stripped down, and of course, I did the same, stealing glances at everyone around me. Nobody was particularly conscious of being naked. We went out onto a playing field where people of all shapes and sizes were playing volleyball. I must confess I didn't get much pleasure out of watching women with big breasts bouncing up and down, nor of watching the potbellied men with their limp penises jumping up and down either. Gradually, however, I found myself focusing on people's faces, voices, and words, and began to lose my own self-consciousness.

That change in perspective came with another awareness—the bugs. I found myself continually flailing my towel around me, and couldn't help thinking, *Is that why horses keep flicking their tails?* Eating was another challenge. We spread our towels on the wooden planks of the picnic table seats, but I felt the scratchy wood beneath the towel. Paper napkins covered our laps. I was hungry, but itchy too, and found making polite conversation a bit difficult.

As soon as we finished lunch, I leaned over to Arnie and whispered, "Can we go for a swim?" Arnie, a sophomore at the University of Chicago, was sensitive and polite. He said to his father, "I think Rhoda and I will go down to the beach for a bit. Okay?" His father, chomping on a barbecued chicken leg, nodded his assent, and we took off.

The water was delicious, and we swam for a long time. We swam close together, our bodies sliding and slipping against each other easily. There was no particular urge for either of us to do more than that. I felt completely sensual without the extra "frisson" of passion. I was aware of my physical self as a wonderful extension of my inner self, luxuriating in the way I twisted and dived, feeling the water rushing through my hair, on my naked body, a sense of joy and exhilaration. I think Arnie must have felt the same. We frolicked like otters and porpoises.

That was my first and last experience at a nudist camp, but the lack of self-consciousness stayed with me. *Years later, when I found myself in Norway on a blistering hot day at the Louisiana Museum, I asked the desk receptionist if there was any place nearby to swim. She looked surprised, and motioned to the sea down below. "Just go down, take off your clothes, and swim!" she said, her face absolutely steady. I did it, of course, and discovered various families all hanging around, nude, no problems at all.*

Arnie and I continued our friendship, only this time on regular public beaches. He liked acrobatics, and I did too, so we used to do all sorts of stunts on the beach. I would often stand on his shoulders and then do a somersault, landing on my feet. We would fall on our faces in the sand, laughing our heads off.

The summer was coming to an end. Arnie went back to the University of Chicago, and I went back to my brother's law office, full of joy and anticipation, knowing that classes at Northwestern would start in a few weeks. Soon I would begin my longed-for new life at Northwestern. I had been accepted, and although I would live at home and commute to the campus, I didn't care. I was on my way!

Chapter Eight:
Northwestern and Yellowstone Park

⌐

W E HAD MOVED TO A SMALLER FLAT on Winnemac Avenue in north Chicago, and I took the El to the Evanston station, from where I walked to the campus. Northwestern was a conservative, Methodist university, populated mostly by North Shore men and women from upper middle-class homes. Most of them were members of fraternities and sororities. As a commuter, I was definitely an outsider, and definitely lower-class, since not only did I work, but also brought my lunch to the campus in a brown paper bag.

The campus "smelled" clean. There were wide paths between carefully tended expanses of grass. Everything was neat, planned, nothing random; the university buildings were stately with vines crawling in an orderly fashion up the red bricks. There was an air of solid respectability about the whole place. I was used to the Chicago wind. But *this* wind, directly off the lake, with no buildings to break up its penetrating blasts, was different. When I walked from one end of the campus to the other, my head down, the wind sliced through my winter coat. And walking into a heated classroom, I would take a minute or two to recover. I wondered if I was the only one feeling buffeted by this gale.

The whole atmosphere of the Northwestern campus was so open. I could look out onto trees, elms, and catalpas flourishing in a casual acceptance of their privileged environment, so different from the sickly trees on my block at home. I felt expansive, as if anything and everything were possible. Here was another world; a world I didn't know existed. Would it be possible that one day, I, a child of Chicago's West Side, would be able to function here as if I belonged? However, I wasn't following the family pattern—working full-time and going to school at night. As long as I was still living at home, my mother expected me to contribute to the family expenses. I had no extra money, so I was determined to find a live-in job on campus as soon as possible.

It turned out to be easier than I thought it would be. I got a job working for my room and board with a wealthy family in Evanston in my second semester, and when anyone asked me where I lived, I gave their posh address, without mentioning that I was a maid. In addition, my studies with the Nathanson Group in high school, especially the projects I did for that group, gave me an aura I wasn't even aware of. The experience of researching the lives of Gauguin and Van Gogh, studying their paintings week after week, doing a paper on the Impressionists, taught me the joy of doing research that was accepted by my peers.

I often sat reading on a bench overlooking the lake, and people would come by, sit down, and begin to talk. Perhaps this was a gift my sister Sara and I shared. I didn't know why it happened, but I grasped every opportunity to pretend that I belonged.

That was how I met Alvin. He simply sat down beside me one day and began to talk. When I found out he was a music major, I asked him what he thought of Bela Bartok. He looked at me, astonished.

"You know Bela Bartok?"

"Well, no, I don't know him. I just think he writes the most beautiful music I have heard in a long time."

"Well! What do you know! I'm writing my master's thesis on Bartok! Do you live on campus?"

Suddenly I decided to be honest. I told him my address and then added, "I'm a maid. I work for my room and board." I paused, and he didn't say anything. Rushing on, I said, "There's a wonderful grand piano in the living room, and no one's home, usually, between four and six every afternoon. Would you like to come over and play some time?"

Alvin looked at me as if I'd given him a large present. He looked at his watch. "Can we go now?"

"Sure, why not?" And that's how we began a long, deep, lasting friendship.

I was comfortable with the routine as a maid, and there was trust between my employers, Mr. and Mrs. Mayberry, and me. Life in that household was orderly, prescribed and peaceful. I wore a black uniform with a white lace-trimmed apron, served from the left and removed from the right, and prepared kidneys soaked in milk overnight for the master's breakfast, promptly at seven-thirty every morning, Sundays included. I had a small room at the top of the house, overlooking an alley, and there was a private entrance at the back that I used.

The Mayberry living room was full of linen and damask upholstered soft sofas and chairs, portraits of scowling, mustachioed men, elegantly dressed women and Bougereau landscapes. There were photographs of a handsome young man in tennis whites on the piano. They were pictures of Humphrey, the Mayberry son.

Alvin sat down at the piano and played a few chords. It was as if he and the piano were talking to each other. Then he swung into part of Bartok's Piano Concerto, and I took a deep breath. Here was real music! At that moment I fell in love. I don't know if I fell in love with Alvin or with the way he played, or with Bartok, as played by Alvin! When he stopped playing, I asked him if he would play something he had composed. He did, and I ignored the feeling of discomfort his composition gave me.

"You're a wonderful pianist!" I enthused.

Alvin sighed. "I'm still feeling my way in composition," he said. "I'm working on a sonata for my graduate thesis. I'll play some of that for you another time. The piece I just played was a nothing—I wrote it when I was a junior."

I couldn't tell him I didn't respond to the discords, and simply said, "Hey, it's five-thirty. I have to get ready for supper. You'd better go before the Mayberrys come home. That was really wonderful, Alvin. We'll do it again." I showed him out, and danced into the kitchen.

Everything was fine for the first three months I worked for the Mayberrys. It lasted until one night in early December. I was studying for finals one evening when there was a knock on the door to my room. When I opened the door, there stood Humphrey, smelling of beer. He pushed into the room and grabbed me, slobbering over my face and neck with wet kisses. I suppose he felt he had the right to assault the maid. Twisting out from under his arms, I ran downstairs and around to the front door. I punched the bell over and over, even though it was around eleven at night. Mrs. Mayberry came to the door in a fury, and looked at me in amazement.

"What are you doing out there without a coat?" She fixed me with an accusative look.

"Your son is in my room, uninvited," I said. "Please ask him to leave," I said, shivering.

Mrs. Mayberry turned around and looked at Humphrey, who had come in behind her from the kitchen.

"Never mind," I said. "I'm giving you two weeks' notice," and I ran back around to the stairway to my room. Once inside, I locked the door and barricaded it. *Was this standard behavior for wealthy sons? I thought of the feudal "droit de seigneur"—the rights of the lords over the peasants. But this was the twentieth century, not the Middle Ages!*

I couldn't go back home, because I had given up my room to Jeanne and Arthur, who had come back from Palestine, broke, and very discouraged. They had gone to Palestine in 1932, which was the height of the depression in Chicago. Arthur was a newly minted lawyer, for whom there were no clients; Jeanne had tried to save her boss from committing suicide and failed—she was now out of a job, and they thought they could make a new life in Jewish Palestine. They were so sure that they could grow tomatoes in a kibbutz, make tomato juice, and sell it to the natives that they stopped in Czechoslovakia on their way to buy tomato juicing machinery. Unfortunately, the seeds they brought from the Midwest produced pulpy tomatoes, totally unfit for juice, and Jeanne hated life on the kibbutz. Subsequently, they moved to Haifa where Jeanne found a secretarial job working for a British company, and Arthur picked up a menial job as a clerk. They were exiles, and they felt defeated, so they came back to Chicago and moved into my room.

My friend Peg, who lived in the freshman dorm, got permission to have a guest in her room for two weeks, while I figured out what to do. It turned out that there were many upper-class families in Evanston happy to have live-in college girls who would do light housekeeping, so I managed to move from one posh house to another by the end of the two weeks. In addition, I had a job on campus under a federal program that included students, called the Works Progress Administration, which paid twenty-five cents an hour. I worked for a political science professor named Colegrove.

There was a lot going on in 1936. The Italians were invading Ethiopia; Spanish Republicans were revolting against Franco; Germany was sending help to Spain in support of General Franco. The German government called the men they sent "observers" and "advisers." That was also the year of sit-down strikes in Chicago and throughout the Midwest, and when there were protest marches on campus, I was an enthusiastic placard carrier. I became secretary for the League Against War and Fascism, and worked to secure housing for refugees from Hitler's Germany. This was not popular at that time, because the mood in the Midwest was isolationist, and the intellectuals on the Northwestern campus pooh-poohed Hitler as a "silly madman." The popular attitude of left-wing liberals was that the war in Europe was something that America should stay out of. Chamberlain, Britain's prime minister, had not yet gone to Munich to negotiate a non-interventionist pact, and while my friends had gone to Spain to fight, promoting total American involvement was against pacifist principles.

I chose Political Science and History as alternative majors to English, and wanted to add Journalism as a minor, but didn't succeed. I always dreamt of being a journalist or a writer, and welcomed my job for Professor Colegrove. He was writing a book called *Militarism in Japan*, and I functioned as a quasi-editor.

Professor Colegrove was an enthusiastic Republican, and I was a vociferous Democrat. I showed up one day wearing a "Tribune Haters' Club" button during the Roosevelt/Al Smith campaign in 1938. Franklin Delano Roosevelt, the Democratic candidate for President, was running against Al Smith, the Republican candidate, and the *Chicago Tribune* was carrying attack ads against Roosevelt, as well as outspoken editorials, full of innuendoes and lies, as far as I was concerned. Dr. Colegrove, greeting me with a stony glare, said, "Political statements do not belong in my office." My answer to him popped out almost automatically.

Placing my hand on my button, which was pinned to my sweater over my heart, I said, "This is a free country, Dr. Colegrove. I'm against the campaign Al Smith is waging against Franklin Roosevelt, using the *Tribune* to do it, and this is how I declare my opposition." Dr. Colegrove gritted his teeth, and didn't speak to me for the rest of the semester. We communicated through written notes to each other.

Colegrove had sponsored a Japanese liberal named Professor Oyama, and was working with him on his book. My job was to take the scribbled in pencil notes by Professor Oyama and translate them into coherent English. Oyama's handwriting was not very clear, and his garbled English was even less clear. Inasmuch as Professor Oyama's primary language after Japanese was German, his English was doubly convoluted. I pored over the scribbled notes and guessed at much of it. Oyama always accepted my translations as "good, good." *How could he do otherwise?* It was an interesting and challenging job. I learned a lot, and I was rather relieved not to have to talk to Dr. Colegrove anyway. I just typed my material in silence.

By this time, I had shoved my envy of all the beautiful girls from the North Shore, with their cashmere sweaters and their confident airs, deep into my subconscious. I tried out for Dance Orchesis, was accepted, and began to relax a bit. Doris Humphrey, Jose Limon, and other dancers prominent in the modern dance world came to Northwestern for special weekend workshops. Our dance instructor had worked with Martha Graham. I loved that dance group, and felt my soul expand.

My job as a maid was beginning to depress me, so I applied for, and got, a job in the cafeteria of the Freshman Women's Dormitory, which carried with it a free room and free food. During the summers of 1937 and 1938 I worked as a secretary for Mandel Brothers Department Store, and learned a lot about merchandising.

The summer of 1937 was special in many ways. I worked in downtown Chicago, but lived on campus. Lena Horne and Walter Kerr were guest performers and lecturers in the Drama Department, and I was able to participate in weekend workshops. The evenings and weekend workshops were magical. *I found out later in my life that working in retail during the week, and experiencing the world of the theater on weekends taught me that no experience is ever wasted.*

Alvin and I had long talks. "You're a snob, you know," he said one evening as we walked along the lake front.

"How so?"

"You think you're better than all the debutantes who go to school here because you're working your way through school. Well, you're not better, you're just different. So you have to work for your room and board, and you're on scholarship. Does that mean you're smarter than everyone else?"

That made me mad. "Yes, I think so," I said. "Did you know that the girls in that sorority over there want me to write their English essays for them so that they can play bridge all day and not have to worry about their grades? They'll pay me for the papers too."

"Just because they're lazy doesn't mean they're dumb. Will you do it?"

"I don't know. It's awfully tempting."

"Then you'll be contributing to a felony. How does that make you feel? More superior?"

His arguments shook me. At the door to the dormitory, Alvin took me in his arms and held me tight. He knew I was on the verge of tears. "Don't cry," he said. "I think you're really smart and brave. I just don't want you to get a swelled head." He squeezed me hard against him.

In 1938, students in the Political Science Department at the University of Chicago staged a Mock League of Nations, assigning different universities in the immediate area different countries to represent. The University of Chicago took the United States and Spain as its two countries, and assigned Germany and the Union of South Africa to Northwestern; Italy and Ethiopia to Wisconsin. When we heard about the assignments, we laughed. Wisconsin and Northwestern were considered football rivals to Chicago, and we usually won all the football games in the "Big Ten." U. of Chicago students also didn't think much of the intellectual abilities of Wisconsin or Northwestern students.

Owen Lattimore was a visiting professor at the University of Chicago in 1938, and he was the guiding spirit behind the Mock League of Nations project. I used to go from Northwestern to the University of Chicago on the

El to sit in on his lectures. He was a charismatic man, tall, imposing, with an authoritative air that entranced most of the undergraduate women I knew, including me. Lattimore told us stories of how he had dyed his skin with coffee and how he had put lemon juice in his eyes to change the color from blue to brown, in order to disguise himself when he went into Tibet. He told us how he had dressed himself in the poor robes of a pilgrim and hunched over his donkey, in order to blend in with other pilgrims. We sat riveted during his lectures. When I heard that Owen Lattimore was going to be the moderator and director of the Mock League of Nations Conference, which was to be held on the University of Chicago campus, I was determined to be a member of the Northwestern team.

I was hoping to go to the conference as a junior member of the Political Science Club. Most of the members who were going as active participants were seniors or graduate students. As it turned out, one of the seniors got sick, and I was promoted to be an active member of a committee. We met every day in one of the dorm rooms on the University of Chicago campus rather than on our own campus because we often had to change our strategies at the last minute. *These guys don't really trust me, since I'm only a junior. I'll say yes to whatever they suggest.*

During a particularly acrimonious committee meeting called by the American and Spanish representatives, I, the representative of Germany, was asked about the status of German troops in Spain. Since I was a substitute representative, one of the graduate students on our team sat behind me and made sure I followed the strategy we had mapped out. For my answer to the statement about German troops in Spain, I said, "We have no troops in Spain. We have observers and advisers, requested by Generalissimo Franco. We are neutral."

I thought the University of Chicago student, representing Spain, would have a fit. The argument went on until two a.m. I wouldn't budge, and there was a vote that was supposed to come out of the committee. Professor Lattimore pleaded with us to compromise, and I remember saying to him, "Dr. Lattimore, you told us that we were supposed to behave as representatives of these countries would behave if this were a realtime conference. Do you want us to act as if this were an ideal situation, or a real one?" Lattimore paused and said, "As if it were a real situation."

"Then I deny everything. Germany has no troops in Spain, just observers and advisers." Lattimore declared an impasse, and the next day, Italy and Germany, represented by Wisconsin and Northwestern students, walked out of the Mock League of Nations.

The host student from Chicago was furious and accosted me in the hallway. "I might have known somebody from Northwestern would behave like that!"

I was also incensed. "Just a minute. We're here in a simulation, and we're following the rules. Besides, you don't know who I am, and just because I go to Northwestern doesn't mean I'm not a liberal. I'm a Jew, and I'm also secretary of the League Against War and Fascism. You guys set up this conference, and Lattimore made the rules. You can't change them in the middle." I walked away and joined the rest of our delegation.

That experience left an indelible impression on me. No one else on the campus was particularly interested in the Mock League of Nations. I wrote a long report which I submitted to the *Northwestern Daily*, but it was cut to two paragraphs, and was buried on an inside page. Even though I had had several articles published in the *Daily*, and harbored a secret desire to be a journalist, I had never taken a course in journalism. The memory of my high school experience as a "muckraking" reporter was always in the back of my mind.

All of the Midwest was in denial about the threat of Hitler. Milwaukee was the heart of the German Bund organization, an organization promoting the myth that Germany was a democratic country. "America First" was an isolationist organization that was vociferously against any "foreign involvement." They held many parades, all of them well promoted, and reflected the general mood of the country.

By May, 1939, all of the talk with my friends in the Political Science Club was about the impending war. We were all suspicious of Chamberlain's attempt to negotiate with Hitler, and we figured that this summer would probably be the last summer of peace. I was just as restless as everybody else. Alvin and I had another of our long talks.

"I think you should transfer to the University of California at Berkeley," he said. "It's a state university, and the atmosphere is a lot different. Why don't you go to Yellowstone and work for the summer as a waitress? Then you could go on to Berkeley from there. I'll be getting my master's in Music in a few weeks, and I'll be heading back home to Stockton. I've been offered a teaching position in the Department of Music at College of the Pacific in Stockton, and I could come through Yellowstone and pick you up, take you the rest of the way to Berkeley. I think there are jobs available in Yellowstone, and waitresses get good tips. Think about it."

I had been nominated for Phi Beta Kappa for the fall, which would be my senior year. *If I left Northwestern now, I would be graduating from Berkeley, two thousand miles away. I had to decide. If I stayed in Evanston and graduated, I would probably be stuck in the cashmere-sweatered ghetto of middle-class Jewish life, and I knew I didn't want to do that. The pattern of revolt that was my life was already fixed. What did I owe my family? Three thousand dollars. What kind of support had I gotten the last three years? My mother took every opportunity to complain about my choice. Was election to Phi Beta Kappa that important? Subconsciously I knew my family would be disappointed, but I was itching to leave.*

I walked over to the Student Union building and found Peg and all our friends from the Political Science Club engaged in deep conversation.

"Let's take a ship to Europe and bicycle through France and Spain," Harry said. A group of all the members of the Political Science Club were sitting in Charlie's Cafe near the Northwestern University campus, talking about summer plans.

"Spain?" Sylvia practically spit out the word. "You're nuts. The Spanish Republicans lost, remember? England, France, Switzerland maybe, but not Spain, and not Italy, either. Not with Mussolini as head of the government!"

"Okay, Okay. But what about the idea of staying in hostels and going around on bicycles?" Much head-nodding and happy murmuring. "After all, who knows how long Chamberlain and the Brits will be able to keep Hitler in Germany? This may be the last summer of peace. I, for one, have a desperate doomsday feeling. I'm restless," Peter said, running his hand through his red hair. He began to pace up and down the room.

There was a heavy silence. May, 1939, was an uncertain time, especially for me and my friends. We all knew boys who didn't come back from Spain in 1936-37; Joe Berkowitz for one, and Richard Modell, the poet who had introduced me to the Nathansons for another. We had participated in marches led by the League Against War and Fascism; we knew war was in the air. The German-American Bund and other isolationists pressured Roosevelt against involvement, and Roosevelt's ploy was to use the Merchant Marine to send supplies to England.

Peg and I, both juniors, were the only ones on scholarship and working twenty-five hours a week in order to pay our fees. I looked at Peg, my buddy, stood up, and said, "Hey, guys, we have to go now. Quiz tomorrow. See you." Peg joined me, and we walked out.

"Yeah," Peg said. "Bicycle through France. Heck, we don't even have bicycles, let alone money for the ship."

I said, "My friend Alvin, who lives in Stockton, California, says I ought to transfer to the University of California at Berkeley. His idea is for me to go to Yellowstone, work for the summer, save up some money, and go on to Berkeley. Are you interested?"

"I don't want to transfer to UC Berkeley," Peg said, "but I like the idea of Yellowstone. Do you think we could get jobs as waitresses?"

"Maybe." I thought about it. "I think Charlie, our friend at the Cafe would lie for us, and say we worked for him. He's a good egg. It's worth a try. Do you know how we would go about applying?"

"I'll check Student Employment tomorrow," Peg said. "See what I can find." Peg and I walked back to the dorm. As we walked through the quiet, tree-lined streets of Evanston, the air seemed cloying, even suffocating.

I don't want to graduate from here. If I do, I'll probably end up marrying a "nice, Jewish boy" and never get to be a real journalist. I'm sure we can get jobs as waitresses. Alvin had the right idea. I could save up my tips and go on to Berkeley. I guess I'll have to send my credits off to UC Berkeley Admissions. Excitement coursed through my veins like an electrical current.

The next day I saw Peg waving at me as I left my English class, and she ran to catch up with me. "Guess what! There was a sign on the bulletin board asking for people who wanted a ride to the West Coast! *And* I got all the information about Yellowstone!" She was jumping up and down with excitement. "All we have to do is get a recommendation from a restaurant or cafe owner saying that we have experience, and I think we'll be okay. Here are the application forms that I got from the employment bureau."

We filled them out immediately and went over to talk to Charlie at the Cafe.

"Okay, girls," he said. "I don't think they'll check. The places that hire college kids for the summer usually train them anyway. Good luck." He grinned at us. "Don't take any wooden nickels!"

We were walking on air. I sent off my credits to the University of California, and we called the boys who had advertised for riders. They had signed up with a company that hired drivers to ferry cars from Detroit to California, to save shipping charges. They warned us that we would be driving night and day in shifts, but they did agree to drop us off in Yellowstone.

I went home to pack, and didn't say anything to anybody about not coming back. That was hard. I simply said I was going to Yellowstone Park to work for the summer, but I didn't say I was planning to continue on to California. I couldn't handle the long explanations I knew would be demanded. *How could I explain the force that seemed to be pushing me?*

Neither Peg nor I had ever been out of the Midwest. We drove through the flat country of Iowa and Nebraska, and when we reached the Rocky Mountains, I felt my heart and mind expand. Those mountains! That clear air! We jumped out of the car at the first sign of snow in the mountains, and lay down to make angels. Imagine! Snow in June! We drove in shifts, stopping only to buy gas and food and use the restrooms at the gas stations. We sang and told stories and jokes, anything to keep ourselves awake. We got to Yellowstone a day earlier than we planned. The boys took off, and we walked over to the administration building.

The manager, a lean woman with dyed red hair, looked us over. "You girls are pretty skinny, aren't you?" was her greeting. "All right, take Cabin 43, put your things away, and report back here in an hour. Since you're here a day early, you'll be able to help get things ready."

When we showed up at the main building, we were handed buckets of water and sponges and put to work cleaning tables and chairs, setting up the dining rooms. More people kept arriving, and we felt as if we were in a big summer camp. There seemed to be an unspoken hierarchy. In order of importance were 1) waitresses and porters; 2) chambermaids; 3) dishwashers. Customers were called "Dudes," and they lived in cabins slightly more luxurious than those for staff. The staff all earned the same base salary, but of course tips were what everybody counted on to make the summer pay off.

There was a lot of bustling around. Inhaling the bracing mountain air, I found myself running from place to place. All of us were in a state of high energy. While we were scrubbing tables and washing windows, we kept checking out who came from where. There were two other girls from the Midwest, from Wisconsin, but most of the other college kids were from places closer to Yellowstone—Montana, Wyoming, Utah. I felt part of a vast community, college kids working their way through school. That was me all right, part of a special world. It was our summer away from parents and siblings; free to explore fantasies and dreams. Since most of us came from working-class families, and many of us were on scholarships at our universities, I didn't feel the same class pressure I'd felt at Northwestern.

We had to be at our stations at five a.m., and since we usually spent the late evening hours at bonfires at the lake, we slept only about three to four hours a night. We hiked around the park on our one day off a week, went fishing, talked and dreamed. The geysers, the mountains all around, the clear air, the bears, created a memory that lives in my mind suspended in time.

There was one incident I've tried not to remember. Somebody brought a case of beer one night to the bonfire. It was a warm night, and after a while, couples began to drift off to bushes surrounding the fire. One boy and I were left. I sat with my knees drawn up, my head resting on my folded arms, and stared into the dying fire. Suddenly I felt a hand on my back, snaking around to grab my small breast. I was not in the mood to make love with someone I barely knew. As I turned around, he grabbed me and started to push me down. All the horror stories about rape that I had heard from my cabinmates flooded my mind, and I kicked him hard, knocking him off his feet. I scrambled up and ran as fast as I could to the road. I kept looking back over my shoulder, but he didn't follow.

Back at the cabin, I fell shakily into bed, drifting off to a troubled sleep. Peg didn't come in for another hour, and I heard her dimly through the fog of my dreams. I didn't tell Peg about the experience, and concentrated on learning how to balance a tray full of food.

I remember my first evening as a waitress. I was tall and skinny, being five feet, six-and-one-half inches and weighing ninety-eight pounds, and the manager was doubtful about my ability to carry a heavy tray of food. I was determined to show her how strong I was that first night. Accordingly, I loaded up my first tray with heavy bowls of soup and hoisted the tray to my shoulder. As I pushed open the door from the kitchen and hesitated in the doorway, getting my balance, I sensed a hush that fell over the dining room. Out of the corner of my eye, I noticed the diners' forks suspended in air, and was aware of their eyes watching me maneuver my heavy tray across the room. When I bent my knees, lowering the tray to the serving table, I heard a collective sigh of relief and the clatter of forks on plates. I had passed, and didn't spill any soup, either.

After dinner, in the evening, we were supposed to entertain the "Dudes." We had to improvise songs and skits, and put on some kind of talent show every night. Luckily, there were plenty of amateur singers, dancers, and clowns, and we arranged to take turns. It didn't take us long to organize ourselves so that no one had to perform more than one night a week.

Peg and I created a song and dance number, reminiscent of the kind of duet popular in musical comedies. We took a tune like "Blue Skies," and wrote lyrics that fit the Yellowstone scene, and created a soft-shoe shuffle to go with it. We also did "There's a Rainbow 'Round my Shoulder," and "The Sunny Side of the Street," changing the words to "the sunny side of the road," for instance. There was a special Fourth of July parade, and the Dudes got to vote on which group came up with the best costume. The dishwashers, called "Pearl Divers," won.

Chapter Nine:
UC Berkeley

⌒

THE SUMMER WAS OVER THE FIRST WEEK OF AUGUST, and Alvin came to pick me up as planned. The entire summer of 1939 I had nourished a special fantasy... that Alvin cared for me as much as I cared for him, that we would drive to Berkeley together, and he would declare his love for me, and... and... I usually didn't get much farther than that. I knew Alvin was older than me, that he was a graduate student in music, a composer, and that he expected to become an instructor in the Music Department at College of the Pacific in Stockton. My dreams didn't include any details. In all of our times together, Alvin had kissed me only once, and although he was affectionate, his attitude was always more like a mentor than a lover. That didn't stop my fantasies.

Alvin arrived about seven o'clock on a full moon night, and we walked a short way out of the campground, across a meadow. The moon was tangible; I felt that I could touch it if I stretched out my hand. Alvin walked next to me, but not close. I was aware of a hesitation in his manner. Then he stopped, faced me, and put his hands on my shoulders.

"I have something to tell you," he said.

Uh, oh, my stomach dropped, as it had done when my brother spoke those same ominous words. I looked up at him, the moonlight strong around us. It was a black and blindingly white universe.

"Yes?"

"When I left Stockton," he said, turning and starting to walk again, "I had an informal arrangement with a girl. I wasn't sure what I wanted to do right then, and neither was she. She wanted to finish her degree in Drama, and I knew I had to write my thesis and complete my graduate work." He took a deep breath. "She came to Northwestern in May after she graduated; we spent the summer together... and... we decided to get married. I thought you ought to know."

I looked away from him. "There's a stream at the end of this meadow," I said, "let's go and sit on the bank." A light breeze lifted my fantasies and spun them away. I took Alvin's hand, and we sat down on the bank, looking at the moon path on the water.

"What's her name?"

"Muriel. She's a lovely person. You'd like her, and she's also a Christian Scientist, like me."

Ah, well. I rolled over onto my stomach and rested my head on my hands. *Too late to go back now. I had sent my credits to UC Berkeley before leaving Northwestern, and I hadn't told my parents or family that I wasn't coming back; I had slammed a door shut behind me.* I sat up and looked at Alvin. He looked miserable.

"You'll still drive me to Berkeley, won't you?"

"Of course! And I'll help you get settled, too! You didn't think I'd leave you stranded, did you? You are important to me. I feel responsible for you!"

Responsible for me? Within limits, I guess. Better keep everything as impersonal as possible. "Where are you staying?"

"Down the road at a motel."

"Well, I can be ready to leave about nine a.m. Is that early enough?"

"Sure. We want to get over the Rockies in the daylight. I thought we could stop at the Grand Tetons on the way."

I was in no mood to discuss our itinerary. We walked in silence back to the campground, and Alvin left me at the door to Cabin 43. Our hugs were friendly, and I resisted the impulse to put my head on his shoulder. I looked at him, nodded, and said, "See you tomorrow." Once inside the cabin, I stared out at the campground, the black shadows of the cabins reflecting my state of mind. Taking a deep breath, I started packing. I had accumulated a little more than three hundred dollars in tips, and I sewed the money into a special belt I wore around my waist. I gazed again at the moon through my window... no point trying to think ahead. Berkeley would be another country.

Alvin and I kept our conversation light and general. He talked about music; I talked about what I intended to do when I got to Berkeley. I had a little money in my pocket, and was full of confidence. Alvin kept assuring me that I would be fine. He was right. I got a job through Student Employment and found a cooperative dormitory on Ridge Road, on the north side of campus. Once I was sure I could pay the out-of-state fees and rent at the dorm, I called home. My family was furious. They felt betrayed, cheated out of celebrating my graduation. It was a stormy conversation, full of recriminations like "How could you do a thing like this?" and "Don't you ever consider anybody but yourself?" There's no answer to questions like that, and I didn't try. When I hung up, I sighed. I had really slammed that door behind me. I was on my own now, and I felt free. I didn't know anyone in California; I wasn't within an hour of home; I had cut the umbilical cord.

My job was to work part-time as a secretary for a social worker in Oakland. That meant I would need a car. I would never be able to work in Oakland and get back to the Berkeley campus on public transportation, if I expected to get to classes on time. I went to the Dean of Women and told her my story. She was wonderfully sympathetic, and helped to arrange a loan. Shopping around, I found a 1935 LaSalle two-seater coupe with a rumble seat for thirty-five dollars. It was a classy car with a long hood and a sleek look. Of course it got only ten to twelve miles per gallon, and I had to put in a quart of oil every time I filled the tank, but I loved that car, and I loved the independence it gave me.

My boss, Mrs. Andropolous, was a psychiatric social worker, employed by the city of Oakland. I was never quite sure where her patients came from, but typing their case histories was another fascinating experience. I always took my lunch and wrote letters to friends on my lunch hour. My boss objected, and I almost lost the job.

Now that I had a job, a car, a room in a cooperative dorm, I was wondering how to fit into the social scene. My roommate, Fran, came up to me one night when I was on kitchen duty.

"Hey," she said. "Going to the New Students' Dance Friday night?" Fran was a transfer student from UCLA (Los Angeles). She was also a senior.

"New Students' Dance? I don't know anybody here. How can I go to a dance by myself?" This was unthinkable by Midwestern standards.

"I'm going." Fran looked surprised. "You know me!"

"I mean I don't know any boys. I don't have a date."

She laughed. "You sure are funny. Nobody has a date at the open dances. Everybody goes stag."

"Stag? Do you mean the boys line up on one side of the room and girls on the other? And you just stand there until somebody comes along and asks for a dance?" I was horrified. "I can't do that."

"Sure you can!" Fran was pretty, petite, bouncy, and totally assured. "You'll see. It's fun. I'll hold your hand." She giggled.

We set off across the campus with Fran literally holding my hand, pulling me along. Wearing the clothes of an ordinary college girl, new bobby socks, new saddle shoes, new blue wool circular skirt and long sweater, I felt as if I were living in someone else's skin. *Oh, what am I doing here? The air is so crisp, so clear, so un-Chicago! Is this really not a dream?* The Women's Gym, a huge structure, was on the south side of campus, about a mile away. We walked through the fragrant night across the campus, the classic buildings ghostly in the fog. The band was already playing when Fran and I walked in.

"Now what?" I asked Fran.

"We just stand here until someone comes along who asks us to dance. Then we say yes or no."

"How do you know when to say no?" I felt helpless and exposed, awkward and stiff, suddenly realizing what a restricted life I had led. I knew how to waltz and do the two-step, but jitterbug? I looked at the gyrating couples on the dance floor and thought, "oh, god, I can't do that!"

Fran gave me a disgusted look. "If you don't like a guy's looks, or he's too short, just say you have this dance promised. Relax. I'm off." She nodded at a boy who approached her and they hopped off. I watched with growing anxiety, and looked around for a pillar to hide behind.

A tall, dark-haired boy approached me. "Like to dance?" he asked.

He was cute, but I hesitated. "I don't know how to jitterbug," I said, hoping he would go away.

"I'll teach you," he said, taking my arm, "I can teach anybody." We went off to a small space at the edge of the dance floor. The band was playing Duke Ellington tunes: "Stompin' at the Savoy," "Take the 'A' Train," "One o'clock Jump." Bill taught me how to do the Boston Stomp. He put his arm around my waist, practically lifting me off the floor. This was partly side-by-side dancing, totally in synch. Budda, budda, budda, stomp! Budda, budda, budda, stomp! Lean toward your partner, lean away. Swing your hips toward him, lean away, keep the rhythm. Think of nothing else. We whirled wider and wider, my skirt flaring above my knees. A group of people gathered around us, and the band played chorus after chorus. Transported, I thought and felt nothing but the rhythm, the in-synch movement of my body. Always aware of Bill, following his lead, I was having the time of my life. We kept stompin', swiveling our hips, leaning in, leaning out. Finally the drummer took a solo—was it Gene Krupa? Could've been… We fell into a couple of chairs, the crowd around us clapping and clapping.

"Hey! I thought you said you didn't know how to dance!"

"Well, I didn't know I could till just now! I've never done this kind of dancing before. Everything's more formal in the Midwest, but this seemed so natural. Where'd you learn to do that fancy stuff?"

"I'm Boston Irish. That's what we do in Boston. I'm in the Merchant Marine. Just here for the weekend. We ship out on Monday. My buddy has a cousin who goes to school here, and he told us about this dance. So we decided to crash. Might be a while before we get to dance again." He watched me carefully to see how I would take this information.

Wow! Bill was actually going to war, in a way. I nodded. "Where are you going?"

Bill's handsome face closed down. "I don't know," he said. "We'll find out when we get there." Bill shook his head as if to clear it. He flashed his captivating grin. "Never mind. Let's dance. I'll show you some new steps."

We were off again. Bill did some fancy stuff, jumping in the air, twirling around. He was good, really good. I caught a wave from Fran. She gave me a big grin, thumbs up.

Later, we sat around over sodas, Bill, Fran, a boy from L.A. Fran had picked up, and me, kidding around, making small talk. Bill leaned across the table.

"My buddy's cousin has an apartment in South Berkeley," he said, looking around the table. "How about going over there for some music and beer?" *A chill went down my back. Oops. He was handsome, all right. But things were happening too fast. I flashed back to that night on the beach at Yellowstone when I had to fight off an overly aggressive boy. My roommates had talked of rape. Agreement was one thing, with someone I knew well, but I had just met this boy. What if Fran said yes? How would we get back? I didn't choose this boy, he chose me.*

Fran shook her head ever so slightly, and looked down at her shoes. *Whew! Saved.* "I don't think so," I said. "We have a one a.m. curfew, and it's almost that now. Sorry, I think we'd better go." I stood up. Everybody got up then, and Bill said, "Well, let me drive you home, anyway. Okay?" He took my arm, propelling me firmly toward the door. We got into Bill's small car, and all squished together, drove slowly to our dorm. Fran and Joe got out, and Bill hung on to me, leaning over. "How about just you and me going over to my cousin's? Look, I only have this weekend, and then…"

I put my hand on the door handle, ducking his mouth. "Sorry, Bill, I have to go now." I leaped out of the car and ran up the steps to the pillared porch, passing Fran and Joe, locked in a deep clutch. From the safety of the screen door I called down, "Take care of yourself, Bill!" and fled into the sanctuary of the living room.

Chapter Ten:

Jim

⤳

"Come in! Come in! Sit anywhere you like! Welcome to our humble abode!"

The boys at the "Men Only" co-op were hosting us that evening. We lived next door, at the women's cooperative, in a house called "White Gables."

We walked tentatively into the dining room with its long narrow tables, noticing that every other place setting was marked with a small card stating "Visitor," and we assumed that each one of us would be flanked by a member of the men's co-op. A tall, thin boy wearing thick glasses approached me. His brown eyes regarded me gravely, and as he bent courteously over me, his light brown hair fell gently across his face. He brushed his hair back and said, "Would you like to sit here?" pulling out a chair for me. He waited for me to sit down and then sat down next to me. "I'm Jim Pack," he said, holding out his hand. "My major is Psychology. I'm a senior, from Grants Pass, Oregon." His hand was firm and dry. *Oooh, I like this guy! He's so polite! Says he's in Psychology. At least he's not an engineer, with a vocabulary limited to technical jargon.*

"I'm Rhoda Curtis," I said. "A senior transfer student from Northwestern. I'm majoring in English Lit."

"English Lit, eh? Are you familiar with poetry by e.e. cummings? I don't quite understand all of it, but I like it. I don't know why."

A psychology major who likes poetry? Yes! I didn't pay much attention to the boy on my right. I was too absorbed by Jim. We talked about poetry and psychology. Jim kept drawing me out, actually listening to me. *I wonder if he's got a girlfriend.* The dinner over, we all stood up and Jim said, "It's my turn to clear the tables, but it won't take long. Is it okay if I meet you in the parlor?" *How polite he is! Of course it would be okay!*

"Yes, sure." I draped my sweater over the space next to me on the sofa in the main gathering place of the dorm. Groups of people clustered in corners, heads together, talking intensely. Girls and boys, pretending to be grown women and men, lit cigarettes with self-conscious airs, blowing smoke rings, puffing nervously. Jim came in and sat down, pulling out a pipe. We had just leaned back against the cushions when Fran came over to us and said, "A bunch of us are going down to the White Horse Tavern on Alcatraz. Want to come?"

I knew that Alcatraz was on the edge of the one-mile boundary around the university that excluded bars. I knew that Fran knew I had a car. I looked at Jim. He grinned (what a nice smile!) giving me a "why not?" look, and said, "Fine with me, you want to go?"

"Sure," I said. *I wonder what the White Horse Tavern is like. If it's anything like those dives on the border between Chicago and Evanston, I can skip it. I really want to spend some time alone with Jim.* "Hey Fran, do you and Joe want to ride in the rumble seat?"—*knowing that Fran wanted to do exactly that.* She liked my 1935 LaSalle coupe, especially the rumble seat.

The White Horse Tavern, filled with smoke, loud jukebox music, with wall-to-wall UC Berkeley students pressed up against each other, pretending to dance, wasn't inviting. Fran and Joe pushed their way to a booth, and squeezed in with a couple of people they knew. Jim and I stood on the edge of the crowd, people shoving past us. Jim made no move to join the crowd.

"I don't dance very well," he said hesitantly.

"Well, there's not much room to do any real dancing anyway," I said, thinking of Bill and the Boston Stomp. "We don't have to stay, you know."

"No?"

"No. Since I have a car, we can drive up to Grizzly Peak and look at the view." He nodded, seeming relieved. "Just let me tell Fran we're leaving." I edged my way over to her, "Excuse me, excuse me," elbows out. I reached

Fran and told her we were leaving. She said it was okay, that she'd catch a ride with somebody, or just walk back to campus.

Outside, the night was cool and clear. I stretched my arms wide, drinking in the crisp air and looked up at the stars. "What a gorgeous night!"

Jim held the door of the car open for me. "I have to say I'm more comfortable out of doors than I am in. Growing up in Grants Pass, my dad broke me in early, camping on the Rogue River."

Thinking about Jim's remark, I shifted into low gear, heading toward Grizzly Peak. "I grew up in Chicago, close to Lake Michigan," I said. "My family had a cabin in the Indiana Dunes, and I used to spend summers there. Haven't done much camping, but I love the outdoors too. That's one of the things I love about Berkeley. Five minutes and you can be above the city, close to the sky."

Jim rolled down his window, letting the cool air blow into our faces. We sang, "Boola, boola, sarsparoola, boola, boola, you're for me!"—making up words as we went along.

Arriving at a spot overlooking the East Bay, we parked and sat looking at the lights in silence. Jim put his arm around me, tentatively, and I snuggled in close, putting my head on his shoulder. Suddenly Jim opened his door, came around to my side of the car, and took my hand.

"It's too beautiful to sit inside the car," he said. "Let's walk up the road and get a better look at the Bay." The night was clear, the stars enveloping us in a benign light. We stood hand in hand, silent, looking at the twinkling lights below us.

"Sometimes I wish I had chosen a career that allowed me to work outdoors," Jim sighed. "Something like geology or archaeology, so I could go on field trips or on digs. I feel so hemmed in, when I'm working in my lab."

"What do you do?" I was getting more and more interested in this shy boy.

"I'm doing research for a physiology professor named Dr. Shock. We do experiments on students, taking blood pressure readings under stressful conditions, which we create." He laughed. "Sounds funny, doesn't it? Create a stressful condition, then measure blood pressure?"

"It sounds to me as if you're using students as guinea pigs. What kinds of students are willing to be part of your experiments? Why do they do it?"

Jim put his arm around me. "I don't know," he said. "But the students volunteer. I don't know if Dr. Shock pays them, or if they get breaks on their grades. Most of them are athletes, I notice. I tell myself it's not my responsibility. It's a job, and I need the job to pay my fees." He noticed I was shivering. "You're cold, maybe we'd better go back to the car."

"Yeah. Race you!" I turned around and ran up the road, then jumped into the car. "You're right. It's warmer in here." I started the car, put it in gear, and we drove down the hill in a comfortable silence. When we got to North Gables, Jim again got out, came over to my side of the car, and opened the door for me. "Will I see you tomorrow?" He looked at me hopefully.

"I usually go to the library after dinner. Want to walk over with me?" *I felt a different kind of shiver up my spine.*

"Sure. I'll pick you up at seven. 'Bye!" He hummed a little tune as he walked next door.

After that, we walked to the library every night and each evening I found myself impatiently going through the dinner chores, continually looking at the clock, which seemed to crawl toward seven. Friday night Jim asked me what I was going to do on Saturday.

"I have a paper to write," I said, "but I think I can finish by five o'clock. Why?"

"Oh, I just thought you might like to have a pizza and go to a movie." He shifted from foot to foot, looking away as if he didn't care whether or not I said yes.

"What a great idea! I'd love to do that." I didn't care what kind of movie we went to. This was a date!

After the movie, we drove up to our spot on Grizzly Peak and parked, looking at the Bay sparkling in the moonlight. Suddenly Jim reached for me just as I reached for him. We kissed hungrily, our breath came faster and faster. I fumbled with his zipper, he reached under my blouse. We stripped down quickly, but the front seat of my car was not exactly roomy. We wrestled around the stick shift, my arm hung out the rolled down window, the rough plush of the seat tickling my behind. I suddenly felt Jim deep inside me. He came very quickly, withdrew, and with a wild whoop, opened his door. Dashing off into the night, he leaped around like a startled faun. Lucky there wasn't another car in sight on this popular "Lover's Lane." I couldn't help giggling, so startled I didn't know what to expect next. *So different from my first experience at sixteen. Then it was a full moon at the Indiana Dunes, a warm summer night, and sand in my crotch. I understood Jim's exhilaration.* He ran back to the car, opened my door and pulled me out, just as he did the first night we came to this spot.

"Feel the air! Isn't it glorious?" He pressed his naked belly against mine, and I could feel him hardening up again. I moved toward the car. He hung onto me. *I wanted everything to last longer.* "A little slower, this time, if you can," I whispered into his ear, as we edged into the car, still clutching each other.

"Mmmm," he muttered. This time it was *much* better! Afterwards, we leaned back, sighing. Jim eased himself out of the passenger side and ran around to the driver's seat, sensibly not trying to crawl over the stick shift. He reached in for his clothes and quickly dressed. I was wiping myself off with my underpants when Jim handed me his handkerchief. I looked forward to a shower.

We drove slowly down the hill, Jim driving, my head on his shoulder, his arm around me. He began singing, "The stars out tonight, something something so bright... deep in the heart of Berkeley!" We laughed together, and as he squeezed my shoulder, I covered his hand, pulling myself closer to him. *Ohh, I feel so safe and cared for with this guy!* At my dorm, Jim parked, came around to my side of the car, lifted me out and we hugged. He kissed me tenderly, and then he seemed to float down the street.

After the wild coupling in my car that memorable evening in October, 1939, we again spent every evening together at the library, and when the library closed, we were off in my car to Wildcat Canyon Road, parking on parts of the road that were seldom patrolled. I had myself fitted for a diaphragm by a cooperative campus health service, and by December we decided to find an apartment off campus. Housing around the campus was still pretty tight in 1939, and when it came to rent, my mother's worried voice echoed in my head.

"Do you think we can find something we can afford?" I asked Jim. "The co-ops are pretty cheap, and my current job ends in two weeks." We were sitting in LaVal's coffeehouse before going back to our dorms.

"I think I can get you a job as my assistant." Jim squeezed my hand. "Don't worry, I'll teach you. It's not that complicated. We're now doing experiments for the Army Air Corps and for the Institute of Child Behavior. You'll see."

I wasn't convinced. "When can I get an interview with Dr. Shock? Maybe he'll need a typist, so if he turns me down as your assistant, maybe he'll hire me anyway." *We're still seniors. We still have to pay our fees. Ma was right. It's a good thing I know how to type and take dictation.*

"That's the spirit." We grinned at each other, full of optimism.

Two days later we were in Dr. Shock's office. "This is Rhoda Curtis. I spoke to you about her yesterday."

"Oh, yes, the English major." From behind a messy desk, he peered at me, spectacles riding low on his nose. "What makes you think you can work in a scientific lab?"

"With Jim as a teacher, I figure I can learn anything." I looked at Jim and then back at Dr. Shock.

There was a pause while Dr. Shock looked at both of us appraisingly. *Does he notice how we're sitting, shoulders touching? I'm glad he can't see our entwined fingers.* Then he said, "We'll give it a try. Jim will show you the protocols for the work we're doing. Mind you, we have to have complete and accurate records on everything you do. Do you understand?"

I nodded, not really knowing exactly what he was talking about. Our combined salary would be about twelve-fifty an hour and we could live on that. We bounced happily out of his office, ran down the steps of the Life Sciences Building, and spun each other around on the grass.

"Wheeee! We're off!" We found two rooms with a kitchenette built into a closet on Delaware Street, about a mile from campus, sharing a toilet down the hall with another couple. There was a washing machine in the basement with a hand-turned wringer attached. We bought a frying pan, some plates, cups, cutlery, sheets, blankets, and towels at Goodwill. We felt very domestic.

As things turned out, I did get more work with Dr. Shock as his typist, so occasionally we were able to afford hamburger at twenty-five cents a pound, but mostly we ate oatmeal or macaroni and cheese. Jim gave me half a pound of bacon and a potted begonia for my birthday. *How I loved that pale pink begonia.*

The LaSalle was giving us trouble, and we decided to look for another car. We drove the coupe in fits and starts to a used car lot, and found a Model A Ford that was in pretty good shape. The dealer even took the LaSalle and gave us twenty-five dollars toward the purchase of our Ford. After that, we were able to drive to the campus in our new old car, which was permanently open, the previous owner having cut off the top. In the winter, we drove with me holding an umbrella over our heads, if we were in a hurry. Otherwise, we walked.

On campus, Jim led me to his basement lab in the Life Sciences building, a narrow, low-ceilinged room and explained our job: "Dr. Shock has several contracts with the Army Air Force," he began, "and the Air Force wants to know how their pilots might react to various kinds of physical stress. We have to measure changes in blood pressure and pulse rate after exercise."

"How do we do that?"

Jim pulled out a blood pressure cuff and stethoscope from a lower drawer in his desk. Putting the stethoscope in his ears, he took my blood pressure and pulse rate and wrote the numbers down on a pad. "Now you do it," he said, putting the stethoscope around my neck. "You'll hear nothing, and then you'll hear a 'thump, thump, thump.' Look at the gauge, and notice the number when you hear that first 'thump.' Keep listening. Then you'll hear a change in the thumping. Look at the number on the gauge. Write down both numbers."

I tore the stethoscope off my neck. "Oh, Jim, I don't think I can do this!"

"Sure you can." Jim the optimist was confident. "Let's do it again." And so we did, all morning, until I finally heard the difference between the systolic and the diastolic blood pressures; the difference between the first "thump" and the second one.

Our number one volunteer showed up the next day, and we went upstairs to the first floor of the Life Sciences Building. "We'll go up to the landing on the floor above the stairs," Jim said to the burly football player who'd shown up. "You run up the stairs, and we'll take your blood pressure and pulse rate." Jim and I trotted up the stairs, our volunteer ran up, we strapped the blood pressure cuff on him, and Jim took the readings. Then we went up to the next level, and this time it was my turn. But I fumbled getting the blood pressure cuff on, and by the time I pumped it up, he was all relaxed, so the numbers were way off. We thanked him, and he took off.

"This is kind of dumb, Jim," I said. "I don't know much about scientific experiments, but it seems to me that there ought to be a better way to do this."

"You're right, English major!" He grinned. "I'll talk to Otto."

A few days later, we had a newly built set of steps that our volunteers ran up and down. At least we didn't have to run up the stairs ahead of the subjects. The steps were installed in our small room, and even though there wasn't much room to walk around, it was better. We watched and waited. When our "subjects" began to pant and sweat, we quickly took the blood pressures and pulse readings. I felt calmer when it was my turn, but I was a bit relaxed when it came to record keeping. Sometimes when I couldn't remember the numbers, I made them up. This was not a good idea, as I soon found out.

One particularly hectic week, when I turned in my records to Otto, Dr. Shock's assistant, he looked at them with a frown. Otto was German and meticulous in everything he did. He prided himself on being exact about everything. Otto was short and stocky, and carried himself as if he were on a parade ground. There were times when I think he expected me to give him a salute. Otto's frown deepened as he looked at the sheets I had handed him and said, through tight lips, "What is this? These numbers don't make any sense!"

"I guessed," I said.

"You guessed?!" The veins on his neck swelled; he almost exploded. I backed toward the door. Otto noticed my backing away, took a big breath, and in a lower voice, asked, "Why did you do that?"

"I just couldn't tell the difference between the blood pounding in my ears and the pulse I was supposed to be hearing. But I had to write down something, so I guessed."

Otto sighed. "My dear girl," he said, "in science, it is better to leave a space blank than to fill it in with made-up figures. Maybe this is not a job for you." He turned away. Relieved, I sprinted out the door.

The following day I approached my appointment with Dr. Shock with a sense of impending doom, but Shock was surprisingly calm. He greeted me benignly and waved me to a chair.

"I guess English majors really can't be bothered with careful recording of scientific data!"

I flushed and looked down at my hands. He was right, of course.

"You said you could take dictation, didn't you?" I nodded. "Well, how about attending my lectures, taking them down, and transcribing them for me? Then I can use my lectures as a basis for my next book."

I was delighted. This was more or less what I had done for Dr. Colegrove at Northwestern. That assignment suited me to a T. One of the odd things that happened was that I discovered Dr. Shock's lectures were full of "hm-mms" and "ahhhs," with long silences while he thought about what he would say next. He didn't seem to prepare very thoroughly for his lectures on the physiology of the human body. I began to edit the lectures and make literary sense out of them, as I had done for Professor Oyama. Unfortunately, Dr. Shock came to believe that the carefully transcribed and edited notes were a literal translation of what he said, and he began to show up later and later for his lectures, and prepare less and less.

I decided to teach him a lesson and one day I transcribed a lecture exactly as given. I waited in my small room off his office for the inevitable explosion.

"Miss Curtis!" he shouted. "Come in here!"

As I walked through the door, he was on his feet, waving my transcription in the air. "What is this? Were you asleep?"

"Dr. Shock," I said calmly. "That's really what you sound like." *I had learned a thing or two about scientific methods, even though he thought I was incapable of careful record keeping.* "I've been spending a lot of time editing your lectures because I knew you were going to use them as notes for your book, and I wanted to be helpful."

He gave me a long, slow look, and took a big breath. Then he sat down, laughed and said, "Score one for you, Miss Curtis. I'll try to come on time and be a bit more prepared from now on. But please don't do any more exact transcriptions. Just keep on doing what you're doing." He came around his desk, patted me on the back and went out, chuckling.

The rest of the term went smoothly, with Jim doing the scientific work in the basement lab, and me being Dr. Shock's private secretary. We all trusted each other, and there was a comradely feeling between us, even with Otto.

Jim and Rhoda at UC graduation (1940)

First home after marriage: 1720 Delaware, Berkeley

Chapter Eleven:
First Marriage and Teaching

⤙

IN JUNE OF 1940, Jim's father and mother came to Berkeley from Grants Pass, Oregon, for our graduation. We had to work that morning, so Jim had made arrangements with his parents to meet afterward in our lab. Jim's father, a lumberman, came to the lab alone. He and Jim talked in the room adjoining our office, where I was working on a report. I could hear his unfamiliar voice through the thin partition.

"She's Jewish, you say? You don't have to marry her, you know. You have your whole life in front of you. You don't want to marry just yet, especially not a Jew."

Stunned, I strained to hear Jim's answer. It was so mumbled, I couldn't make it out, but it evidently didn't suit his father. His father's voice rose to a shout.

"Don't be such a stubborn idiot! It will never work! You think that because you've graduated from the university, you're an adult! You don't know anything about life. You're still a child! I'm not going to say anything to your mother about this. She would simply have one of her headaches. Never mind dinner tonight. Your mother and I will go right back home this afternoon." Mumble, mumble. "No, I don't want to spend any time with her, not under these circumstances. We'll go out to the car now; you make some excuse to your mother about having work to do. Come on."

The door slammed. I put my hands over my ears and tried to tell my brain to ignore what it had just registered. It didn't work. Jim's face was flushed when he came into the office. He grabbed me and held me tight. Burying my face in his shoulder, I swallowed my tears.

"It doesn't matter what he says," Jim said slowly. "I think we should get married as soon as possible. We're supposed to work during summer break, but I think the boss will give us some time off."

We stood holding each other. Time stopped. Jim took my face and kissed my eyes, my nose, and my whole face tenderly. "Don't cry. He isn't worth it."

"Okay." Shaking, I sat down and put my head on the desk. I had been passing as a non-Jew ever since I needed to get a job after high school, simply by not declaring my origins. I hadn't joined any Jewish groups at Northwestern, and spent most of my waking life either working or studying at UC Berkeley, when I wasn't with Jim. Apparently, as a Jew I was a non-person as far as Jim's father was concerned. Did it matter? How "Jewish" was I, anyway? Jim knelt beside me, his head close to mine. Time began to move again. Sighing, I sat up, took his face in my hands, looking deep into his eyes. We rose together and held on tight. We took off our rented graduation robes, walked out of the Life Sciences Building, our bodies moving in unison, Jim's supportive arm around me.

"Let's eat out tonight, Rhoda. Someplace other than La Val's Pizza Parlor!"

Still teary, I pressed his arm against me, and we wandered down to Shattuck Avenue, looking for something a bit more upscale than La Val's. I didn't want to talk about his father's attitude toward me and toward Jews in general; I didn't know anything about Jim's mother. *I pushed my feelings into my gut.* Jim didn't say anything either. As far as Jim and I were concerned, the graduation ceremony was just something to be gotten through. We talked mostly about work we had to do the next day. We had both already signed up for courses in our respective postgraduate fields—Jim in his field of Applied Psychology, I in my field, Education. I was working toward an M.A. in Remedial Reading; Jim was working with Dr. Jones in a special Institute for the Study of Child Behavior headed by Dr. MacFarlane. We were both involved in a study of twins, as well as research into the reaction of adolescents to different kinds of visual and auditory stimuli.

The next two months passed in a blur. One evening in August, in the library, Jim reached over to me and ceremoniously closed my book.

"We have to talk about something serious. Let's go."

It was a windy, cold, foggy evening, and I buttoned up my sweater. Jim sat me down on the library steps, out of the wind. "Do you remember what I said about getting married? I think it's time."

I looked at him in astonishment. "Really?"

"Yes, really. Pretty soon we're going to be working harder than ever, and this may be our only chance for a two-week vacation. Don't you have a friend in Sacramento? Fran what's-her-name?"

I laughed. "Yeah, Fran Harrison. She moved to Sacramento right after graduation." I took a deep breath. *Odd, I had become so accustomed to living from day to day that I had succeeded in wiping out everything about that traumatic day in the lab. I had also wiped out the memory that I hadn't received any cards or congratulatory letters from my own family.* "I guess we could stay with her. Let's go home, I'm freezing. We can call her tonight."

After talking to Fran, we went to Sacramento that weekend and stayed with Fran. She introduced us to a Protestant minister she knew. Jim, a Christian Scientist and I, a Jew, agreed to have this man marry us. I don't know why we didn't go to City Hall, it just didn't occur to us. But the pre-wedding conference was wrenching for me. The minister preached to us about God and the Good Life. I came undone afterward, crying through the night. The not-to-be named God I knew was connected to men praying separately from women, swaying back and forth, hidden under prayer shawls. That God was also connected to candles on Friday nights, the smell of fresh braided bread. It had nothing to do with the death of a human being, being tortured on a cross, or having died for sins I didn't commit. Alone, so alone, I wept and wept. *What was I doing? Who was Jim Pack? We had lived together for more than six months, but what did I really know about him? I didn't know anything about his parents or his family. What am I committing myself to?*

The next morning cold water did little to diminish my puffy red eyes, and I sniffled through the vows. That's how I became Mrs. Jim Pack, thinking of myself as Rhoda Pack, no longer Rhoda Curtis, Jewish girl from Chicago. As we walked out of the minister's study, I knew I was walking into a different life.

When we came back from Sacramento, we looked for a place where we didn't have to share a toilet. We found an old water tower in the backyard of a big house on the corner of Grove and Hearst Streets. It had been remodeled into small living quarters by the owners. The tower was a wooden structure with a curving stairway, at the top of which you fell into the bed that occupied the entire space. There was no room to stand up. One window in the slanted wall gave a view of the Golden Gate Bridge between housetops; the other window on the opposite wall presented a view of the stars and the moon. When we opened the two windows, there was a lovely cross draft. There used to be a real water tower on the roof, so the insulation protected us from the sun's heat. There was a small but decent kitchen on the first level, a toilet tucked under the stairs with room for a handheld shower. It had a cozy, tree house feeling. We studied on the kitchen table, stacking our books underneath.

I wrote my parents about my marriage. Opening the mail one Saturday morning, I found this letter from my father:

"Rhoda... you are dead to me. Don't come to my funeral. I will erase your name from our family book. You have disgraced all of us. Signed, Mayer Curtis."

Jim had gone to the Lab to finish up some work. I was alone. I sank down on one of the two chairs in our tiny kitchen, and stared out the door into the garden. Dry-eyed, I read the letter over and over. *Oh, Pa, did you really write this letter? I didn't think you would do this. But here is the letter, in your hand. Pa, you cannot erase me, a name in a book is not a person. I know I chose to leave; I chose to marry Jim, but still...*

When Jim came home, I showed him the letter. He dropped it on the floor, picked me up, sat down, and held me on his lap. "What was it you told me Jews say when you have to make a hard decision?"

"Choose life," I mumbled.

"All right, then," he said, stroking my hair, "let's choose life. Come on, let's go for a walk on the Marina. We need to smell the sea."

We walked the length of the Marina, and then sat silently on a rock, looking at the sunset, our arms tight around each other. Jim kissed the top of my head from time to time. We didn't have to talk. Staring out at the bay,

I willed myself onto one of the sailboats, tilting into the wind. *Oh, the lovely smell of the sea, the high keening of the wheeling gulls.* I melted into Jim's encircling arms. Sitting on the Bay Shore, my head on Jim's shoulder, memories of my father swam over me.

There I am, on his lap, his voice murmuring in my ear, "Shana maidele, mein shana meidele (beautiful little girl, my beautiful little girl)." There I am, sitting on the rim of the claw-footed tub in our bathroom, watching him strop his razor, shave carefully, wax and shape his red mustache, pat his face with Bay Rum aftershave lotion, his blue eyes twinkling at me in the mirror.

Jim's voice roused me from my reverie. "Let's go over to that motel restaurant and have some clam chowder. What do you say?" I sighed, straightened up, inhaled deeply. Still in a daze, I wasn't ready to face strangers in a restaurant. "Let's get chowder to go, and eat it at home."

Back in our cozy water tower house, we ate our chowder with French bread we had picked up from a local bakery on the way home. Suppressed tears filled my throat, and I drank my soup with slow sips.

"You know," Jim said, quietly meditative, "both of our fathers seem to object to our marriage because of the difference in our religions. I wonder why they're so upset."

I struggled to find the right words for my psychologist husband. "My father, his brothers, and his father hid in the cellar of their house in Romania during pogroms by soldiers," I said. "The women covered themselves in shapeless black clothes and pretended to be mourning the dead when the soldiers came. They were persecuted just for being Jewish. They escaped from Romania and traveled in an overcrowded freighter to get to the United States. My father is invested in his religion, and feels threatened when members of his family don't agree with him. There's a story by Sholom Aleichem called *Tevye and His Daughters,* that I've always liked. It's about a peasant who has three daughters, and one of his daughters wants to marry a non-Jewish Communist and go off to Russia with him. Tevye is tormented, torn between his love for his daughter and his dismay at what he sees is a flouting of tradition. In a long soliloquy he debates whether he should disown her, and in the end decides not to. My father has four daughters; three of them married Jews. I was the only one who didn't. Maybe my father feels like Tevye, but unlike Tevye, my father did disown me. Why does your father feel the way he does? Is he very religious?"

"No," Jim replied thoughtfully, "my father isn't actually very religious. It's my mother who goes to the Christian Science services every week. I don't know why he's so anti-Semitic. Maybe he's never known any Jews. Anti-Semitism is a mystery to me."

We were silent. I stirred my soup around in my bowl. *How can I explain the feeling of being excluded to someone who has always felt included in the mainstream of the society we live in? How to explain the push and pull of assimilation to someone who has never felt it? Someone who has never felt the push to conform and the pull of traditional holidays, food and music? What would make sense to a non-Jew?*

"Jim, anti-Semitism is a mystery to me too, and I've been fighting it a good part of my life. One of the ways I cope is to pretend I'm not Jewish, duck all conversations relating to religion. When I was looking for a job at a department store in Chicago, I was asked to state my religion, and when I said I was Jewish, I didn't get the job. That's the kind of slap in the face that's hard to live with."

Jim looked at me, astonished. *I kept talking and found I was getting rid of pent-up anger I didn't know I had.* "There's more, and I think it's even deeper. I grew up in a family where I also felt on the outside. My mother was forty and my father fifty, and I had four older siblings. It was as if I had four bossy parents and two grandparents. When I was twelve, we moved to a non-Jewish neighborhood."

Jim leaned forward and took my hand. "Why was it so important to live in a non-Jewish neighborhood? If your parents were so committed to Judaism, it seems strange to me."

"It's odd, isn't it?" I replied. "I think my parents really wanted to be mainstream Americans, and I know my sisters and brother did. Somehow there were mixed messages when I was growing up. On the one hand, my mother kept a kosher house, separate dishes for meat and dairy dishes; we celebrated all the holidays. My father prayed facing East every morning and went to the synagogue on Saturday mornings. We lit candles, ate braided bread, freshly baked by my mother every Friday, and yet there was a sense that our Jewishness needed to stay within the walls of our apartment. My sisters worked downtown on LaSalle Street for non-Jewish bosses, my sister Fay was a schoolteacher. We didn't mix much with our neighbors. Children pick up hints from what is not said out loud. It seemed to me there was something hypocritical about our Jewishness. Perhaps my sisters or brother made fun of friends who didn't speak English without an accent, I don't remember." I put my empty soup bowl to one side. "Is any of this making sense to you?"

Jim reached for his pipe. "My life was so different. Religion and religious customs weren't really part of it. I never knew any Jews, or Catholics either. My friends were either churchgoers or not, it didn't seem to make much difference. Being Jewish seems to be a social as well as a religious part of your life. You seemed to think being Jewish was a handicap."

"That's it!" I clapped my hands. "Yes, definitely a handicap and I resented it. My mother forbade me to have a non-Jewish boyfriend, so I went to my boyfriend's house after school without her knowing it. My sister Fay couldn't go to the high school prom unless she had a Jewish boy to go with, so Jeanne and Al went with her to the prom. It all seemed so unfair. My brother had a non-Jewish girlfriend whom he really loved, but everyone in the family put pressure on him not to marry her. I think my father could not accept the thought that his only son might marry a non-Jew. I think my marriage was also unacceptable. You know, I never told anyone I wasn't coming back to Chicago from Yellowstone. I waited until I was settled at the University of California. The whole family must have felt betrayed." I sighed.

Jim came around our small table, and lifted me. "Come on, kiddo, let's go to bed. It's been a long day."

We climbed up the winding staircase and fell into our bed. We always undressed upstairs, piling our clothes in the small space between the bed and the wall. We stared into the sky through the open window and watched the fog slowly blank out the stars.

The next morning, I awakened feeling fresh, as if relieved from a huge burden. I was ready to think about practical things. Like my mother, I worried about money. We were still in graduate school, and our part-time jobs barely covered our expenses. I confronted Jim at breakfast. "Jim, we're running short. Why don't I leave the graduate program and apply for a teaching job? I'm only one course shy of getting my degree; I can always pick it up next summer, and I already have my credential."

Jim was stunned. "But Rhoda, isn't the M.A. important to you?"

It really wasn't. Not unless I wanted to teach in a community college or a university, it didn't matter much. I said, "I don't get more money teaching in an elementary school if I have an M.A. And anyway, if I decide I really want to take that last stupid course, I can do it next summer. I've already submitted my thesis to the *Journal of Educational Psychology,* so I figure I've already done the important work. Listen, I'll go around tomorrow to all the school districts within a fifty-mile radius of Berkeley and leave applications. Something is bound to turn up."

Jim leaned across our small table and smiled. "I know you're itching to teach. You already have a teaching credential. What the heck. It's worth a try."

I went all over the Bay Area, even to small districts in Marin without much luck. All my friends said, "Don't even try for Oakland, Berkeley, or San Francisco. They all want experienced teachers." But I decided to try anyway. After several discouraging interviews, I got an interview with the superintendent of the Oakland Public Schools. I didn't know it, but he was newly appointed and wanted to make a difference in the district.

"Why do you want to teach in the Oakland Public Schools?" he asked me, a standard question all administrators ask, and I'd become accustomed to it. It was easy to answer him, because I passionately believed what I was saying.

"At Northwestern, we studied the school districts of different states, and there were two which impressed me—Wisconsin and California, particularly Oakland. You have a fantastic program. You have a school nurse in every school, a psychologist on call. You have music programs, art, a library and librarian at every school, and you also have a school lunch program for poor children. This is a school district I want to teach in. There's nothing like it in Chicago. Evanston has a good program for middle-class children, especially gifted children. I know, because I did some practice teaching at New Trier."

"I see you did your practice teaching in second grade and sixth grade in Oakland." Mr. Grover was checking the papers in front of him carefully. He was actually reading the letters of recommendation. "I see the *Journal of Educational Psychology* is considering your paper on 'Reading Preparation Strategies for Children.' How would you feel about teaching a fourth grade?"

Was he actually offering me a job? Better not get my hopes up. "That would be fine," I lied, since I didn't know anything about fourth graders.

Mr. Grover rose and offered me his hand. "Thank you, Mrs. Pack. We'll be in touch." I walked out of his office, hoping that the forty-five minute interview was a good sign. *I liked him, he looked me right in the eye when he spoke to me; he wasn't deprecating, and treated me like a human being, not a supplicant. No comparison to the interview in San Francisco, where the superintendent implied that he was doing me a favor just by talking to me.*

I did get the job, at Piedmont Avenue Elementary School, and that meant steak and lamb chops instead of hamburger and macaroni and cheese. That fourth grade was a real challenge. The third grade teacher had been a veteran of thirty years of teaching in a rigid, authoritarian manner, and those students were ready for a change.

In the mandated curriculum for fourth graders in California, children are supposed to learn about California, its varied climate, its different topography, and the differences between urban and rural life. One of the suggested activities was to have the students create a relief map of California, using papier mache. I had done my practice teaching in second grade and sixth grade in Berkeley, but I wasn't really prepared for fourth grade in Oakland.

My only trip to southern California had been taken hunkered down in the small backseat of a Volkswagon on a three-day trip over a school holiday. All I could see of California through the small back window of the car were the brown California hills. *They gave me the impression of huge breasts in which ancient giants would nestle and snuggle.* We did go to the beach in Los Angeles, but that was about all I knew personally about California. My students, on the other hand, had taken vacations in Yosemite Park, Lake Tahoe, and had driven back and forth to Los Angeles many times.

My attempts to have my students create a relief map of California using papier mache, while well intentioned, ended in disaster. Papier mache is made with scrunched-up newspaper mixed with white paste. It is an excellent source for creating solid, squishy balls to hurl at friends and enemies across a classroom. Many of those missiles also end up with a splatter on the blackboards. My classroom was a study in bedlam, and I spent hours after school cleaning up the mess before the custodians arrived.

One lunchtime period in the teachers' lunchroom, I overheard a conversation about upcoming citywide and countywide tests for fourth graders. Nobody talked to me in the lunchroom. It was widely assumed that I was a stooge for the superintendent, since none of the older longtime teachers at the school had had any input on my hiring. I was curious, however, so I asked boldly, "What tests are you talking about?"

After a short, stony silence, one of the younger teachers turned to me and said, "These are standard tests for fourth grade students in Alameda County to see if they are performing up to grade in mathematics and reading."

"Oh," I responded, "and what do these tests cover? Can I see one of them?"

One of the older teachers leaned over to me and said, frostily, "Of course you can't see the tests. That wouldn't be fair. I'll tell you, though, that in math, it covers long division."

Uh, oh. I had followed the dictum instilled in us in our Education classes to "take the child where you find him, and bring him up to required standards" literally, believing implicitly that then the child would be able to function with the background he needed. Accordingly, I had divided my class into rows of students who could do only addition and subtraction (one row), multiplication (another row), and a few students who were beginning long division. There was no way my students struggling with addition and subtraction would be able to handle long division. On my way back to my classroom, I knew what I had to do. I opened the classroom door, then closed and locked it behind me. The students were suddenly quiet. I strode to the front of the room and made this announcement:

"There is going to be a state-wide test in arithmetic in two weeks, and you are not ready for that test." They gasped, their eyes riveted upon me. There was a breath-held silence. My words fell like stones into a quiet lake.

"I have an idea, but I will have to have your full cooperation." They nodded obediently. "I suggest that we do nothing but arithmetic every morning from nine until twelve, and art and music in the afternoon. We will drill and drill and drill every day; it will be like what your brothers and sisters do in college when they cram for exams. How many of you have brothers or sisters in college?" More than half of the class raised their hands. "Okay, you've heard how they spend time studying for their exams, haven't you?" Enthusiastic nods. "All right, that's what we're going to do. We're going to cram, and you will pass those tests."

Nothing disturbed the hushed silence in that room. I pressed on. "The only thing is, you are going to have to take a vow *to tell no one about this plan!*" I paused dramatically and stared at them. "Now, I want you all to stand. Place your left hand on your heart and raise your right hand. Repeat after me: 'I solemnly swear not to tell anyone about my special program at school.'" When they had all repeated the vow, I added, "Now say this: 'I swear I will not tell my mother or anyone in my family. This is a solemn vow.'" Then I said, "Now, cross your heart and bow your head." As one, they followed all my directions. If I could have had them prick their fingers with a pin, and bleed onto a piece of paper, I would have done it. "All right," I said, "that's fine, now I'm going to read you a story. When you go out for recess, are you going to tell anybody about what we just did?" Every head shook a vociferous "No."

We drilled on arithmetic problems every day for the next two weeks; they loved the art and music sessions in the afternoon—we had put the relief map of California in the cloakroom—and when the day came for the test, I crossed my fingers.

The principal, a formidable dragon lady in her sixties, considered me an uppity kid with highfalutin ideas. (This was not my imagination; I had heard her say those exact words to one of the other teachers in the school.) She came to my classroom to make sure I didn't give the answers to the children while they were taking their tests. She patrolled the aisles with me. We were allowed to read word problems to the students, but that was the only help we were allowed to give.

After the test, I went back to my original organization of the classroom. I knew that the students who were weak in basic things like addition, subtraction, and multiplication would not have learned what they needed to learn through the rote and drill routine we had just been through. The rigid concentration helped a little, however, because some of the students I had despaired of began to pay closer attention and to move ahead faster than I expected.

The results came in the following month. Our fourth grade class placed right where it needed to be, in the upper percentile of schools like ours. Miss Trimble, the principal, couldn't figure out how I had done it, but after all, she had been in the classroom with me, and she knew I hadn't cheated.

I had no discipline problems for the rest of the semester. The strong and happy rapport continued, even extending to trust between me and the fourth grade girls. A committee of five had come to me one day and complained about the boys chasing them at recess. They wanted me to keep the boys in at recess. I looked at them and said, "Do you want the boys to chase you?"

"No-o-o," they said. I looked at them and said, "If you don't want the boys to chase you, don't run." They regarded me in silence and filed out. It was a win for me.

My students performed in a play we had written, and they participated in the Christmas pageants in the auditorium. I left for the winter break holiday feeling happy and vindicated.

When I got home, all elated by my first semester's successful teaching, Jim greeted me with a letter from his parents, which included an invitation to come to Grants Pass for Christmas.

"Shall we go?" I asked him. "After your dad's violent reaction to me, why do you suppose they invited us?"

Jim hesitated. "I think they want to do the proper thing. Now that we're married, there's nothing they can do about it. Both my mother and father like to be seen as doing what's proper. Their personal feelings are not what counts. It's how their behavior looks to others, or at least how they think it looks. They behave the way they think others will judge them. I'm not sure who those others are."

"Well, I guess they decided if they wanted to see their only son, they would have to accept us. How long do we have to stay?" I was focusing on details.

"We'll drive up, spend Christmas Eve and Christmas Day, and then drive back the following day." Jim leaned over, held my face between his hands, and kissed me tenderly. "It'll be all right. You'll see."

I wasn't convinced. "What about presents? I don't know anything about your parents. We can't give your dad a tie or socks, can we? And what about your mom?" *I didn't know anything about presents at Christmas. The only presents given at Hannukah were to children, and those presents were mostly fake money made out of chocolate, or once in a while, a real quarter.*

"Let's give them a plant, a California plant," said Jim. "Something that we know will survive in Oregon."

"Great! That's neutral enough."

So we went. It was a surreal experience. I felt like I was living in someone else's movie. We ended up getting a tie, anyway, for Jim's father and a beautiful scarf for Jim's mother. Carrying the wrapped presents, we arrived on Christmas Eve. We survived Christmas morning and sat down cheerfully to the festive Christmas dinner of turkey, stuffing, yams, and green peas. I watched Jim's dad drink gin with a beer chaser, and wondered how those flavors mixed with turkey. I told myself to suspend judgment. Tense with the effort of being conscious of what I said, how I sat, how I smiled, how I talked, my back ached. My efforts paid off though. Jim's dad warmed to me and began to flirt a bit as he got drunk.

Jim's mother, Arlene, was a small-boned woman about one-third the size of her husband, with a thin, refined manner. She kept referring to her childhood home in South Carolina as if she were Scarlett O'Hara mourning a lost plantation. She pursed her lips in disapproval as her husband poured himself additional portions of alcohol, but kept silent. We were all playacting that weekend, but I was the only one without a script. When we escaped to our room, Jim told me that his mother was "lace curtain Irish," and that his dad had rescued her from genteel poverty. I never did get the full story. Christmas Day we went to a Christian Science church with Jim's mother, which featured testimonials about how prayer had cured illnesses. Jim's dad slept late.

The weather was awful, but we decided to drive back to Berkeley the day after Christmas anyway, pleading work pressures. Jim's mother packaged left-over turkey for us, we left with cheerful waves and promises to write soon. My muscles unwound as we drove south through a pouring rain.

Jim's father invited us to spend part of our Spring break camping on the Rogue River outside of Grants Pass, and we said we'd let him know. We talked about it on the way home. "We won't have to spend much time with them," Jim assured me. "We'll be camping for ten days. I think we might as well go." I agreed, snuggling closer to him.

Chapter Twelve:
Camping on the Rogue River

⏤

THE FOLLOWING AUGUST, 1941, we went back to Grants Pass. I was twenty-three years old, with limited experience of backpacking or camping, but looking forward to new adventures. Jim's father dropped us off on the edge of a path leading down to the Rogue River outside of Grants Pass, Oregon. Jim and I planned on camping out for ten days. It was our first real vacation. I had never camped out before and I was carrying a heavy pack: only twenty-five pounds, it felt like forty. I weighed one hundred and eighteen pounds, and I was five feet, five inches tall.

The previous weekend, Jim's dad had taught me to fish with a hand-tied fly, and I was anxious to try my new skill. We had gone to a quiet part of the river three days earlier, because Jim's dad decided I needed to know how to fish. During our lessons, I managed to catch and land more fish than he did. Beginner's luck, his dad had said, with grudging acknowledgment of my success. Actually all I did was watch him closely, doing exactly what he told me to do.

On Monday, Jim's dad drove us to a marked place on the road where we were allowed to enter the forest on the edge of the Rogue River. "Don't drink the water!" Jim's dad yelled at us as we slid down the steep bank. "I'll pick you up here in ten days." We barely heard him, our packs bouncing along the rocks and earth. My pack began to feel really heavy when I stood upright and started trudging along the river trail behind Jim. The Rogue at this part is a wild, fast river, full of boulders, jutting through the swift current. The loud music of that river drowned out any attempt at conversation. We were in a steep canyon, with pine trees growing down close to the banks on each side. Occasionally I glimpsed bits of intense blue which looked like wild irises. I made a mental note to ask Jim the names of the plants and flowers we passed. Our narrow path followed the curves of the river. Suddenly Jim stopped, bent down and patted the earth, patted what looked like a brown lump.

"What are you doing?" I asked Jim.

"Checking bear scat."

"Bear what?"

"Bear scat. Poop. Shit. To see how warm or cold it is."

"Oh, and... "

"It's cold. That's fine; it means that any bears that were here have moved on."

"Will they come back?" I was Chicago-born, what did I know about bears? And the only river I'd ever seen was a calm stream in a suburb of Chicago called Fox River. Also, this wild place was nothing like the Indiana shores of Lake Michigan where my family and I spent summers at a cabin. That had been my experience with the Great Outdoors. Even Yellowstone Park was relatively calm compared to where I now found myself—not prepared for wilderness, trying to cope with the unexpected.

I grinned to myself. *I'm having an Adventure, capital A! What fun! Forget bears! Take a deep breath, Rhoda. Enjoy the glorious air! Stretch your legs!* I lengthened my stride.

"To answer your question," Jim spoke over his shoulder at me, "the bears who dropped that scat probably won't come back. But that's not to say that others won't come around. I'll hang our food high in the tree when we camp." He paused at a fairly level place near the river, and looked around. "I think this is a good place. We'll camp here."

Jim was carrying double my load. He had the tent, the cooking pots, canned food, and one sleeping bag. I had the other sleeping bag, extra clothes, and our fishing rods. I knew Jim had grown up in this area, camping with his father on the Rogue, since I had heard lots of stories about adventures he'd had as a child. Jim loved the outdoors, and I was awed by his knowledge and expertise. I trusted him.

We planned to catch and eat trout most of the time we were camping, the canned meat was for emergencies. Jim and I had gone ocean fishing in San Francisco Bay and trout fishing at Lake Merced from a boat, using fish eggs as bait. But this was different. Here there was no salt smell of the sea, no gulls shrieking, no pounding of waves on a sandy shore. And neither was there the cloistered, protective, calm Lake Merced, ringed by tall concrete apartment buildings, the hum of street traffic in the background. Oh, this was very different. Steep, wooded cliffs around us, a clear, piney smell, the music of the river creating a different beat. I looked at the water boiling around the rocks with awe and respect. I remembered fishing with Jim and his dad the day before, remembered the feel of the cold water through my waders, and was anxious to try it again.

Jim dropped his pack and unrolled the tent. It was noon by this time and I was hungry.

"Can't we have lunch before we set up the tent? I made sandwiches."

"No." Jim was firm, all business. "First things first. We have to get the tent up, store our bags, and then make a fire. Won't take long. Here, give me a hand with these pegs."

The weather was gorgeous, hot sun, cool shade. I wanted to take off my hiking shoes and paddle my feet in that rushing stream, but I followed orders. We got the tent up, stored our zipped-together sleeping bags, and Jim went foraging for wood. I cleared a space for our fire, gathering stones and arranging a kind of cooking space, remembering scenes from cowboy movies.

Jim went down to the river and came back with a pot of water, made a tripod of twigs, and sat the pot on his well-constructed fire. Jim made sure the water was boiling hard before he made the coffee. It was amazing how quickly we had established a cozy little nest. Ready for food, I unpacked the sandwiches and fruit.

We didn't fish the first day; instead, we opened a can of beans and went to bed early. Sleeping in a tent in woods by a river that burbled and babbled in my ears, snug and warm, I was in heaven. We were up at dawn, and, shivering a bit, went down to the bank and cast our lines. Whop! A strike! Jim pulled in a beauty of a rainbow trout, Whop! I pulled in another, and we ran back to camp. Jim built up the fire, and I watched closely as he cleaned and fried the trout. Oh, that trout was good! We sat contentedly drinking our coffee, snuggling closer together. I noticed how quickly it got cold and dark in the woods.

Jim was an avid lover without much practice, and sometimes it took a couple of times before I came to climax. Jim came each time, but was perfectly willing and able to perform again and again until I was satisfied. There was very little, if any, foreplay.

Three days went by in this idyllic fashion. One morning, after our tumble in the tent, we decided to go for a hike. We cooked an extra trout, packed a small lunch, including a small bottle of boiled water, some dried fruit, apples, and rye-krisp. We picked up our fishing rods and set off, Jim checking the temperature of the bear scat, each time reporting on its warmth.

The upper part of the river that we set out to explore was more rugged. The trail, such as it was, took us up the mountain away from the river. After climbing a few miles, I flopped down near a huge boulder.

"You know, I'd rather go back down to the river, find a quiet pool, and go for a swim. How about it?"

Jim was on his back, gazing at the clouds. "Sounds good to me. We can have a swim, check the pools, maybe fish a bit on the way back." He rolled over, and grinned at me. "Having a good time, city girl?"

I gave him a punch. "I'm not complaining. Let's go."

It was a lot faster going down than it was coming up. When we got to the river, we took off our boots, tied the laces together and hung them around our necks, pulling up our jeans and wading in shallow water near the bank. We didn't go very far. Stopping at the first quiet pool, we stripped, piling our clothes on a rock, and jumped in, gasping as the cold water hit our sun-heated bodies.

"Whee!" Jim stopped and, cupping his hands, took a long drink of the cool water. A bell rang in my head. *Didn't Jim's father say not to drink the river water?*

"Hey! Your dad said not to drink the river water!"

"Oh, my dad, he's so full of orders. Look how clear it is. It's all right."

"Yes, but..." Jim went splashing out into the river. "Come on," he said.

"Don't be such a worrywort!" *Well, too late to do anything about it now.* We climbed out and let the sun dry us off. Dressing leisurely, we sauntered back to camp on the river trail. That was the beginning of the end of our wilderness idyll.

After our dinner of rice, trout, and coffee, Jim went crashing off suddenly into the brush, then came back looking pale. "I don't feel very good. Can you clean up? I'd like to lie down."

I took our pots and dishes down to the river, scrubbed them clean, came back and banked the fire as Jim had taught me, then crawled into the tent. I found him curled into a ball, shivering. *Dear god, I'm not prepared for this.* Neither was Jim. We had a terrible night, and by morning Jim was alternately vomiting and shitting, sometimes both at the same time, often not being able to get very far from camp. I was scared green.

"I'm going for help," I said. "You told me there were homesteaders in these mountains. People who build a cabin, plant and tend a garden for five years, then they get title to their cleared land for fifty dollars. Isn't that right?"

He nodded, moaning, clutching his gut. I looked at the mountainous slope opposite our campsite. It didn't look as steep as on our side, and the river was not all that deep right where we had camped. I tucked Jim into the sleeping bag, left him with some boiled water, and waded into the river. On the other side, I found a narrow trail and began to climb, stopping often to look back, trying to locate our camp. It had quickly disappeared.

Rounding a bend in the trail, I looked up and saw a thin thread of smoke in the clear air. I pushed up faster. Suddenly a man stood in my path, holding a rifle casually in his hand. He was wearing overalls over an undershirt. He looked to be about thirty years old, with a small black beard, and serious brown eyes. He was about my height. He raised his eyebrows when he saw me.

"Who are you? What're you doing here?"

"Oh," I gasped. "Do you live here? I need help."

He looked me up and down, changing his grip on his rifle, lowering it. "Where'd you come from?"

"I'm camping with my husband, he's sick." I waved in the direction of the river.

Turning abruptly, he waved me on ahead of him. I climbed up the trail, and we soon came into a small clearing. We were met by another man holding two dogs on leashes. The one with the rifle motioned me to a stump.

"Where's your walking stick?" asked the man with the dogs.

"Walking stick? I don't have one. Just pulled myself up with my hands when I needed to."

"Not what I mean. You need a stick like this, for rattlers." He picked up a heavy stick, forked at the end. "This here's my brother, Hank," he said. "I'm Jeb. We're settin' a stake here."

I took the callused hand. "I'm Rhoda. My husband Jim is sick, and I don't know what to do. He's vomiting, has diarrhea, and I'm scared."

"Wha'd he do? Eat some bad meat?"

"No, he drank some water while we were swimming. River water."

"River water? Why'd he do that?" they said in unison.

"He said the water was clear where we were, that it would be all right."

They snorted. Jeb looked at Hank. They seemed to have a silent communication system. "I'll go down to the campsite with this little lady here. You go over to Malcolm's, rig up a stretcher. Meet you at the river. Come on." He stood up, handed me a stick, and we set off on the trail. "No time to lose."

Halfway down the trail, Jeb stopped. Whack! He struck at something just off the path, then lifted his stick. A dead rattler was caught in the fork. "Didn't you hear the rattle?"

I shook my head, numb.

"That's why you need a stick! Rattlers make good eatin'. Nice skin, too."

Shuddering, I swallowed hard. When we got to the camp, we found Jim huddled in the tent, moaning, bent over, and still shaking. He looked awful. Jeb took one look at him, felt his head, and stood up.

"Let me go get Hank and Malcolm. Me and Malcolm will fix the stretcher. Hank will help you break camp. Malcolm's got a boat. We can make better time down river than walkin'. There's an old man downstream knows just what to do in cases like this. Don't worry, little lady, we'll take care of your man." Jeb acted like I was some small kid, and I suppose that's what I looked like. He must have been all of thirty-five or so. I had no way of telling.

I put a cloth dipped in the cold water of the river on Jim's head and started to pick up our gear. Hank picked Jim up gently, laid him down a little way off from the campsite, came back and swiftly took down the tent. By that time, I had rolled up the sleeping bags, packed up the cooking stuff, and started to stamp out the fire. Hank came over, threw damp leaves on the fire, and began to sweep the earth with some branches. Boy, he was efficient!

Jim crawled off into the bushes, where we heard him retching. About that time, Jeb and Malcolm appeared with the stretcher. It consisted of a piece of canvas stretched between two long, hand-hewn poles. They loaded Jim on it and we set off on the trail with Hank bringing up the rear. When we got to where the boat was tied up, they carried Jim down, laid him in, and folded up the stretcher. The plan was for Jeb and Malcolm to go downriver to where the old man lived, and carry him up there. Hank and I would walk, and meet them at the old man's place. We loaded as much gear as was safe into the small boat, and Hank and I started walking.

"What're you doing here?" Hank asked, the same question put to me by his brother.

"We're here on vacation," I said. "Sort of a delayed honeymoon. Jim's father lives in Grants Pass. He's a lumberman, do you know him? James Pack, II."

"Nope."

"Jim and I are graduate students at the University of California in Berkeley," I said. "We just got married three months ago. When did you and your brother decide to come up here?"

"Oh, we been here a year now. 'Course we don't stay full-time in the summer. Come out on weekends. Law says we have to tend the garden, and after five years we have title to the land we clear, maybe a couple acres. We aim to clear as much as we can, and plant at least two gardens. Then we'll bring our wives and kids, live full-time."

"What do you do in the winter?"

"Work in the lumber mills. It's a good deal. The bosses know they can count on us. Things are slow in the summer anyways. Everything picks up in the winter, even in the rain. We get real busy; me and Jeb have good jobs. It works out." He gave me a sideways glance. "Figured you was university kids," he said. Then, shaking his head, he muttered, "Drinkin' river water, what a fool thing to do."

I thought we'd never get there; the straps of my backpack were beginning to bite into my shoulders. Then a patch of clear sun shone ahead, and we looked up the hill to a fairly big clearing, a sturdy looking cabin, and a fenced garden.

Hank waved at Jeb and Malcolm as we spotted them climbing the hill with the stretcher.

"That wire fence is to keep the deer out," he said. "But sometimes they jump right over it. Eat ever'thing in sight. Stubborn critters."

"Just who is this old man?" I asked Hank as we started up the road.

"Name's Grady. Been here longer than anybody. Grows all kinds of herbs. Knows a lot. Knows how to set a broken bone, suck out the poison from a rattler's bite, all sorts of stuff. Good man."

Jeb and Malcolm set Jim down on a patch of grass in the yard under a tree. Mr. Grady bent over him, felt his forehead, and took his pulse. Dressed in faded blue coveralls, Mr. Grady was tall and lean, with a black beard lightly flecked with grey, and a round bald spot on his head like a monk's tonsure. He stood up, went into the house, and then came back with a bottle and a spoon. Holding up Jim's head, he poured the stuff down Jim's throat. Jim coughed, sputtered, made a face, then spit. Grady laughed.

"Good sign," he said. "Guess I'll make some garlic soup."

Garlic soup? Yuck. I hope Jim isn't too conscious when he tastes it! We unrolled the sleeping bags, and said goodbye to our rescuers. They were full of "aw shucks, never mind, we only did what anybody would have done," but I was weeping with gratitude.

We got through the night fairly well. Jim managed to get to the outhouse with my help several times, and by morning he seemed much better. He had downed the garlic soup, and taken two more doses of Grady's magic medicine. I wondered what was in it, but wasn't inclined to ask Grady for the recipe. I started to think about how we were going to walk out, up a steep mountain trail. *Relax, Rhoda,* I said to myself. *The worst is over. We'll get out.*

Up early the next morning, after a good breakfast that Jim held down, we started our climb out. This time I carried most of the load, Jim was still very weak, and we stopped often to rest. We didn't have a clearly marked trail, and just kept pulling ourselves up by grabbing onto the brush. *Boy, I'm glad I have that stick Jeb gave me, not that I know how to use it against a rattler, but it helps me climb. My pack is getting heavier and heavier. Are we ever going to get out of here?* We sat against a tree to rest, and drank some boiled water. I looked at Jim carefully. *Don't faint, Jim, don't faint.*

"It's okay, kid, I won't pass out." He grinned weakly. "Sorry about all this." I was too tired to say anything. It was noon by the time we reached the road. We were both hot, sweat pouring off our foreheads, and panting from our efforts. We had finished all of our water, and I didn't even have any spit to swallow. Of course, Jim's dad hadn't planned to pick us up for another four days, so we had to thumb a ride. Jim was very pale by this time. He slumped down by the side of the road, looking as if he might fall over at any minute.

I jumped into the middle of the road, waved my arms frantically in front of the first car that came along. It screeched to a stop.

"What's going on? What's the matter?"

I motioned toward Jim, sitting by the road, his head hanging between his knees.

"My husband's ill," I panted. "We've just climbed up from camping on the Rogue. I need to get him to a hospital. I'll phone our parents from there. Please help."

The driver looked at the woman sitting next to him, at the two kids in the backseat. It was a station wagon, so there really was enough room for us.

"Okay, you kids, climb over into the back, make room." And to us, "All right, get in. We're going into Grants Pass, and we'll drop you at the hospital."

I roused Jim, got him to the car, picked up our stuff and got in.

"Thank you very much, you've saved our lives."

"What happened?"

"Jim drank some river water, had a terrible reaction and some men who were homesteading helped us. They were wonderful, built a stretcher and carried him from our campsite to where we were able to climb out. We've been lucky... first those guys, now you." I choked up and began to cry.

The driver, a man in his forties, nodded. We drove in silence for a while.

"Are you sure you'll be all right?" he asked. "Will his folks be at home?"

"Yes, I'm sure. Jim's dad is a lumberman, but he's not working right now. Do you know him? James Pack, II?"

"Nope. We're newcomers. Moved here recently from Medford. Well, here we are. Good luck."

We got out at the hospital, and I walked Jim up the steps, leaving our gear at the curb. After I got him inside, I ran down and picked it up, dragging it behind me. The clerk at the emergency desk took one look at Jim's face and took him behind a partition.

When she came back, I asked, "May I use your telephone? I need to call his folks."

When Jim's dad answered the phone, I was brief. "We're at the hospital. Jim got sick and we came out early. Can you come over? We're in the emergency room. I'll tell you more when you get here." I hung up as quickly as I could. *Let Jim handle the excuses with his dad. I didn't want to get into <u>that</u> scene!*

I waited in the Day Room while Jim's dad went into the hospital room and closed the door. When he came out, his face was grim. "He'll be ready to go home in about an hour," he said. "They want to do some more tests, and make sure he doesn't have any parasites. Where's your gear?"

"It's in the closet in the room." I gestured toward the closed door. "Do you want to wait? We could get some coffee. Or... do you want to come back?"

"I'll come back." He turned on his heel and left abruptly. I went into Jim's room. He looked shriveled in the bed.

"What happened?" I asked. "Did he chew you out?"

"Oh, boy, I'll say." He turned and looked out the window. "Nothing new, really. Just gave him an excuse to tell me what a stupid asshole I am. Been telling me that all my life. That I'm a weakling, that it was too bad it was my younger brother who died in the boat accident when we were young, instead of me."

Younger brother! That was news to me. "Was the accident on the Rogue?"

"Yes. My brother was fourteen, I was sixteen; we got caught in some rapids. The boat overturned, I hung on to some rocks, Billy got swept away. Dad never got over it. He made me feel that if one of us had to die, it was too bad it wasn't me."

My god. I sat on the bed and held Jim in my arms. *Why do we do such terrible things to each other?*

The next couple of days were spent in an atmosphere of strained politeness. Jim's father towering over his wife, at six feet, two inches, with a big head and a bluff manner, he made Jim's mother seem even smaller. Her wistful expression and soft voice created an atmosphere of long-suffering delicacy in the presence of boors.

I got up early the second morning we were there, and was on my way into the kitchen for some coffee. Passing through the dining room, I walked past Jim's dad, who was pouring himself a half glass of gin from a bottle on the sideboard. He glanced at me, tilted his head, draining the glass.

"Helps the appetite. Sets a man up for the day." He made that statement to the air, not looking at me. Then he walked out of the dining room. I kept on going, made some instant coffee, and took the mug back upstairs to our bedroom. Jim sat up, drinking the coffee gratefully.

"You look better. How do you feel?"

"The coffee's great. I think I'll live. Anybody awake downstairs?"

"Just your dad, getting a pick-me-up in the dining room." *No point elaborating, no point telling him how upset I was by his dad drinking straight gin before breakfast.*

"Ohh, yeah. He does that. Look, honey, we'll leave tomorrow. Just one more day, okay?"

I sighed. "What'll we talk about? The lumber business? The war in Europe?"

Jim leaned back against the pillows. "I generally let him choose the subjects, and I never talk politics. He's a Republican, hates Californians, thinks all Californians want to move to Oregon, and thinks union members are out to kill the lumber industry. We can talk about fishing. He's never done any ocean fishing. Don't worry about it. I know how to steer him onto safe subjects."

Jim was right. His dad had a few more drinks before dinner, a large meal held at two in the afternoon, and he carried on more or less of a monologue, all through the roast beef and boiled potatoes. After the apple pie, I helped

Jim's mom clean up. While I was drying the dishes, she asked about our work at the university.

"What exactly did you and Jim work at in your lab?" she asked. "I've always been curious."

"We did physiological tests on athletes, research for the Army and Navy. In our offices we had a set of steps on which our subjects ran up and down. Then we checked their blood pressure and pulse rates. It was interesting. We had to keep careful records of everything we did." That was the longest speech I had made in two days.

"My, my," she murmured. "I had no idea you were doing such important work."

Jim's dad burst through the swinging doors, his two-hundred-and-fifty-pound bulk filling the kitchen. "Let's take a swing around town, show Rhoda the sights. You'd like to see what a lumber mill looks like, wouldn't you, Rhoda?"

"Sure. My idea of a lumber town is mostly from educational documentaries."

"All right!" he bellowed, picking up his wife and swinging her around the kitchen. "Let's go!"

He was in an expansive mood as we zoomed out of the driveway, and I fixed a smile on my face, determined to keep it there for the rest of the afternoon. The mill was deserted, and Jim's dad strutted around showing us how the machinery worked. I was appropriately impressed, the afternoon ended without any unpleasant incidents and no accidents. A few close calls, with Jim's dad swearing about "damn fool drivers," but otherwise, home safely. We all took a nap, and supper was quiet, just soup, bread, and salad.

We drove back to Berkeley the following day, both of us subdued. Neither one of us talked about the ordeal we had just been through. Jim didn't want to talk about it, and neither did I. I had learned enough about surviving in the wilderness to last me forever.

War Years: The Pumphouse

Jim in 1942

Chapter Thirteen:
The War and First Pregnancy

⟿

OUR RETURN TO BERKELEY marked a change in our lives. I decided that I didn't want to continue teaching at the Piedmont Avenue School, and I contacted a principal in the slums of Oakland, near the railroad tracks, for an interview. He welcomed me enthusiastically, and I transferred to Tompkins, a newly opened elementary school near McClymonds High School. Oakland was experiencing a surge in population of people moving north from the segregated South and dust-bowl refugees from Oklahoma moving west to work in the fields of California.

We were eating breakfast in the water tower on Sunday, December 7, 1941, with the radio tuned to H.V. Kaltenborn, on CBS, when suddenly there was a break for "an important announcement." We heard President Roosevelt's voice: "Japanese planes have bombed Pearl Harbor."

War! We stared at each other and turned the volume up. I don't remember what we talked about. We walked around, stunned. At school the next day, there were special faculty meetings, teachers milling around, trying to figure out what we should tell our students. We ended up not doing anything. By Tuesday, bulletins began arriving from the main office of the Oakland School District. However, the teachers at Tompkins Elementary decided to wait until parents and/or students asked questions. In the meantime, it was business as usual. Weird, I thought.

About a week later, Jim reported that the attitude in the Psychology Department was pretty much the same. "Wait and see," he said, "that's the attitude on campus." Then he exploded. "Damn it! Jones wants me to try Factor Analysis on the data I've collected. That's in addition to all the other statistical analyses I've tried. It won't make any difference! Why can't he accept the negative correlations? If he weren't such an egotist..." he left the rest of the sentence hanging. "Ahh, he doesn't want to admit that maybe he's on the wrong track. I'm fed up." Then he suddenly stood up, grabbed the file containing his thesis, and went into the backyard. He threw the thesis into the trash can and set it on fire, "I've had it!" His bitter voice penetrated my spine. "Jones rejected my last figures. He wants me to go over the data once again to show something that's not there. I won't do it." I watched in horror as three years of work burned, and shuddered as he turned toward me, his face full of despair, anger, and frustration all mixed together. I had never seen such a look on his face. He waved a hand.

"See you later." He ran out of the garden. I heard our car cough and sputter as he ground the gears and took off. I puttered around our tiny kitchen all day, listened to the radio, wandered into the garden and back again, wondering where he had gone. When he came back that evening, around seven, his face still tight, his words came out in a rush.

"I've signed on at the shipyards as a Liberty Ship worker. They're working twenty-four hours a day, seven days a week. I'll be on the day shift, and I'll be working weekends too, if necessary. I figure that I'll be ineligible for the draft since I'm so nearsighted... what's the use of all that research anyway...." We walked out into the garden, holding on to each other like drowning swimmers. What could I say? All those years of work, all those dreams and hopes, gone, ashes now, the ground shifting beneath our feet.

Later on, in bed, staring at the moon through the window in the slanted wall, Jim said, "Oh, I forgot to tell you. Dr. Shock is in Washington. He's a major in a new agency, called the Office of Strategic Services. I guess he's a big shot now." (O.S.S. morphed into the C.I.A. after the end of World War Two.) "Well, he had all those connections with the Army anyway," I reminded Jim. "Remember all those tests we did? That seems so long ago." I sighed. *We're in a whole new world. Jim a shipyard worker? He's an intellectual! At least he hasn't been drafted. More money, I guess.*

Maybe we can move out of the water tower into a decent apartment with Jim's new salary.

And that's just what we did. We found a one-bedroom apartment over a garage in north Berkeley, definitely a step up. Still, I was filled with anxiety. *Okay, so here we are. How secure are we really? What if Jim gets drafted anyway? Goes to war? Doesn't come back?*

One night I couldn't hold back any longer. "Jim, I want to have a baby. Who knows what's going to happen? You may be drafted anyway." He didn't answer; I took his silence for agreement and put my diaphragm away. We made love fiercely, even desperately. Six weeks later I knew I was pregnant. *Hey! Nobody told me I would be nauseated all the time! Help! In spite of the nausea, I felt triumphant, and would have proclaimed my new status to the world with a megaphone, if I could have.* I was twenty-four.

I ate crackers and sucked lemon drops. Jim was careful to prepare non-smelly things to eat, since the smell of anything frying, even meat or fish broiling, was enough to send me running to the toilet, hand over my mouth. But none of that could diminish my joy at being pregnant. I even thought about learning to knit.

About the same time as the nausea tapered off, Jim got a draft notice for the Construction Battalion, known as the lowest denomination in the Navy. All the Construction Battalion did was to dig trenches. I was appalled. *How could they do this to him? He's one of the most brilliant men in his department! They need people like him in Washington! Damn it!* Jim was stoic, refusing to get upset.

"Listen, it's safer than the infantry. I'll be at Vallejo for a while, and then who knows. So what. So I'll be digging ditches, not carrying a gun."

That wasn't enough for me. Shortly after Jim left for the Navy, I got Dr. Shock's address from the Physiology Department, and sent off a strong letter. "Can you do something about this? What a waste of talent!" I wrote. "Jim, with his expertise in Applied Psychology, ought to be invaluable in Navy Personnel. Please try to get him out of the ditchdiggers' brigade!"

Dr. Shock's reply was guarded, but he promised to do what he could.

Now that I had done what I felt I needed to do, I thought about myself. I had an urge to go "home," wherever that illusory place was. I wrote to my parents, to my sister Fay and to my brother, choking back my pride. These were the answers I got:

"Sorry, our apartment is too small." This from my mother, ill at sixty-five, caring for my father who, at seventy-five, had had a small stroke.

From my sister Fay, married to Henry, "Sorry, we have only one extra room, and if you come, Sylvia and Alice would have to share a room, and they would fight all the time. Besides, that room is the maid's room. Too small for you and a baby!"

"Sorry, you made your bed. Now lie in it." That from my brother Al. Sara, at forty-three, was in Knoxville, Tennessee. Jeanne, thirty-eight, was in Washington, D.C. I knew that their attitude toward having children was strictly negative. There was no point in writing to them. Jim and I had never discussed the possibility of my giving birth when he wasn't around; everything had happened so fast.

I wrote to Vernon and Edna in southern California, who were old friends. Vernon had grown up with Jim in Grants Pass, and the four of us had spent many weekends together on their small farm in Colfax, California, before they moved to Burbank. Vernon was now working in the airplane industry; Edna was a school counselor.

Edna called as soon as she got my letter. "Of course! Come as soon as you can. We'll be delighted to see you. We have three dogs. You're not allergic to dogs, are you?"

"No," I laughed. "Today's Saturday. My principal knows I'll be leaving as soon as I can make arrangements for a place to stay. I'll take the night train two weeks from tonight. We have a month-to-month lease, but no thirty day notice required. I'll just rent a storage locker and put our stuff in it. We don't have much, anyway. It'll be great to see you." *Oh, Edna! Thanks for the life raft!*

I was seven months pregnant, and the train was drafty. I caught cold, and coughed steadily during the next months. Edna kept dosing me with all sorts of special remedies she concocted, but nothing helped much. Since Jim was in the Navy, I went to the Naval Hospital in Burbank for prenatal care and eventual hospitalization. The doctors gave me some sort of chalky stuff to drink, to ease the pain in my chest. I wondered who I was; the life I was living didn't seem to belong to me.

I got a terse note from Jim close to the time of my delivery. "I don't know what happened, but one day I was yanked out of the drill yard and told to report to the colonel. He notified me that I was being transferred to Officers' Training School. It's all a mystery. So I'll be in Virginia until further notice."

Aha! My letter to Dr. Shock paid off! We were all delighted by the news. "It's going to be all right, Rhoda. You'll see." Edna gave me a big hug.

One of Edna's Airedales was also pregnant. I looked at Nellie and she looked at me; we seemed to commiserate. When contractions began, Nellie ran back and forth between me and the door, whimpering, coming back to lick my hand. She laid her head in my lap, looking up at me. If she could have used the telephone, she would have. When Edna came home from school, we drove to the hospital, but after a few hours the contractions stopped, and I came back to the house. Nellie checked me out carefully, and lay down at the foot of my bed. A few days later, contractions began again, and we went back to the hospital. Things did not go well. I was in labor for a long time, walking up and down the hospital corridors, the contractions starting and stopping. Finally, in bed, amniotic fluid pouring down my legs, I heard someone say, "No dilation yet, she's getting weaker. We'd better go."

Dimly, I felt myself rushed down corridors, doors opening and closing, a mask pushed down over my face, told to count backward from one hundred, then oblivion. I don't remember waking up in intensive care, but I do remember waking up in a ward with three other women.

"Where's my baby?" I asked, looking at the nurse who was taking my pulse.

"He's in an incubator. He weighed only five pounds," she said. I wanted to see my baby, but I didn't get an answer to my question about when I could see him.

"You've had a caesarian, you know. You're still pretty weak, you're lucky to be alive." She left, and I had a terrible feeling that something was wrong. A heavy foreboding silence hung in the room. I was suspended in a dim, unreal, foggy place.

Someone from the Red Cross came to see me and handed me a telephone. Jim was on the line. "I can get leave," he said, "and come to see you."

Suddenly I didn't want to see him, didn't want to see anybody. I wanted to hold my baby, to see him. Full of anxiety, I said, "Oh, Jim, something is wrong. The baby is in an incubator. I haven't seen him." I started to cry.

"Don't cry, sweetheart. Listen, I'm still waiting for my commission. It should come through any day now. I've been told I probably will get a desk job in Washington, and won't be sent to sea because of my thick glasses. I can be in Burbank in a few days."

I hesitated. A strange voice in my head spoke. *If he comes here, the commission might get lost in paperwork. If he comes, and the commission falls through, what then?* I have to do this by myself. Out loud I said, "Jim, maybe you'd better stay in Washington. As soon as the baby comes out of the incubator, I'll start nursing him and get my strength back. Then the two of us will come to Washington. I'll do my job here; you take care of things there. Don't you think that's better?"

There was a long painful pause. "Oh, Rhoda, are you sure? It doesn't seem right." His voice was full of tears.

"Vernon and Edna will take good care of me. I'll probably be in the hospital for another week at least. Call me tomorrow, I'll be stronger then. I love you." I handed the phone to the Red Cross worker and fell back against the pillows. I didn't hear his final words; instead I felt myself sinking into a deep pit. When I woke up again, I was in a private room with tubes in my nose, an oxygen tank next to my bed. Edna was stroking my hand.

"Where's the baby?" I said, feeling my engorged breasts. "I need to feed him."

"He's still in the incubator," Edna said. "I tried to see him, but he was in a special ward, and they wouldn't let me in."

"Edna, something is wrong. Nobody will talk to me. Will you try to get hold of someone to come in and tell me when I can nurse my baby?"

Edna came back with a doctor I'd never seen before. He had a solemn look on his face. He took my hand, but his overly solicitous look put me on guard.

"Mrs. Pack, your baby is coughing. It is not a good sign. He is a child at risk."

"What are you saying? Can't I see him even if he's coughing?"

He sighed. "No, it's too dangerous to take him out of the incubator. Even though he was full-term, he weighed only five pounds and he has lost weight over the past three days. My recommendation is that you rest now. I'll be back tomorrow." He left.

I stared at Edna, hardly seeing her through my tears. She sat on the bed, held me close, and then stood up as a nurse came in with a hypodermic needle. "Have to go now, kiddo. I'll be back later."

I never did see my baby. He died the next day, coughing, they said. The solicitous doctor came in early to see me. "Mrs. Pack, I'm sorry. We couldn't save your baby. He died early this morning. I'm sorry." He motioned to a nurse standing behind him, and I felt the jab of another needle in my arm.

The next time I woke up a nurse was standing beside my bed, a huge piece of canvas in one hand, a pill in the other. "Here, take this," she said. "It will help dry up your milk."

"Why can't we pump out the milk and offer it to women who don't have enough?" I had romantic ideas from nineteenth century novels about peasant women feeding other women's babies, and I had an illusion of being an anonymous wet nurse.

"We don't do that these days," she said flatly. "Take the pill. I will also bind up your breasts." *I will smash your face; tear up that binding cloth...* I gave her a murderous look.

When Edna showed up later, I was in a foul mood.

"I have some questions for you," I said. "One, how soon can I get the hell out of this prison? Two, did anybody call Jim? Three, how do I go about getting an autopsy? I already named him Stephen. I want to know exactly why he died. It's all too mysterious. Why wasn't I allowed ever to see the baby? I feel betrayed."

Edna's voice was studiously calm. "I spoke to Jim last night and gave him the news. He still wanted to come, but he doesn't have the commission yet, and I know how important that is to the two of you, so I told him to hang in there. He'll call you tonight."

I clenched and unclenched my fists. "On top of everything else, I have terrible cramps. Find out, will you, when I can start going to the toilet by myself and what I can do about these terrible gas pains. See if you can find an intelligent nurse to talk to." *I was choking on my rage.* Edna gave me a re-assuring pat and disappeared. She came back with a stout, motherly looking aide who took one look at me, nodded, and said, "Okay, time to get up and start moving. Your gut has been exposed to air, and exercise will help work out the gas."

I heaved myself out of bed. "Let's do it." She walked me to the window and I doubled over. Edna held me up and the aide massaged my back, until I stood up, gasping. We walked around the room a couple of times.

"Now listen," said the aide. "This is what you have to do. You have to walk as much as possible. Drink lots of water. Move your hips around like this: knees bent, move your hips left, back, right, front, like a striptease dancer. Do squats and knee bends. Can you do that?"

"Sure. When can I get out of here?"

She laughed. "You have to talk to the powers that be," she said. "I just work here. I'll bring you some orange juice."

After she left, I looked at Edna and said, in as strong a voice as I could manage, "I want an autopsy. I want to find out why the baby died. Can you find out what I have to do?"

"I'll try. Be back in a minute." I stared out the window, wondering how long I had been cooped up in this nightmarish place. *Maybe this is someone else's dream. Ah, I wish it were. It's only too real. But Rhoda, you mustn't give up.*

Edna came back loaded with forms. "There seems to be a lot of red tape to get through. I brought the forms anyway."

The door to my room opened and both the doctor and the day nurse came in.

"It's really not necessary, you know," the doctor said in his patronizing way, motioning toward the forms. "I think it's best for you to concentrate on getting your strength back. The baby's lungs were compromised. We couldn't have saved him."

I stared at him. *Who are you to tell me what's best? I need to know, I don't want bland reassurances.* "Why wasn't I allowed to see my baby? Just tell me what I need to do to get the autopsy done. How long will it take?"

He sighed, never answering my question, and exchanged a glance with the nurse. "A few days. We can mail you the results. You'll be ready to leave tomorrow, if you feel you want to."

"Yes, I do want to get out of here, and I can do the exercises the aide showed me at home." I looked at the nurse. "Will you help me fill out the necessary forms? You won't have to mail them. Either Edna or I will pick them up. You have my friend's address and telephone number. Just call us when they're ready." My voice was icy. The doctor left; the motherly nurse, Mrs. Carlson, came over to the bed and gave me a hug.

"Hang in there, honey. Don't worry. We'll do it." She wiped my face. "Your friend will fill out the forms and we'll bring them back for you to sign. Take this pill now. It will help you rest." Once again I dropped into a deep pit.

Edna was still there when I woke up to a darkened room.

"What time is it? Have you been here all afternoon?"

"No, I went home to feed the dogs and tell Vernon what was going on. We'll come for you at noon tomorrow. Has Jim called?"

"No, not yet. He should be calling any minute now. Will you stick around?"

"Sure."

Just then the phone rang. It was Jim.

"Hi, sweetheart. How are you?"

"Do you know about the baby?" I started to choke, and Edna picked up the phone.

"Hello, Jim. Yes, I thought you probably talked to the people at the nursing station. She's pretty weak, and we're going to get an autopsy. Here, I think she can talk now." Edna handed the phone back.

"Hi." I took a deep breath and wiped my face. "What's happening with the commission? Oh, great! It came through! Will the Red Cross pay for my ticket to Washington? Okay, Okay, I won't worry about that. Yes, I thought I'd like a compartment. I'll be going home tomorrow at noon. I feel so groggy. It's probably all the pills. Maybe I'll be ready to travel in about ten days. I just don't know." I sighed. "Oh, Jim, I love you so. Yes, I'll talk to you tomorrow. Here's Edna again." I dissolved in tears once more.

Edna talked quietly for a while, and then hung up. "Look, here comes your dinner. Don't shake your head. You have to eat. I'll come back in an hour or so and we'll walk around the corridor."

I shifted the tight bands around my breasts, and reluctantly tackled the drab food. "Yes, Ma'am," I managed a weak grin. Walking around the corridor later, I asked Edna about the dogs. She said that Nellie had had three puppies, and that one of them was for me. The puppies had been born last week. *At least one pregnancy went well.* "What about the autopsy papers?"

"I have them right here. Just sign them, and we'll start the process going. I don't know why people seem so reluctant about such a routine thing." She shrugged.

Next day, after I got back to Edna's house, and was lovingly installed in bed, Nellie immediately came over and put her nose in my hand. I got up, and she led me to where three little puppies were squirming around in their basket. I couldn't help smiling, picked up one of the puppies and held her against my face. Nellie watched me carefully. This was an important connection for me. The air was cool, no hospital smells, and I slept without medication. Jim called the next night.

"Hi, sweetheart. The commission came through. You have an open ticket, compartment included. It's in the mail. Come as soon as you can, I miss you so," his voice shaking.

"I miss you too," I sputtered, crying into the phone. Gulping air, I continued, "I wrote to my sister Fay and asked her if she wanted an Airedale puppy for Alice. No way can I bring the dog to Washington. Fay thought a dog for Alice was a great idea. So I'll bring my dog, make a stop in Chicago. I can see my folks too. I'll call you just before I leave. Bye, love." Every time I talked to Jim, I collapsed into exhaustive weeping. *When will this end?*

My puppy, which I'd named Josie, pushed close against my legs, trying to climb into my lap. I picked her up, felt her rasping tongue on my neck, and laughed through my tears. "Oh, you are a funny dog. How do you know what I'm thinking?" I hugged her tight and set her down, wiping my face. "Okay, Edna, let's do some more of those fancy exercises, and then go for a walk."

The results of the autopsy came through in the next three days. The autopsy stated: "Male child, four pounds, eight ounces, born to Mr. and Mrs. James Pack III, February 16, 1943. Died three a.m. February 26. Cause of death: Heart failure due to lung collapse." *Was I responsible? Was my child's death the result of the cold I had caught on the way to Los Angeles? Why had I not been able to relax? My heart was a heavy lump in my chest.*

Ten days after leaving the hospital I was on a train for Washington, D.C., with a stopover in Chicago. In the compartment, I set up a nest for Josie on one side of my bunk that she could sleep in, and set up another box, covered in several layers of paper, for her own private toilet. I put her water bowl and food bowl near her sleeping place. Josie knew instantly which space was for which purpose, and she never messed up, all during the three-day trip to Chicago. Whenever the train made a stop of any length, Josie and I were out of the compartment in a flash, walking up and down the platform. The steward of our car was captivated by my well-behaved dog, and brought her little tidbits from the dining car. I took most of my meals in the compartment, and relaxed.

Resting on my bunk, idly watching the countryside clicking by, I read mystery novels, slept, dreamt, deliberately not thinking about anything. Once in a while, I invited Josie to snuggle next to me on the bunk, but she never leaped up without being invited.

I'm alone. No nurses, no solicitous friends, just Josie.

Fay and seven-year-old Alice met me at the station.

"How was your first trip back?" Fay greeted me. Alice's eyes were riveted on Josie.

I ignored the nudge about "first trip" and replied, "It was very comfortable, and I want to tell you, this is one smart dog." I patted Josie. "I've written out all the instructions for you. Remember, she's a puppy; she's going to have to get to know you. But she's well trained to paper; she knows what to do on a walk. I think it would be a good idea if you and Alice took a dog-training course." It was hard to let go of Josie. She looked at me, quietly sitting as I handed the leash to Fay. I knew Alice was only seven, and I had no idea what they knew about dogs.

"How are things with you?" I was carefully casual, as was Fay. We were very polite. On the way to Fay's house, Josie and I sat in the back of their Buick, Alice swiveling around to look at me and the dog. Dinner was full of small talk, "How are you feeling?" kind of thing, and "Fine, making a good recovery, thanks, looking forward to seeing Jim as a new second lieutenant," all that stuff, being studiously offhand. I went to bed early, in the small spare room.

The next morning at breakfast, I asked Fay about Ma and Pa. "I thought I'd go over and see Ma and Pa this morning, especially since I plan to take the night train to Washington. How are they?"

"They still fight all the time, and since Pa's stroke, things are worse. He's become very demanding, which drives Ma crazy. They come over for dinner Friday nights, which Ma loves because there's a truce, for that night anyway."

"How far away is their place? Not walking distance, I suppose."

"No, not walking distance, but you need to take only one streetcar." She gave me directions, and I left, a bit apprehensive.

My mother did not greet me with enthusiasm. Sitting at the kitchen table, we tried to talk. "So how is Pa?" I asked.

"All right." She paused. Then, without preamble, she looked at me over our tea and said, "Be glad the baby died."

I froze, my cup halfway to my mouth.

"Children are a nuisance," she continued, in a flat, even tone. "No matter what you do, they always disappoint you."

What is she saying? "Didn't you want me?"

"I never wanted you. Tried to get rid of you." Her voice didn't change. "But nothing worked. I threw myself down the stairs. Nothing happened. Not even a broken bone. I drank vinegar. Nothing. You came anyway."

I'm cold. I'm not really here. I am above this table. Who is that down there? That's my mother, in her print housedress, sitting at the oilcloth-covered table; that's me, my cup halfway to my mouth; there's my father, snoring in his rocking chair in the small living room, the newspaper dangling from his limp hand.

I put down my cup. *No way to answer her. I have to get out of here.* Standing up, I said, "I'd better go now, Ma," leaned over and pecked her soft, wrinkled cheek. Her lips were a thin tight line, her small black eyes fixed on my face, challenging me. *I don't know what is in your head, Ma. I wish I did.* "Bye."

Staggering down the steps to the street, I stood for a minute, taking deep breaths. What was her message? Was it her kind of "tough love"? Remember the acts of love, Rhoda. Remember the way she made apple strudel, stretching the dough over the cloth-covered table, spreading apples and cinnamon only, no nuts, over a special section for you. Remember the holiday strudel, made with candied fruit, and a special bit with no nuts. Was that not love? I shook my head to clear it. Another wound to heal. I took the streetcar back to my sister's house.

"How'd it go?" Fay greeted me.

"Fine. Dad's pretty much out of it, it seems." I kissed her. "I'm leaving early tomorrow morning," I said. "Don't bother getting up. I'll call a taxi to get to the train station. Be sure you sign up for dog-training school with Sylvia and Alice. I'll write you from Washington. Thanks for everything, Fay." *I still felt cold and distant.*

Chapter Fourteen:
Washington, D.C. and the O.W.I.

⌒

I FELL INTO JIM'S ARMS AT THE STATION, and we stood, holding each other, not saying a word. Finally, having piled my suitcases into a trolley, we walked slowly to the curb. Jim had booked a hotel for us off the beaten track. Once in our room, we shed our clothes quickly and spent the next few hours wrapped in each other's arms and bodies. We didn't leave our room for at least twelve hours, having all our meals in. We came up for air Sunday morning.

"Hi, sweetheart. Want to go for a walk in Rock Creek Park? Have breakfast out for a change?"

I grinned at him. "Yes, let's go. I've put the nightmare of the last six weeks in a box. Look, I'm going to throw the box away." Opening the window, I pretended to toss something out. It was pure bravado, but I wanted to erase the worried look on his face. "It's cherry blossom time, and a beautiful day for a walk." We stood by the open window, arms around each other, and I felt a loosening of the tightness in my chest. "When we get back, I should telephone my sister Jeanne and let her know I've arrived. I know my sister Fay has already written her that I'm on my way."

"Okay. Later."

Jeanne and Arthur came into our hotel room about three p.m.

"How are you?" Jeanne reached awkwardly to embrace me. If anyone could maintain distance while giving someone an embrace, it was Jeanne. Arthur, her husband, was even less demonstrative.

"You look pretty good, actually," was his contribution. Arthur worked in the State Department, as an adviser on the Marshall Plan project and seldom smiled. Jim stepped forward, offering a box of candy we'd bought, taking their flowers with his other hand. We stood awkwardly in the small room.

"Find yourselves some chairs," I beckoned vaguely around the room. Jim and I sat on the bed. "I'm pretty tired, but okay, thanks. This is one of the lower priced hotels in Washington. We're not sure how long we'll have to stay here." Conscious of their silent eyes on me, I felt awkwardly formal.

"Doesn't the Navy provide housing for its officers?" Arthur looked at Jim.

"My unit is currently based in Virginia, so we may end up there. Everything is so confused right now; I don't even know what my assignment will be. Until the Navy decides where it wants to put me, I'm sort of in limbo."

The small talk moved along in fits and starts, and suddenly Jeanne said, "Would you like to come for dinner Friday night? It's Arthur's turn to cook." She gave Arthur an arch look. He gave a start of surprise. "We live in Arlington," she added. "There's good public transportation."

"Sure," I said, glancing at Jim, who nodded vigorously. "What time?"

"Say seven o'clock?" Arthur stood. "It'll be a simple dinner. Probably steak and potatoes." He laughed.

After they left, Jim sat down on the bed. "They're kind of formal, aren't they?"

"I guess so," I said. "I really don't know either one of them very well. I was still in high school when they got married, then they went to Palestine. I haven't seen either Jeanne or Arthur since 1936. I have no idea what we'll talk about, but I'd like to get some inside information about how things work in Washington. Arthur must have connections somewhere, but who knows? We'll just have to play it by ear."

We showed up at my sister's apartment promptly at seven o'clock Friday evening, and handed her the bouquet of flowers we had bought at the train station. "Mmmm. Smells good," I said.

"Come in, come in, dinner's just about ready," Arthur greeted us at the door. "But we have time for a drink first. Martini okay?"

We sat down on a comfortable Swedish modern sofa while Jeanne put our flowers in a cut-glass vase. Arthur came out of the kitchen with a tall martini pitcher and two crystal martini glasses. Jeanne followed, carrying two more glasses, and sat down facing us. When the drinks were poured, we all clinked glasses, and Arthur turned to Jim.

"Do you know what your orders will be?"

"It's all very mysterious," Jim replied. "I was in the Construction Battalion, and one day I was pulled out of a drill line and told to report to the Colonel. He didn't seem very happy to see me, but said he'd received a directive from Washington to transfer me to Officers Training Camp. He wanted to know if I'd requested such a transfer, and didn't seem to believe me when I said no. I have to say Officers Training Camp was a lot easier than the Sea Bees!"

Arthur shrugged. "Who knows? Anyway, with your background in Applied Psychology, and the fact that you have to wear such strong corrective lenses, you'll probably be assigned to some desk job in the naval office." Arthur always spoke in complete sentences, biting down hard on his consonants.

"That seems to be the rumor—scuttlebutt—I'll feel better when I know for sure."

Jim kept glancing at me, as if to say, "Am I doing all right?" *Everything about Jeanne and Arthur, their apartment, their body language included, was proper and formal. I found myself uncrossing my legs and sitting straighter in my chair. I was dying to know what had really happened in Palestine, what the kibbutz was like, how they had ended up in Haifa. I remembered that Jeanne had worked in an office, but that Arthur had not been able to work as a lawyer. Did they both speak Hebrew? But obviously, tonight was not the time or place for that particular conversation.*

We had another drink, and Jeanne told some amusing stories about her job, her boss, and how everybody in Washington was constantly name-dropping. "The game is to pretend to know everybody who is anybody, and to carry it on until you get caught." She laughed, easier now that she'd had a few drinks.

We left about eleven p.m. with a definite glow, having had wine with our very good steak, on top of the martinis. I felt we had held up our end in the small talk dinner conversation.

"Well, that wasn't so bad, was it? Once you get your orders, we'll find a place to live, and I'll look for a job. Washington might be fun." We hugged and did a little jig, as we hopped aboard our commute train.

We were optimistic about our future, but six weeks later, Jim was sent to the South Pacific, for duty aboard a destroyer. All our assumptions about logical assignments were totally wrong. We were devastated. Everything happened so fast. One day we were making plans for a solid life together, and the next thing I knew Jim was gone. I looked around the half-empty hotel room, sat down on the bed, and tried to concentrate on what I had to do next. *How to find a job? How to find a place to live?* I decided a place to live had priority, and checked out the addresses of several rental agencies. I went to five different places, and at each one received the same message: long lists, long waits, but I put my name down everywhere. Next I checked out the YWCA, only to find there was a seven day limit. I decided to call Jeanne.

"Jim's been sent to the South Pacific," I said. "Can I come over tonight? I need to talk to you and Arthur."

She hesitated. "We only have leftovers for dinner," she said.

"That's all right. Do you want me to pick up anything? Dessert? Ice cream? How about a bottle of wine?"

"Whatever," she said. "Come about six-thirty."

I stopped at a delicatessen and picked up some tarts and a bottle of wine, heaviness in my heart. She had sounded so offhand.

Arthur greeted me at the door. "Jeanne's having a bit of a rest," he said. "Can I offer you a drink?" He had a glass of whisky in his hand.

"Sure. On the rocks, please. Arthur, how do things work in Washington? What kinds of jobs are available?"

"Civil service is better than working for congressmen. You take a test for a professional category, which is for people with university degrees, or a clerical job. Either one pays about the same at the lower levels." Anticipating my question, he added, "Political connections don't make any difference in civil service jobs."

"I hate tests. Are there employment agencies? If I decide against civil service, what else is there?"

"Employment agencies are always looking for people. You go for an interview, fill out a Form Fifty-Seven, listing all the experience you've had, and the personnel officer makes the decision. That's one of the things your sister does."

"What's one of the things I do?" Jeanne came in from the bedroom.

"Make decisions about who gets hired and fired. Rhoda was asking me about how to go about getting a job in Washington, and I was telling her what kind of hoops she will have to jump through."

"Just be specific about what you've done, and you'll be all right." She looked at Arthur. "Shall we eat now?"

At dinner I brought up another subject that was on my mind. There was no point in being subtle. "I've been to several housing offices, and there's a wait for everything. One of the agents I talked to said that you couldn't stay more than seven days in any one temporary place, like the YMCA or a residential hotel. Is that true?"

"Yes, you know the old story. Fish and guests begin to stink after seven days. Where are you staying now?" Jeanne poked at her macaroni and cheese, helping herself to wine.

Her remark struck me as deliberately distant. Well, I was getting to know my sister. "I moved into the Y, but I have to move out by Sunday. I lucked out before I came over here. I had put my name in at an apartment house on J Street near DuPont Circle, while I was wandering around the neighborhood, and I had a long chat with the landlord. He told me there was a possibility for an apartment on the fourth floor, a walk-up. But he said it wouldn't be available for another ten days."

Jeanne looked at Arthur, who nodded. "I guess you could stay here for a week," she said. "The couch is long enough for a bed." This wasn't the most cordial invitation I'd ever received, but I wasn't in a position to be choosy.

"Thanks, Jeanne, thanks, Arthur. I really appreciate it." Heavy silence. "Would you like to try the tarts I brought?" *Might as well stay within the limits they set up.*

The first employment agency I went to on Monday found me a job with the Office of Price Administration, working under Abe Fortas. Fortas was an engaging man, later to be the first Jew to be nominated for the Supreme Court by Franklin Roosevelt. He also withdrew his nomination after he saw what vitriolic opposition that nomination caused. He was enough of a politician to realize that sticking with the nomination would divide the Democratic Party. I didn't know anything about how Washington worked at that time; all I knew was that it was August, it was hot, and the O.P.A. offices were not air-conditioned.

There was an outbreak of polio in Washington that year, and when I passed out in the office, and found myself in a hospital bed in Bethesda, I agreed to a spinal tap to find out if I had succumbed. The test was negative, but the experience was awful; I couldn't sit up for twelve hours and was told that I would get a horrific headache if I did. After that, I decided that I didn't care where I worked, as long as the office was air-conditioned!

Back to the employment office, where I conveyed my priorities. Apparently, my typing speed and stenographic transcription skills were strong enough to give me several choices. I chose a job working for a congressman. Working as a third secretary (the lowest position) in a congressional office gave me fantastic insight into how the government really worked.

Congressman Allen was from Lima, Ohio, and he was a conservative Republican. Talk in the office ranged from pornographic jokes about Eleanor Roosevelt to trashing of Franklin. There was much speculation about their sex life, considering the fact that Franklin lived in a wheel-chair. I was disgusted, but learned to keep my mouth shut. As an ardent liberal Democrat who had campaigned for Franklin Roosevelt and worshipped Eleanor, biting my tongue took heroic effort.

I spent every lunch hour sitting in the Visitors' Gallery in the House of Representatives, watching and listening to the debate over the G.I. Bill of Rights. I was appalled at the pettiness of the debates, the haggling over small details. The gallery was also full of discharged soldiers, many of them on crutches or with their arms in slings. They also followed the arguments with intense interest. It was 1944; we were fighting on two fronts, in Europe and in the South Pacific. The atmosphere was tense in Washington.

Along with the tension, which was palpable, there was a frenetic energy in the city. You could feel it everywhere. Mr. Allen had one executive secretary, an office manager, and two third secretaries. Sybil, the other third secretary was also a "war widow," as we were called, and we hung out together. We never talked politics, since Sybil was more interested in a social life than in politics.

"Let's go over to the Shoreham for a drink," she offered one Friday night after work. "It's fun, and there are always a lot of cute guys in town for the weekend, especially officers." She winked.

Suddenly I was back on the UC Berkeley campus in 1940, remembering Bill, the Irishman from Boston, and I had the same sinking feeling in my stomach, a premonition of disaster. "Well, just one drink. I'm not in the mood for a pick-up."

Sybil tossed her head. "Suit yourself. Let's go."

The Shoreham Lounge was crowded, as she had said, with Army and Navy lieutenants, all eyeing the unattached women hungrily. I felt as if I were in a live meat market. We sat down at a small table. I ordered a Manhattan. Suddenly, an Army lieutenant appeared at our table.

"Would you ladies join us for a drink?" He motioned to a table nearby, where two more Army men were sitting. Sybil was on her feet in a moment. I stood too, but said, "I'm going to the ladies'. I'll be right back." *Let Sybil pay for my drink, I thought. I've got to get out of here.*

After two months in Congressman Allen's office, I decided to try for a job with the Office of War Information, and made my way to the personnel office on my lunch hour. I filled out the regulation Form Fifty-Seven, but left the space marked "religion" blank.

The personnel officer zeroed in on that blank space. "Are you Jewish?" she asked.

"Yes."

"Can you be anything else?"

I gulped. "Unitarian?" I offered.

"No," she said, emphatically, "Unitarian is code for Jewish; Jews who want to pass say they are Unitarian."

"Oh," I replied, and after a brief pause suggested, "Christian Scientist?"

"Yes, that's perfect. I'll put down Christian Scientist." She gave me a shrewd glance, and I met her gaze with a straight face. It was my stomach that flinched. She smiled thinly, stubbed out her cigarette, and asked, "Anything else on your mind?"

Her name was Helen Kerry, one of five women reporters on the *Chicago Tribune* and I was familiar with her interviews with survivors of trauma. Those stories were usually assigned to women, and the writers were known as "sob sisters." Helen Kerry had a low raspy voice, and kept a cigarette constantly either in her mouth or in her hands throughout our interview. Her office was a small cubbyhole with head-high partitions. I could hear the murmur of other voices, and registered the differences in the voices of the interviewers and the interviewees—the easy assurance of one, the hesitancy of the other.

I focused on the main reason I was there. I wanted a writing job of any kind, especially if it was in an air-conditioned office. "Yes, what is really involved? I mean, how much writing will I be doing, and if Kurani approves of me, what then?"

"Habib Kurani is our Middle East specialist, and he's from Lebanon. He's fixated on the fear that the Jews in Palestine want to take over Lebanon. He wouldn't even want to look at you if he knew you were Jewish. Yet I think you will be the right person for Habib. He is in charge of planting information in Middle East newspapers. We have operatives in Beirut, Cairo, and Baghdad. We supply them with information favorable to the United States, and they place this information in local newspapers. That means that your primary job will be as an executive secretary for Dr. Kurani and doing some writing, preparing material to send overseas."

My journalism experience in high school and at the university had prepared me to distinguish between propaganda and information. The description of my job sounded like propaganda, but I knew that the line between the two was pretty thin, especially during a war. I nodded.

"Can you come in for an interview with Dr. Kurani at nine-thirty tomorrow morning? The F.B.I. will investigate your background, and when you pass, you'll go to work."

I let out the breath I'd been holding. "Okay. Yes, sure. I'll be in Dr. Kurani's office at nine-thirty sharp." I took the piece of paper with Kurani's office number on it and danced out of the office. Then I went right downtown to buy an interview outfit. Since it was late August and I was south of the Mason-Dixon line, I bought a wide-brimmed white straw hat, a demure blue and white striped cotton dress, and white cotton gloves. I already had blue leather pumps and a blue handbag.

Thus equipped, I showed up at Habib Kurani's office the next morning. We exchanged evaluating looks. I noted his gentle brown eyes and eyebrows raised at a querying angle. I noticed his sagging shoulders and saw him as an academic, stuck in a bureaucratic job. He half-rose from his swivel chair and gestured toward a chair next to him. I hoped he saw me as a competent future assistant.

"Please sit down. Tell me about your experience."

I sat upright on the chair he offered, my knees together, and a pillow of air between my spine and the back of the chair. "I've been in Washington since the end of March. My husband was shipped to the Pacific six weeks after I got here, so I had to find a job right away. I worked for the Office of Price Administration under Mr. Abe Fortas, and as a third secretary for a Republican congressman from Lima, Ohio. I really want a job where I can use my writing skills, but I know how to type and take dictation, and I really know how to organize an office." Rushing on, I told him about my experience teaching in Berkeley and Oakland, California, and also about my journalism experience in high school and at Northwestern University.

He listened carefully, his brown eyes behind their glasses never wavering. "Well, Mrs. Pack, I'm sure we'll get along just fine. We have to wait for security clearance from the F.B.I., but I don't think that will take too long. Maybe ten days at the most."

"Thank you, Dr. Kurani. I look forward to working with you." I wasn't so sure about how fast my clearance would be since I had been secretary of the League Against War and Fascism at Northwestern University and was probably on a list somewhere as a communist sympathizer. Newspapers in 1943 and 1944 were full of articles about "quislings" and "fellow-travelers." Vidkun Quisling was a Norwegian who collaborated with the Nazis; in fact, he helped prepare the way for Hitler's invasion. "Quisling" became a word synonymous with "traitor." Communist sympathizers, labeled "fellow-travelers," were people who marched in demonstrations supporting Spanish loyalists or who voiced support for sit-in strikers. I was a marcher and an organized labor supporter. I wasn't at all sure I would pass the F.B.I. litmus tests.

I called the personnel officer about a week later. "Have you heard anything about my clearance?"

"Dr. Kurani is having a fit about the delay," she said, "and he is hounding the F.B.I. He has asked his chief, Dr. Badeau, the head of the Office of Strategic Services for the Middle East, for help in getting you approved. I think you'll see some action next week." I knew that Dr. Badeau's office adjoined Dr. Kurani's.

I had already told the congressman I worked for that I hoped to get a job with the O.W.I., and he had agreed to let me leave whenever the job came through. I had to admit that while I disagreed with that congressman's politics, he was a decent guy and really represented his conservative constituents. The call from Personnel came through the following week, and I showed up in Kurani's office the next day.

"Good morning!" I hung up my straw hat and looked around the office. *I heard the voice of the executive secretary in the law office where I'd gotten my first job in my head. Molly's words echoed: "The first thing you do when you get a job is to reorganize the files. Then no one else will be able to find anything, and you will become indispensable. That's power, kid!"* Aloud I said, "Shall I organize your files?"

Dr. Kurani looked relieved. "Oh, would you? I haven't had any help for more than two weeks, and everything has piled up." He pointed to a stack of papers on his desk. "We get a copy of all non-confidential material relating to the Middle East, but I'm not sure it all gets filed in the proper places." He then pointed to the bottom left-hand drawer of the filing cabinet. "I keep my lunch in there."

We smiled at each other. I picked up the pile of papers and put them on my desk. "Besides the filing, what's the most pressing item you would like addressed?"

"I need to present a report to Dr. Badeau this afternoon about the work of our men in the field. I've been writing it out in longhand."

I picked up my shorthand notebook and sat down next to him. "Why don't you dictate to me? I'll type up a first draft and you can edit it. Will that help?" He looked at me as if I'd just thrown him a lifepreserver, and he began to talk.

By the end of the day, I had a pretty good idea of what my job would be, and it would be a lot livelier than that of a third secretary in a Republican congressman's office!

I felt protective toward Habib Kurani, even nurturing. After all, I was in charge of that office; I could make decisions; I felt the surge of power Molly had talked about.

One of my jobs was to read, actually scan, four New York papers and two Washington papers, for news items relating to the Middle East. I was to clip them out, summarize the important ones, put the summaries into a coded form of telegraphese, and present them to Kurani. He would take a look at the ones I had discarded, check the summaries of the ones I had selected, okay the language, and I would then send them out by special courier. After a few days, his review of my summaries became more and more cursory, and the confidence between us grew.

When our overseas agents came back from Beirut, Cairo, and Baghdad, Dr. Badeau held debriefing sessions in his office. Dr. Kurani had spoken of me so highly to Dr. Badeau that I was invited to sit in and take notes. For some reason, Dr. Kurani trusted me more than he did Dr. Badeau's secretary.

I remember a completely horrifying report session in January 1945. All three agents were assembled in Dr. Badeau's office, and they were assessing the situation in the Middle East. There was a lot of talk about how the Western Allies (meaning America and Britain) should contain the "Jewish invasion"—those were the words they used—of Arab lands, and what to do about the Zionists. There were also many references to support of the Arab communities, especially Saudi Arabia, the United Arab Emirates, and all of the countries surrounding the area that would later become Israel. The entire area was a British Protectorate, known as Palestine.

I kept my head down, concentrating on my notebook. I found myself pressing down so tightly on my pencil that the point snapped, and I had to quickly pick up the extra pencil I kept with me. I knew all about the Zionists. I remembered the recruiting sessions when I was a teenager. We were invited to attend special camps where we would learn to dig ditches, plant gardens, and get our fingernails dirty. We were told we would be building a new land; learn to work together in a communal setting. I was more interested at that time in building a more equitable society in the United States, and was not all that committed to a Jewish homeland. Nevertheless, there was no way I could relate to the offhand way the agents, Dr. Badeau and Dr. Kurani brushed off the Jewish refugees from Europe as "invaders," as well as the denigrating way they talked about "the Arabs." It was as if neither the Jews nor the Arabs were people, but instead were impersonal chess pieces in a game not of their choosing.

I felt like a spy who would never be able to report to anyone what I had heard and what I knew. That knowledge seared my brain like a hot iron, and remains as a scar.

The months passed, and the news from the South Pacific was not encouraging. I heard from Jim sporadically; brief letters spelling out his loneliness, his sense of isolation.

"Since I didn't go to West Point, and am not a career officer," he wrote, "I am treated as if I'm not there. When I walk into the eating area, called 'the mess,' (and sometimes it is), other officers stop talking or look meaningfully at each other and change the subject. Also, I'm having trouble with my glasses. On deck they get fogged over by spray, and when I take them off to clean them, of course I can't see anything. Oh, I miss you so..."

Much of the letter was blacked out, so the censors must have noticed something they didn't like. Anyway, some time in November of 1944, his letters stopped coming altogether. Three months went by, and I couldn't get any information from anywhere. It was as if a blanket had descended on the South Pacific. We knew some terrible battles were being fought, but I wasn't sure exactly where Jim was. My mind was full of horrible scenarios. Battle scenes on television became personal; I saw him on a ship being blown up; I saw him hanging onto a life raft, perhaps drowning. I didn't sleep well and had lost my appetite for food.

Then in February 1945, a letter postmarked Mare Island, California arrived. Jim's handwriting was so shaky I could hardly decipher it. I showed the letter to Habib Kurani. "What do you think?" I asked him.

"I think he is very ill. He says he is in the hospital, but he doesn't say why. He doesn't mention an injury. Just that he is happy he has his glasses back." Dr. Kurani handed the letter back to me. "You have to find out what happened to him."

"How do I do that?" My eyes filled with tears.

Dr. Kurani was very specific. "You must go to see the admiral and find out what the diagnosis is."

"The admiral? Of the Navy? Me?"

"Yes. In America, the members of the government work for you. You are the boss. You have the right to get information about your own husband. You should call the Naval Office and ask for an appointment with the admiral."

I stared at him. *What an amazing concept! That the admiral of the Navy worked for me! I loved it.* The call was remarkably easy to make, and I made an appointment for the end of the week. Dr. Kurani told me not to worry about taking time off.

There I was, at twenty-six, in the middle of World War II; I, Mrs. Jim Pack, was off to challenge the admiral of the U.S. Navy. *I felt the same rush of adrenaline that carried me across a rough lake in 1930 when I was twelve years old.*

I walked into the admiral's office and sat down opposite this imposing man, grey haired, with gold stripes up his sleeves almost to his elbows, his grey-blue eyes fixed on me.

"What can I do for you, Mrs. Pack?" His hands were folded on his desk.

I handed him Jim's letter. "I'd like to know why he is in the hospital, and what the diagnosis is."

The admiral had a folder in front of him that must have related to Jim. He opened it. "Your husband has been diagnosed manic-depressive, acute depressive, and has been in the psychiatric ward under a suicide watch. However, he has responded well to treatment, and is doing better."

I swallowed. "That doesn't sound like Jim," I said. "He is a brilliant man, a psychologist, and if he was depressed, there must have been a good reason for it. I would challenge the diagnosis. And, also, as far as I know, when a member of the Naval Services is confined to a hospital, he is sent to a hospital nearest his closest kin. That's me, and I'm here in Washington, not Berkeley."

Admiral Johnson leaned back in his chair. "I have no way of verifying his diagnosis," he said. "What do you want me to do?"

"I want Jim transferred to Bethesda," I said, "and to have him diagnosed there. I want him to be close to where I can visit him. If you care about the health of your sailors, as I know you do, I think he'll do better here than in Mare Island."

"I can do that, Mrs. Pack," the admiral replied. "I'll cut an order for his transfer."

I made no move to stand up, but sat firmly in my chair.

"Is there anything else?"

"Yes, I would like you to cut that order now." I couldn't believe what was coming out of my mouth.

"Now?" His eyebrows lifted.

"Yes. Now." I was firm and calm.

Admiral Johnson compressed his lips, and pushed a button on his desk. A male secretary appeared, and Johnson proceeded to dictate something to him. The words were not clear to me, but the intent was. "There. The order has been cut and will be sent today."

"Thank you, Admiral Johnson. How soon may I expect Jim to arrive at Bethesda?"

Johnson could barely control his impatience. "Within ten days, I should say. Give or take a day or so."

I stood up and extended my hand. "Thank you very much. I'll look forward to hearing from the hospital at Bethesda within two weeks," I said. "I'll let you know when he arrives. Thank you for your help." Johnson's mouth was a slash in his face.

When I walked out of his office, my legs shaking, I realized that I had been holding my breath. *Did I really do what I thought I had done?* I went back to my office in a daze. Dr. Kurani was waiting for me. "How did it go?" He wanted to know.

"Admiral Johnson agreed to have Jim transferred. He said Jim was manic-depressive, acute depressive. I can't believe it. That's not the Jim I know. But anyway, he's supposed to be at Bethesda in about two weeks. I'll feel better once I can see him for myself." I couldn't hold my feelings in anymore; I put my head down on my desk, all the held-back tears pouring out.

Dr. Kurani didn't say anything; he just left the office quietly.

Admiral Johnson was true to his word. Ten days after my visit, I got word from Bethesda that Jim had arrived, and I tore over there. He was a shadow of himself, thin, drawn, his head sinking down into his shoulders. I held him a long time. We sat in the "Day Room," and talked.

Jim sat hunched over, his hands on the table in front of us. He kept twisting and untwisting his fingers. "I've been offered a discharge," he said tentatively.

"A medical discharge?" I was leery of that designation.

"I don't know."

"Tell me the proper procedure. Do I see the doctor on the ward? The chief petty officer? I'd like to get a straight story."

Jim looked at me. "A straight story? From the Navy? Good luck." He paused. "Well, you're a civilian, you might get a different story than I would. Might as well try. Ask for Dr. Gibbons, I think he's the one who signs the discharge papers."

I leaned over and gave him a hug. "I'll be right back."

Dr. Gibbons was very specific. "We can release Lt. Pack into your custody, but you must understand his health is not robust." *The understatement of the week!*

"I accept that charge," I said. "What about his discharge? Will it be qualified, or will it be honorable?"

Dr. Gibbons looked at me for a long moment. "I understand you," he said, giving a small sigh. "It will be an honorable discharge."

I let out my breath, stood up, and extended my hand. "Thank you, Dr. Gibbons. I appreciate this." He looked embarrassed, and dropped my hand quickly.

"We can arrange the paperwork in a few days. Mr. Pack will be ready to leave on Friday."

I rushed back to the Day Room and found Jim with his head on his arms, his eyes closed. "Jim! It's all set! You'll be getting out of here on Friday! I'll come for you about eleven a.m. What do you think about that?"

He lifted his head and stared at me. A slow grin spread over his face. "You're a genius, kiddo!" I blinked away tears and put a smile on my face. "Okay. See you Friday. 'Bye, love." And I danced out the door.

Friday afternoon, we stood in the tiny living room of my fourth floor walk-up on Nineteenth and Dupont Circle and looked at each other, not really believing that we were finally together again. As I held him close, I could feel his bones through his jacket.

"Let's go to bed," I whispered, and, holding each other close, we moved to the bedroom. We lovingly removed each other's clothes. Time does stand still, once in a while. It had been a long year and a half.

It was dark when I woke up. Jim was still asleep, breathing lightly but in a deep, quiet way. I rose quietly and tiptoed out of the room, closing the door gently. I was hungry, and I figured he would be hungry too. I felt giddy, apprehensive and relieved, all at once. He was alive, but he was so different. How had he changed? We had both changed; we would have to get to know each other all over again. I made some coffee, pulled out eggs, milk, and opened a can of mushrooms. I heard the bedroom door open.

"I think I'll take a shower. Okay?"

"Sure. We'll have an omelet when you come out." I had taken ten days leave from my job at the O.W.I., and that gave us some time to sort things out and decide what we wanted to do for the rest of our lives. An omelet never tasted so good. Then Jim stood up, saying, "I want to show you some of the things I made in the craft shop at Mare Island, even in the few months I was there." He went into the bedroom and came back with beautifully crafted handbags and belts.

"Jim! These are beautiful!" I immediately put on one of the belts. "There's nothing like this in the shops. Maybe there's a market for your work! I have a friend from high school who lives in New York. Her name is Beatrice, and she has all kinds of connections. Maybe we should go to New York." I stopped, caught by a cautious look on Jim's face. "Shall I call her?"

Jim hesitated and sighed. Then, straightening his shoulders, he said, "Sure, what do we have to lose?"

So I called Bea, and asked her for help. She said she would get us an interview with a famous bag maker named Phelps, and we should bring samples of Jim's work. I told her that Jim's handbags were laced and carved, but the shapes were not at all traditional. They didn't look artsy-craftsy; they were different from anything I'd seen in the current fashion magazines. I told her that Jim's work was meticulously elegant. So we went to New York for an interview with Phelps.

The showroom was impressive. Black leather couches, a free form-glass coffee table, photos of models with Phelps's bags on the walls, blowups of pages from *Women's Wear Daily*. This was obviously "big time." We showed Phelps all of Jim's drawings for other designs, and he was impressed.

"You have real talent," he said to us. "But my advice would be to go back to San Francisco and make your name from there. New York is very competitive. It will chew you up and spit you out." Jim was twenty-seven, I was twenty-six. We must have seemed like babes in the wood to him. I don't know what we expected, but it seemed like a brush-off to us, and we said as much to Bea later.

"Oh, I don't know," she said. "You don't know how tough New York is. It's hard to break in anywhere without connections, and I don't think you want to work as a laborer in Phelps's factory, do you?"

Jim shook his head. Suddenly I leaned forward. "You know, O.W.I. has an overseas branch in San Francisco. If I could get transferred there, we'd have a base. We'd have an income, and we could develop a leather business without having to worry about working for peanuts, working our way up from the bottom somewhere. What do you think?"

"Rhoda, you've got it!" Bea exclaimed. "That's exactly what I meant. If you have your base secured, you can afford to take a chance on a new field. Besides, you know the Bay Area, don't you? Didn't you both graduate from UC Berkeley?"

"Yes, and we used to go to San Francisco on weekends. I love San Francisco." I turned to Jim. "What do you say? I can start the wheels turning when I go back to the office on Monday."

Jim was silent. He'd been staring out the window of the cafe we were sitting in, watching the wet snow splat against the window. "It'll be warmer in California," he said.

He seemed to have withdrawn into himself, and was lost in reverie.

"Great! That's settled." We stood up, Bea and I shook hands, and grinned at each other. *We both remembered carrots and a sleepover in Chicago when we were sixteen.* "Take care of yourself, Bea. We'll let you know what happens."

On the train back to Washington, Jim fell asleep, and I began to plan. The first thing to do was to tell Dr. Kurani what we had decided, ask his advice, and find out what was available in the San Francisco office. I trusted Dr. Kurani completely, and knew that he would understand why we had to leave Washington.

The next day I spoke to Dr. Kurani. I told him that Jim and I wanted to go back to the San Francisco Bay Area, and that neither one of us wanted to go back to the academic world. I told him how much I really liked my work for O.W.I. and asked him what he knew about the overseas branch in San Francisco.

Dr. Kurani looked at me for a long time. "I'll be sorry to lose you," he said. "But I can tell you what you have to do. First, you send an exploratory letter to the head of the department in San Francisco, include a short resume and say exactly why you want to relocate. You have to find out which departments have openings for reporters."

"Reporters? Wouldn't I have to submit a piece of writing?"

"Ah, yes, I forgot. Better talk to Larry in the China Department. He'll know what to do. Wait, I'll call him right now."

Within half an hour, I found myself talking to Larry Davenport, a short, intense man in rolled-up shirt-sleeves, a pen behind his ear. He looked like a character out of a movie called "The Front Page."

"I happen to know that there might be an opening on the Indonesia Desk," he said. "What you need to do is write a piece, maybe a book review, or a think piece, then we'll circulate it around the desks in San Francisco, and if somebody there likes it, you might get an offer of a job. Tell you what. Write a review of *Cannery Row,* as a window on American culture. Don't spend too much time on it. Just dash it off and bring it to me tomorrow. I'll check it out and let you know if it would encourage me to hire you."

I sweated over my book review. After the fourth rewrite, I decided I was ready to show it to Larry. He took one look at my painfully created bit of writing, picked up a blue pencil, and swept through it. "You're writing for translation!" he said, wielding his pencil like a sword. "No clauses. No prepositional endings to sentences. Nothing but subject, verb, object. No descriptive adjectives or adverbs. Simple sentences! Simple sentences! Here, rewrite it; bring it back tomorrow."

I gripped my copy, and went back to my office. I had too much work to do that day, so I worked at home far into the night. I went back to Larry the next day and tentatively handed him the copy.

"Better," he said, using his dreaded blue pencil sparingly. "One more rewrite, and I think we'll have something we can send out. Everybody pretends they're submitting a first draft, but what the hell."

Two days later, Dr. Kurani got a phone call from San Francisco, and he handed the phone to me with a smile. "Yes?" I said.

"This is Professor Compton of the Indonesia Desk," the voice said. "Mr. Corcoran of the China Desk put in a request for you, but I need you more. How soon can you get here? I'm short a reporter, and I need one right away."

"I've given Dr. Kurani two weeks notice," I said. "I have to find him a competent replacement before I leave. The earliest I could be there would be about three weeks. Also my status has to be upgraded and I think the paperwork might take that long."

Mr. Compton sighed. "All right. Do the best you can. Call me when you get to San Francisco. Now let me talk to Habib."

I handed the phone to Dr. Kurani and walked unsteadily back to my desk, feeling slightly unreal. I pinched myself to make sure. Wait till I tell Jim!

I ran up the four flights of stairs to our DuPont Circle apartment, and burst in, panting. "I got it! I got the appointment to the San Francisco Office of the O.W.I.!" I grabbed Jim and hopped up and down. "Now, with your discharge, we can go to San Francisco and start a new life! Goodbye, Washington, hello San Francisco!"

Jim was cautiously enthusiastic, but nothing could dampen my spirits.

Chapter Fifteen:
San Francisco, Grant Avenue, 1945

⊸∋

T HE THREE-DAY TRIP BY TRAIN from Washington, D.C. to San Francisco became a bridge to our new world. Jim didn't want to talk about
the war at all, so we sat in our compartment, dreamed, and talked about
what we would do when we got to the Bay Area. The Navy had provided
transportation to Jim's city of induction into the armed forces, and the compartment gave us needed breathing space. We had already decided to live
in San Francisco. We had Jim's discharge pay of three hundred dollars, and
my job for the O.W.I. Overseas-office. That was our capital. We had several
handbags and belts Jim had made for me in the naval hospital, encourage-
ment from Phelps in New York, and we were full of hope.

During our years at UC Berkeley, we had spent a lot of time in the pubs of
North Beach, and knew that North Beach was the place for us. Getting off
the train in Oakland, we crossed the Bay by ferry. It was a glorious day. The
waves sparkled in the sun, sea gulls wheeled and cried. I imagined them talking to each other in sea- gull language, *Hey! Do you see any fish down there?*
Yes! Over near the third tower, etc. The windows of San Francisco's skyscrapers
reflected the sun's rays, a magical city on a hill, beckoning us. We stood on
the ferryboat deck, inhaling the fresh sea air, feeling our lungs expand with
hope and joyous expectation.

From the Ferry Building we made our way to Union and Stockton, where
we found a small motel, and then we wandered down to Grant Avenue. Our
search was for a place where Jim could set up a workshop, ideally somewhere

with living space, as well. We planned that I would work downtown during the day, and Jim would make leather handbags and belts in the shop. Then I would help finish things in the evening.

As we walked up and down Grant Avenue, we noticed an empty store at 1541 Grant between Union and Filbert that looked possible. Inquiring at the bar next door, we found out that the Italian landlord also owned a parking garage on the corner of Filbert and Grant. He turned out to be a taciturn man, chomping on a big cigar, who answered all our questions in monosyllables. He said the rent was twenty-five dollars a month, which sounded just right. Mr. Torelli acknowledged that there was a toilet and rooms in the back we could live in, but he didn't seem to care whether we rented it or not. He gave us a key, and we promised we'd let him know in an hour.

The store at 1541 Grant was an odd place. There was a partition between the front and the back, and there were small rooms behind this thin wall, all separated from each other by doors. There was a small bathroom with a toilet, but no bathtub, and there was a room with two laundry tubs and an old gas stove. The back door, opening from the laundry tub room, led to a small yard, a weedy patch of grass.

Our imagination transformed the bare rooms. The front part of the store could be a combination workroom and showroom, and one of the back rooms would serve as a bedroom. The room with the stove would become our kitchen. We told Mr. Torelli we would take it, and gave him a month's rent. Full of confidence, we walked down Grant to Figoni's Hardware and Plumbing Shop. The Figoni who owned the hardware shop was one of the three famous Figonis in North Beach, important men in the neighborhood. One of the brothers owned and operated a night club, called "Finocchio's", on Broadway, featuring transvestite performers. The other Figoni owned the New Tivoli Restaurant on the block between Green and Union. Salvatore Figoni, at the hardware store, was friendly and talkative.

"Hi," he greeted us. Looking at Jim, who was still wearing his Navy uniform even though he was officially discharged, he said, "Hey, did you know your commander-in-chief just died?" The date was April 12, 1945.

"You mean Roosevelt?" Jim and I looked at each other.

"Yep. Harry Truman is now your president."

Jim automatically removed his hat. We stood there, not knowing what to say next. *I felt a stab in my heart. Franklin Delano Roosevelt had been my president for twelve of my twenty-seven years; my father had accepted him as a worthy substitute for Norman Thomas, the perennial socialist candidate. Harry Truman, who was he? The war in Europe is over, but what about Japan?*

The awkward silence grew. Then Figoni, in a fake cheerful voice, said, "Well, you didn't come in here to talk about Roosevelt, did you? What can I do for you?"

We told him that we had decided to rent 1541 Grant Avenue and make it into a shop to sell handmade leather bags and belts like the one I was wearing. We told him we planned to live in the rear of the store, and we needed paint and pots and pans.

Figoni looked at us and laughed. Then he said, "Do you kids know what your place used to be?"

"No, what?" We said in unison.

He paused for effect. "A whorehouse! That's what! The whores have moved upstairs!" He laughed again, watching us to see how we would react.

"Oh!" I said. "That's why all the little rooms in the back of the partition are separated from each other by doors! Oh, well, if the whores don't bother us, we won't bother them." We were academics, after all. Whores were an intellectual construct.

Walking back up Grant Avenue, I looked with different eyes at the houses and shops we were passing. All the buildings were jammed close together, so close it seemed as if one building's side wall must also be the other's side wall too. *Hmmm. There must be a layer of extra brick between them; otherwise you would be able to hear everything that went on in your neighbor's apartment!*

Apartments were located on the second story of the buildings, with shops on the ground floor. We passed an Italian bakery on the corner of Grant and Union, an Italian delicatessen across the street. Iacopi's Meats was next to an Italian dry goods shop, next to the New Tivoli, next to Peter Macchiarini's jewelry shop. The only non-Italian place was a Chinese laundry next to an Italian-owned stationery store.

From open windows in the apartments above the shops, buxom Italian mamas and grandmamas leaned on their windowsills, gossiping cheerfully back and forth, a second-story backyard fence exchange. There was a place on Vallejo near Grant called "The Spaghetti Factory," but it looked deserted. Maybe at one time there was enough business in the neighborhood to keep a spaghetti factory going, but the only place that still advertised homemade pasta was a small store next to Figoni's hardware. The whole neighborhood was Little Italy, San Francisco's version, and we liked it.

As we marched back to 1541 Grant, our new home, we nodded to several people giving us the once-over. *We're newcomers to the village all right!* Next to the shop we had rented was a bar/restaurant advertising bocce ball courts in the rear. As we walked into our dingy storefront shop, we nodded to the men hanging out in front of the bar. We waved cheerfully; they grunted.

The radio broadcasts were all about Roosevelt, Truman, memorial services, and the war. Roosevelt's death was half expected, of course, but Jim and I were so immersed in our own painful journey, we felt detached from the national mourning scene. We were both trying to recover from our own traumas.

Jim had been released into my custody. It was a bargain I had struck with Dr. Gibbons in Bethesda. I wanted Jim to get an honorable discharge, not a medical discharge, afraid that if he went looking for a job, employers would question the reasons for that designation. I knew how the average person reacted to anything that hinted of any kind of mental disability. Yes, I was protective, and yes, it was not a healthy way to begin a different sort of relationship. The death of my child still haunted me, but I buried it. I talked to myself. *Don't think about how Stephen died. That was 1943. This is 1945. San Francisco. Concentrate. Make things work.*

We bought a few cushions, a mattress from Goodwill, and slept on the floor in our newly painted back room, which looked out over our patch of grass. "I've got to go back to work on Monday," I said to Jim. "Our savings are disappearing like the fog." We were on our backs, staring at the ceiling, late evening sunlight drifting into the room.

"I'm just thinking about where to put up some shelves, and building a work-table," Jim said, as if he hadn't heard me. "I'll need to get some tools and find a lumber yard that's close."

We're traveling different tracks, I guess. But they have to intersect, or we're lost. I'd better switch over.

"Why don't you go talk to Figoni? I bet either he or a relative owns a lumber yard. Anyway, he seemed to like us. See if he'll help you."

"Right." Jim roused himself. "What time is it? Five-thirty? I'll go talk to him right now."

Jim left. I sat up and began to make lists. Jim built shelves, I made lists.

Monday morning I left Jim hammering away at his shelves and work-table, and took the bus downtown to 111 Sutter Street, the headquarters of the U.S. Office of War Information Overseas on the twelfth floor.

Full of apprehension, I walked into the O.W.I. Overseas Newsroom and looked around. There were several long tables set up in the room, and reporters sat facing each other. All men. All conversation stopped as I walked in. Eleven pairs of eyes followed my progress. The Desk chief nodded at me.

"You must be Rhoda Pack, from Washington, D.C., right?"

"Yes," I said. "I've been working for Dr. Kurani, in the Middle East section."

He didn't introduce himself, but simply pointed to a chair, a typewriter, and waved at the ticker tape machine in the corner. "That's the tape machine," he said. He walked over to it, tore off some paper. "Rewrite these stories," he said, and walked away. That was all. *Well! I had been warned that the situation in San Francisco would be different from Washington, but no one had been specific. This crowded room, full of people working close together, the clatter of typewriters—this was nothing like the calm, carpeted room in which I worked at my own desk in a spacious office with only one other man, where I had had some status!*

For two weeks I was totally ignored, "in Coventry," as we used to say. That phrase comes from a way of punishing nonconformists in a British coal town named Coventry in the nineteenth century. During a particularly acrimonious strike, anyone who walked across the picket line was subjected to this punishment. Entire families were isolated, even children. No one spoke to the isolated family in Coventry. In the San Francisco Office of the O.W.I. no one spoke directly to me. People spoke across me, over me, everyone avoided eye contact. My boss left notes on my typewriter, outlining my assignments. I wrote my feature pieces silently, handed them to the Desk chief silently, and seldom had to rewrite. I ate my lunch at my own small space in silence. If the men in that room were waiting for me to break, they came close to achieving it.

I knew that all the reporters took news off a ticker tape and rewrote it for translation. This meant that we had to write simple, clear sentences, no dependent clauses, no adjectival clauses. One of the pieces I wrote, a review of Norman Cousins's essay, "Modern Man is Obsolete," came out "Modern Man is Ready for the Ashcan."

On the Indonesian Desk, the material we wrote was translated into Dutch and Indonesian. The U.S. section was sandwiched between the Dutch and the Indonesians, and all material had to pass three censors: the Dutch, the Indonesians, and the U.S. Even though the U.S. Intelligence censors had the final say, there were subtle things the U.S. censors missed. For instance, I picked up an article from the ticker tape about how the Filipino fighters had prepared for a land invasion by the Japanese by placing poisoned stakes in the roads along which they thought the Japanese would come. They intended the stakes to be traps to be used in ambushes. *I thought of the English defenders in the tenth century placing spikes in the stone walls of their narrow country roads on which the horses of the French would be impaled. Are these lessons of warfare learned or mysteriously acquired through some form of osmosis we're not aware of?*

I copied the information off the tape and included it into a piece I wrote for broadcast to Indonesia, knowing full well that the Indonesians, who were planning to revolt against the Dutch, would file that information away and use it against the Dutch, who were, after all, our allies.

At the end of two weeks, the senior reporter in the room, a gray-haired, grizzled veteran reporter on the *San Francisco Examiner,* met my eye, reached across the table, and offered me an apple. I often wondered why he did that. Maybe, as the senior reporter in the room, he decided that I had passed the initiation. Whatever it was that motivated him, it brought me out of "Coventry." That's when I almost broke down. Everybody was watching. I swallowed hard, took the apple, managed a grin, and said "Thanks." Choking down the apple, blinking back tears as I grinned, I heard a small buzz all around me. Chairs scraped, someone offered me coffee, and I felt a pat on my back. My boss came over, saying, "This is an interesting story. Try your hand on this one."

I stood up, rushed to the toilet, sagged into a booth, and let the tears flow. *So this is what it takes to be "one of the boys"!*

Back in the newsroom, people began talking to me. They started coming over, peering over my shoulder at what I was writing, telling jokes, and consciously editing their language while always letting me know what they were doing with side-long glances or throat clearings. George Harris, the veteran reporter from the *Examiner*, took me out for a drink after work, and offered some advice.

"Watch your back, kid," he counseled. "Those guys won't give you an inch. Keep your ears open for when the tape starts clicking, and hop over there right away. Right now you're getting the crumbs, the special feature stuff nobody wants. If you're satisfied with that, okay, but if not..." His voice trailed off.

I remembered his advice when I transferred to the China Desk. When the atom bomb was dropped on Hiroshima in August 1945, I was the first one at the ticker tape machine, and had my hand on the copy.

"Hey, Rhoda! This is an important story! Let me help you on this one! Hey, Rhoda! Are you sure you can handle it?" The other reporters crowded around me. I brushed past all of them, the tape in my hand, and began to type furiously, ignoring the anxious reporters clustered around me. When I finished, I ripped the pages out of the machine, turned around, and handed them to my boss. "Check it out," I said, and grinned at him. *Thanks, George!*

I left the office that evening in a state of euphoria, and was glad for the long walk home. It gave me time to move from one mind-set to another. I was living in a sort of unreal dual universe. During the day I was a reporter, concentrating on being "one of the boys," and in the evening I was struggling to be Jim's partner in our fledgling leather business. When I left the shop in the morning, I was in my reportorial persona; when I walked home, I would consciously become Jim's wife. I felt strange, almost, but not quite schizophrenic.

We had painted the partition dividing our selling space from our work and living space a neutral off-white, and then put ornamental hooks onto the partition. We hung handbags and belts from the hooks, and we also bought used bricks from a local brickyard which became back-drops for display in the windows. People kept coming in, wanting to buy the bricks and ignoring the handbags. *So much for innovative window dressing!*

The United Nations Conference convened in San Francisco on April 14, 1945. I wasn't accepted as a full working member of the newsroom staff until the end of April, but by May 25, I was hanging around the Conference headquarters with the rest of the staff. Women are treated as subservient to men in Saudi Arabia, and do not have equality with men on any level. Since I was female, even though armed with a press pass, I was not allowed onto the penthouse floor of the Mark Hopkins Hotel, where the Saudi Arabian group was quartered. However, I had gained the confidence of the *TASS* representative from Russia, and met him every day at the bar for daily briefings. He pumped me, and I pumped him. George Harris, my pal at O.W.I., had a different assignment, but we arranged to meet every day for coffee, and I passed on the information I had acquired. I didn't know what to do with that information, but I figured George would know. I just went along for the ride.

There was a heady feeling of hope among all of us in the newsroom, and yet I kept having a feeling of dèjá vu, remembering the fiasco of our mock League of Nations project when I was a junior at Northwestern University in 1938. Maybe things would be different this time, I told myself. Whatever happened at the United Nations, I wouldn't be part of it. My time with the O.W.I. would be over whenever the war with Japan was over.

Meanwhile, there was the reality of life with Jim in our cold water flat-cum-working studio—a reality to which I was still trying to accustom myself. Taking a bath required a bit of maneuvering. There were two concrete laundry tubs and an old-fashioned gas stove in the room we had designated our kitchen. The stove had four burners and an oven with a pull-down door. We had a big kettle for boiling water, and we put our dishes and glasses on some shelves that Jim had built. We decided that we would fill up the tubs with the water heated in the kettle; I would put my bottom in one of the tubs and my legs in the other. After I soaped up, Jim would pour more warm water over me. So that's what we did.

We always turned on the oven, and even though the windows steamed up, the whole system wasn't really so bad. Jim washed my back and kept pouring warm water over me. After rinsing off, I stood up, and Jim handed me a towel. Stepping out onto another towel, I didn't have to put my clean feet onto the wooden floor. When it was Jim's turn, I did the back scrubbing and the water pouring.

After bathing, we would make our way to the bedroom. Our intense, frequent, passionate lovemaking was part of the glue that held our marriage together. We would fall asleep happily entwined.

One morning, half awake, I fell into a reverie. *I love the feel and smell of leather, the sensuous texture and the way it drapes, I thought. Perhaps it's true that talent and artistic intuition are inherited traits. Did I inherit that interest in clothes from my mother? Oh, I remember that beautiful reversible silk scarf I bought with my money from my first job in my brother's law office. It was long and narrow, heavy silk, beige on one side, large brown dots on a beige background on the other side. It was wonderfully flexible. That scarf transformed the two suits I had that I wore to work. Twisting it one way, it softened the neckline; folding it another way it brought out the soft brown tones in the tweed suit. I had bought it with the small amount of money left over after I paid my mother for room and board.* I smiled at the memory. *I was delighted with my scarf, but my mother and sisters were appalled at what they considered a waste of money; my father loved it, and my brother paid no attention.*

Another image drifted into my mind. *That belt Jim was working on—it should curve, conform to the shape of the body. Belts shouldn't be just straight— that's a man's idea. Must talk to Jim about that later.*

I woke up Saturday morning all fired up by the vision I had had about shaping a belt to fit a woman's body, allowing the leather to dip down in the back, curve over the hips and straighten out in front. I made a rough drawing and showed it to Jim.

"What do you think? Will it work?"

He looked at it, and smiled. "Yes, I think so. Let's try it." He cut a piece of paper and spread it across my back, then drew the curve and cut out a pattern. We played around with the design until we got it the way we wanted it, then Jim got out his cutting knife and cut a sample belt out of the steer hide we had bought. Then it was just a matter of rounding and shaping the edges, stitching on a buckle, punching the holes, saddle-soaping the belt. Voilá!

"Hey! I like it! It's very comfortable!"

We had forgotten all about breakfast, we were so excited about the new design. I don't know where our creative instinct came from. Our hands and minds seemed to be telling us what to do. It was so satisfying to feel the leather and realize the power of the tools, to watch something emerge. For me, this was a sensation no academic work ever matched. I don't know whether Jim felt the same.

At that time we bought all of our leather retail from a handcraft store on Ninth Street near Mission, using what was left of our savings for our meager inventory. We bought a few books on leather craft from a company that eventually became the Tandy Leather Company. The books were full of designs for carving and lacing, but I didn't want to create handbags that looked "handcrafted." I wanted to produce something that looked commercial, well made but not like something that came from a "Western Leather and Craft Show." I wanted a handmade bag that was elegant and looked as smooth as if it were made by machine.

Perhaps the nature of the creative process involves the beginning of an idea, a vision of how we want something to be, or to function. Then our minds enlist memories of music we have heard, images we have seen, images long buried. We begin to experiment, keep what we like, what appeals to our inner sense of aesthetics, and we keep refining our skill. I am convinced we all have the impulse to create something. It doesn't matter how it begins. Perhaps the inspiration is the color of leaves in the autumn or the spring, a pattern of light and shadow we have observed and absorbed without conscious knowledge. After the awareness comes experimentation, whether in wood or leather or cloth or clay, or in words, a poem, a song, a story. Then comes the hard part. Refining, modifying, trying again. At this point, all the aesthetic information we have stored up in our subconscious comes to the surface, and we apply that knowledge. That knowledge allows us to evaluate our work with a new perspective, and to try again. I think the craftsperson's hands create what the mind and heart dictate, and that's what Jim and I did.

The books on leather craft were valuable. They gave us good information on types and thicknesses of leather, and on tools we might need. We were very careful with everything we bought, choosing only what we needed. Every time Jim cut into a hide, he figured out how to cut carefully, wasting as little as possible, saving all of the scraps. We had no apprenticeship, no experience; we just felt our way along. It was exhilarating. We were full of optimism. Each day was an adventure, and each day, as I walked through Chinatown on my way home, I looked forward to what new ideas might be awaiting me. At that time, it didn't matter to me that I would also find a stack of stitched handbags, waiting for me to finish them somehow. I had to design and complete the bag; Jim had a difficult time finishing anything. Whenever he arrived at the finishing time for a handbag, he would put it down and build another shelf.

When the atom bombs were dropped on Hiroshima and Nagasaki in August 1945, all Chinatown erupted. I walked from 111 Sutter Street to 1541 Grant Avenue ankle deep in exploded firecracker paper, the smell and smoke filling the air, bumping into ecstatic Chinese residents singing and dancing in the street. Everyone in Chinatown knew all about the Japanese atrocities in China, especially in Nanjing. They knew that the heavy Japanese occupation of China was finally over. The Italian section, on the other side of Broadway, was relatively quiet, but excitement was in the air there.

"I guess I'll be looking for another job pretty soon," I greeted Jim. "Not much use for American propaganda now that we've won. Any drop-in customers today?"

"Wish you could just stay here with me and work on the bags," Jim said. "Right now the only people who come in want to buy the bricks we have in the show windows."

"Ah well. We'll just keep working. We have so many designs in mind, we can just keep going. We've only been open a few months. Meanwhile, I'll write some sample radio commercials and make the rounds of advertising agencies. I think I'll be getting a paycheck from O.W.I. through October, anyway."

Late August and early September were important months for our Italian neighbors for other reasons than the end of the war. It was time for wine-making, and the gutters ran red with the dregs of the results. There was a huge press that trundled up and down our block, which was between Union and Filbert Streets, filling the air with the pungent smell of fermenting grapes, plus clouds of gnats.

That pungent smell brought back another memory. *I remembered my own parents, in our second floor flat on Chicago's West Side, squeezing black Michigan grapes by hand over a large tin tub in our kitchen.* I sat dreaming until the little bell we had installed over the door to our shop tinkled. Both Jim and I walked around the partition to greet a young couple.

"Hello," the tall young man said. "We're the Reynolds. This is Eileen and I'm Rossi. We're potters; we live up the street, on Edith Alley." Rossi was tall and thin, his lanky body curving slightly over his petite wife. His sparse brown hair was combed carefully over a bare spot on his head. Eileen's brown eyes sparkled behind her horn-rimmed glasses, her long black hair hanging loose around her face.

We were delighted to meet fellow artists. Jim invited Rossi to see the workroom and the two men disappeared. Eileen ran her hand over one of the belts.

"Your work is just beautiful," Eileen said. "How is it going? Are you getting any customers?"

"Not many," I admitted. We sat down on one of the benches Jim had built for customers to sit and chat. "Do you have a studio? How do you sell your work?" I wanted to know how they survived.

"Our studio is in a shed behind the flat we rent. We have a small kiln, and we sell at art fairs. It's hard; Rossi and I teach in the San Francisco Adult Schools; he teaches art, I teach English. That's how we stay alive."

Responding to the subject of staying alive, I explained that I was still working for the O.W.I., writing propaganda for China, but that now, with the end of the war, I wasn't certain what I would do. I told her that Jim wanted me to work with him full-time, making the bags and belts, but I didn't know how long our savings would last. I decided to change the subject.

"Look," I said, "here's a new bag I designed last week. It's not laced, it's stitched by hand. I did some research at the library—this is a seventeenth century English saddle-stitch, made with two needles. How do you like it?"

Eileen turned the bag over and over, caressing the leather. "It's beautiful, Rhoda, and it looks as if it will last forever! I would love to have a bag like this. What are you going to charge for it?"

"I don't know. If you like it, maybe we can trade the bag for pottery. What do you think?"

"A trade for pottery? What a great idea!" She wrapped her arms around the bag, holding it close against her, smiling happily. We walked around the partition to tell Jim and Rossi about our plan. They were examining the latest shelves Jim had built. One of the things that Jim did when he couldn't face finishing any of the bags he'd designed was to build another shelf. I never talked about this aspect of Jim's mental state; I simply praised the way our tools, leather pieces, and half-finished work were meticulously organized, with shelves all over the place.

We continued into the bedroom and kitchen area behind the workroom. Eileen looked around the kitchen area, and looked at the laundry tubs with a board laid across them. She had a puzzled look on her face. "Where do you take a bath?"

I lifted the board and there the tubs were, revealing their gray knobby surface. Eileen put her hand over her mouth, trying to stifle a horrified look. I laughed, and told about how I sat in one of the tubs and dangled my feet in the other.

"It's not so bad," I said. "Jim pours warm water over me; we turn on the oven for heat, and the room gets steamy. It's better than nothing."

I replaced the board and filled the kettle, preparing tea. We sat at a small table we'd bought at Goodwill, pulling up our rickety kitchen chairs. We talked about how we planned to make a living from selling our bags and belts, and about how long we could hold out. Eileen didn't participate in our conversation, her eyes fixed on the laundry tubs. Finally she suggested that we come up to their place for dinner and a shower. *What a thoughtful person! I felt as if she had just thrown me a life jacket.*

"Yes! Why not?" I stood up. "Jim, why don't you and Rossi start walking up the hill? Eileen and I will clear up the tea things; we'll catch up with you." Eileen and I connected on a level beyond words. I knew we were going to be close friends. She picked up her new handbag, and I tucked our towels, soap, and shampoo into a paper bag. I felt buoyant and optimistic as I locked the door of the shop.

The Reynolds's apartment was in the rear of a small house on Edith Alley, a dead-end street off Grant Avenue, up the hill. They had a shed that housed their potter's wheel, their kiln, and shelves for drying pots. They had a small display shelf for finished pottery, which I examined closely.

I liked it immediately, "Hey, I love your pots, Eileen. I wouldn't mind doing as many exchanges as you can afford. We'll work out the retail prices and base our trade on that, okay? We need dishes and mugs, and you tell me what you think would be a fair exchange for the bag you selected." This was our first commercial transaction, and I felt empowered by the exchange. For me, it was validation of the worth of something I'd helped to create.

After our shower, we sat around drinking the local wine and talking about the neighborhood. The Reynolds's had lived there for three years, since Rossi had had a 4F deferment. Flat feet and poor eyesight.

"Do you know about 'The Blabbermouth Cafe?'" Rossi asked. "They meet every other Thursday night in a store-front right across the street from your shop."

"No," I said. "What is it? We're usually in the back of our shop, in our bedroom in the evenings. What do they do?"

"A bunch of local poets and writers assemble there and read their poetry and prose. They have a strict time limit, which varies from week to week. Sometimes it's ten minutes. Sometimes five. We've heard several outstanding poets. One of them is a guy named Kenneth Rexroth. He's a very good poet; his images are wonderful, and he's very dramatic when he reads his poems. It's smoky and noisy, but fun. Sometimes Henri Lenoir comes by. He's not a poet; he's an entrepreneur. He places artwork in restaurants and bars in exchange for food and drink. Works the commission angle from both ends. I think he used to sell silk stockings door-to-door, made by a company named 'Realsilk.' There's a story about Henri that Bob McChesney used to tell. It seems that one evening Henri asked Bob if he had a chance to sell two paintings instead of one, could he offer a two for one bargain. Bob couldn't believe his ears, and told Henri that a painting is not like a pair of stockings. He said if Henri had a chance to sell two paintings instead of one to the same person, he should raise the price, not lower it. Henri is a funny guy, always wears a beret. We should to go over to the Cafe together some Thursday evening."

"The Blabbermouth Cafe is a kind of gathering place for artists too," said Eileen. "Bob McChesney, who lives at the top of Union Street, often comes by, and so do other artists who live at the top of the hill. You might call our neighborhood Greenwich Village West. You've seen Peter Macchiarini's shop, of course. His jewelry is spectacular. He's a real craftsman."

I nodded. "We noticed his shop the first day we came here. I liked the feel of the street from the first. When we walked along Grant, looking for a place to rent, I felt we could have been in an Italian village. There's a neighborly feeling about all the blocks between Broadway and Filbert Streets that's really special."

"Well," Rossi continued, "there's more. You know that bar next to your shop, with the bocce ball courts in the back?" Jim and I nodded. "It's the payoff place for some of the San Francisco cops and the local mafia!"

"I heard that gossip too," I said. "And we noticed the Black Maria (a pickup van for arrested and suspected criminals) parked outside on Friday nights. But I wonder about the gossip. How do we know it's a payoff place? Maybe the cops are just stopping in for a drink when they go off duty. I hate rumors, but I might be naive."

Rossi gave me a gentle smile. He cleared his throat. "Well, I haven't seen any money changing hands, but everybody around here thinks that's what's happening. That's the gossip in the Italian delicatessens, the bakery, and Iacopi's Meats on the corner of Grant and Union." He shrugged. "I figure the natives should know what's happening. According to the Examiner, the cops have a tight hold on the city, and that's why crime is fairly low. There seems to be an agreement between the cops and the petty criminals that works."

I laughed. "Well, I guess the cops and the crooks have their world; we have ours. Like the whores who live upstairs at our place. They work at night, we work in the daytime!" We stood to leave, and I invited them to come for dinner the following week. "We do pretty good spaghetti," I said. "And we'll be eating on your plates, drinking out of your mugs!"

The next day, Saturday, I was arranging some belts on the partition wall when our little bell tinkled, and a stunning young woman came in. "Ooooh," she said. "Do you make these things here?"

"Yes," I said, noticing the smooth sheen to her hair, the way she stood and walked. "Is there something special you're looking for?"

She was already trying a belt on, cinching it around her narrow waist, whipping it off, and reaching for another one. *She's serious!* I went behind the partition and pulled out some of the more exotic belts we'd been working on. "Here are some new shapes we've been experimenting with," I said.

"Yeah! These are interesting! What colors do they come in? And how much are they?"

"We can do any belt you want in natural, black, brown, or navy, and they cost twelve-fifty, made to order." I just chose a figure out of the air. It hadn't occurred to us to do any comparative shopping to see what belts cost in stores like I. Magnin or Joseph Magnin or Roos Brothers, downtown.

She gave me a look I couldn't fathom, and said quickly, "I'll take five of them, this one, and this one, and... ." She laid them down lovingly on the little brick supported bench we'd built. Two were in natural leather, two black and one brown. "Can I take them with me?"

"Sure." I buckled them around her, marked the places for the holes. "But they are so long. I'll have to cut and finish them. Maybe you could get a coffee down the street and come back in half an hour?"

"Okay. Here's a deposit." She handed me five ten dollar bills. "I'll be back."

Our first real customer! I gathered up the belts and went around the partition. Then my knees gave way, and I sank down on the bench in front of the cutting table. I handed the belts to Jim. "Jim, look! I sold five belts! But we have to trim them, and she's coming back in half an hour! How shall we do it?"

Jim put down his hammer and picked up the belts. He decided that it would be faster if he trimmed them from the tip end. He agreed to cut and finish the belts. Then we would put in grommets to protect the buckle holes and dye the edges of the belts. My job was to punch the holes and put in the grommets. We were both trembling with excitement.

Janet Gomberg came back on time, and she had a friend with her, equally beautiful, equally poised. "Look," she said to her friend, picking up a belt. "Isn't this gorgeous? And this one!"

While they were oohing and aahing, I went behind the partition and brought back the five belts Janet had ordered. She was looking at one of the newer handbags I had designed, with interior stitching instead of lacing. "How much is one of these?"

How much? I had no idea. I didn't remember the cost of the hide from which we had cut several belts, and I had designed the handbag around the pieces that were left over. The time spent punching the holes and stitching with two needles and waxed linen thread—do I count that? How much would I spend for a handbag? I'd better choose a number—"Thirty-five dollars?" I offered.

She cocked her head appraisingly. "Could you make it a bit longer?"

I looked at the bag, figured we could add two inches and it would not destroy the aesthetic balance of the design, and nodded. "That would be forty dollars," I said, boldly.

"Perfect!" she said. "Here's a twenty dollar deposit. When will it be ready?"

I thought quickly. Time to make a new pattern, cut the leather and the thinner lining, glue the two pieces together, punch, stitch, finish, put in the snap closure, stitch in the lead weight on the flap—I made a show of looking at a calendar, and chose a date ten days later, which included a weekend. "How about November twelfth?"

Janet consulted her calendar. "The fifteenth would be better for me. I'm doing a show on the twelfth."

"Oh? What do you do?" I asked.

"I'm a model, and I want an elegant bag that will hold a small makeup kit, you know, last minute things in case I don't have my regular kit with me. Also, I'm tall, and I think a longer bag would be better." She turned to her friend. "Helen, what do you think? Two inches longer?"

Helen cocked her head to one side, held her hand below the bag and looked in the mirror. "Yes, I think that would look fine." She turned her attention to the belts. "The belts are great. I'd like this one in black. And that one in red. And the one that curves in the back. I'd like that one in natural leather."

In a state of controlled calm, I took out my tape measure, and measured her waist. "Would you like them on the twelfth—or the fifteenth?"

"Oh, I'll come with Janet on the fifteenth," she said, waving her hand. "How much for a deposit? Twenty dollars?"

"Yes," I said. "That's fine."

They twinkled out the door, and I went behind the partition and collapsed, the money crumpled in my hand. I couldn't believe it. In half an hour, we had enough money to buy several hides and do some further experimenting with different leathers and different designs. I shoved the money into Jim's hands, grabbed him and began to dance around the shop. "Let's eat at the Gold Spike tonight." I was slightly delirious.

Jim grinned at me. "You're being pretty reckless, aren't you? Let me see exactly how much we have. Let's set aside the money we need to buy the leather and the fittings, make sure we have enough for the rent, and see if we can go out or not."

I pouted, but didn't say anything, and we began sorting out the money, putting it into different piles. "Don't forget we still have some inventory, and we have some savings, too." I was not enthusiastic about this particular chore.

Jim stopped counting, swept the deposits into a pile, took out some bills, and put the balance into a cigar box we kept under one of his shelves. "I guess we need to celebrate," he said. "Let's go." We locked the shop door, walked down to Union Street, turned the corner and headed towards Stockton. The pavement felt spongy under my feet. I wanted to bounce up and down. Maybe we would make it!

Neither Jim nor I knew that the two beautiful young women who had just ordered belts and a handbag were two of San Francisco's top models. Within the next year, we would be designing handbags, belts, and sandals for them and their friends. Once they started wearing Pack belts and bags, almost all of San Francisco's models would begin showing up at our shop.

Chapter Sixteen:
The Leather Business

᠕

BETWEEN NOVEMBER 1945 AND JANUARY 1947, our trade and reputation grew. Working with the models became an educational experience. They knew exactly what they wanted. They knew what the fashion trends were, and I absorbed all their ideas like a sponge. I began to buy fashion magazines, French and Italian as well as *Vogue* and *Harper's Bazaar,* and started going downtown to check out the merchandise in the retail stores. I soon realized that our prices were below what was selling in the exclusive shops, and I could see that we were doing something different. With each new challenge, my confidence grew, and the designs became bolder.

I learned the painstaking routine of gluing thin "skiver" leather to the underside of the exterior heavier leather, then punching holes along the perimeter. We used a four-hole leather punch made of steel. I punched four holes, then placed the end of the punch in the last hole, and punched three more. Once the holes were punched, I threaded two upholstery needles with waxed linen thread, put the needles through two holes, crossed the thread, and brought one needle up through the second hole, pulling the stitch tight. I stitched through four thicknesses of leather, plus a welting strip. I soon developed significant upper arm muscles!

Once the bag was finished, we hung it on our partition wall. That gave us a sample for future sales. In the beginning, when we got an order, we would make two bags, one to deliver to our customer, and one to keep as a sample. As our inventory grew, we managed to keep more and more samples on our wall.

I found a joy inside myself I hadn't known existed. There was something so satisfying about seeing an idea come to life beneath my hands. Maybe my mother worked out her frustrations by designing and making clothes for her four daughters. I learned that the creative process demands inspiration, skill, and discipline. My hands and arms ached, but with each bag that I made, my confidence grew. My new skills allowed my imagination to soar. I began to design sandals as well as bags and belts, using our friendly models to practice on.

As our business expanded, I began to get more and more fed up with our limited cooking and bathing facilities. "Jim, I think it's time we looked around for a better place to live. We need more room. Maybe we could even hire some people to help fill our orders!"

Jim looked up from the bag he was stitching, and surveyed the half-finished work that surrounded him. He agreed, and I decided to walk down to the butcher shop. Bruno Iacopi was always helpful. I picked up my umbrella and went out. By this time we had made friends with everybody on the block. Our older Italian neighbors treated us with bemused respect, with a certain formality in their greetings. Perhaps they just didn't know what to make of us—two "kids" making belts and handbags by hand?—I sensed their curiosity, tempered by their paternalism.

There weren't many customers in the meat market that morning, and after I bought my hamburger, I spoke to Bruno directly, and asked him if he knew of any empty stores in the neighborhood. I mentioned that our place at 1541 was getting too small.

Bruno Iacopi leaned his hefty bulk across the meat counter, and said in a confidential tone that he thought the store across the street at 1461 Grant would be vacant soon. He suggested that I check it out with Tony, the owner of the dry goods store next to the meat market.

Tony was actually co-owner with his brother of that narrow little store. It was a dimly lit, crowded place that sold thread, socks, needles, buttons, all sorts of "notions." Tony usually sat on a stool near the door, smoking a thick cigar, his wife sequestered in the dim recesses of the back of the store.

"Hello, Tony," I said, as I closed my umbrella. "How's business?"

"Not bad." Tony removed his cigar, tapped his ashes into a tray near his hand. "Need something?"

I bought a package of upholstery needles, and then brought up the main reason I had come into the store. I asked Tony if he knew anything about the store across the street. I said that Bruno had mentioned the possibility that the store might be vacant in a month or so. Tony didn't answer right away. He regarded me soberly, and then said guardedly, "I don't know. My brother owns that property. I don't think they will move until February or maybe March. You want to look at it?"

Of course I did. "Yes, I do. Can you show it to me?"

He put his cigar back in his mouth, took a long, slow pull on it. "I have a key, but Mario has the final say. He's in Napa today, checking out how much damage the rain has done to our grapes. He'll be back tomorrow, but we can go look at it now, if you want. There's nobody there."

I could hardly control my impatience. "Yes, I'd like to look at it now. Does it have any living space in the back? I saw shelves, but no real partition. Does it go back to the alley?"

Without answering any of my anxious questions, Tony turned to the back of the store. "Sonia! I'm going out for a while!"

We walked across Grant Avenue to 1461, and as soon as I walked through the door, I liked it. It was twice as wide as our current shop, and I walked past the shelves with a mounting sense of excitement. The back part of the store had real living quarters. I noticed a living room to my right, and a bathroom opening off it to the left. I looked inside. Hey! A real bathroom! With a full-size bathtub! The bedroom was behind to the left, and the kitchen was off to the right. There was a window in the bedroom, and stairs leading down to a door that opened onto the alley behind the store. There was a door that opened onto a stairwell, with stairs leading down to the basement, and up to an apartment upstairs. Two big windows in the front provided great visibility for everything. We would have much more space—about three times what we had at 1541 Grant, plus a bathtub! We would have to take out the shelves and build partitions, clean the place and paint, but it was really do-able.

Tony looked at me. "What do you think?"

"I think it's great. Do you know what your brother wants for rent?"

"You better talk to him. He'll be back tomorrow. Come over about ten in the morning. It's his place. He has the final say."

I practically ran back to our place. Darting around the partition, I excitedly called out to Jim. "I think I've located a good place for us to move to!"

Jim was punching holes in one of the new handbags a customer had ordered. It was a black drawstring pouch, made of a new, softer cowhide we'd just found. He looked up, grinning at me. "How much is it?" He wanted to know.

I told Jim all about the new place, which was how I already thought of it. "We'll find out tomorrow. Tony's brother owns it, and he'll be back tomorrow morning. Jim, it's got a real bathtub! And a real kitchen, with a sink and cabinets, a refrigerator and a stove!" I was giddy with excitement. "I'd say it's about three times as big as this place. It's got real possibilities. But I don't think we'll be able to move until March or April."

"That's okay. It's December, we need to concentrate on making and selling stuff during Christmas. We don't want to move in the rain, anyway." He put down his tools, stood up, and put his arms around me. We stood holding each other, trembling, our bodies remembering all that had gone before this moment. We knew we were moving into another phase of our adventure. As I rested my head on Jim's shoulder, a tremor of fear went through me, but I felt hopeful and exhilarated at the same time.

I thought back over the distances we had both traveled in the past six years; for me, it had been gut-wrenching, requiring all my strength to survive the war years. I fought to retain my sanity through a lonely pregnancy, delivery, and death of my first child, through writing for a government agency, to a new career in creative fashion design in leather. What a journey!

And the journey for Jim had been traumatic as well. From a promising academic career in Applied Psychology to shipyard worker, to boot camp, to Officers Training School, to becoming a lieutenant junior grade with poor eyesight on a destroyer in the Pacific, to hospitalization, to working with his hands on creative projects while all the while fighting the depression that overcame him from time to time.

Each one of us was recovering in our own way, but every so often I shud-dered with a premonition that Jim was carrying a heavier burden than I real-ized. He still had trouble finishing projects.

The rent on our new store/living space at 1461 Grant wasn't much more than the rent at 1541 and we were making enough money from our retail sales to handle the move. We signed the lease in March 1947, and spent all of our free time cleaning and painting. By April, we had a large clean empty space, and got ready to move. Sending out a call to our artist and customer friends, they all showed up—the Reynolds, Macchiarini, the models—and we were ready for them. We had packed everything into small boxes, easy to carry, and our little army of porters paraded down Grant Avenue, from 1541 to 1461, carrying boxes in their arms or on their heads, safari fashion. They filled up our future living and working space from back to front, packing it so tightly that we could hardly open the front door.

To celebrate, we all congregated at the New Tivoli Restaurant across the street, and happily toasted each other. Joe Figoni, the owner, treated us to zabaglione, a fantastic Italian dessert, made with whipped egg yolks, sugar, and Marsala wine. We were suffused with a sense of shared camaraderie, an intense energy of possibilities. Both wars were over, exuberance, joy, and hope filled the air. There was talk of a new Medici in San Francisco, a new buyer at Gump's, who was interested in buying and supporting local crafts-men. Gump's was famous for its imports of magnificent antiques from Chi-na and Japan, but the word was out that the import business was not reliable, and Gump's wanted to keep their exclusive clients happy. Any new retail outlet for our work was a cause for celebration.

We staggered across the street after midnight, and wove an unsteady path through the boxes to our bedroom in the back. I had put down our mat-tress, along with sheets and blankets early in the day, and we fell happily into bed.

I woke early the next morning, and pawed through the labeled boxes. Where were the coffeepot and the coffee? Ah, yes, in the orange painted box! Out came breakfast essentials, and I woke Jim with a steaming cup of strong Italian coffee.

"How did you do that?" He muttered.

We spent the following week unpacking, sorting things out, building two partitions. One partition separated our workroom from the showroom; another separated the workroom from our living quarters. Jim was in heaven, building tables and shelves. I sorted out and stored the leather, the fittings, the tools, and built displays for our bags and belts in the windows and the front area. I still remember the surge of happiness and satisfaction in designing the showroom space.

The more I worked with my hands, the more confident I became. I decided to make a wool suit. I, who had refused even to sew on buttons during my adult life, holding skirts together with safety pins, suddenly decided to sew an article of clothing! I was finally ready, in my late twenties, to throw off an inhibition that had haunted me all my life.

When I was in grammar school, enrolled in a Home Economics class, I was supposed to make an article of clothing as a final project. I chose the simplest thing I could think of, a slip. One day, as I labored on the foot-pedaled Singer sewing machine in our flat, my mother looked over my shoulder, and suddenly put her hand on the wheel, stopping the machine.

"Here," she said, "Give me that." She pushed me off the chair. "You're making a mess of it. You're hopeless. I'll finish it." She ripped out my stitches and started over.

"But Ma," I remember wailing. "It's my project! I'm supposed to do it by myself!"

"Never mind. This way you'll get a good grade." She continued sewing for a few minutes, whipped the now beautifully stitched garment off the sewing machine, and handed it to me triumphantly.

I didn't realize how long I had carried that sense of humiliation until I stood in my own workroom and decided I could, and would, make a suit for myself. I called Eileen.

"Eileen, I want to make a suit. Will you come downtown with me and help me pick out the fabric and a pattern?"

"A suit? Rhoda, you can't start out making a suit! A simple skirt, maybe, but not a jacket with set-in sleeves!" Eileen protested.

I needed a suit, not a lecture. I bit my lip. "Look, Eileen, I need a suit, not just a skirt. Will you come with me, and help me or not?"

Of course Eileen agreed, and even offered to loan me her portable sewing machine. We decided to go downtown the following day.

We bought tightly woven tweed and a simple Vogue pattern and came back to the shop to work. Poor Eileen! I fought her every step of the way. "Why do I have to baste it? Why can't I just pin the two pieces together and pull out the pins as I go? Why does it have to have five-eighth inch seams? It seems like such a waste of material!" I didn't realize I was fighting the ghost of my mother during the entire endeavor. However, I managed to finish the skirt, complete with zipper and button closing, as well as the jacket. As I struggled with the shoulders and the set-in sleeves, I decided that if I ever made anything again, I would stay away from set-in sleeves! Eileen did the hand-bound buttonholes, and I found some bone buttons at Tony's store that I liked. It was a triumph, and my mother's ghost retreated.

Chapter Seventeen:
Monsieur Bertrand

⌒

OUR BUSINESS EXPANDED WITH THE MOVE, as did our social life. We became frequent visitors to friends who lived at the top of the Union Street hill, young physicians like Jep and Bill Hunter, who worked for the newly organized Kaiser Group, a cooperative at that time; Bob Winston, a jeweler; and of course, Bob McChesney. The McChesneys hosted parties to which Robert Howard, a painter and sculptor, and his wife, Adelene Kent, also a painter came, as well as famous potters, Edith and Brian Heath, and Jean and Virginia Varda. Jean, a renowned painter of collages and his wife, Virginia, lived on a houseboat in Sausalito.

One evening, we were invited to a party honoring a Frenchman who, we were told, had survived the occupation of Paris. We didn't know anything about him, and got to the party late. The room was very crowded. The only empty seat was on a couch next to a very pale man who was buttoning up his vest over a heavy sweater. I didn't know he was the guest of honor, and after I sat down, wondering what to say, remembered an item I'd read in the morning paper.

"Do you think it's true that the new minister of culture in France will close all the brothels?" I said to him with a bright smile.

He stopped buttoning his vest, and instead slowly unbuttoned it. He turned to me, fixing his intense blue eyes upon me. "Where did you read that?"

"It was in the morning paper," I said, disconcerted by his intensity. "The article also said that there was quite an uproar over the impertinence of her action."

"It will never happen," he said, in heavily accented English. "It's ridiculous. She is a fool." He looked away for a moment, and then turned back to me. "Who are you?"

"I'm Rhoda Pack, my husband and I have a leather shop at the bottom of the hill. We make handbags, shoes, and sandals by hand."

Just then a few people came up to him, and began to warble about how wonderful it was to meet him, and how honored they were to make his acquaintance, and how they were looking forward to seeing more of his work. Suddenly I realized that I had been speaking to the guest of honor! He was the Frenchman who had survived the occupation of Paris by the Germans! All the stories I had heard about him suddenly clicked. It was rumored that he had survived by eating Vaseline and hiding in a cellar. I felt like a fool, and started to get up.

"No, don't go," he said, putting his hand on my knee. "The party is just starting to get interesting."

"Tell me about your work," I said, retreating to safer ground. "And how you happened to settle in San Francisco."

"Ah, well, yes. But first, will you get me another glass of wine?" He held out his glass to me. For the next half hour, he talked about how he had created a leather mosaic wall for the Isle de France luxury liner, and how he made suede evening bags, hand-embroidered with jet beads and gold thread. Jim pulled up a chair. Monsieur Bertrand told us about his sponsorship by a famous San Francisco socialite, how she had helped him find a studio. He was happy that he had more orders than he could handle, but was worried about not being able to finish them on time. He was worried about his health. Apparently he hadn't done much talking before we arrived, and now most of the guests were leaving. But our Frenchman didn't want to stop talking.

"Would you like to walk down the hill with us and see our shop?" I asked. I found him fascinating, and wanted to know more about him.

"Yes, that would be fine!" He stood up, buttoned the vest he was wearing over his wool sweater, and shrugged into a heavy overcoat. It was quite warm in the room, and balmy for San Francisco. I wondered why he was so cold.

By the time we got to our shop, Monsieur Bertrand was breathing heavily and said he was very tired. He complimented us on our work, but said he wanted to go home. He asked us to go with him to the streetcar stop, and also asked us to do him a favor on the way.

"Is there a drugstore near here? I need to get some bromides for my stomach."

When we got to the drugstore, it turned out that Mr. Bertrand bought several bottles for himself, and then asked us to buy some extra bottles for him. It seemed that there was a limit as to the number of bromides the druggist would sell to any one person.

We became friends with Francois Bertrand, and visited him in his studio. Over time, we discovered that he used an awful lot of bromides. I never knew what there was in them that he needed so much. *Perhaps the Vaseline had damaged his stomach. Why Vaseline? Did he think he needed the oil? It didn't make sense, but no matter.* His studio was in the attic of an old, beautiful Victorian house on Pacific Avenue. The light from the north window illuminated his worktable, full of half-finished, exquisite work. He used a sixteenth-century French feather stitch, and I watched him closely as he worked. Later I used those stitches making the soft pouches I designed.

When we visited him, we always brought French bread, cheese, wine, and two bottles of bromide. Mr. Bertrand seemed so sad, going off into reveries in the middle of a sentence. He would often regard us silently, shaking his head from side to side, as if he couldn't quite figure us out. Like Jim, he also suffered from being unable to finish his bags. He would take hefty deposits, but he knew that when he finished them, he would have to give them up. He seemed reluctant to do that. When he died, just before Christmas, 1948, the San Francisco matrons who were his customers nearly rioted, fighting over which bag was whose. I missed Monsieur Bertrand. He left a lasting influence on my designs.

Chapter Eighteen:

Expanding Designs

◠

O UR EXPANDED SOCIAL LIFE led to more exposure of our work, and we became inundated with orders. Perhaps the block between Green and Union Streets was a better one for foot traffic; perhaps it was the New Tivoli Restaurant and the quality of Peter Macchiarini's clients, as well as the proximity of Peter's shop, across the street from ours. We needed help to fulfill our orders, and we spread the word among our friends and clients.

Caroline, one of our customers, called one day. "You said you needed people who would be willing to work with their hands, and didn't need to know anything about how to stitch leather. Did you mean that?"

"Yes," I said. "We can teach anybody to punch and stitch our bags. We taught ourselves. We can teach anybody else! Do you know somebody who would want to work for us?"

"I have a friend visiting me, and she says she wants to stay in San Francisco. She's very bright, but she's bored. I think she'd like a chance to do something with her hands."

"Great! Ask her to come over, any time tomorrow."

Alix, a small, cheerful blond woman with a twinkle in her eye, showed up the next morning. "Hi, I'm Alix Taylor," she said. Her handshake was firm. "Caroline told me to come over and here I am."

I liked the firmness of her handshake, and I noticed that her hands looked strong and capable. I told her that she would be stitching steerhide bags with two upholstery needles and waxed thread. I picked up a bag that I was working on and showed it to her.

"Do you think the work would be too hard on your hands?"

Alix laughed, started to say something, and then checked herself. "I don't think so," she said. "I've been around horses a bit. That toughens up your hands. When can I start?"

"We can pay only two dollars an hour right now," I said. "If that's all right, you can start right now." I didn't know that Alix was a debutante, with money of her own, and that she thought of this job as a hobby. She had graduated from Bryn Mawr, and had been considered a bit of a rebel. After Alix came Betty from the University of Washington, and Evelyn from Sausalito. We now had three employees, and I began to think about expanding our line. I could see that our handbags would never wear out; our sandals and belts would last almost forever, nothing would become obsolete. The only thing to do was to expand—into clothing. I was getting bolder, and contemplated making a dress out of suede.

Suede was the only thin, flexible leather available for clothing at that time. Voris, a designer for the movies in the forties, used suede in some of her designs, and I decided to try it. I leased a leather sewing machine, a Singer 3120, which I still have, and thought about what I would try. We had been invited to an opening at the DeYoung Museum, and I decided to make a green suede dress.

I bought a *Vogue* pattern for a dress that looked like it could be adapted to leather, and also bought four skins of green suede from our favorite retailer. The dress was in two pieces, a top and bottom, which seemed eminently suitable. The bodice was in four pieces, two for the front and two for the back, and the wonderful part was that the front pieces included the front, dolman sleeve, and collar all in one piece! There was a dart, of course, on the front pieces to create space for the breasts, but it looked simple enough for a novice like me. However, when I lay the skirt pattern down on the hide, I could see several problems.

When an animal hide is dressed to create leather, it is stretched out, so that the firm part of the hide is down the center, and the sides, which were the belly, are not firm at all. In fact, if you attempt to cut a straight line down the side of the hide, it will emerge as a curve. I noticed that there was a part of the hide that would give me a straight line, if I pushed the leather under the bottom part of the pattern. I decided to try it, and it worked like magic. I managed to get a straight line over the hips, and the front of the skirt billowed slightly just over the thighs and knees. No fabric would ever fall like that.

I learned something else when I made that dress. I couldn't pin it, because my pins bent, so I cut a sample in muslin first, tried it on, and then put the muslin on top of the leather, holding it down with lead weights. I cut the leather carefully, trying not to nick the edges. I used a stapler to hold the leather pieces together when I stitched them.

I cut a wide cummerbund to wrap around the waist of the dress. When I tried on the finished dress, I looked at myself in the mirror, and felt like Cinderella going to the ball.

Jim and I went to the opening at the DeYoung Museum. I wore my dark brown hair long, pinned up at the back in a French twist, and tried to look as if museum openings were things I did all the time. Jim went off to get me a glass of champagne, and I was standing by myself when a good-looking older man came by and started to speak to me, bowing first.

"Perdonnez moi, Mam'zelle," he said, "I simply had to speak to you. You look like a Modigliani painting. May I get you a glass of champagne?"

I was absolutely charmed. I smiled at him and said, "Thank you, but my husband is getting me a glass. What do you think of the exhibit?"

"Oh, for a contemporary painter, he is quite good. Are you an artist?" He was quite good-looking, and his suit looked hand-tailored.

"No, not exactly. My husband and I make leather handbags, belts, and sandals by hand, on Grant Avenue, near Union Street."

"Indeed!" He became quite animated, and reached into his vest pocket, producing a card. "This is my card. I am Paul Verdier, the president of the City of Paris. I would be most interested in seeing your work. Please come to see me." He bowed again, and walked away.

Paul Verdier was a descendant of the original Verdier brothers, who had come to San Francisco in the 1820s, and had established the City of Paris department store in 1850. I knew that Mr. Verdier had a strong influence on the cultural life of San Francisco in the 1940s and 1950s. He encouraged local weavers and jewelers and was on the board of two Museums of Art, the Legion of Honor in Lincoln Park, and the DeYoung Museum in Golden Gate Park. In addition, the Verdier Cellars were known throughout San Francisco for their excellent selection of French and local wine, plus cheese and sausages. I felt a surge of pride that Verdier had singled me out.

Standing there quite stunned, I stared at his card, and when Jim came back with the champagne, I couldn't wait to tell him what had just happened. I showed him the card. "What do you think? Isn't that exciting?"

Jim's response was not what I expected. "I think he was trying to pick you up. That's what I think! Where is he?"

"Oh, Jim! Don't you think he was impressed by my dress? He's the president of the City of Paris! I'm going to call and make an appointment to see him!"

Jim glowered, but just then Alix Taylor and her friend Caroline Thompson came up to us. Caroline was a member of the Museum's board, and they flanked a beautifully dressed woman in her fifties.

"Rhoda, this is Mrs. Ganz. She is intrigued by your dress. I told her it was your creation. We love the way the skirt falls. Turn around." I swirled around, and Mrs. Ganz wanted to know if I was willing to take an order. Was I! Without hesitating a second, I asked her to come for measurements on Tuesday, figuring I would have time on Monday to pick up samples of suede to show her when she came.

I was walking on air as we left the museum, but Jim was unusually quiet. "Well! What do you think, Jim? What an exciting evening!"

"I guess so." He didn't say any more, and I was too exhilarated to pay much attention to his subdued mood. *Why was he so sulky? Why wasn't he as excited as I was?*

Tuesday brought Mrs. Ganz and two friends, who all wanted suede dresses, and they didn't seem to mind that I had only one design to show them. The problem was that they were all different sizes. My dress was a size ten; they were size twelve, fourteen, and sixteen. I took their measurements, and made appointments for fittings in three weeks. Patterns for garments are graded according to a set formula, but I had made so many changes to the Vogue pattern that there was no way I could use Vogue's formulae.

What to do? I went downtown to Stacey's bookstore and bought a book on how to grade patterns according to standard formulae, and set to work. There was no point in trying to go to a fashion design school; I didn't have enough time for that. I would have to slug it out by myself. I made patterns out of heavy butcher paper, but I didn't trust the muslin to hang the same way that the leather did. I cut the bodice in muslin and the skirt in leather. Mrs. Ganz, size fourteen, was the first one I called. I had cut the skirt and held it together with staples. It was almost right, and I used chalk to mark the changes.

By this time, I had hired a seamstress named Miriam Harris, because I didn't trust myself to sew the clothes with the precision I wanted. Miriam was very good, and very careful. We went over the problems in sewing leather. "You can't make a mistake when you stitch leather, you know, every hole shows. It's not like fabric; if you make a mistake in fabric, you can rip out the stitches, but there's no way you can do that in leather. You also have to watch out for oil stains from the machine too. That will ruin suede faster than anything."

Miriam understood, and practiced on scrap suede until she felt comfortable tackling a dress. We sweated over every garment we made, but once our three customers picked up their dresses, with exclamations of joy and praise, we relaxed.

Everything seemed to be happening at once. We were getting more and more orders for handbags, and one day a buyer from Joseph Magnin came to visit us. Acting like a regular customer, she had bought a handbag several weeks before. She had a proposition for us.

"I've shown your bag to Mr. Cyril," she said, "and he's very intrigued. "Could you come down tomorrow with your entire line and show it to him? I think he might want to carry your bags in our store."

I looked at Jim, he looked at me. *Wholesale? What price would he offer? How many bags would we have to produce? How would we get paid?* Jim spoke first. "Do you know how many bags Magnin's might buy? And what price would they pay for the bags? I guess we could meet with Mr. Magnin, and work something out. Did you say he liked the bag? And did he realize it was all hand-made?"

The buyer, a well dressed woman in her forties, patted Jim's hand. "Don't worry," she said. "Mr. Cyril is a very fair man. I'm sure you'll work something out."

"All right," I said. "We can make it at ten-thirty tomorrow morning. Where do we come?"

"Come to the seventh floor. We'll be waiting for you."

After she walked out, I said to Jim, "What about Mr. Verdier? We forgot all about him. Don't we need to see him first?"

"I think he's mostly interested in you, not in our line. He didn't even mention the bags, you did." *Oh! I felt a stab in my heart. Jim was jealous! Why?* I couldn't think of anything to say, and decided that I would call Monsieur Verdier by myself, after we'd seen Cyril Magnin.

Cyril Magnin was a small, compact man with glasses and a twinkle in his eye. He spoke almost exclusively to Jim, and I watched Jim expand with the attention. Jim was very articulate as he turned our bags inside out and demonstrated how we created them. Mr. Magnin liked them, which was obvious. The big question was the price, and how many we could make. He offered a price that was half of what we were charging, and I was appalled. Jim didn't say anything, and I couldn't keep quiet any longer.

"I'm sorry, Mr. Magnin," I said, "but we couldn't make our bags for that price." I mentally subtracted twenty percent from our selling price and offered him that. His eyes lost their twinkle. Jim spoke up at that point.

"How many would you order? And would you put a down payment on your order?"

Mr. Magnin laughed. "You mean give you an advance on our order? We don't operate that way."

I could see we had arrived at a stalemate, and decided to step in.

"Mr. Magnin, we don't have enough capital to buy supplies in quantity. We have enough inventory of raw materials to make twelve handbags right now. If you can pay us upon delivery, we can then buy enough material to make more, but it would have to be on a pay upon delivery basis."

There was a heavy silence in the room. "Twelve handbags? That's all?" was Cyril Magnin's initial response. He was obviously on a totally different track. When I mentioned twelve handbags, once again it was a number I picked out of the air. I really had no idea how much leather we had on hand, it just sounded like a good round number to me. Words hovered in the back of my mind, words like "markups, discounts, promotion, sales figures." They were memories that floated, insubstantial, shadowy. As for Jim, he looked completely surprised by my statement.

"I'll have to talk to my staff," Mr. Magnin said. "Two things. Can you leave your samples? What is your delivery date after you receive the order?"

I waited for Jim to answer, since Mr. Magnin directed all of his attention to Jim, and only looked at me when I spoke up. Jim hesitated, and finally said, "Yes, we can leave some of the samples, and we'll tell you the delivery date after we get your order."

I could see that Cyril Magnin was not satisfied with Jim's answer, so once again I stepped in. "If you're planning to order anywhere from ten to twelve bags, we can promise two weeks delivery," I said boldly. "And you don't have to limit your order to one style. We make each bag one at a time, they are all unique." Mr. Magnin hadn't really responded to my request for payment on delivery, but it didn't seem like a good time to bring it up again.

He stood up, offered Jim his hand, and said, "I'll let you know by the end of the week." He nodded at me, and we left.

We stood outside the closed door and looked at each other. We walked slowly to the elevator. "What do you think?" I said. "Do you think he'll pay on delivery, if he orders?"

"I don't know," Jim said, not meeting my eyes. "I almost wish we hadn't come. There's going to be a lot of pressure on us."

I put my hand on his arm. "Let's check out the handbags on the first floor," I said, "and see what the price range is." Jim followed me silently out of the elevator. I wondered if he was worried about the time pressure or was stunned by the possibility of success, but I knew we had moved into a different realm. Cyril Magnin had directed all of his attention to Jim, but Jim had missed a lot of signals he was sending. *I shrugged off a vague sense of unease. We were still a team, weren't we? That was all that really mattered.*

Outside on the sidewalk, Jim turned to me. "Do we really have enough leather to make twelve handbags?"

I took his arm as we walked back toward the shop. "Look, it doesn't matter. If we don't have enough black or natural or whatever, I think we can show our suppliers the order from Magnin, if we get it, and they'll probably advance us the leather. We're good customers, and we always pay cash. What the heck, it's worth a try. We just have to be careful about the price. Let's try to figure out just how much the bags cost us to make."

We walked along silently, each of us alone in separate contemplation. Alix and Betty greeted us with happy anticipation, and wanted to know how it went. I told them that we were still negotiating, and warned that we might have to turn out twelve handbags in two weeks! I asked them if they thought we could do it. Their response was an unequivocal yes! I also mentioned that I had no idea what they were going to order. "They seemed to like the basic shoulder bags best. They might choose different designs." I was feeling more hopeful by the minute. Jim had gone directly to our leather bins, and began to sort out the hides by color.

I sat down beside Alix. "Listen, Alix, we have to figure out how much it costs us to make a handbag. So we're going to have to keep track of how long it takes to cut the exterior, the lining, glue them together, punch, stitch, and finish. Will you try to keep track? I'll try to time Jim and myself in the cutting, gluing, and punching, and you keep track of the stitching. Okay?"

She grinned at me. "A time/management study, eh? I don't mind, but I think I remember something from an economics class I took that had to do with allowing for time to go to the toilet and stuff like that."

"Yeah. Well, we have to start somewhere. I need some numbers to put down on paper," I said. I needed to get an idea for our next round of negotiations with Cyril Magnin. From what I saw at his department store, a handbag selling for thirty-five dollars or more was close to the appearance of our bags, even though their handbags were machine-made. *If Magnin's wanted to buy our bags for seventeen-fifty, we wouldn't be able to do it.*

As I stood talking to Alix, I was suddenly back at Mandel Brothers in the summers of 1937 and 1938. *Of course! I remembered working in different departments of the store, and in the executive offices. Buyers of different departments had certain percentage markups on the items they carried, so that when they had sales, the sale price would still provide a profit over the price they paid for it. I remembered putting figures together for the accountants, and how the different departments I worked in had different rates of markup, depending on how high their sales were.* No wonder Magnin hesitated. He didn't have all those figures at his fingertips.

I went out to the showroom and sat down at my desk. How to figure the cost? We had been figuring only the cost of the leather in our bags, and hadn't added in the cost of our labor. Now that we had employees, we would have to figure that in too. In our naive approach to business, we never figured in the rent or anything called "overhead." We had relied on guesses up until now, and on what our models offered to pay us for the bags they bought. As I sat writing down numbers and crossing them out, thoughts of Monsieur Verdier floated in and out of my mind.

If we sold handbags to Joseph Magnin's, would we be able to sell to the City of Paris also? And what about my suede dress? Was Mr. Verdier interested in carrying suede dresses? I wasn't really interested in making dresses, a jacket maybe. And I didn't really like suede that much. It was so delicate. What about glove leather? Glove leather was washable, wasn't it? I liked the feel of some cowhide we had bought recently. It draped nicely, too heavy for a jacket, of course, but it made up into some lovely drawstring pouches. What about deer hide? Didn't American Indians make dresses and jackets out of deer hide? And didn't they wear them in all kinds of weather? I put down my pencil and let my mind wander.

Almost without volition, my hand picked up the telephone, and I dialed the number on the card Mr. Verdier had given me. His secretary answered, and after I gave my name, with the added information as to where we had met, he came on the line.

"Ah, Madam Pack," he said. "How nice to hear from you!"

I reminded him that he had said he would be happy to talk about our leather products, and asked for an appointment. He turned me back to his secretary, and we made a date for 11 a.m. two days later. *You did it, Rhoda. What are you going to wear? Think about that later. First things first. Better finish figuring out how to price the handbags.*

I went back to talk to Jim. "What do you think we can charge for the bags, Jim? I'm not getting anywhere with my figures. I wish we could get a better price for the leather."

Jim walked back into our living quarters. I followed him, and we sat down on our secondhand couch. I knew we had a problem. Currently our bags sold for thirty-five dollars. If we sold them to him for that price, I was sure he would charge at least forty percent more. Then we would have to increase our retail price in our own shop, and I was afraid we couldn't sell them here for more money. I said to Jim, "Suppose we limit the designs we sell to him... maybe one, at the most two, as an exclusive, and don't sell those designs here. We didn't bring him everything we have, and we can always make subtle changes in our best designs." My mind was whirling with possibilities. "Let's decide on the minimum price we will accept, and see what kind of deal we can make. Then, if we can afford to buy in greater quantity, we might get a better price on our leather."

Jim shifted uncomfortably on the couch. "Are you sure we should do this? We're really doing all right with our business here. We're getting a lot of free publicity, maybe we don't have to sell to Joseph Magnin."

"Why can't we do both?" I took a good look at Jim. He had slumped back on the couch, and seemed to shrink. Was he scared? I moved closer to him and put my arms around him. "Let's wait and see what happens," I said. I didn't say anything about my appointment with Mr. Verdier, and in a few minutes we both got up and went back into the workshop.

Those postwar years in San Francisco were halcyon days for small craftsmen. Department stores like the City of Paris, I. Magnin, Joseph Magnin, Gumps, were all hungry for quality merchandise that was different. None of the top-end stores were able to get access to their markets in Asia or Europe, and they all wanted to cash in on the exuberance of postwar consumers. French couture hadn't recovered from the war yet, a few American designers like Claire McCardell were beginning to make an impact on fashion, and fashion editors were all over the place. They were looking for new ideas, new people to exploit. Jim and I were young, photogenic, and articulate. With Jim's beard and scholarly air, my tall dancer's shape, we attracted attention. We were both modest, and we presented ourselves as ordinary people who worked with their hands. Now that all of the top models in San Francisco were wearing our products, fashion editors saw us as good copy.

People like Paul Verdier and the new buyer at Gump's saw themselves as contemporary Medici. There was a temporary but vital love affair going on between the artists and craftspeople of San Francisco and local retailers. I knew we had something special, something unique. I felt invigorated by the challenge.

I sat at my desk in the front of the shop and started to dream. Picking up my pencil, I began thinking about adapting the lines of the top of the dress I had just designed into a jacket. If I kept the idea of the front and sleeve in one piece, adding inches to bring the bottom of the jacket to hip length... I stopped myself. *Not now. Back to work. First things first.* I walked back around the partition and sat down at the worktable, picked up a punch, and began to work on the next handbag.

The next morning, after breakfast, I took a deep breath and said to Jim, "I've decided to see Paul Verdier at the City of Paris."

He looked at me as if I were a stranger. "Why?"

"We need to have an alternative to Cyril Magnin. If we don't like his terms, we might get orders for bags and belts from Verdier. I don't know, but it's worth a try."

Jim was glum. "What will you wear? That green suede dress?"

"No." I took another sip of coffee. "That's too dressed-up for the middle of the day. I'll wear the tweed suit Eileen helped me make, and one of our newest handbags. I won't wear a bag we've already shown to Cyril. I don't know who the people are who shop at the City of Paris, but I'll bet they're not the same people who shop at Joseph Magnin. I want to find out."

Jim was silent, and pushed his cold scrambled eggs around on his plate. "When are you going to see him?"

"Tomorrow at eleven. He's a wheeler-dealer in San Francisco, Jim, and I think we can learn a lot from him."

Jim put down his fork, and raised his head. "Be careful," he said. "I don't trust him. He's French."

Oh, god. How deep do prejudices go?

I dressed carefully the next day, and chose our most conservative armbag, which I had named the "Helen." Armed with photographs of our other handbags, plus samples of leather, I took the Stockton Street car downtown, and showed up at Mr. Verdier's office ten minutes early.

Paul Verdier came out to greet me as soon as his secretary told him I was there, and he ushered me into his elegantly furnished office, decorated with original Impressionist paintings, including one by Monet which I particularly liked.

"It's a pleasure to see you, Mme. Pack," he said. "I was very impressed with the dress you wore to the De Young Museum opening. The fall of the skirt was very impressive. How did you do that?"

I smiled, relaxing instantly. "Ah," I said. "You can only do that in leather, because of the way the hide is tanned. It's an effect you cannot get in fabric without piecing, and even then, you would have to cut the material on the bias. I'm not good enough to know how to do that, but I know how leather works."

Verdier nodded. Instantly on a convivial footing, he said, "You and your husband have a shop on Grant Avenue?"

"Yes, we make everything by hand." I showed him my handbag. "And we have a variety of designs. Our clientele so far is limited to people who walk by the shop or who are recommended by other people. We haven't tried to solicit business wholesale, because, frankly, I don't know how much we could produce, and also because we don't have any capital." Suddenly, I felt free enough to be quite open with him, which I had not felt with Cyril Magnin.

Paul Verdier leaned back in his leather chair, and placed his tapering fingers in a small pyramid. He looked at me thoughtfully, raising his bushy eyebrows. He had a thin mustache and sandy hair combed carefully over a receding hairline. His mouth turned up slightly at the corners.

"We buy most of our handbags and belts from a reliable supplier in France," he said. "Now that the war is over, I am sure they will be shipping us merchandise again soon. I don't think we have a market in our store for your handbags or belts." He shifted in his chair. "However, we might have a market for a jacket. Do you have anything in mind along that line?"

I was bursting to share my ideas. "Yes!" I said, leaning forward. "I have an idea for a simple, easy-to-move-in jacket, similar to the way I designed the top of the dress," I said. "But I really don't like suede. It's so fragile. I wish I could find some smooth leather that might be washable. I keep thinking about glove leather. A hide has two surfaces, a smooth, skin side, and a rough, flesh side. Why wouldn't it be possible to use the smooth, skin side for a jacket? It's used for gloves, isn't it? And gloves are washable."

Mr. Verdier laughed. "That's an interesting idea," he said. "But most smooth garment leather these days is made from horsehide. That's the leather that the German army used for the overcoats their officers wore, and I don't think you would want to use horsehide for a fashionable jacket for women."

I shuddered. I had an image of SS officers, booted and leather-coated, an image fed by the movies. "I was thinking of something softer, more sensuous, maybe deerskin. Indians made dresses, boots, and jackets out of deerskin. Something like that, but I don't know if deerskin is really washable."

Mr. Verdier's eyes lit up. "I just thought of something." He picked up a pen and began to write on a notepad. "I have a friend in the leather business," he said. "His name is Paul LeGallet; he and his brother have a tanning company in San Francisco, near Bayshore Boulevard. The man who handles all their skins is an Italian named Moon Giovanetti. He's very knowledgeable, and I think you can get a lot of information from the LeGallets as well as from Giovanetti. Here, here's a note to Paul from me. Let me know when you have a jacket for me to look at." He stood up, gave me his hand, bowed, and I left.

I stopped at the handbag counter to check out the display, and I could see what Mr. Verdier meant. They were on a level of elegance that we could never match, nor would we want to try. He was right. The City of Paris clientele would consider our bags the kind of thing they might buy at a Paris flea market.

Chapter Nineteen:
Beginnings and Endings

⌒

PAUL VERDIER HAD TREATED ME SO COURTEOUSLY that I felt validated and upbeat. In addition I now had a possible connection to a leather
resource other than our retail people downtown. The shop was unusually
quiet when I walked in. No response to my cheery, "Hey, I'm back!" As I
walked around the partition, Alix and Betty were stitching away, but Jim
was nowhere to be seen.

"Where's Jim?" I wanted to know.

"He said he needed some air, and went out about an hour ago," Alix said.

"Oh. Any calls?"

"Two. One from Alice Martin, wanting to know when her bag would be
ready, and one from Mrs. Rosenberg, at Joseph Magnin."

"Oooh. I'd better call her right away." I moved to the telephone, and then
hesitated. "I wish Jim was here. What if she wants to place an order? Oh, well."
I dialed the number. Yes! Joseph Magnin wanted to place an order for two
dozen bags! That meant Jim would have a big job to oversee, and would free
me up to concentrate on finding suitable leather for clothing.

I was so elated that I decided to call the number on the card Verdier had
given me even though it was four-thirty. Somebody at LeGallet Tanning
Company answered. When I mentioned Verdier's name, Mr. LeGallet came
on the line.

"Hello," he said. "You are a friend of Mr. Verdier?"

"Not exactly a friend," I said. "He gave me your name and suggested that I come to see you. My husband and I make handmade leather handbags, belts, and sandals. And I am beginning to design leather clothes. He thought you might be able to help me find the kind of skins I am looking for."

"Ah, well! So! All right, when do you want to come to the tannery? Do you know where we are?"

"I'm not sure," I said. "I can look on the map. Should I come by car, or is there public transportation available? We live in North Beach."

"Ah, no." He laughed. "You'd better come by car. It would take you half a day otherwise." He gave me explicit directions. "Come on Friday at eleven. Then I'll take you to lunch at the Old Clam House."

I had the feeling that Paul Verdier had called Mr. LeGallet before I managed to contact him, but no matter. I felt ten feet tall.

I was peeling potatoes when Jim walked in, about six. He gave me a perfunctory kiss on the cheek, looked around the kitchen. "What's for dinner? Hamburgers again?"

"No, meat loaf." I put down my knife. "Something's eating you. What is it?"

"I don't know." He sat down heavily, put his head in his hands. "I feel like a failure. We work our tails off, and we're barely breaking even. I feel like a drink. Do we have any bourbon?"

I shivered. *He has that look he had when I first saw him in the Day Room at the hospital in Washington. The difference is that now he's wearing blue jeans and an old navy pea jacket rather than hospital pajamas.*

"Have you been out for a walk?" I asked, taking a bottle out of our cupboard. I brought out two glasses and some ice, and poured us both a drink.

"Yes, I walked up to the tower at the top of Telegraph Hill, hoping to get some perspective on our life." He looked at me sadly. I raised my glass.

"Cheer up, Jim. Mrs. Rosenberg from Joseph Magnin's called, and we have an order for two dozen handbags! What do you think about that?" I hurried on. "Also I saw Paul Verdier today. He gave me an introduction to people who run a leather tanning company near the Bayshore Freeway. Come on. Let's drink to progress!"

Jim smiled uneasily, and we clinked glasses. He leaned back against the couch, downing his drink in several gulps. He straightened his shoulders, and I felt relieved. I stood up and continued to make dinner. Jim poured himself another drink.

Looking back, I wish I had paid more attention to Jim's mood swings. Instead, I was so energized and excited by being able to create something with my own hands that I couldn't concentrate on anything else. Everything was a challenge. How to take an abstract idea, develop it so that it became a concrete product, how to reproduce it, adapt it if necessary; then how to sell it, how to promote it. All those elements whirred around in my head. I didn't want to be sidetracked. I focused deeply on the problems and challenges in front of me.

I realize now that this was a pattern with me. That was why I had such a good time at the O.W.I. Satisfying Dr. Kurani and Dr. Badeau as well as myself, I was energized by proving I could be a good secretary and preserve my integrity. In San Francisco I loved proving to the reporters in that newsroom that I could write a decent article, and now I was feeling exhilarated by mastering a new craft. What an exciting, invigorating period this was for me!

As I expanded emotionally, creatively, Jim was beginning to shut down. He became more and more morose. I didn't know what to do, or how to deal with his sulky moods. I missed the depth of Jim's despair. One evening we were having dinner with Elizabeth Hanna, a customer who had recently become the owner of a gallery on Post Street. Elizabeth had become a good friend, and toward the end of the evening Elizabeth commented on Jim's behavior.

"Rhoda, does Jim usually drink this much?"

I responded, "Well, we usually have a drink before dinner, and sometimes he has a couple after dinner." I looked over at Jim, passed out on the couch. "He has been very moody lately."

"There's something bothering him," Elizabeth said. "Have you thought about taking him to a psychiatrist?"

"A psychiatrist? No. Where would we get the money?" I suddenly remembered the diagnosis from the Navy report, "manic-depressive, acute depressive," which I had dismissed as invalid, and probably due to stress. "How do you think a psychiatrist could help him?"

Elizabeth paused, searching for words. "I have a degree in counseling," she said, "as well as a degree in Fine Art. In the three months I've known you, Jim seems to be sinking into a deep depression. Artists do go through periods like this."

I sagged. "Elizabeth, I don't think I can deal with this. We have an order for two dozen handbags for Joseph Magnin and I'm working on a design for a jacket in smooth leather. I'm trying to figure out how to get hold of glove leather, or cowhide or deerskin, and I need Jim as a partner. Are you telling me that psychiatric treatment will help to pull him out of his depression?"

"It's worth a try. I have a friend who's an analyst, who might be willing to take Jim on. He has helped other artist friends of mine, and maybe he could help Jim as well."

She put her hand on mine. "I'll pay for it," she said. "Think of it as a gift from me to the two of you."

I shook my head to clear it. "I can't suggest the therapy to him," I said. "Will you talk to him? I think he might accept the idea, coming from you."

Elizabeth stood up and walked out onto the balcony of her apartment on Potrero Hill. I followed her. "All right," she said. "Take him home now. I'll think of a plan and let you know. I've decided to carry some of your more unusual bags in my new gallery. I consider them art pieces; one of a kind, and I'll invite Jim to supervise their display. Don't worry. I'll think of something."

When we walked back into the living room, Jim was sitting up. "Is there any coffee around? I could use some."

After a couple of cups of coffee, we went down the steps, got into our old second-hand Ford and I drove us carefully back to North Beach. That was the beginning of two years of agonizing Freudian psychoanalysis, during which time Jim's mood swings became more and more extreme. It was tough, but he didn't talk about his therapy sessions and I didn't probe. Instead, I joined Anna Halprin's dance group when she was partnered with Welland Lathrop and escaped into dance and design.

I followed through on my introduction to the LeGallets, and spent a lot of time with Moon Giovanetti. He taught me about leather; showed me why deerskin couldn't be "skived" (put through a machine that would reduce its thickness), because the hide would tear apart in the machine. I also learned about the hierarchy that existed in the manufacture of leather.

The manufacturers of glove leather in aptly named Gloversville, New York, had a monopoly on the machinery for creating glove leather, the skiving machines, the vats and chemicals for tanning, the drums for dyeing. There was an agreement among the manufacturers not to ship any of those tools west of the Mississippi. Hides that were bark tanned (using oak trees from Virginia and the Carolinas) were shipped west, and machinery to produce leather for shoes, briefcases, luggage, called "saddle leather" was also shipped west. Machinery to process smaller hides that came from China or Portuguese East Africa (Angola), used for glove leather, was available only east of the Mississippi.

Moon had adapted much of the machinery available to the LeGallets to process deerskin, and he did a good business processing hides that hunters brought to him, but not much was available in the commercial market. He did sell me some of the lighter-weight skins, and I was able to experiment with them. We couldn't spot clean them, however, and I spent a lot of time talking to him about the kind of skins I wanted to work with.

"What I want," I said to Giovanetti one day, "is a soft, pliable skin with some sort of finish on it so that it can be wiped off. You know, like the way you can wipe off an oilcloth cover on a kitchen table."

He laughed. "You can't drape oilcloth, of course, and the problem is that anything you spray on deerskin would make it stiff. It would crack. No, any kind of chemical treatment would have to happen during the tanning and dyeing process, and it would have to be a certain kind of leather. Horsehide can't be skived, it will rip apart in the machine; neither can steerhide. I'm not sure about cowhide."

We sat in his small, windowed office above the tanning floor, where he could watch everything that was going on. I stroked the cowhide I was holding in my hand, testing it, folding and unfolding it, enjoying the sensuous feeling of the soft skin. Moon had gotten hold of some cowhide he thought might be thin enough for me to use.

"Moon, do you have any connections in Gloversville? How do they process their glove leather? I've noticed that I can wash my leather gloves, just as you said I could wash deerskin, but it takes forever to dry. I'd like to be able to just wash off spots without immersing the whole thing."

Moon thought for a minute. "I know a guy in the Wood & Hyde Leather Company in Gloversville. Yeah, his name really is Hyde, who might be interested in your idea. And Gloversville is on strike right now, so it might be a good time for them to do some research."

"Gloversville is on strike?" I felt the hairs on the back of my neck rise. *Would I have to deal with strikebreakers?*

"Well, the tannery workers knew that the owners made a lot of money during the war, and they decided they should have a part of it. So they struck for a higher minimum wage, and the tannery owners locked them out. The tanneries are closed. They aren't even negotiating with the union."

I digested that information slowly. "Are you suggesting that Mr. Hyde might want to invest some money in research? Maybe I should write to him. I guess there isn't much I can do from California to affect a tannery lockout in Gloversville, New York. In the meantime, can you get me a few more hides like this one? It doesn't have too many scratches on it."

Moon said he'd try, and I walked thoughtfully back to the car, clutching my two precious cowhides. When I got back to the shop, Jim was busy putting up a few more shelves; everybody else was busy stitching or punching, with loud music blaring from the radio. I could hardly wait to spread out my hides.

At that time, I worked in muslin on a dress form, pinning and shaping the fabric on one side of the form, working with the leather on the other side. Then I unpinned the muslin, laid it down on butcher paper and drew the pattern on the paper, adding margins for seams. After I had the pattern worked out, I laid it on the leather and cut around it. I soon found out that this was a dangerous process. My cutting knife would nick the edges of the paper pattern, and I would continually have to repair them. Looking in the yellow pages of the phone book, I found a company that advertised commercial templates and decided to visit them. They made templates for working on steel, but they quickly analyzed my problem and offered a solution.

"We can transfer your paper patterns to this heavy cardboard," Harvey

Weinberg said, "then we can bind them with brass. The brass is soft enough for us to bend, and sturdy enough to resist the nicks your knife makes in the edges." That sounded great, but the price made me gulp.

"Let me work out my best design," I said. "Can we start with just one pattern? It will have about four pieces. Consider it a sample for future orders." I hoped I didn't sound too pleading.

Harvey gave me a knowing look. "Working on a shoestring, eh? Okay. We don't usually work this way, but I'll do it for you. Things are a little slow now, anyway. Come back at the end of the week."

After I got the brassbound patterns, I used them on the cowhides Moon had secured for me, and took my first jacket to Paul Verdier. I modeled it for him, and he was pleased by the look of it and the workmanship. Then he called one of his store models to try it on. She ran her hands down her arms and gave herself a little hug. Verdier smiled, and gave me an order for six jackets, a size range from ten to sixteen. He asked me if four weeks would be enough time. *What a thoughtful man!*

Jim was sitting in our living room when I got back, having made himself a drink. It was about five p.m. *Uh, oh, it's going to be a long evening.* I walked over to him, gave him a long kiss. I knew that today was his day with the analyst, and he looked miserable. I sat down and proceeded to tell him about the plan for the patterns, and for the orders I'd just gotten from the City of Paris. He nodded, staring off into space.

After dinner, three or four drinks later, Jim and I went to bed. The alcohol didn't affect our sex life, but he didn't sleep as well as he used to. Sometimes he would sit bolt upright in bed, clutching the sheets, his entire body rigid. After calming down, he would often get up and wander around the shop, sometimes making himself another drink. I didn't sleep much either, on those nights, and wished we could talk about our fears. But we didn't. I was too afraid to acknowledge my fear that our marriage was falling apart, and I was reluctant to interrupt whatever process he was going through with his psychiatrist. Jim became more and more unapproachable. I remembered his father's morning gin pick-me-up. Was that pattern inheritable?

The patterns Harvey made for me were made of heavy blue cardboard, bound with brass, and they definitely made cutting easier. As soon as I laid the pattern on the cowhide, I could see what a difference it made. The weight of the cardboard and the brass edging made it possible to plan the layout in a much more efficient way.

The thing that bothered me was that as I became more and more absorbed with the working out of my designs, Jim became less and less involved with our business. We were still "Jim Pack Designs in Leather," and we were still going to art fairs to sell our products, but Jim spent less and less time actively working in the shop. He would disappear for hours at a time, saying that he had gone for a long walk, and sometimes he came back smelling of beer or whisky.

Business was improving; we were getting more and more orders every day, from both retail customers and from Joseph Magnin. Magnin's had given us a special display in their San Francisco and Palo Alto stores, and I spent a lot of time talking to the buyers, showing them the difference between a hand-made bag and a machine-made one. I talked up the quality of the leather we used, and showed them how we actually stitched the bags, hoping my sales talk would rub off.

Fashion editors began visiting us. Bernadette Snyder, the fashion editor of the San Francisco Examiner, came in one day, and left after ordering a suede leather suit. I agreed to make the suede suit for her, which she wanted to wear to New York, provided I could make her one of my newer jackets in deerskin as well. I said I wouldn't charge her for the jacket, if she would agree to wear it to one of the showings. I called it "The Flyaway," since I wanted to get the jacket seen in New York.

The year was 1949, ten years into our relationship, and by that time Jim and I were barely speaking to each other. It didn't seem to me that the psychoanalysis was working very well. It was almost as if we lived on different planets. We ate our meals together, went to bed, had perfunctory sex, much of the passion gone, and were careful but distant with each other. I couldn't put my finger on it, but often felt that a chasm was widening between us. I went to see Elizabeth.

We met at her gallery on Post Street and went to a nearby cafe for lunch.

"Elizabeth, things are not going well. Jim is becoming more and more detached. I can't get through to him, and I'm choking on my own anxiety. On the one hand, I feel stronger than ever about my designs, but on the other I am worried about Jim's lack of involvement. He does practically nothing. Oh, he cuts the bags, and does a lot of the punching, but Alix and I do most of the working out of new designs for handbags. Jim is becoming an automaton. What can I do?"

Elizabeth sighed. "He will just have to work it out. Sometimes analysis takes years."

"I'm not sure I can wait." I shifted in my chair. "Maybe it would be better if we divorced. I'm bursting with new ideas, with energy; and whenever I try to share any enthusiasm, his lack of response drags me down."

"Don't do it, Rhoda," Elizabeth said. "Give him another six months, at least. Leave him alone. Let him work out his own problems. He'll do as much as he can right now. Best if you don't push him."

It was my turn to sigh. "You don't know what it's like. I feel responsible for him. I was the one who pulled strings to get him out of the Construction Battalion, and when he got his commission, we thought our troubles were over. Maybe they were just beginning. He went to sea—what happened on that ship? Then when he came back, and was in the naval hospital, I pulled strings again to get him a regular discharge. He was discharged in my custody. What did I do?" Both elbows on the table, I clutched my head.

Elizabeth ordered another round of martinis. "Listen, Rhoda, Jim is having a hard time now. It's tough, going through psychoanalysis. I know, I've been through it. It took five years, but I've gotten rid of my demons. Jim will make it, and you will too."

I looked at her. "I wish I were as confident as you are." I lifted my glass, took a deep drink. "I resent the downward drag," I said. "I love what I'm doing. I just wish Jim and I were on the same track." I finished my martini and stood up. "I'd better get back to the shop," I said. "We have to finish the Joseph Magnin order by Friday. Come by the shop, Elizabeth. Take Jim out for lunch or something. Okay?"

"Sure," she said. "I'll come by next week. See you then."

Elizabeth did come by, but her visit didn't change anything. I don't know what I expected, but I kept hoping for a miracle. Elizabeth was still paying for Jim's therapy, but I didn't see much progress.

Bernadette Snyder, the Examiner's fashion editor, came back from New York, full of enthusiasm. She came by the shop one day.

"Rhoda! The fashion editors loved your jacket! And I got compliments galore on my suede suit. They loved the way the skirt fell. I think you've got a winner there. The top editor of Hearst Magazines will be in town next week, and I've told her about you and Jim. I'll let you know when she gets here, and then I'll bring her over."

I pumped her hand. "Gosh, Bernie, thanks. Give me a couple of hours warning, so we can clean the place up."

"No, no! Leave it just the way it is. It's fine, it's fine!" She bustled out the door.

Jim shrugged when I told him the news. "What're we supposed to do? Turn handsprings? Bow three times before the great editor?"

I couldn't speak. There wasn't anything rational I could say. I knew that the kind of publicity we might get was publicity that we could never buy. We had just gotten the kind of validation that made all our hard work worthwhile, but Jim was too swallowed up by his own misery to get any joy from our new prospects.

Bernie Snyder brought Meredith Robertson, the chief fashion editor of all the Hearst magazines, and a publicist named Harry Cole to the shop the following week. We shook hands and I took them behind the partition, so they could see our operation. Suddenly it all looked very small, as I tried to see it through the eyes of the fashionably dressed New Yorkers. But I showed them how we made our handbags, including the way we soaped and polished them. They nodded, ahhed and hmmed. I couldn't tell if they were impressed or just being polite.

Meredith took a good look at the Flyaway jacket and at my green suede dress.

"Would you like to come to New York, Rhoda? We could place you with a large leather garment house, and I'm sure Lord & Taylor would carry your designs, especially with our backing."

Jim had gone into our living quarters to prepare some coffee, and I was alone with them in the front part of the shop. *Go to New York? Without Jim?*

"I don't know," I said. "We have so much invested here. And I'm not sure Jim would want to go to New York."

Meredith looked at Harry, then back at me. "We think the clothes have more promise than the bags and belts," she said. "Phelps has a good solid grip on that market, and he's beginning to do sandals, too. We were thinking of promoting you as the newest up and coming designer of suede and leather clothing. You'd be close to the leather sources and to the market."

Whoa. But I knew this was no time to leave Jim. "Give him six more months," Elizabeth had said.

Just then Jim came in with the coffee and some cookies. "I'm not sure," I said. "I'll have to think about it. How long will you be in town?"

Harry answered. "We're staying at the Mark Hopkins," he said. "We'll be here for a few more days, through Sunday." He handed me his card, with the room number of the hotel penciled in. "Give us a call."

We drank our coffee, made small talk about places to go in North Beach, things to see while they were here, and they left. Jim and I took the coffee things back to our kitchen, and sat down to talk.

"What did they say?" He wanted to know.

"Meredith asked me if I wanted to go to New York and work for a big leather garment firm as a designer."

"Well, do you?"

"No. In the first place, I've never been to design school; I don't know how to draw in the way you're supposed to. Everything I've done has been experimental, and I really don't know what I'm doing. The real truth is that I wouldn't want to live in New York. I don't like the weather; the frantic pace of life. Also, I don't want to leave you, or the shop. I think it would be a mistake."

Jim stood up and took me in his arms. There were tears in his eyes. "I'm glad you said that. She didn't invite me to go, did she?"

I shook my head. Then I held him tight. "We'll stick it out here. Phelps said we should make our reputation from San Francisco, and that's what we're doing. I'll call them tomorrow and say thanks but no thanks. Let's go tell our staff what happened."

I called Mr. Cole and thanked him for their confidence in me, but that

I decided to stay in San Francisco. This incident marked another shift in my relationship with Jim. We were becoming more and more popular, more and more well known. Our bags were selling well, both at Joseph Magnin's and from our shop. Even though I had turned down Meredith Robertson's offer, word about us traveled quickly among New York's fashion editors. Many of the editors who went to the trade shows in Los Angeles came to San Francisco to play. They visited our shop, exclaimed over us, and they brought photographers with them. We showered everybody with complementary handbags, belts, even made sandals for many of them. They insisted on paying something, so we charged them nominal fees, enough to cover the leather.

Television was in its early stages in 1949 and 1950, and we were invited to do a show on CBS. I had seen a stage production where an actor took a bolt of cloth, wound it around a scantily clothed model, and created a gown on the stage. I was impressed, and decided it would be fun to try the same thing in leather. One of the fashion editors I talked to thought it was a great idea, and we were invited to do it.

We lined up two of our most beautiful models and showed up with several cowhides and a few deerskins. Herb Caen was on just before us, and we watched him promoting white bread. He was squeezing the bread, and he said, "I wish you could see just how fresh this bread is!" "Cut!" yelled the director. "Herb! This isn't radio! People can SEE you squeezing the bread! Try it again." We realized we were watching a rehearsal. But our performance wasn't a rehearsal. We were doing our stunt live.

When it was our turn, our models appeared in their cotton coveralls, and suddenly every TV crew member in the studio materialized, waiting for the models to disrobe. We were positioned on the stage, the director motioned us to begin, and somebody introduced us. Jim and I worked simultaneously on the two models; he draped one and I draped the other. Then we switched. He wrapped a belt around one of the models; I twisted a piece of leather on one shoulder and secured it with a large ornamental clasp. Rounds of applause erupted from the entire crew. We gathered up our hides and left, sharing grins of congratulation all around.

The free publicity helped, of course, and while I was almost giddy with success, Jim's gloom lifted only slightly. Our evening cocktail degenerated into two or three drinks for him before we went to bed, and our lovemaking began to feel more desperate. Jim was still wandering around at night, and running the shop became more and more my responsibility.

In December, 1949 Jim's mother wrote, asking us to come to Grants Pass for Christmas. Remembering the first Christmas we had gone to Grants Pass, and our disastrous backpacking trip on the Rogue River, I really didn't want to go. The weather was usually terrible, and I resented taking the time away from the shop. We did most of our business in December, and by the end of the month we were usually exhausted. I hated having to think of presents for his parents, to take time away from getting out orders to design something they would like, or spend time shopping. The whole Christmas celebration seemed like a charade to me. I knew Jim's father would drink too much, the exchange of presents would again be a meaningless formality. The turkey would be overcooked and dry, the gravy thick and tasteless. Of course we went.

I slept during the rainy trip on the way up, and insisted on driving part of the way back. As I expected, we received gifts like tablecloths and napkins we would never use, an apron, and a hideous cut glass vase. Jim's dad drank too much and reminisced about fishing trips he had taken with his two boys. Jim winced every time his dad spoke lovingly of the dead brother. Jim was even quieter than usual, and conversation around the holiday dinner table creaked and groaned. I counted the minutes impatiently until we left. We didn't talk much on the way home. As I drove through the sleety rain, I kept thinking about new ideas for jackets, turning up the radio while Jim slept. We both relaxed once we got through our door, welcoming a return to our regular pattern of living.

After taking off my jacket, I sat down to check the mail. There was a letter from Meredith Robertson. "Jim! Meredith writes that my jacket, 'The Flyaway,' will be featured on the inside of the front page of *Harper's Bazaar* in the February issue! She asks us to verify the names of the stores that carry the jacket! What do you think of that?" I was hopping up and down with delight. "I'd better call Paul Verdier right away, and also Littler's in Seattle!" Littler's and the City of Paris belonged to the same retail buying service. We had sent each store a range of sizes, from ten to sixteen, six jackets to each store.

"That's great, Rhoda. Is there a check from Magnin's for our last shipment?" I rifled through the mail. "Nope. But it might come in tomorrow." I stared at the letter from Meredith. What a wonderful boost this would be! *Harper's Bazaar!* I could hardly believe it. I called Eileen and also Elizabeth. "Let's celebrate!" I said, after sharing the news. "How about we all go out to dinner tonight at the New Tivoli? Joe will want to help us celebrate, too, I'll bet." Jim's lukewarm response hardly registered with me.

I bought several copies of the *Bazaar* when it came out in February, and spread them all over the front window. By that time, I had two or three other designs I had worked out, and the strike in Gloversville was over. I was working hard with Mr. Hyde on the finish for the skins he was importing from Angola. American cowhide was simply not reliable. Many of the skins were so scratched by barbed wire that they were not usable. Local sheepskins had the same dr awback.

Mr. Hyde sent me hides from Gloversville with different finishes on them, and I submitted them to various tests. I measured their thickness, tested them for pliability, and also sponged them off with soap and water to see how well I could spot clean them. Then I sent the hides back with carefully detailed comments.

One day a hide arrived with all the criteria beautifully satisfied. I fired off a letter to Mr. Hyde. "You've done it!" I wrote. "The hide I just received is exactly the right thickness, and I can spot clean it with a damp cloth. I think we're on the right track." I was using the "we" form because I felt so much a part of the process. *It never occurred to me to ask for any kind of fee for the work I was doing. It was research for me, something I was accustomed to doing.*

As the interest in the garments grew, Jim's depression became deeper. Our business was flourishing, but our marriage was dying. Pretty soon I was the one wandering the shop at night, and finally I couldn't bear it any longer. I got the name of a psychiatrist from Elizabeth, and after the first visit, came home with a prescription for Nembutal. She was not an analyst, and I never went deeper in my therapy other than on an intellectual level. We met once a week.

On a foggy Saturday in June, after lunch, I asked Jim if we could go for a walk. We climbed the Union Street hill to Coit Tower, and sat on a concrete bench, watching the setting sun slowly emerge from the fog.

"Jim, I have to tell you something." I stopped, stole a look at him. He was staring out at the Bay. "I can't take the pressure any more. I think it would be better for both of us if we separated, maybe got a divorce."

He turned to look at me. "Do you have any idea of what I've been going through?" He began to weep. I put my arms around him. I don't know which of us was more miserable at that time. "I've been living through those final days on the ship, over and over. I hardly know where I am, most days. I sit in the analyst's office and talk and talk. He never says anything. I have terrible dreams. I keep trying to sort out what happened."

"Do you want to tell me about it? I promise to talk back."

We sat there on the cold concrete and Jim finally told me what had been haunting him all those years.

"Maybe I should never have become a lieutenant," he said. A stab went through me. "Once I got onto the destroyer, it was like I was the man who wasn't there. I was the only officer who had been commissioned straight from civilian life, and none of the other officers treated me with any respect." I thought of my initiation on the news desk of the O.W.I., and nodded. I knew what he was talking about.

"I'd walk into the mess, and the buzz of conversation would stop. Oh, some of the guys would talk to me, but it wasn't the same." I stroked his hair. "Then, it was the Battle of Peleliu," he said, his voice quavering. "I was sent down to the gunnery section in the bottom of the ship. It was our job to cover the men who were landing on the beach with protective fire. We had to focus through telescopes and give the orders to fire." He shuddered. "With my glasses on, I couldn't focus the telescope carefully, because I couldn't bring the glass close enough to my eyes, and with my glasses off, I still couldn't focus clearly, because the telescopes weren't built with corrective lenses. It was awful. I would give orders to fire, and I never knew whether the guns I ordered to fire were hitting above our men or maybe landing on them. I never did find out."

"How awful. How long were you cooped up in that place?"

"It seemed like forever. And then it was time for me to go up on deck for my turn on the watch. I hadn't had any sleep for maybe 48 hours, and I was very depressed. The captain was standing watch with me. It was a clear night, unfortunately, and we could hear the guns, but couldn't see the beach from where we were. The captain asked me how I felt and I told him I felt like killing myself, because I felt like such a failure. The next thing I knew I was in the brig, my glasses taken away."

"My god, Jim! They threw you in the brig? Just because you confided in the captain about how you were really feeling?"

"Yeah." He slumped over his clasped hands. "You're not supposed to do that if you're 'true Navy,'" he said, bitterly. "Then I was transferred to a hospital ship and sent back to Mare Island."

"So that's what happened to you," I said. "I didn't hear from you for three months, and was frantic. Then when that letter came from you, in a handwriting I could hardly believe was yours..." I didn't finish my sentence. We both stared unseeing into the fading light.

"Well, we're here now." I had to say something. "We left Washington in 1945, and it's now 1950. We have a new life. Where do we go from here?"

"I don't know. I feel as if I'm in a pit, and I can't climb out. I don't know what to do."

We walked silently down the hill, silently into the shop. I went into the kitchen, made us both a stiff drink, and we sat down on our couch. "Listen, Jim," I said. "Somehow we have to get through this. The landlord told me that the apartment upstairs is vacant. Maybe if we moved upstairs, got away from the shop entirely for a few hours, we might be able to rest a little better. He gave me the key. Let's go take a look at it." *I was always one for immediate physical action when I felt that words weren't leading anywhere.*

We went up the back stairs and into the kitchen at the back of the flat. It was a typical North Beach railroad style tenement flat, with the back porch leading into a kitchen. Then a long hall leading to a bathroom with a bathtub and an overhead shower; there were two little rooms in the front with bay windows opening onto the street. "We'll need lots of shelves," I said, hoping Jim would see the humor of my remark. He didn't. He shrugged.

"Whatever," he said. "How much is the rent?"

"We can afford it," I said. "I offered him one hundred dollars a month for both places. Told him we'd clean it up, paint the walls, and we'd pay for scraping the floors, everything. He grumbled, but finally agreed."

Jim seemed to welcome the physical work that the new flat called for, and spent most of his time upstairs. My three employees and I worked closely together. I cut the leather for the bags and for the jackets; Miriam cut the linings, and Betty, Alix, and I punched and stitched the bags and belts. Miriam stitched the jackets, and we worked together pressing the seams of the jackets open, using brown paper between the leather and the iron. We used rubber cement for the hems, but I wasn't satisfied with it. It wasn't until the following year that the white glue which later became known as "Elmer's" was developed.

I handled all the billing, and Jim continued to spend little time in the shop. I called Elizabeth, and asked her to meet me for lunch.

"Elizabeth, things are not going well. I'm not sure this psychoanalysis is helping Jim at all. It's been almost two years since he started. Have you talked to your friend?"

"No, I haven't. Analysts don't usually discuss their patients."

"Yes, but you're spending an awful lot of money on Jim, and I don't think he's getting any better. In fact, he's getting worse, and I'm at the end of my rope. Sometimes I think we would be better off without each other. He's getting more and more dependent on me. I'm not his mother, Elizabeth, and he's not my partner any more." The more I talked, the clearer the situation became. "We could separate. Now that we have the flat upstairs, I could live there, and he could live downstairs, at least for a while. I mentioned divorce to him once, but didn't get much of a response. A different arrangement might make it real." Elizabeth didn't say anything, and I rushed on. "Maybe he'd rather live upstairs. I don't care. I just think we ought to separate."

Elizabeth sighed. "Whatever you do, make sure Jim has time to talk it over with the analyst. He may seem worse to you, but to me he seems stronger than he was last year. Maybe a separation would be a good idea."

I walked back to the shop without noticing where I was going, and almost tripped over a curb. *Once more I am going to be the initiator of a change. Whatever decision I make now will affect both of our lives in ways I can't predict.* I found Jim hammering away on new shelves in the kitchen when I went upstairs.

I was consumed by a sense of urgency. "Jim," I said, "I have to talk to you."

He put down his hammer, and we sat down on the back porch, which overlooked the alley behind the shop. I stared into space and sat on my hands to keep from wringing them. "I've been seeing a psychiatrist, too," I said, and hurried on. "I think we might both feel better if we separated. One of us could live here and the other could live downstairs, for a while."

Jim nodded. "We were separated before, during the war," he said. "How will this separation be different? What do you really want to do?"

I hesitated. Then words came tumbling out before I could stop them. "I want a clean break. If I'm going to run the shop, I want to run it by myself. You're there, but you're not there."

There was a long silence, and finally Jim said, "You sound like you want a divorce. You brought this up once before. Is that what you want?"

I have to do this. I took a deep breath. "I don't want to hurt you, but yes. I want to run the shop by myself."

His glance was cold, his voice calm. "Well, let's talk to Elizabeth. Maybe she can find us a lawyer who would take care of all the little details."

Was he relieved? Had I underestimated him? Maybe Elizabeth was right. Maybe he is stronger than I thought.

We met with Elizabeth that evening, and Jim arranged to move into the bottom flat of the house she owned on Potrero Hill. All of a sudden, things seemed to move very fast. We met with a lawyer Elizabeth found for us, and he worked out the legal aspects of division of property. There wasn't any money to divide, and I agreed to take on all of the debts and responsibilities of the business, in exchange for full ownership. A date was set for a court hearing.

I hadn't been sleeping more than two to three hours a night, and was so tense that I felt brittle. My psychiatrist kept prescribing sleeping pills, but I resisted taking them. They made me groggy the next day, and I didn't like that feeling. I needed to be alert. I didn't tell the psychiatrist that I was using the sleeping pills sparingly. During our sessions, I talked about responsibility, and how I felt guilty for feeling exhilarated by taking charge. I told her about feeling responsible for getting Jim out of the Construction Battalion. I recalled Dr. Shock's intervention, which I had asked for, and how that intervention probably resulted in his commission as a lieutenant. Was that a mistake? Later I had been responsible for Jim's transference to the Bethesda Naval Hospital from Mare Island, and finally I had maneuvered his discharge without penalty. The memory that he was "remanded" into my custody still bothered me. Now I felt I was deserting him, and told her that.

Dr. Durban didn't like that line of reasoning, and kept reassuring me that Jim was perfectly capable of living his own life, that I had acted out of my own need for him.

That was a message I didn't hear. I was so wrapped up in my own guilt that it never occurred to me how much I needed to be the decision-maker. Now I dreaded the appearance in court, even though that was the result of an action I had initiated.

Eileen went with me on the fateful day, and the judge asked me if I wanted alimony from Jim... *alimony? From Jim?* When I answered, "No," I was told that I had to accept something, so I replied, "One dollar." And that satisfied the judge. *Weird.*

I was silent on our way home. My head was spinning, my eyes burning with unshed tears. Eileen and I parted at the door to the upstairs apartment. "Are you sure you'll be all right?" she asked anxiously.

"Yes, I'll be fine," I replied, gritting my teeth, and walked upstairs. I pushed the door carelessly behind me, and walked in a daze straight down the hall to the bathroom. Doors don't always latch when you push them behind you, and the door to my apartment hadn't latched tightly. In the bathroom the bottle of Nembutal sat on the shelf, staring at me. Moving as if in a dream, nothing in my mind; I opened the bottle, dipped the pills into my hand and swallowed all of the seventy-five tablets in the bottle. It took a while to get them all down. I gagged, but persisted. Then I walked down the hall to the bedroom in the front of the flat, but didn't make it, collapsing on the floor.

When I woke up in a bed in San Francisco General Hospital, in a dimly lit room, a nurse seated beside me, I am told I asked, "Where am I? Who are you?" And the nurse answered, "You're in San Francisco General Hospital; you tried to kill yourself."

And then I was told I answered, "Then it didn't work. I'll jump out of the window," and promptly fell asleep again.

I do remember what happened next. I woke up, my arms tied to the bed, the sides of the bed raised as if I were in a baby's crib, and a nurse was seated beside me. "Why are my arms tied?"

"Because the last time you woke up, you said you were going to jump out the window."

I remember looking up at the bars covering the dingy window. "That's a dumb thing to say. How would I ever get out?" And fell asleep once more.

The next time I woke up, the room was bright, my arms were not tied, but I was aware of a transfusion apparatus tied to one arm, and a nurse beside me. "How do you feel?" she asked.

"I'm hungry," I said.

She smiled, closed her book and got up. "I'll be right back."

She came back with a doctor and another nurse. He checked my pulse, shined a light into my eyes, nodded curtly to both nurses, and left. I was presented with a menu, and ordered scrambled eggs on toast, fried potatoes, and coffee. The tray arrived with my order, plus a slice of ham, jam, and cream.

"Your psychiatrist wants to see you as soon as you feel strong enough," the nurse said. "You can use this telephone if you want to. Her telephone number is right here." She seemed anxious to deliver the message.

"Okay. I'll call her as soon as I finish eating." I felt remarkably healthy and really wanted to know what had happened. How was it I was still alive? I decided to call Eileen first.

Eileen's voice was joyful, and she wanted to know when she could come to see me. We made a date for that evening, and then I called Dr. Durban, who said she would be over at three p.m. The intravenous drip, which contained heavy doses of vitamins, was removed, and I had time to take a shower and wash my hair. I put on a clean hospital gown and some lipstick. I felt rested and in control.

Dr. Durban arrived, bristling with anger. "How dare you do this?" She demanded, seating her large bulk in the chair next to the bed. "Don't you realize what a hostile act you have committed?"

I wasn't prepared for this onslaught. "Hostile to whom? Hostile to myself, yes. I felt like a total failure, and I also felt that I didn't deserve to live," I said defensively.

"I spoke to your brother, who called me. He was the one who used that word."

My brother? The brother who had refused to help me when I was pregnant? The brother who said "no" whenever I asked for help? The brother who gambled away my college money in the stock market? And I was hostile to him?! I stared at her. "How come he called you?"

"The hospital notified your family, as well as me, and your close friends. I gave my number to the hospital, saying I was available for counseling." She continued, "You realize, I suppose, that committing suicide is against the law. You will be charged with attempted suicide and you will have to pay for the ambulance and for your stay here."

If Dr. Durban had intended to shock me into facing reality, she succeeded. "How soon can I get out of here? If I'm going to have all those bills to pay, I'd better get back to work!"

"I want you to promise to see me in my office at least three times a week," she said. "We have to get to the bottom of why you felt so desperate. I'll talk to the physician on call, and you can probably leave tomorrow."

Why is she so angry? I felt bullied and I resented having to defend behavior that I had already decided was stupid. I called Elizabeth and reported the encounter with Dr. Durban. "Is she correct about the hospital costs and all that stuff about having to face charges?"

"I think she was deliberately trying to shock you," Elizabeth responded. "I think we can get the charges dropped, considering the circumstances. I'll talk to her and to some of the people I know at City Hall. Don't worry about the money. We'll work something out."

"How's Jim? Did you tell him what happened to me?"

Elizabeth said that he was stunned, that Jim couldn't believe I would do what I did. "He said he guessed that you finally understood how he felt that night on the bridge during the Battle of Peleliu; only you tried it, and he couldn't. That was all he said."

Eileen came at eight that night, and I got out of bed so that we could talk more easily. We walked down the hall to a little visiting room at the end of the corridor. "Tell me what happened," I demanded.

"I wasn't comfortable when I left you outside of the door to your upstairs flat," she said. "You looked funny. I can't describe it, but you didn't look like yourself. Then, when I got home, I tried to call you, and there was no answer. Rossi was teaching that day, and I went over to the shop by myself. No one there had seen you or talked to you, and I rang your bell. No answer. So I went across the street to the restaurant and called our friend, George Kosmak. I told him I thought something was wrong, and asked him if he could come over. His studio is at the top of Telegraph Hill, he was close.

When George came, we tried your doorbell again, and you still didn't answer. So we rang the bell of the people on the third floor. They were at home and buzzed us in. We explained who we were, and then we went up the stairs and tried the door. We couldn't get in at first, but George pushed and pushed, and when we got in, we saw you on the floor. George felt your pulse and hollered to me to call an ambulance, which I did. The ambulance came, they put you on a stretcher, and here you are."

I groaned. "I suppose all the neighbors were gathered around. It must have been a rare event... someone being carried out on a stretcher, not pregnant and not dead! Oh, boy!"

"You must be feeling better," Eileen smiled. "If you're worried about what the neighbors think!"

I thought about what she said. It was true that for some strange reason I felt well, healthy, and peaceful in a relaxed way. Perhaps I needed that long sleep. "Eileen, I don't know why I did it. I don't know why I was willing to turn my back on life. The roses you brought me... why didn't I think of what it would mean to never smell a rose again? Obviously, my mind was closed down. I suppose I'll have to go into all of this with Dr. Durban." I paused, not sure of how to tell Eileen I really felt quite good. "Anyway, I'm glad you're here."

My good friend reached over and embraced me. We didn't say anything. Then she leaned back and said, "You're strong, Rhoda. I don't know why you did it either. You must have felt really desperate. I'm sure you weren't thinking clearly. You looked as if you were in shock when I left you at the door. That's why I was so worried." She took my hand again. "I'll help you all I can."

The night nurse interrupted us, and Eileen rose to leave. She wanted to know what time I would be able to leave, since she and Rossi planned to come and take me home. I told her I'd call her as soon as I knew. She gave me a thumbs up as she left.

Rossi and Eileen came to pick me up around noon the next day, and Rossi told me that he and Eileen had decided that I was to come home with them for a few days. "We don't want you to go back to the flat alone," he said, "and that's that."

I was anxious to get back to work, but relieved that I wouldn't have to sleep in what I viewed as a haunted space. "What's been happening at the shop? Have you been there, Eileen?"

She smiled. "You'll be delighted by the way your people have been managing. Alix is handling the books, they are getting the orders out, and they're working together as a team. Betty has been doing the cutting, and they've all been working overtime. I know they'll be glad to see you back."

It was at that point that I started to cry. I sat back in the car and let the tears flow. Eileen and Rossi were quiet in the front seat, and then they began to talk in low tones, ignoring me. By the time we got to their house, I was gulping and hiccuping, and they still acted as if whatever I was doing was perfectly all right. I have never felt so accepted and so protected at the same time. Eileen handed me a batch of tissues, picked up a paper bag full of toiletries and we went upstairs to their flat. Without another word, Eileen opened the door to their bedroom, ushered me in, and closed the door.

Several hours later, I went to the bathroom, washed my face, and joined them in the kitchen. Rossi was reading the newspaper, and Eileen was washing the dishes. When she saw me, she opened the oven door and took out a covered plate with my dinner on it, and set it down in front of me in the most matter-of-fact way possible.

Rossi put down the newspaper. "How about a glass of wine? We'll join you."

How could I resist? Then Rossi revealed the plan that he and Eileen had devised. "We—that is, all of your friends—have decided that you cannot go back to live in the flat as it now exists. So we're going to have a meeting this Sunday. We've contacted everybody—George Kosmak, Jean Coria, Boris Gutmann, Bill Donovan, Nobuo Kitagaki. Counting Eileen and me, that makes seven of us. I think that will be enough. We're going to talk about how to remodel the flat. Eileen has already talked to the landlord, and he said to check with him after we'd decided what we wanted to do. Eileen told him that our friends included architects and interior designers, and he was impressed."

"Mr. Torelli said to tell you he was sorry you were so sick, and he hopes you are better now," Eileen put in.

I was stunned. Tears came again to my eyes, and I swallowed hard. As I opened my mouth to stammer some kind of thanks, Eileen put her arm around me. "What we decided was that we'll do the work, and your job will be to feed us. We don't plan to make any changes to the kitchen. Okay?" She laughed. "It will be fun. We can work on weekends. You'll see."

I looked at them. "When did you cook up this deal? Whose idea was it?"

"When George and Eileen came back from the hospital," Rossi said, "we started to talk about your situation, and Boris was the one who said you would need a redesigned space. So we called Jean and George and Bill; Jean got in touch with Kit. We all love you, Rhoda—now don't start crying again—have another glass of wine."

The week passed in a blur of activity. Eileen was right. The shop was humming. I couldn't believe the tight organization my team of three had created. Alix had kept a careful record of the money that came in, and the money that went out. The lawyer Elizabeth had found for us took care of deposits and payroll. I couldn't believe how efficient they were. They were glad to see me, of course, and I plunged immediately into the work at hand. Betty went back to stitching, and I began to cut leather.

Working with my hands had always been therapeutic, and now I felt doubly strengthened by the support and love that surrounded me. The connection was deeper than family. I was part of a team, and we all understood how much we needed each other.

Chapter Twenty:
A New Life

⟶

THE FOLLOWING SUNDAY MY FRIENDS AND I GATHERED in the front
room of the upstairs flat at 1461 Grant Avenue—eight of us—Eileen,
Rossi, George, Jean, Boris, Bill, Kitagaki, and me—to decide on how to re-
design my living space. The door to the flat opened onto a long corridor, connecting the two small rooms in the front with the kitchen and dining room
in the back. There was a back porch and steps leading down to the workshop
on the first floor. We sat around on the old couch and chairs we had brought
up from the shop's living quarters in one of the two small rooms overlooking
the street.

Jean and George were both architects and interior designers; Boris was an
insurance broker with an office on Montgomery Street; Bill was a lawyer; and
Kitagaki was an artist, a Japanese screen and furniture maker, working with
his father, a master carpenter.

Both Jean and George had decided that we needed to take down the wall
separating the two front rooms, and create one large living room. Kit would
design and create a screen that would make part of the living room space into
a bedroom. That area had a window that opened onto the space between our
building and the building next door that housed the Chinese laundry.

There was much discussion about how we should do this. Eileen had already gotten Mr. Torelli's approval for changes we wanted to make to the flat,
and George had assured us that the wall in question was not a bearing wall.

He did say that we still had to support the ceiling at either end. That was one of the biggest projects. One of the other projects was to install a gas stove in the fake fireplace on one wall of the room.

We made a list of the projects. George Kosmak, the eldest and the most experienced of all of us, made up a list of things to do, and we sorted out the assignments. One was to put in bookshelves on either side of the new fireplace; another was to remove the pressed-metal wallpaper that covered the walls and ceiling of the corridor; pressed-metal wallpaper being the rage for old buildings like ours. The deal was that I would provide food and drink, and they would work. My friends called our weekends "work parties," and that's what they became.

Pretty soon the flat was filled with the sound of sledgehammers on the wall, the pounding of nails and the smell of wet plaster. I escaped to the delicatessen on the corner and came back with ham, salami, eggs, mushrooms, pickled herring, bread, butter, and coffee. We had brought up a small table and chairs from the shop, and I set the table with the Reynolds's mugs and plates. As soon as the smell of coffee wafted through the flat, my friends gathered in the room adjoining the kitchen.

Kitagaki and Jean looked thoughtfully around that room. Jean decided I needed a dining room table, and Kit decided I needed a screen to cover the windows that looked out onto the dreary back porch. They put their heads together, and began to make drawings on a paper towel. I noted that everybody seemed to be completely absorbed in creating a new environment for me.

We decided to work a few more hours, and then go across the street to the New Tivoli for dinner. I promised to cook a real meal for the following Sunday, so we decided to get together at twelve-thirty, work about four hours or so, and then have a proper dinner in what would become the dining room. Jean said not to worry about a table; she had an idea she wanted to try out, and Kit said that he also had something in mind. They were a little mysterious, but I didn't care.

The following Sunday Kit arrived with a completed screen that covered the back windows of the room. It was not an ordinary shoji screen; Kit had created a linear design, resembling a Mondrian painting, with black strips of wood dividing the sections of Japanese rice paper. The screen was beautifully elegant. Kit also showed me his design for a long cabinet for the opposite wall, using light tan stained wood for the sliding doors, the drawers and top stained black. The colors in the dining room would be white, light tan, and black stained wood.

Jean and Kit also carried in the table. The frame was a long rectangular box with a narrow base that sloped upward, supporting a four by eight piece of plywood. That meant that diners would have completely free legroom—no table legs to duck around. It was a brilliant design. We all clapped our hands with delight. Everybody trooped into the front part of the flat to work, and I began to cook.

Bruno had provided me with his special ground beef. He trimmed off T-bone steaks, porterhouse steaks, and other choice pieces of beef, which he supplied to the New Tivoli and other restaurants, and then ground up those lovely pieces into hamburger. He charged me twenty-five cents a pound. I chopped garlic and onions and sauteed them in olive oil; then I put the special lean ground beef into the pan. Adding fresh tomatoes, cilantro, Italian spices, and red wine, I covered the pan, letting everything simmer on a low flame. Then I boiled fresh spaghetti from the pasta shop down the street, adding olive oil and fresh basil. While waiting for the spaghetti to get to the proper "al dentro," I steamed fresh Italian green beans with ginger and baby green onions, which provided our vegetable dish. Then I sliced a long loaf of fresh French bread from the bakery on the corner, spread garlic butter and freshly grated Parmesan cheese on it, and put the loaf in the oven. We were just about ready. I opened another bottle of red wine and set it on the table.

I had to see how far my work crew had gotten before I announced dinner, and I marched into the living room to survey the scene. I couldn't believe my eyes. The support of the ceiling was in place, and the indirect lighting nestling in the cove of the support was all hooked up. The bookshelves were in, and George was working on the fireplace flue. "I'm going to hire a chimney sweep," he announced. "I think we have a working flue here, and I don't think we'll have any trouble connecting a gas stove." He looked up. "Hey!

Something smells good!"

"Yes!" I clapped my hands. "You guys are fantastic! Let's eat!"

The transformation of my flat reflected a transformation in me. Cause and effect were interchangeable. I was part of a group, included, accepted, and loved. The whole process became a mammoth healing of both spirit and mind. I was on the inside of a group that had formed itself around me; no longer was I outside, wanting to belong.

Invigorated and inspired, I was thrilled by the use of the four by eight piece of plywood as the top of my new dining room table. George told me to sand the plywood diligently, paint it with black paint and wipe it off, allowing the grain to rise; then repeat the process several times. I followed his directions and sanded, painted, wiped off the paint, sanded and applied varnish, doing this several times a day for a few days, until the patina of the wood and the gloss on it made it look like a rare piece of wood.

On our last working weekend we gathered around the table and admired it. George said we ought to photograph it and send it in to *Arts and Architecture* magazine.

"We'll call it 'Psuedo Tsuga Tioga from the shores of Juan de Fuca.' In other words, it's plywood from a lumber mill in the state of Washington! But when we give the table that Latin name, it sounds pretty impressive!"

When anyone asked me what that beautiful wood was, I used the Latin name for it, and nobody asked me to explain. I thought that was pretty funny. I bought place mats for my new table, and was delighted to discover that I could easily wipe off the glassy surface with a damp cloth. It was the most beautiful and practical table I have ever had.

We installed a new small stove of George's design, and put a piece of wavy green fireproof plastic behind it. We painted the new bookshelves, and Kit produced the screen for the bedroom area, the cabinets for the dining room, plus cabinets for my new bedroom. We had removed the wallpaper from the corridor and painted the entire place warm light beige.

After the furniture was in, with a simple small couch, two armchairs, a rug, and a coffee table I had bought at Goodwill, the room was warm and inviting. Kit's screen, separating the living area from the bedroom and George Kosmak's modern gas stove with its glass front provided an extra artistic touch. The three curved bay windows let in the right kind of light for my favorite prints and paintings on the walls. I looked around my elegant room with a deep sense of satisfaction. I was able to plan a flat-warming party within a month of my brush with death.

Rhoda laying pattern on leather

Chronicle Publicity

Rhoda in 1959

Chapter Twenty-One:
Rhoda Pack Leathers

⤸

COMPLETION OF MY BEAUTIFUL, RENOVATED FLAT stimulated me. I felt liberated and supported, free to create new designs. Along with renewed energy and confidence, as well as having new customers almost every day, I began to feel like a real business owner. I realized I would have to hire more workers, and decided to call the Leather Workers' Union. Locating the number in the phone book, I called and asked to speak to the union representative.

A deep masculine voice answered, and when I told him my name, that I had a small business, and that I wanted my employees to join his union, there was silence on the other end. I heard him clear his throat, and he asked me to repeat my name. He seemed to be incredulous that an employer would be calling a union. He asked me if the union shop was my idea, and if so, why. I remember what I said.

"I'm the owner of a small business, making leather clothing for women, and I have three employees. The reason I want to have a union shop is that if I need to hire a cutter or stitcher, I could call you and you would send me a qualified person. Isn't that how it works?"

How could I do otherwise? With a father who was a union organizer, I felt obligated. Besides, Pa would have been proud of me.

Geraldo, the union representative, had to admit that that was how it worked, in theory. I asked him to come to the shop the following morning, and told him that it was up to him to make a sensible pitch to my employees. The choice to join the union would be up to them.

The following morning a bulky man, medium height, with the build of a middleweight boxer, stomped heavily into the shop. I shook his callused hand, and led him around the partition. "This is my staff," I said, introducing Alix, Betty, and Miriam. "I'll be upstairs," I continued, "I'll put the 'closed' sign on the door, and Alix, just ring the doorbell when you're finished. I'll come down." Then I walked out, leaving them to their discussion.

When I came back down, about forty-five minutes later, I found a tense atmosphere in the workroom. Geraldo said that my workers would think it over, and would tell me their decision in a few days. We walked around the partition and sat down on the customer's bench in the front of the shop. The union representative was curious about why I had called him, especially since I only had three employees. I put it to him as clearly as I could.

"I believe that unions benefit employers and employees. Look," I said, "I need to have some security if I'm going to meet deadlines for orders. I've heard that leather cutters tend to be eccentric, independent, and that sometimes they show up for work and sometimes they don't. If this happens, I want to be able to call you and have you send me somebody I can trust to fill in. Can you do that?"

He was slow to respond. "Theoretically, we can do that. But we might not have somebody we could send."

I jumped in before he could continue, and insisted that it was the union's responsibility to provide me with reliable workers, just as it would be my employees' responsibility to pay their dues. We parried back and forth for a while, and then Geraldo agreed to present my case to his board of directors. I repeated that I wanted some sort of agreement between us that the union would send me responsible people, and that if they weren't capable, I would be able to send them back. I agreed to provide documentation in writing, and we left it at that.

When I walked back into the workroom, there was still a certain amount of tension in the air, and I tried to relieve it. We all sat down, and I told them about my background. I told them about my father; how I'd grown up, and how I believed in fairness for everybody who worked everywhere. I said I didn't believe in paternalism, that things weren't going to change in the shop, and that mainly I was trying to set up some sort of security for all of us.

"You guys were wonderful while I was recuperating from that suicide attempt," I said. "I can't tell you how much I appreciate your teamwork. We're still a team, and if we do join the Leather Workers' Union, everybody he sends is going to have to be approved by you. Every new person will have a trial period of two weeks, and if we don't like a person, and we decide to reject that worker, we'll have to say why in writing. We have to maintain our integrity. It shows in our product." There was silence for a minute, and then Alix spoke up.

"We feel we have a personal stake in what we make here. We were worried that if we joined a union, there would be a separation between you and us. Of course we're employees, but we felt that we are more than that. We realize that you have to hire more people, and as long as we have a say in whoever comes to join our team, we have decided to join the union."

We all stood and embraced. I was close to tears, but I felt I had done the right thing. That was Wednesday. I knew we had to finish two jackets and four handbags by Saturday, but I figured we could do that, and told everybody that I was having a flat-warming party Saturday night. We could close the shop at five-thirty and just go upstairs for the celebration party. They laughed, and we went back to work.

The years from 1950 to 1953 were exciting years. I was giddy with accomplishment, with expanding horizons, with a heady sense of liberation and freedom. The mood in the shop was upbeat. We were getting steady orders for jackets and coats, handbags, and belts. The call for sandals was diminishing, but that didn't matter.

I hired a cutter, Arturo, who came from Cuba, and a finisher, Anna, who came from the Philippines. Both of them were approved by the staff. With five employees, the atmosphere in the workroom changed, and over the years I realized that an employer is always viewed as "the boss." If I thought of myself as an equal, that was my illusion, and I hung on to it.

My routine was simple. I would confer with Arturo, about the designs we had to turn out within the week. He sorted the skins needed for a jacket or coat by laying them out on a sawhorse, making sure that the skins matched in tone. Working with leather adds a layer of precision not needed when working with cloth. Each animal's hide is different, and although the tanning and dyeing process is mechanized, each skin takes the chemicals and dyes differently. The skins also have to be scrutinized for flaws, and the cutter has to make sure that whatever flaws exist are buried under the arms or inside pocket areas.

After the hides are selected, the cutter lays the brassbound, heavy cardboard pattern pieces on the hides, taking care to cut as expeditiously as possible, using the backbone, the heaviest part of the hide, in the center, for the straightest cuts. I continued to cut dresses and skirts, in both suede and smooth leather, because I was the only one who really understood how to use the edges of the hide to advantage.

Once the design was cut, it was rolled up with a tag, showing the size and the name of the customer, and whether it was for a department store or an individual. I had hired a cutter for linings, since I was now running back and forth between the retail part of the shop, doing fittings and selling things, as well as working on new designs. The lining cutter also worked as a finisher and sort of a shop foreman. She would look over the jackets that were ready to be stitched, note the number still to be cut, and try to cut more than one size of lining at a time. The leather had to be cut one at a time, but fabric could be piled up and several sizes could be cut at once. We still cut everything by hand.

Then the jacket was bundled with the lining and given to one of the stitchers. All of my seamstresses made the complete jacket and signed their initials on the back of the Rhoda Pack label that went into each garment or handbag. The finisher pressed open the seams, using a piece of brown paper between the dry iron and the leather, glued the hems with the special white glue I had helped to develop, and checked the garment before hanging it up on the packing rack.

The handbag makers had their own particular routine, which we'd perfected by that time. We had decided that we needed to suntan the "natural" bark tanned leather before we stitched it, so I took the cut and punched handbag up to the roof of our building. I left it there during the day, brought it down, treated it with saddle soap, and then turned it over to our stitchers, who used waxed linen thread for the stitching. Our customers would lift the flap on handbags hanging in the shop and complain that the leather looked "faded." We knew that this was what happened to bark tanned leather, but we thought it was easier to forestall a complaint than try to convince a customer that it wasn't a matter of fading. Once the leather had been exposed to sunlight and subjected to the saddle soap treatment, it was less likely to show the effects of sunlight.

There is a myth that if you own your own business, you are free, and don't have to work to please a boss. That is an illusion. Instead of having one boss to please, you have a multitude of bosses—each one of your customers becomes your boss, and you are constantly aiming to please, placate, and satisfy all of them. The customer often has fixed ideas of what she wants, and it's often impossible to talk her out of them, even when you know the result will be disastrous. Like the customer who ordered a beige suede dress with matching bolero jacket.

I warned her that the suede I had available would shed, and tried to get her to buy the design she wanted in smooth leather. I explained that short-haired chamois was no longer available from China, because the flooding of the Yellow River had wiped out all the short-haired sheep that used to provide the beautiful non-shedding skins I had previously bought. The new skins came from Portuguese West Africa, as did the smooth leather, but I didn't like the suede, and used it reluctantly. My customer insisted on the suede, and she did look wonderful in the dress. I had a twinge, though, when I delivered it to her, and was not surprised when I got a tearful call two weeks later.

"You were right! Can I bring it back?" What could I say?

"Bring it back. I'll see what I can do." She showed up with the dress on Saturday, and explained that she had worn it to a dance with her new boyfriend the previous weekend. He had worn a blue wool suit. *Uh, oh.*

After one dance, she said, he had looked down at himself in horror, and fled. I smothered a laugh, and lifted the dress from the box.

"Tell you what I'll do. A salesman brought a special spray for suede that he asked me to try out. It will flatten the nap somewhat, but it won't change the softness. If you're willing to let me try it, I'll spray it, and you can look at it. I don't know whether it will make the leather stiff or not. I tried to warn you, but, well, never mind. What do you say?"

My customer looked at me sadly. "I just love that dress. Yes, do what you can. Do I have to pay you anything more?"

I was so relieved that she didn't ask for a refund that I reassured her all the experimentation would be on my part. She sighed and said she'd be back the following Saturday. The spraying did make the suede a little stiffer, but I worked it with my hands, thinking about the Inuit women who chewed the seal hides bit by bit before they stitched them into their own clothing. The spraying worked out, and at least I didn't have to chew the suede!

As the business expanded, my position shifted. In addition to conferring with Arturo about layout of the skins, I handled special orders and selling. I also had to order the leather, linings, fittings, file the taxes on time, and make sure I could meet the payroll every week. Luckily, most of our business was retail, and we could sell most of our samples whenever I decided we needed some ready cash. It was up to me to create a sale. I could feel the pressure building, but that dark cloud evaporated when I concentrated on creating a new design. That was the fun part. That was the aspect of the business that I really enjoyed. I found myself working after hours more and more, enjoying the quiet of the shop, losing myself in the intricacies of the design. Much of my best work was done in that period.

Chapter Twenty-Two:
Ma's Funeral

⌒

IN MARCH 1951, I received a letter from my sister Fay that my mother had died suddenly after suffering a heart attack. I knew that she and Pa had moved to the Jewish Home for the Aged, but I hadn't known she was ill. We all expected Pa to die first. Fay gave me the date of the funeral, and I knew I would have to leave right away.

Calling the staff together, I told them I would have to go to Chicago for a week, and asked them if they wanted to carry on while I was gone. They looked at me as if I'd gone mad. Of course they wanted to carry on. So I asked Alix to take care of the front of the shop, set up work for the week, and left that night.

It had been eight years since I'd seen my sister Fay and my father, when I stopped in Chicago on my way to Washington, D.C., in 1943. It had been sixteen years since I'd seen Jeanne and Sara. A lot had happened in those intervening years.

My sisters, Jeanne and Sara, were staying temporarily with Fay and Henry. Al and his wife, with their two daughters, lived in a suburb of Chicago. Sylvia, Fay's eldest daughter, was seventeen, Alice was thirteen. Fay's house was really full. Conscious of my status as the black sheep of the family, the one who left without saying goodbye, the one who not only married a non-Jew but divorced him, the one who chose a commercial career rather than one in academia, I was apprehensive when I walked into Fay's house. I wished I was an armadillo, protected by a hard external shell, but I wasn't. I took a deep breath and braced myself. To my surprise, everyone behaved as if the years of separation had never happened, and we were all back to 1936. It was weird.

We all took turns in the bathroom, and one by one, we all washed our hair. Coming into the kitchen with my hair wrapped up, I didn't expect their reaction.

"Good Lord, look at her!" Jeanne exclaimed. "The rest of us simply wrap a towel around our heads, but Rhoda creates a fashion turban! I can't stand it." They all laughed.

I didn't know whether to laugh or cry. *Would our worlds ever intersect?* My eighty-five-year-old father and my forty-four-year-old brother were at the funeral parlor when we arrived, and I didn't know whether my father would speak to me or not. After all, he had written me when I first married Jim that he had disowned me, that he didn't want me to come to his funeral, and that he had taken my name out of our family book. He didn't look at me during the service, but I didn't expect him to. He was weeping most of the time. We got through the services and the trip to the grave, and then assembled at Fay's house.

The custom in Jewish families following a death is similar to an Irish Catholic wake. People come to offer condolences, bringing food, cake, and other goodies. It is a time of tension and deep emotion. Pa was the only one to weep steadily, with great, gasping breaths. Sara and Jeanne sat on each side of him stroking his hands, rubbing his back, prodding him to drink some tea. Finally he stopped, and simply sat quietly, looking at the floor.

We were all deeply affected by Ma's death; Sara, Jeanne, Fay, and I wept quietly, but Al fell apart. We were all sitting around Fay's living room as various people, friends and relatives, came and went. Suddenly Al, who had been standing next to the table laden with food, collapsed, and we all thought he had had a heart attack. Dr. Abrams happened to be there, and after checking his pulse, declared it to be "an anxiety attack." Al shifted himself to Fay's side and put his head in her lap. *Al was the one most visibly affected by Ma's death, and went into psychotherapy shortly after the funeral.*

Pa and I did manage to talk. After the guests left, we went for a walk in a nearby park. It was a blustery March day, but the wind was warm. We sat down on a bench.

"Don't bother to come back for my funeral," Pa said. "I'll be dead in two months."

I took his soft old hand and stroked it. "I'm sorry I hurt your feelings, Pa," I said. He didn't seem to be listening to me, but I went on talking anyway. "You know I loved Jim very much. I think if it hadn't been for the war, and everything that happened after that, I might still be married to him."

He heard that part. "What? You're not married anymore? What happened?"

"It's a long story, Pa. I'm glad I got to see you again, anyway." He nodded and changed the subject. Sighing, he said, "The ball of string has run out. It's time for me to go. Do you remember the story I told you about how we live out our time on earth? About the ball of string we all start with? Well, my ball of string is finished. Let's go back to the house. I'm tired."

I remembered then the story he had told me when I was a child. He said, "We are all born with a full ball of string, and as our life uncurls, the ball of string unwinds. When it is empty, we die. No one knows how big that ball is, or how long it will take to unwind. Some people have balls of string with lots of knots, and they have many troubles; others have string that is smooth. But no matter what the condition of the string, when the ball is finished, it's finished."

As we sat on that park bench, my father didn't talk about forgiveness or past grievances. He was too engrossed in his own loss to remember anything that happened between him and me so long ago. We hugged and said good-bye, and Henry drove him back to the Jewish Home for the Aged. He died two months later, as he said he would.

After the funeral, Fay and Henry invited me to the Dunes for the rest of my stay in Chicago, and we sat on the sand in front of the cottage while the girls played in the water, even though the water was cold. The air was soft and warm for March, the sand slipped easily through my fingers. I remembered the berry picking in my girlhood, the bonfires on the beach, the drifting, easy feeling of the long summers we spent at the cabin we rented at the

Dunes. I remembered the sense I had then of wanting those summers to last forever, yet knowing that they would end. I thought about the turbulence of the years between 1942 and 1951.

"I wish I could find someone steady and calm like you, Henry," I said. Henry looked at me fondly. "Rhodabike," he said, using his favorite nickname for me, "you would never find someone like me in the places you hang out! If you're looking for someone like me, you're looking in the wrong corners."

Fay chimed in. "I think you would be bored to death by Henry," she said. "We're pretty stuffy, ordinary conservative folks. I think you need more excitement in your life, and you'll just have to get used to the ups and downs." *She was right, of course, and deep down, I knew it. In fact, I could hardly wait to get back to San Francisco. But there was always that push and hold back in me; my father's spirit saying, "Go for it! Take a chance!" And my mother's cautious, bitter voice, saying, "Be careful. You could fail. Keep the day job." I heard both of the voices of my parents, and I heard Fay and Henry too. It was another goodbye for me.*

Chapter Twenty-Three:
Varda and Skiing

⌒

I FELT MY SPIRITS RISE AS THE PLANE TOUCHED DOWN in San Francisco. Driving into the city from the airport, I thought San Francisco never looked or smelled so good. I feasted my eyes on the sparkling bay, and inhaled the air as if it were the finest ambrosia. Chicago's air is heavy, moist, and vaguely threatening when it's cloudy. San Francisco's fog is like living in a cloud. I let go of Chicago, and embraced my new home, one that I had helped to create.

Walking into the shop, I was delighted to see that the windows were clean, the customer area had been dusted and swept, and Rhoda Pack Leathers looked welcoming. As I walked around the partition, everyone turned to face me and shouted, "Welcome back!" *What a homecoming!* There were new orders for jackets and handbags, and Alix showed me a list of the garments that had been shipped to stores as well as delivered to customers. She also showed me a list of orders that had to be filled that week.

"I'm glad you're back," she said. "Here are names and phone numbers of customers who want your special attention. And we're running behind on these orders."

I took my bag upstairs, changed clothes, and went down the back steps to the shop to get to work. Checking with Arturo, I saw that he was sorting the skins not only for subtle variations in tone but for weight and texture, which was exactly what I had told him to do. *What a lovely feeling! This is real power—a group of people who work together toward a common goal, without constant supervision.* Moving through the shop, I checked on who was doing what, and decided that the most important thing for me to do was to call the customers who wanted special attention, so I went around the partition and sat down at my desk.

However, as soon as I settled myself, the bell tinkled, and a tall, thin man appeared at the door with a stunning woman beside him. He looked familiar, and then I realized it was Herb Caen!

"Hi," he said. "Didn't I see you and your husband at KCBS last year? Doing a design thing on models, using leather as cloth?"

I laughed, remembering the squishy bread commercial. "Yes, that was Jim and me. What would you like to look at?"

"This is my friend Marilyn. How about a jacket for her?"

That was the beginning of a lasting friendship between us. Whenever Herb acquired a new female companion, he always brought her around for a handbag, a coat, or a jacket. He was a good friend, and gave me the kind of publicity I needed. Other columnists on the *San Francisco Chronicle,* like Stan Delaplane, began to send customers to me. Word of mouth travels swiftly in small social circles. I did brown suede trousers for horseback riding with a short jacket to match for Mrs. Zellerbach, and a different outfit for Mrs. Haas. According to Who's Who, both Mrs. Zellerbach and Mrs. Haas were members of San Francisco's two hundred important families; Mrs. Zellerbach was connected to the Zellerbach Paper Company, and Mrs. Haas to the Levi Strauss family. They were wonderful clients, and of course told all their friends about Rhoda Pack Leathers.

Working with the orders they gave me I learned how important it was to trim the suede with smooth leather wherever there was contact between cloth and leather, or between human skin and animal skin. For example, I put smooth leather lapels on the collar and cuffs of suede jackets, and smooth leather trim around the pockets of suede trousers and skirts.

Photographers like Ginny Stoll, Harry Stearns, and Rondal Partridge were friends who were willing to photograph my products in exchange for clothes and handbags. I met Rondal through his mother, Imogen Cunningham, who was also a friend. Imogen and I had long talks about the nature of the creative process, as well as about what it takes to survive as an artist. Her ready wit and down-to-earth pragmatism was a stimulating antidote to a lot of the high-flown language of some of the artists who hung around the shop. I talked to Imogen about how I felt the need for some sort of catalog of my creations. Many of the jackets, suits, and coats that I made were special orders, and once the orders were delivered, I didn't have a record. Imogen suggested that I contact Rondal, her son, and that connection turned out to be wonderfully productive. Rondal's eye was so sharp, so intuitive, that his photographs became small masterpieces. Now, with the photographic catalog we produced, I had a record that I could show prospective customers. When I really liked a particular design, I would make a sample in size ten and one of my favorite models would pose for Rondal, and we would add it to the catalog. It was fun, and my confidence expanded as the orders continued to come in.

I went to museum exhibit openings, to the theater, to parties, always wearing one of my own creations. My hair was long at that time, and I wore it up in the back in a French twist, using a beautiful handmade piece of jewelry to hold it in place. Bill and Boris often accompanied me to these events, and it was fun, being aware of the attention we drew. I was five feet six at that time and weighed about one hundred and twenty pounds, so I could wear all my samples.

I remember an opening at the DeYoung Museum of a show by Jean Varda, a Greek collage artist. It was the middle of October 1951, the same year that Lawrence Ferlinghetti opened City Lights Bookstore. I was absolutely captivated by one of Varda's paintings, called "The Secrets of Eleusis." That collage depicted the women who created a temple of worship on the mountain opposite Apollo's temple, for their own secret rituals. I coveted that painting, but after looking at the price tag, knew I could never afford it. *Exchanges worked with the Reynolds's and other artists. Would it work with Varda? I decided to take a chance.* I walked over to Varda and boldly told him how much I wanted that painting of his. I asked him if he would like to make a trade, offering to make him a white leather suit as an exchange. He laughed, said exchanges were fine, but he didn't want anything for himself. He'd like a jacket for his daughter who lived in England, and maybe a coat for his wife. I couldn't believe my luck, and agreed immediately. Privately, I decided to make him a leather vest in addition to the coat and jacket for his daughter. I measured him with my eyes, but decided he would have to come to the shop, along with his wife.

Just then Virginia, Varda's wife, appeared. Virginia was almost six feet tall, taller than Varda, and I knew immediately she would be a marvelous walking advertisement. I whipped out my appointment book and looked at them expectantly. Virginia and Jean exchanged glances and she said she'd call me on Monday to make a date. I insisted that Jean come along to help decide on the right design for his daughter. He nodded, and I walked away, feeling about ten feet tall.

Virginia did call on Monday, and both of them came to the shop late Wednesday afternoon. Varda had brought a photograph of his twenty-four-year-old daughter, and Virginia supplied additional information, so we were able to choose a jacket we thought would be right. I insisted that if she didn't like it for any reason, she was to return it, and that I would include a catalog of other designs that she could select instead. Then Virginia had to try on every coat I had on the sample rack, and we finally selected a design, making an appointment for a fitting. Then I brought out the muslin I had made up for Varda, and the golden yellow skins I thought would be fine for him. He protested, but I could tell by the smile through his bronze mustache how pleased he was.

The fit was pretty close, and as they were leaving, Varda turned to me and said, casually,

"By the way, I'm having a costume party Saturday after next, on the houseboat in Sausalito harbor, Pier 39. It's Halloween. Please come and bring a friend or two. Eight o'clock." They waved, and left.

I called Bill immediately to tell him about the invitation. Then I called Boris and Jean Coria and Kitagaki. I invited them all for dinner Friday night, so we could plan our costumes.

Deciding that I would go as a witch, I told my friends that I would wear my black long-sleeved leotard with its black leggings and a black wool hooded cape. I had the leotard, and decided to make myself the cape. Then I asked them what they thought about my painting out my eyebrows and drawing two black curved lines up and out to the corners of my forehead. They thought this was a hilarious idea, and Kit immediately offered to embellish my leggings by painting designs on them.

After dinner, which included some excellent red wine, I put on my leotard, leggings and all, and we trooped downstairs for Kit to perform his magic. I stretched out one leg and then another, and with my friends cheering him on, Kit created a most interesting design. I watched, fascinated, as a green vine with thorns crept up my legs, and then the most astonishing blossoms appeared, here and there. They looked vaguely like malevolent orchids. The vines continued up my waist and ended at approximately where we thought my heart was located. Kit's hand never wavered, even though Boris kept refilling our glasses.

The following Saturday we gathered at the shop. Bill showed up with a gorilla costume he had rented, Boris with a lion's mask, Jean in harem pajamas, and Kit as a Japanese samurai, complete with cardboard sword. We climbed into Bill's car, and as we approached the toll plaza at the Golden Gate Bridge, Bill suddenly pulled on his gorilla head, and slowly extended his gorilla hand to the toll taker. Then he stepped on the gas and we sped off toward Sausalito. All of us craned our necks to look back at the man in the tollbooth, who was leaning out, staring at us.

At the pier where Varda's houseboat was anchored, we found the party in full swing. It was full of exotic looking creatures, and as the evening progressed, the masks came off, musicians brought out their guitars and drums, and the dancing commenced. At one point, I sat astride Bill's gorilla shoulders, balancing a large wine jug on my shoulder with my right hand. I'd lean over someone holding a raised glass and carefully fill it, and then we'd move through the room, filling glasses, not spilling a drop. I had to admire Bill's ability to maintain his balance on the uneven floor; he never wavered. I got off his shoulders on the other end of the room and asked Bill if he wanted to get out of his costume, since he was sweating profusely. He couldn't, he said, because he was wearing only his underwear!

Before the night was over, several people fell overboard and had to be rescued with long poles. The water wasn't very deep, and some people didn't want to be rescued, preferring to swim around the boat, but Varda was worried, so we pulled them in anyway.

We drove Jean and Boris home, and then Bill drove me home. Bill had an apartment on the top of Telegraph Hill and we often shared meals. Bill was five years my junior, and we had a lovely, friendly relationship.

In February 1952, we decided to celebrate my birthday at Squaw Valley. It was a three-day weekend that year. Bill was an accomplished skier; I agreed to take lessons. I borrowed everything from friends, even ski clothes, including a beautiful jacket with the emblem of the ski patrol over the pocket, not realizing how ironic that was. Eight of us crammed into Boris's Cadillac, and off we went. We had rented a chalet from one of Bill's friends, and we were planning to rent skis and boots after we got there. Even though I had never skied in my life, I was sure I could learn.

I spent the first day on the "bunny slope," along with ten-year-old kids who would race to the top of the small slope way ahead of me and would ski down with full confidence. I skied down more cautiously, carefully following every bit of instruction. However, I became bolder with each successful "snow-plow" and decided to try the main slope on the next day, which was also my birthday. That evening, in the warm and cozy atmosphere of the ski lodge, I simply smiled mysteriously when anyone commented on the ski patrol logo stitched on my breast pocket.

The next day, filled with confidence, I went up on the ski lift, and when I clumsily got off the bucket seat at the top, I wanted to grab that chair and ride back down. Too late. I gripped my poles, got into position, rehearsing in my mind everything I had learned, and took off. Wheeee! I made it! I was so delighted that I waved my poles in the air as I skied to a perfect stop. Bill immediately chided me for that silly display.

"You don't do things like that! You could hit somebody with your poles! No! Don't do that again!" He was really upset. Then he grinned. "I know how you feel. Want to go back up?"

This time we rode the ski lift up together, and again it was a successful trip down. The afternoon was getting colder, and after we came down the fourth time, I looked up the mountain and wondered if I should try it one more time. We were planning to go back to San Francisco the next day. Bill had already gone up, and I decided, yes, I would go up one more time.

As I skied down, the snow cover was already icing up; I slipped and fell, starting to slide down the mountain on my bottom. Digging my poles in didn't impede my progress as much as I hoped it would, and I couldn't get up on my skis. I thought, "What the hell. Going down on my rear end is just another way to get down the mountain!" Except that just as this thought flitted through my mind, I saw the steel ski lift stanchion over my left shoulder, and then I crashed into it, left hip first. I remember yelling and then passed out.

I came to in an ambulance on the way to a hospital in Truckee, Bill sitting beside me. "We heard your yell all over the mountain," he said. "How do you feel?"

"I don't know. Numb, really." I was probably still in shock. The X-rays showed that while nothing was broken, my left hip was knocked out of its socket. A doctor at the hospital put it back in while I was under an anesthetic, and when I came to, he kept advising me to see an orthopedist as soon as I got home. He gave me a lot of painkillers, and I stretched out in the backseat of the van that took us back to the chalet, my head on Bill's lap. I spent the evening on my stomach while we all toasted my birthday with champagne and tidbits from the bar. I spent the next eight months in a flexible, corset-like brace stretching from my armpits to my hips, sleeping on a board. After the brace came off, intense daily physiotherapy made it possible for me to move without pain. The following winter I went back to skiing—but cross-country this time—never downhill again.

In the fall of 1952, I was asked to do a fashion show at the Del Monte Country Club for the Robert John shop in Carmel, and Bill went with me. Bill said he knew somebody who knew Henry Miller, who was living in Big Sur at that time, and he asked me if I would like to meet Miller. Of course, yes, so Bill made the necessary phone call, and we went up the mountain to Henry Miller's house after the fashion show.

The small house seemed to be carved into the side of the mountain, and it was surrounded by the Big Sur Redwoods, with a beautiful view of the ocean. Henry was a small cheerful man, radiating energy. He greeted us as if we were old friends, and after the second martini, came right to the point.

"I've seen your work at the Robert John shop," he said. "Will you make me a pair of leather pants? I'd like them in the same creamy color as the jacket you're wearing."

I looked at the woman who was living with Henry and decided that she had better be the one to make the pants. I told Henry that I was going to be in Carmel only a short time, and if Vera had a heavy-duty sewing machine, she could stitch up the pants herself. I said I would send him the cut pieces, the paper patterns, with instructions clearly marked, and Vera nodded enthusiastically as we shook hands. Over a fourth martini, Henry offered me a painting in trade, which I accepted.

Chapter Twenty-Four:

Baba

⌒

BY THE SPRING OF 1953 Bill decided to go to Harvard to study Urban Planning, and I was lonely. I was ready for a diversion of some sort.

One day, one of my customers asked me casually if I knew anyone who might want a black standard poodle, free. Suddenly the idea of a dog was very attractive. Happy memories of my dog Josie, when I was pregnant with my first child, surged over me. I plied my customer with questions. How old was the dog? Was it housebroken? On and on. She held up her hand to stop me, gave me a name and a number, and left.

I rushed to the phone and talked to the owner of the dog, which was named "Baba." The owner's name was Emily, and the reason she wanted to give the dog away was that she had just gotten a new job in New York, where she was going to live in an apartment that absolutely would not tolerate pets of any kind. She had had Baba since he was a pup, and didn't want to sell him. She wanted to find the right owner and the right place for him. She was willing to come over and let Baba decide. She said Baba would have to decide whether or not I was the right person for him, since he had already turned down four other people. We made a date for five o'clock the following day.

Emily and Baba arrived promptly, and I felt as if I were being interviewed. Baba walked sedately into the shop, looked at me, circled around me, sniffed my legs and feet, then went back to his mistress and lay down. Baba was a big standard poodle with his black curly hair trimmed in what was called a puppy clip, but I preferred to think of it as the way poodles were trimmed when they were used as hunting dogs in France.

"Let's go for a walk," Emily said. "I'll give you the lead, and we'll see what happens." I locked the door and took the lead from Emily. Baba looked at me and I looked at him. I leaned down and scratched his ears. "Hello, Baba," I said. "We're going for a walk." He looked up at Emily, who was gazing into the distance. I thought she was going to cry. Then the three of us set off for Washington Park at the corner of Union and Stockton, a block and a half from my shop. Baba dutifully stopped at every corner, didn't strain at the leash, in fact, he acted as if he were leading me. When we got to the park, I asked Emily what she usually did when they went for a walk.

"I just take him off the leash and let him run and do his business," she said. "Try it, then call him and see if he comes back."

Before I took the leash off his collar, I leaned down and gave Baba a hug. "You'll come back when I call, won't you, Baba?" I whispered into his ear. Then I stood up. He gave himself a little shake and trotted off, turning to look at us from time to time. We sat on a bench watching him, and I asked Emily what kind of food he ate and where he slept. I also wanted to know if he was at all aggressive, and if he barked a lot. He seemed very polite, but I needed to know if this dog was neurotic in any way. He was, after all, about five years old.

Emily hesitated. "He's rather possessive," she said. "If he decides he likes you, he'll follow you around everywhere, and he will snap at anyone he thinks might hurt you."

I was worried about his behavior in the shop. "How does he behave around strangers? Is he likely to attack people who come into the shop? That wouldn't be good for business."

She said she took Baba to work with her, and he was perfectly behaved at her office. She worked in a travel agency, where there were people coming and going all day, and there had never been any trouble. "Except—" she said, and paused. I held my breath. "One day a street person came in and Baba leaped up, his ears laid back, and he uttered the most ferocious growl I'd ever heard. Then he sort of pointed, like a bird dog, but that street person backed out of the door so fast, he seemed to disappear." I laughed, relieved.

"Okay," Emily said, "try calling him." So I did. Baba stopped, looked around, looked at me, looked at Emily, and turned away. Emily then stood up too, and called, waving her arm. I decided to wave my arm too, and Baba came loping up to us.

"Here," Emily said, "give him this treat." She reached behind my back and slipped the treat into my pocket, as if trying to fool the dog. I held out my hand and Baba took the dog biscuit, giving my hand an extra lick.

We walked back to the shop, and Emily said she thought I'd passed, but maybe she'd better come back tomorrow, and just leave Baba for a few hours with me. "I think he likes you, but let's make sure. I'm not leaving until the end of next week."

Emily brought me Baba's eating dish and his drinking bowl, and we put them in the kitchen at the back of the shop. Baba checked them out and then made a careful inspection of the entire shop. He looked at Emily and he looked at me. When we walked into the front of the shop, he followed us to the door and stood waiting. Emily leaned down, scratched his ears and told him to sit, which he did, his whole body tense. She gave him a final pat and left. I kneeled beside Baba and we both watched Emily get into her car and leave. I gave Baba a treat and stood up. My arrangement with Emily was that she would leave Baba with me for a day and a night, and see how we got along. She would come back the next day and we would go for another walk. I felt as if I were on probation.

He watched me carefully as I opened a can of dog food and put it in his bowl, then filled his water bowl and set it down. He finally condescended to eat it, lapped up some water, came over and lay down near where I was working on a new design. Resting his head on his paws, he watched me carefully.

I decided to take him for a walk to the park, but I would keep him on the leash. If I let him off the leash in the park, would he run off and try to find his way back to Emily? I couldn't take a chance. As soon as I picked up the leash, Baba was up and at the door before I could get my coat on. We walked sedately down to the park, and then on to the grass. Baba seemed to know he wasn't going to get off the leash, so he sniffed around a few trees, left his mark, and finally squatted. I gave him a treat, and we walked companionably back to the apartment. Upstairs, he sniffed the entire apartment very carefully, checking each room, especially the bedroom, where he located his special blanket at the foot of my bed. He reassured himself that it was really his by scuffing it with his paws, circling it a few times, then lying down with a small sigh. Baba was obviously not a barker, but when neighbors who lived upstairs came clumping up the stairs, he raised his head and gave a low growl. I liked that evidence of awareness. He finally stretched himself out and went sound asleep. I was reassured, but I knew that the real test of his acceptance would be if he came back when I called.

Emily called early the next morning, wanting to know how it went. I told her that everything seemed fine, and that Baba was adjusting. She came over at five-thirty; Baba was happy to see her, but he seemed a bit reserved. Emily noticed this too, and told me she felt relieved.

"I'd like to try something," I said. "When we go to the park, I'd like to take him off the leash, and you hide somewhere, maybe behind a car or something. Then I'll call him, and if he comes back to me, we'll know he has made the connection, and he won't run off. But if he doesn't come back, you'll have to call him, and we'll know he's decided I'm not the right owner for him."

Emily put her hand on my arm. "I can see you really want to have my dog, and that makes me feel good. But you're right, if he's going to run off, it won't work. We'll just have to try it."

Off we went, the three of us. I walked ahead, holding the leash, and Emily sometimes walked behind us or in front of us. When we got to the park, I took Baba off the leash, and Emily turned around and walked away. He bounded off and I held my breath, watching him carefully. After he had performed his nightly ritual and was just snooping around, I called and waved my arms. He looked up, looked around, and came loping toward me. I threw my arms around him, hugged him, and scratched his ears, feeling silly and happy at the same time. Emily came out from behind the parked car where she'd been hiding, patted Baba, and we both grinned at each other. That lovely poodle with a mind of his own had decided for us.

Now that my dog had decided he was going to live at 1461 Grant Avenue, he became part of the family. Gradually, he took it upon himself to check out every person who came or went into the shop. He found himself a spot in the showroom, lifted his head as the staff came into work, and checked them out. However, if a stranger came in, he was up instantly, sniffing politely, and if he felt the customer was okay, he would go back to his place and lie down, his head on his paws, his eyes following every move. I found his presence reassuring and comforting.

Baba also made himself at home in the neighborhood. I decided to let him out every morning to roam the streets around the shop. I knew he would come back and lie down in the sun in front of the shop or scratch on the door window if he wanted to come in. I found out from Bruno, the butcher, that Baba made the rounds of every delicatessen in the surrounding two blocks. His first stop was Bruno's. He would pause in front of the door of the butcher shop, sit expectantly and happily take his daily handout of a bit of meat or a bone. Then he would go across the street to the deli, where he would get a bit of prosciutto or salami. If he was satisfied, he would come back to the shop. If not, he would trot down to Green Street and check out the shops there. He strode his territory as if he owned it, and since there were no other dogs around, he really did.

Baba lived until he was twelve years old, adjusting to my second husband, Ric Skahen, our move to Berkeley, and to my son Ricky. He never wavered in his complete devotion to me and took the changes in our lifestyle in stride.

Chapter Twenty-Five:
Mona and Betty Lou

⏤

O NE DAY A LARGE, HANDSOME WOMAN walked into the shop, and was greeted by Baba in his customary manner. This customer passed, and Baba retreated to his corner of the shop.

"I'm Mona," she said, extending her hand. "I own the bar around the corner, on the alley, a third of the way down from the corner of Union and Grant. You know where it is?" Mona had an authoritative air about her, as well as a commanding presence.

"Yes," I said. "I pass it every night when I take Baba out for a walk." *I hope she's interested in ordering a jacket.*

"How much is that jacket in the window?" Mona wanted to know.

The jacket was the Flyaway, designed for a much smaller person. That was the *Harper's Bazaar* jacket, which was how I thought of it. *How to persuade her it would be totally wrong for her?*

"It's fifty-five dollars, but I don't think it's the right design for you."

"No? Why not?" She challenged me.

"You need something longer, with straighter lines. Look, I'll show you what I mean." I brought out a different design, longer, a more tailored look. And I took the Flyaway out of the window. *It won't even fit over half of her, but she might as well see for herself.*

Mona gave me a long, appraising look. I hurried on. "Tell you what. I'll take your measurements and draft a jacket in muslin that I think will look just right on you. You can try it on, we can make whatever changes you like, and then we can choose the leather." I waited.

She smiled, and suddenly she was less threatening. "Okay, kid, do it."

I brought out my measuring tape, and we stood in front of my full-length mirror. She watched me carefully. I measured her bust, her waist, the distance from the back of her neck to her waist, the length of her arms. Holding my hands around her waist, she pirouetted in front of the mirror. "I have a pretty good shape, don't you think?" I freed my hands and stepped back, not saying anything. "How long will it take before I can come in for a fitting?" Every question was like a challenge.

"Today is Friday. I can have it ready for a fitting on Monday. All right?"

"Sure, kid. Here's thirty dollars as a deposit. Why don't you stop in at the bar tonight for a drink? On the house."

"Fine! I'd like that! Thanks a lot."

She gave me a wave, and moved grandly out, a ship in full sail. I closed the shop about seven p.m. and walked around the corner to the bar. As I stepped in, I looked around and saw only women. *Oh, it must be ladies' night! Hmm. Oh well, what the hell.* I sat down at the bar, nodded to Mona and ordered my usual rye, straight up with a soda chaser. I had learned that by drinking rye whisky in California I would get hundred-proof, and by ordering soda on the side, I could sip the whisky all night. I had also noticed that when I did this, people were impressed and got the idea I was a two-fisted drinker. Far from it! I was just saving money. Also I had learned that bourbon and scotch made me sneeze. As I sat down at the bar, two women approached, one on either side of me, and scooched their bar stools close to me. *How nice, what friendly people! And most of the women in the bar seemed to be very friendly. Some of them were sitting very close together, with their arms around each other. They must be part of a club or fraternal organization.*

"Hi," said the woman on my left. "I'm Lucille."

"Hi," I gave her my hand. "I'm Rhoda Pack."

The woman on my right leaned over toward me. "I'm Betty. You live around here?"

"Yes," I said, *sensing a chance to recruit more customers.* "I have a custom leather shop around the corner on Grant. I make custom leather clothes for women."

"Is that so?" They inched closer. Suddenly Mona leaned over the bar and, fixing my new friends with a heavy glare, remarked, "This lady is a friend of *mine.*"

The two women reacted as if they'd been stung. Lucille said, "Oh, excuse me, I have to go now." She slid off her stool and faded away. Betty, on my right, moved her stool away a bit, patted me on the shoulder, saying, "See you around, kid," and also disappeared. *I was a bit disconcerted at the time, but didn't think much about it.*

"I'll have that muslin ready for a fitting on Monday," I said to Mona. "Thanks for the drink." Mona waved at me, giving me a big grin. "Any time, kid."

It took me fifty years to figure out what was really happening that night. Mona's Bar turned out to be one of the first openly lesbian bars in San Francisco. At the time, I thought the event was a bit mysterious, but put it out of my mind.

Mona was delighted with my new design, and ordered a skirt to go with it. She became one of my best promoters, and I began to get a lot of women customers after that. I don't know whether they were lesbians or not, it didn't matter. They were good customers who appreciated my work.

One of Mona's friends turned out to be a mining engineer who had inherited the business from her husband. She always brought a bottle of whisky with her, and would come just before closing, so we would have a chance to talk after her fitting. She was not very tall, but husky, with a strong Texas accent. She had dyed red hair, a husky voice, and a deep, lusty laugh. She loved to tell stories about the men she worked with, how she managed to let them know who was boss. I listened avidly. Here was a woman who enjoyed men, and even more, enjoyed her power. She could pick and choose a partner for the night, the weekend, or even longer, she said. This was real role reversal, and I was fascinated.

Betty Lou was perfectly at ease with her life. She told me about her husband, who had died in a mine accident, and how she was determined to carry on.

"It was tough," she said. "Nobody believed a woman could do this job. But I put on a hard hat and went down into the mines with the men. I was the one who paid them, and money is a strong tool when it comes to building respect. I listened to their gripes, and I understood personally their worries about safety. I listened to the women too, the wives and girlfriends. I never pretended to be a man." She took a long swallow of her drink, and helped herself to the salami, bread, and cheese I had set out for us.

"You know, I knew about the business end too. I was the bookkeeper, and Frank shared everything with me. We had a real working partnership. I wonder if I'll ever have that again." Then, changing the subject, she said, "I really like the quality of your products. Will I really be able to wash off the dirt and grime? Not that I'll wear this beautiful coat or jacket to work, but just in case..."

"I can't guarantee anything," I said. "But if you're willing to stay in touch, I'd like to know just how well real dirt and grime washes off. From my own tests, this new stuff called 'Woolite' works really well." I stood up. I didn't have Betty Lou's capacity for drink, and I was starting to feel a bit light-headed. "I have to take Baba for a walk," I said. "Can you come by next Thursday to pick up your garments?"

She gathered herself together, corked the bottle with a firm tap, and slung her new handbag over her shoulder. "Right," she said. "I'm going back to Texas on Saturday; I'll be winding up some contracts this week. I'll be glad to test your jackets with some real dirt!" She laughed, and we walked out together. Baba was already standing eagerly by the door.

I never expected to hear from Betty Lou after she picked up her order, but I got a wedding announcement from her later, which said simply, "I decided to let someone else go down in the mines! And by the way, the Woolite does keep my jackets clean. How's your dog?"

Chapter Twenty-Six:
The Cape-Stole

‿

B Y 1953, I HAD TWO SEAMSTRESSES, two handbag stitchers, a finish-er, and a cutter. I still did the entire pattern making, and sometimes cut linings as well. Once in a while I cut a jacket or dress, but not often. The shop was full of containers of white glue, which I was testing for the manufacturer, as well as samples of detergent, among them Woolite, which I tested for stain and spot removal from the smooth Angola leathers we used.

I needed a sample maker, someone who had imagination as well as an in-terest in trying new things. The two women who currently sewed the jackets and coats we produced were happy to do their assigned work and go home. I wanted someone I could talk to about possibilities, someone with more sew-ing skills than I possessed.

I had joined the Fashion Group, an organization of women designers and manufacturers in San Francisco, and I talked to them at one of our monthly meetings. I had learned from experience in teaching and at the O.W.I. that networking can get you anywhere you want to go.

Isabel Collins, one of the most creative women in the group, came to my rescue. She told me about a sample maker she had recently interviewed, a woman who was currently working in alterations at I. Magnin, and how impressed she was by her. Isabel said that she didn't need a sample maker, but she thought Elaine would be perfect for me, and she gave me Elaine's phone number.

Elaine and her boyfriend, Kelly Thomas, showed up around five-thirty Friday afternoon, and Baba greeted them with his usual careful checkout. They passed easily, and he relaxed. I was a bit surprised that Kelly came along, but it was Friday, after all, and they probably had a date. Kelly was about six feet two, with muscled, tattooed arms, and he hovered protectively over Elaine, a slim woman of medium height, with curly red hair and a confident air. Kelly wore an open-at-the-collar shirt with the sleeves rolled up, but Elaine was dressed conservatively in a blue gabardine suit. They looked appreciatively at the clothes in the showroom, and then we went into the empty workroom. Elaine immediately picked up a jacket and inspected it minutely.

"This is very careful work," she said.

"Yes, that's how I built my reputation, and we all take pride in what we do. We work as a team." I looked at her closely to read her reaction. "I need someone who will help me realize my designs, someone who can take a partly thought out idea and help me bring it to completion. In other words, I need a sample maker. Does that kind of job interest you?"

Elaine's eyes lit up and she gave Kelly a swift glance. "It's the kind of job I've been looking for," she said. "It's just that I've never worked with leather, but I like a challenge. I'm a pattern maker too, and I know how to adjust patterns for custom work as well."

I could hardly believe my good luck. I asked her what she was currently earning, and we decided that she would start at that figure, and if all worked out well, we'd increase it at the end of a month. We all beamed at each other, and Kelly spoke up.

"We were going into Chinatown for dinner. Would you like to join us? I have some business to do with Chingwah Lee, a collector. You might like to meet him. He's an interesting character."

I liked the idea, and after feeding Baba, the three of us walked to Chinatown, which was only about six blocks away. Walking south on Grant Avenue, we plowed determinedly through window-gawking tourists and Chinese shoppers with bulging net shopping bags. We turned, finally, into Old Chinatown Lane, a quiet alley that housed Chingwah's studio, and I felt as if I had entered another world. Pigeons swarmed all around us. *I wondered if some of them ended up in Chinese restaurants as broiled squab.*

A bell tinkled as we opened the door into a quiet, lushly carpeted room, jammed with statues, huge vases, glass cases filled with rare porcelain, masks and paintings on the walls, incense tickling our noses. Chingwah was a collector of porcelain and rare Chinese antique pieces of all kinds; furniture, artifacts, paintings, knickknacks. I stood riveted. I knew all about the "don't touch" rules in museums, but here was a museum where everything seemed to invite touching!

Chingwah came toward us, arms outstretched. a cheerful, round-faced man, dressed in a silk mandarin coat, his eyes sparkling behind gold-rimmed glasses. He looked like a Buddha statue come to life, with the same roundness of shape. Chingwah ushered us into his back room that housed a small sink, stove, table, and a cot in one corner. I realized that the main studio was where he really lived, surrounded by his treasures, and the small back room was just a convenient place to rest. Kelly had told me that in addition to being a respected elder in Chinatown, Chingwah was a Greyhound Tour leader, as well as a consultant to the Avery collection of Chinese art at the DeYoung Museum. I wasn't prepared for this gentle, courteous man who treated us as if he had known us all his life.

Kelly took out a small package from an inside pocket and laid it on the table. Chingwah unwrapped it carefully, and held a small ivory figurine to the light.

"This is beautiful," he said, smiling. "You have a good eye, Kelly. What else did you bring me?"

"You asked for some Xing Dynasty porcelain," he said. "And I'll bring that by tomorrow. I also have a small Ming vase that I think you will like."

Chingwah clapped his hands. "I'm sure I will!" He beamed. Looking at me, he said, "Kelly is with the Merchant Marine, and he makes frequent trips to China. The U.S. hasn't established an open trade with China yet, but there isn't anything illegal about private trade, especially when it's all in cash." He laughed. "Well, shall we go have something to eat?"

We walked out into the quiet alley where tall brick apartment buildings lined the sides and it was so still that the people who lived there must have been either out shopping or working. The quiet space conveyed a sense of closeness and security. Laundry hung from windows and the usual clouds of pigeons hovered overhead. We emerged onto Grant Avenue and walked down to Kearny Street. Along the edges of Washington Square, old Chinese men played "Go," dominoes, or chess, ignoring the hooting horns on Kearny. Children rolled around on the grass and throngs of shoppers conversed in high-pitched voices. The amazing thing about this square was that the moment you stepped into the grassy area, the voices seemed muted.

Going back up Kearny, we made our way to Sam's restaurant. Sam's was one of the oldest in Chinatown, and one of the few that catered almost exclusively to Chinese customers. We walked through a narrow aisle alongside a row of chattering Chinese cooks, slamming frypans, stirring noodles, our noses filled with heavenly smells, to a twisting iron staircase at the rear of the kitchen. Upstairs was the eating area, where the food was brought up on a pulley from the cooks downstairs.

A beaming waiter greeted Chingwah, and after chatting a bit, he seated us at a round table and brought Chingwah a pint of whisky. This was, apparently, a standard routine. Chingwah poured us all a shot of whisky, then raised his glass.

"To friendship!" He paused, and then added, "To business!" He touched his glass to Kelly's and tossed off his whisky. "Do you have any special requests?" Not getting an immediate response, he asked, "Shall I order for you?" We nodded, and I spoke up.

"Just make sure you have at least one dish without nuts, especially not almonds," I said. "I'm violently allergic to peanuts too—really all nuts. If they fry with peanut oil, I'll have to have anything that's steamed, broiled, or boiled. Sorry about that, but you don't want to be around if I have an attack!"

Chingwah spoke hurriedly to the waiter, and they pored over the menu. "It's all right," he said to me. "We will have enough variety so that you will be okay. Can you eat Peking duck?"

"I think so. I've had it before, and it was fine. I really like it."

Chingwah nodded at the waiter, and leaned back in his chair. "Where did you go this time, Kelly?"

As Kelly and Chingwah launched into what was obviously a business discussion, Elaine and I continued to check each other out. I found out that she was born in St. Louis, Missouri, and had come to San Francisco the previous year to escape what she considered the stifling atmosphere of her town. She had taken a few art courses at the San Francisco Art Institute and soon ran out of money. She had been working at I. Magnin for six months, and had met Isabel Collins when Isabel was showing her line to the Magnin buyer. I had come along at just the right time for her.

We talked about plans I had to expand the range of items in the collection. Since joining the Fashion Group, I had learned to refer to the things I made as my "collection." I was beginning to feel like a professional! Elaine told me that while she would be helping to make alterations on the exclusive designer models I. Magnin carried, she would often make secret sketches on how she would have handled a particular cut of fabric or the shape of a jacket. Her eyes sparkled as she told me of some of her ideas. We were so engrossed in our conversation that we didn't notice Kelly and Chingwah had stopped talking and were staring at us as we gestured, pulling at our sleeves or collars to make a point.

"Oh!" We exclaimed together, and laughed. "Are we ready for dessert?" I asked, innocently.

Chingwah reached over and took our hands. "You two were really off in your own world," he said. "I was wondering if you would like to come back to the studio for a nightcap," he said. Kelly was nodding his head vigorously, so both Elaine and I agreed. But as we walked back up Grant Avenue, I began to have second thoughts. It was getting late, and I wanted to walk Baba before going to bed. When we got to Old Chinatown Lane, I stopped and begged off.

"I really ought to go home," I said. "I still have to walk the dog. You go on, and Elaine, I'll see you tomorrow. Thanks, Chingwah, I hope to see you soon again."

"Come any time, Rhoda. You will be welcome."

They disappeared into the darkness of the alley, and I walked through Chinatown, across Broadway and up Grant Avenue to home. San Francisco's North Beach and Chinatown were safe places to walk alone. There were always people around, all day and all night, it seemed. It was midnight, and the streets were crowded with people coming and going into nightclubs, bars, and restaurants. Music from coffeehouses filled the air; there was a cheerful hustle and bustle to the evening. I held back the urge to dance my way down the street, although no one would have paid any attention to me anyway.

Baba was happy to see me, and we ran down Union Street to the park. I loved the smell of the neighborhood. I held the smell of baking bread from the Venetian Bakery on the corner of Grant and Union in my nose and throat and then inhaled the perfume of freshly cut grass in the park. It was a heady combination. The fog was slowly drifting through the trees, softening the streetlights. I had had so much to drink that I didn't feel at all cold, in fact, it felt good to run along with Baba.

Elaine called the next morning to say she had a hangover, and asked if it would be all right if she came in at one o'clock instead of ten. Of course it was all right with me, and I took advantage of the extra free time to call Elizabeth Hanna. Elizabeth and I had remained friends after my divorce from Jim, and she had left me a message, saying she had some important news for me. I knew that Elizabeth had recently returned from Sweden on a buying trip for her exclusive art gallery on Sutter Street, and I wondered what kind of treasures she had found.

We made a date for lunch, and Elizabeth showed up at eleven-thirty with something rolled up in brown paper. Her brown eyes glittered as she thrust the package at me. "Open it!" she demanded.

I did as she commanded, and was astounded by the hides that fell out. There was a small, exquisitely soft piece of white capeskin, and a piece of black textured leather. I looked at her. "Are these samples of Swedish leather?"

She grinned, practically jumping up and down. "Yes! I met the representative of the leather company that produces these hides, and I told him about you. He would be very happy to send you some sample hides for you to try out, and if you like the way they handle, we might be able to do some business. This would give you an alternate resource."

I was full of "yes, buts"—and started to ask about prices, delivery, minimum quantities, payment, shipping, but Elizabeth interrupted me.

"Never mind the details right now," she said. "I'll explain over lunch. I just think these are beautiful skins, and there's a Swedish leather trade show coming up that I'll tell you about. Wait till you hear my idea!"

There was no stopping her, so I told Alix I was going across the street to the New Tivoli with Elizabeth for lunch, and if anything important came up, she could come and get me.

It turned out that Elizabeth had gone to a Swedish Trade Fair to buy some rare sculptured glass and had met this leather representative there. He had noticed Elizabeth's leather coat and wanted to know where she had bought it. As Mr. Holmgren looked at the photos in my catalogue, and listened to Elizabeth's story about me, he became more and more interested. He said that Swedish designers didn't understand the possibilities of the leather he was processing, that they were stuck in what he called a prosaic point of view. He and Elizabeth worked out a deal whereby he would include any number of sample hides I wanted to order along with the Swedish glass she bought, to save shipping charges and tariff duties. Then after I worked with the leather, we would see about further business. Inasmuch as Elizabeth had an importer's license, I wouldn't have to worry about buying the leather directly. I would work with and through Elizabeth.

What a deal! I could hardly take it all in. But there was more to come.

Elizabeth said that Mr. Holmgren was particularly interested in promoting the use of his leather by fashion designers, and he was hoping I could produce a design that he could submit at the next Trade Fair in December. It was now August.

I looked at the white capeskin hide Elizabeth had brought me. It was small, soft, exactly the right thickness for a design I had been thinking about.

"How soon can you get me a dozen hides of this white capeskin?" I asked her.

"I can wire him today, and ask him to ship them by air," she said. "You could have them next week. Do you have something in mind?"

I was too excited to eat, and pushed my spaghetti aside. "Boy, do I! And I think this capeskin will just do it. I already have a prototype in muslin that I've been working on, and the size of this skin will be just right. What kind of leather is it? It feels like goat, but it has a smoother texture."

Elizabeth didn't know, but guessed it was some sort of sheep, from Finland, maybe. She really didn't care; she was more interested in the final product. We ordered coffee, and allowed our unspoken thoughts to fill the air around us. I sighed, and reached out to grasp Elizabeth's hand. "What a good friend you are. You have never wavered in your support of me and of Jim. I don't know how to thank you."

"Just keep working. That's thanks enough."

As soon as I got back to the shop, I began to sketch my idea for an evening wrap that would be a stole with pockets. I don't draw very well, and do better with muslin in my hands, draping fabric or leather on a form, but I needed to work out some of the layout problems in my head. For years I had been bothered about where to put my "stuff" when I went out in the evening. I hated carrying a handbag, never knowing whether to leave it on my chair or table when I got up to dance, and not wanting to have something dangling from my wrist or shoulder as I cavorted around the floor. I had to have a place to put a handkerchief, a compact, plus lipstick and a comb, money, a driver's license, and my keys.

I had in mind an all-purpose evening wrap that would have pockets to hold my small essentials. I came up with a cape-stole that crisscrossed in front, held in place with an attached belt. That meant that the wearer could put her hands in the pockets (one on each side), and also have her arms and hands free for whatever. The pockets were deep enough to hold everything I needed.

I was so excited that I worked straight through dinner, and only came up for air when Baba nudged me to say it was time to take him for a walk. Munching on some bread and cheese, my poodle and I went to the park. When we got back to my apartment door, the bocce ball players were beginning to come out from the court in the back of the New Tivoli restaurant across the street. I unlocked the door leading to my upstairs apartment, and Baba and I went home. *What a lovely way to live!*

When Elaine arrived the next morning, I showed her my sketch, and the tentative pattern I had laid out. Part of it was already in muslin on the dress form, and I asked her if she thought it would work. We fiddled around with the proportions, finished laying it out in muslin, and she stitched it up. My excitement grew as I watched the idea take shape, and I decided to try it in suede. I had a few skins left over from an order, and Arturo cut it for me. It was beautiful! I could hardly wait for Elizabeth's Swedish skins to arrive, so that I could see if it would work as well in capeskin. This was the most satisfying part of my life. I really didn't like selling, although I liked working with individual people. The thing that stimulated me was working through a design that fulfilled a purpose, a design that also incorporated simplicity of line and movement.

When the skins from Sweden arrived by air the next day, Elaine and I could hardly wait to unwrap the package. The hides were even more beautiful than the sample, evenly skived (which many of Wood & Hyde's skins were not), soft, and supple. We gave Arturo the paper pattern and asked him to be extra careful in cutting. I called Elizabeth and asked her to come over that evening to see her "Swedish" design.

As the shop bell tinkled, I buttoned the belt on the cape-stole and walked around the partition, my hands in the pockets. I was gratified by her gasp of admiration. We decided to ship it immediately by air to her agent in Sweden, because the annual trade fair in Stockholm was due to happen in about three months. I had another sample stitched up and hung it up for display in the shop.

There was a special car show scheduled for Monterey that month, and Ron Partridge happened to come by on a day when one of my customers, an intern in a law firm, was trying on a few jackets. She was quite beautiful, and Ron asked her to try on the cape-stole, as well as several coats. Sylvie was delighted, and as we sat around chatting, Ron brought up the subject of the foreign and special car show in Monterey.

I suggested we cover my two-cylinder Renault in perforated black Swedish leather as an entry in the show, but we decided it would be too complicated, and besides, I didn't have enough of that leather in stock. Instead, Ron suggested that he and Sylvie take the cape-stole and several coats to the show, where he would photograph her in that setting. I was too busy to go, although it was certainly tempting. Ron and Sylvie made arrangements to go, and I put several garments together in a garment bag for Sylvie to take with her. The photographs that Ron took were simply sensational. I had them enlarged and put them up on the walls of the shop.

As soon as the cape-stole was shipped, I put it out of my mind, and began to work on a few suits I planned to show at the San Francisco Art Show, to be held in Union Square. One day in late December, Elizabeth burst into the shop with a telegram from Mr. Holmgren.

"Rhoda! Guess what! Your cape-stole was awarded first prize at the trade fair, and Mr. Holmgren presented it to the king of Sweden! He also mentioned that the king intended to present it to his mistress, but that was an item to be kept in strictest confidence."

I laughed. "Maybe the cape-stole wouldn't fit the queen. Are we going to get a photograph?"

"Of course! And Mr. Holmgren is going to send an official letter with a photo of the king accepting the garment."

Wow! I sank into a chair in the showroom, digesting this information. *What did all this mean? It meant more publicity, but it wouldn't mean any more operating capital; I was still operating on a shoestring, and paying myself just enough for rent and bare essentials. Maybe I should get a bookkeeper, or some advice about pricing. Decisions, decisions! Life was getting too complicated. I wished I had someone to share my problems with. Part of me liked the independence, and part of me wanted some solid support. Virginia Woolf wanted a room of her own, but she already had money and family support. I wondered if I would ever find a mate who would give me both.*

Chapter Twenty-Seven:
Ric Skahen

⤸

O NE EVENING IN LATE DECEMBER 1953, the phone rang. It was Felix Rosenthal, a friend of Jean Coria's, who also was an architect. I didn't know Felix very well; just that he was an Austrian Jew, who had barely escaped from Austria as Hitler was marching in. Felix had been on an ill-fated refugee ship that was refused entry into U.S. American ports and roamed the ocean for months before being allowed to off-load its passengers in Cuba. Felix had spent a couple of years in Cuba before he made it to San Francisco. However, he was an optimistic person, who never talked about that experience. Jean had told me his story, and also that Felix had closed off that part of his life, especially since his parents hadn't made it out of Germany.

"Hey, Rhoda! How would you like to come over for dinner? There's someone here I'd like you to meet. Yes, and I have some good steaks. Will you come?"

Well, of course I would go. I walked up Union Street to Felix's apartment on Kearny, happy to be walking through San Francisco's special evening light, stopping to look back at the fog rolling in over the Golden Gate Bridge. When I opened the door to Felix's apartment, wonderful smells greeted me, and there was Felix, a spatula in his hand, wearing an embroidered cooking apron he'd bought in a flea market. A wiry man about my height, with a drink in his hand, rose from the couch.

"I'm Ric Skahen," he said, his grip hard and solid. "A friend of Felix from way back." Holding onto my hand, he drew me down on the couch beside him. I shrugged out of my coat and leaned back for a longer appraisal. He had sandy hair, an intense look in his pale blue eyes, a half smile on his face. "You're Rhoda, right? Felix has told me a lot about you." And then, calling to Felix in the kitchen, "Hey, Felix, how about fixing Rhoda a drink?"

Just exactly what had Felix told Ric about me? I found his comment unnerving.

Felix brought us a tray with a bottle of Scotch, three glasses, a bucket of ice. He drew up a chair, informing us that the dinner was ready, simply warming itself, waiting for us. He looked at Ric and then at me, beaming. Launching into a long speech involving Dr. Richard Skahen's accomplishments as a physician, he said that they had first met several months previously, at a concert at the Goethe Institute on Post Street. The Goethe Institute was the cultural arm of the German Embassy, offering avantgarde films as well as monthly performances of quartets playing primarily German music. Ric smiled deprecatingly at Felix's compliments, and then started telling us stories about his years in postwar Germany, where he served as a physician with the Army. He was a chain-smoker, lighting a fresh cigarette from the still-burning butt of the previous one. He seemed exotic, an inhabitant of a different, glamorous world.

Ric became more voluble as the evening wore on, and he and Felix began to reminisce about castles on the Rhine, and the superiority of Rhine wines over those of France. I was beginning to feel the effects of all the alcohol, and decided to go home. It was almost midnight, and Ric rose also, saying he would take me home. I was looking forward to walking down the hill in the cold San Francisco night, but Ric insisted that we drive down, because he would then continue on to his own apartment in the Fillmore/Union Street district. He was remarkably steady driving down the hill, double-parked in front of the shop, opened my door, and escorted me to the doorway of my upstairs flat. He said Felix had given him my phone number and that he would call.

The next day I phoned Felix and asked him to tell me a little more about Dr. Richard Skahen. I wanted to know if he was married, what kind of physician he was, whether or not he was in private practice, things like that. Felix told me that Ric had been married, that he was now divorced (which turned out not to be true), that he'd gotten his medical training by enlisting in the army, that he worked for the Veterans Administration, and was studying for his Board examinations in Pathology.

I thanked Felix and hung up. I didn't tell him that I was fascinated by Dr. Skahen, but that I was uneasy about him. I had been struck by his penetrating blue eyes that could be steely or twinkly. He was a captivating storyteller, compelling my attention by keeping his eyes on my face. He seemed so wired; I wondered what he did for relaxation.

When Ric called the following evening, I wanted to see what another encounter would bring. I told him to pick me up about seven, and to ring the bell at the doorway next door to the shop, number 1463.

We went to an elegant restaurant on Pacific Avenue where the headwaiter recognized him. Walking to a secluded table, I noted the upholstered red plush walls, punctuated by gleaming mahogany panels, the soft amber lights, and the general atmosphere of Victorian depravity. The place looked like a movie set.

Ric ordered oysters on the half shell and gin martinis, then, with one raised eyebrow, he asked me if he should order. Since his manner implied agreement, it was easy to nod yes. The waiter hovered obsequiously and Ric ordered steaks rare, baked potatoes, and salad. Then he and the wine steward huddled over the two-foot high-menu, while he selected exactly the wine he wanted. Settling back into the padded banquette, he fixed me with his intense eyes and asked, "So what are your goals in life?"

Speaking spontaneously, I responded, "I want to continue living a creatively intense life, but I also want to marry and have five children. I'm sure I can manage both. What are your goals?"

At that point the waiter arrived with the wine, and Ric never did answer my question. He sampled the wine, rolling it around on his tongue, making a big show of hesitating before deciding it was suitable, and then waved acceptance at the waiter. While I was rapturously eating my oysters, Ric polished off his martini in two swallows, pushing his oysters listlessly around his plate. I love oysters, so I happily appropriated the ones he didn't eat.

Then Ric launched into a long story about where the particular wine he had ordered came from, and how he had wandered the German countryside, tasting wine. He liked hearing the sound of his own voice, and I didn't mind his talking while I ate. He polished off most of the wine, eating very little of his steak. We finished the meal with our salad and Ric ordered Calvados, an apple brandy for dessert. I was slightly dizzy from all the alcohol, but Ric didn't seem to be affected by it at all. He simply became more animated. I was relaxed, floating along, buoyed by food, wine, and stories, feeling happy to be slipping around in a mellow haze. When Ric suggested going to visit a friend in Chinatown, I agreed readily.

We parked in the Chinatown garage, and as we walked up Grant Avenue, the neighborhood suddenly was familiar. When he turned into Chinatown Lane, the location of Chingwah Lee's studio, I knew where we were going, but decided not to say anything. Chingwah opened the door, greeted Ric with a cry of surprise, and then, turning, embraced me, saying, "Rhoda! How good to see you again!"

Ric looked from Chingwah to me, trying very hard to keep his composure, and finally blurted out, "You know each other?" His tone indicated disappointment and disbelief.

"Oh, yes!" Chingwah chuckled. "We are very good friends. Come in! Come in!"

He waved us to two comfortable chairs at the back of the room, disappeared and quickly reappeared with a bottle of whisky and glasses on a tray. I wondered how these two men had connected, amused by Ric's reaction. It turned out that Ric had met Chingwah when he was a medical student at UCSF medical center, and a friend had introduced him to Chingwah. Ric liked the warm, comforting atmosphere of Chingwah's studio, and apparently came often to study there.

As they talked, Ric asked Chingwah about his brother. It turned out that Chingwah had a brother who owned a bar in the next alley parallel to Old Chinatown Lane, and Ric suggested that we go there for a nightcap. *Another nightcap? Oh, well, I could still walk, and neither Ric nor Chingwah seemed to have any trouble with their feet, so I might as well go along.*

We walked to the back of the lane, down some steps, along a fence, and then up some more steps, and we were in another alley very much like Old Chinatown Lane. There was a neon sign proclaiming the simple word "Bar," and we opened the heavy paneled door. Chingwah had mentioned that his brother didn't drink, and that he measured every drink he made very carefully, but he didn't prepare me for the art on display. Explicit, erotic sculpture was displayed all along the walls of the room, in elegant cases, well lit. There were sculptures of erect penises, carefully detailed vaginal labia, as well as sculptures from India, depicting women and men copulating in a number of different positions. I was astonished, and went from case to case, studying the exhibits closely. This was a very private museum.

Ric and Chingwah were already sitting at the bar, drinking brandy, chatting with Chang, Chingwah's brother. They were talking about business, and Chang, with his glasses and serious manner, was alert and watchful, keeping his eye on a customer who seemed to have fallen asleep on his arms at the end of the bar. I sat down between Ric and Chingwah, curious about who owned the erotic sculptures.

"Oh, those are all mine," Chingwah said. "I figured Chang needed some art to liven up this place." He nodded at his brother, raising his glass in salute. Chang regarded his brother sourly, and we left soon afterward.

Standing outside in the cool fog, I announced that I needed to go home before I fell down, and Ric and Chingwah each grabbed my arms solicitously. We walked to Grant Avenue; Chingwah left us to go home, and Ric and I walked to the garage. It never occurred to me that Ric might be too drunk to drive. He was ebullient, animated, and still electrically charged. I was happy to be going home.

Ric wanted to come up for coffee, but I said no, thanks, and stumbled up the stairs. Baba greeted me ecstatically, and I groaned. I put my head under the cold water tap, wondered if I could let Baba out alone, decided I couldn't, and dragged myself down the stairs and out to the park. Remarkable how resilient the human body is! We made it to the park and back, and I thought again how lucky I was to have Baba.

On my next date with Ric, I decided to invite him to dinner, and to try to really get to know him. Ric showed up at five-thirty on a Saturday night, with flowers, a bottle of wine, full of cheerful exuberance. Baba greeted him warily at the door, and hovered at his heels as they walked down the hall to the kitchen. I had prepared hors d'oeuvres, pickled eel on crackers, along with some aged Roquefort cheese, and Ric wanted a Scotch on the rocks with the appetizers. Of course I joined him, and turned the heat down on the roast beef in the oven.

Baba followed us into the living room and lay down near us, his head on his paws, never taking his eyes off Ric. I remembered Emily's warning about Baba's possessiveness, but I had dismissed the idea. I asked Ric about how, where, and why he had joined the Army, and I especially wanted to know about his decision to specialize in pathology.

He said he'd been born in Minneapolis; his mother was a young Polish immigrant and his father was an elderly Irish lawyer. He explained that his last name was the same as a river in Ireland, and that he never knew his father. "My father died soon after I was born," he said. "I think he was probably in his seventies, and my mother, who was the cleaning woman in my father's office, was in her twenties. Well, at least he married her." He took a big swallow of his drink, and changed the subject.

"I went to undergraduate school in Seattle, Washington, and then came to UC San Francisco for postgraduate work. That's where I met my good friends, Stuart Lindsay, Salvatore Pablo Lucia, also Henry Kaplan and his brother Richard. Henry is a famous radiologist and Dick is a lawyer. You'll meet all of them, they're wonderful people."

I could smell the roast beef, and decided we should eat. So we went back down the hall to the dining room. Thank heaven, the roast beef was just right; the fresh asparagus not overcooked, and the potatoes were done. Ric opened the wine he'd brought, again making a big show of smelling the cork, swirling the first taste around in his mouth before pouring my glass. He told me that his friend, Dr. Lucia, was a past president of the Gourmet Society, and was extremely knowledgeable about wine. He said that "Sal" could tell which province a particular French or German wine came from, and that he, Ric, was trying to be just as knowledgeable. I thought this was pretty funny, but the wine really was delicious, wherever it came from.

I had assumed that since Ric was always talking about wonderful restaurants and cafes he'd visited in Europe, that he was a gourmet when it came to food, and that was one reason I was so careful with the dinner. It turned out that Ric was a true gourmet. He cared more about the quality of what he ate than he did about the quantity. He was also more interested in the quality of the wine that accompanied the food than the food itself. As far as I was concerned, the food I cooked was a top priority. For me, cooking was an expression of love and respect for my guests.

We walked back into the living room after dinner, and Ric embraced me passionately. Unfortunately, Baba immediately inserted himself between us and pushed his heavy body into Ric, knocking him off balance. And then Baba mounted his leg! Ric was furious and raised his foot to kick Baba. I knew that would be disastrous, so I grabbed Baba, scolded him and led him into the dining room, closing the door. We had already cleared off the table, so I knew Baba wasn't likely to make off with any leftover roast. I stood for a minute outside the closed door, smothering laughter, composing myself.

In the living room, Ric had lit a cigarette and was staring out into the street. I sat down beside him, gently stroking his face, trying to apologize for Baba and for my hidden laughter. Suddenly he grabbed me, kissing me with deep, almost unbridled passion. I leaned back, holding him at arm's length, and told him to get undressed and get into bed. I said I had to go to the bathroom and I'd be right back. I needed to put my diaphragm in before we went any farther.

This was a different kind of lovemaking. It was rough, demanding, intense, without any of the gentle foreplay Bill and I had created. Nor was it the naive, clumsy suddenness of my early experiences with Jim. This was commanding, take charge, ownership lovemaking. It was not give-and-take.

After he came to climax, and we were lying quietly next to each other, Ric asked me to get us a drink. *I was not prepared for the suddenness of the lovemaking nor was I prepared for the feeling of being used. I felt detached and uneasy.* I put on a robe and went into the kitchen, taking a good look at Baba, who was lying peacefully under the dining room table. He lifted his head as I came through the door, acknowledging me. I brought a tray with glasses, ice, and the Scotch back to the bedroom.

Ric patted the space beside him. "I'm sorry," he said, stroking my back as

I sat down. "I got carried away." He nuzzled my neck, and the stiffness in my spine slowly softened. We began to talk, and I heard more about his early life. Ric's mother, a young widow, had inherited enough money from her elderly husband to buy a house and start a new career.

Ric said he didn't remember much about his very early years, but he did remember that when he was five, he was sent away to boarding school, and often he was one of just a few boys who stayed at the school over the holidays. Later he went to military school, where he learned to drink and smoke. Feeling close to tears, I began to caress him, holding him close, stroking his thin shoulders, feeling compassion wash over me. I felt tension seep out of his back, and as he relaxed against me, we began to move together in closer collaboration. This time I too came to climax, and we smiled at each other. *He's so thin! His body is almost like a boy's. His hip bones dig into me. What a difficult life he has led!*

I kissed him gently, and sat up. "I have to take Baba for a walk," I said. "Let's finish our drinks, then we can walk down to the park, and you can tell me more about your life." Ric looked a bit surprised, but didn't say anything, and I quickly stepped into my clothes. I wanted Baba and Ric to get better acquainted, since I had a feeling I would be seeing a lot more of Ric Skahen.

Outside on the sidewalk, I handed the leash to Ric. "Get to know him," I said. "He's a good dog, just a little protective." The night was clear and cool, a half- moon hung low over the trees. As we sat on a bench in Washington Park, gazing at the Catholic church on the other side of the park, Ric began to talk again.

"When I graduated from high school, I applied for a scholarship from the University of Washington, and got it. I wanted to get as far away from the Midwest as I could." I nodded. I knew that feeling! "Two things happened. I met an older woman, a professor of Biology, and married her. I was only nineteen, she was thirty-five. She taught me a lot, and not just about biology." He gave a harsh laugh. Standing up, he began to pace back and forth. "The marriage didn't last very long. My mother came out to Seattle, and created a scene. Tried to get the marriage annulled, called my wife a child-stealer." He stopped, and said, "Let's go back. That's enough about me for a while."

I called Baba, and he came running. "Pat him," I said to Ric. "And give him this treat." I fastened Baba's leash, but he came around and sat beside me, ignoring Ric.

Ric spent the night, and the next day we all went out to Drake's Bay, over the Golden Gate Bridge, through Marin County, out to the Pacific Ocean, where Sir Francis Drake is said to have landed. Baba charged over the sand, chasing the sand pipers, dashing in and out of the waves, jumping and twirling in ecstasy. Ric and I walked along the beach, inhaling the salt air, savoring the wind in our hair. Ric took my hand, and we climbed a small rise, sank down on the sand, and rested our backs against the rocks. I spread out a blanket I had brought, and weighted down one end with my picnic basket, the other end with some rocks. Once we were settled, Ric began to talk again.

"I look at this sea, which seems so pure, yet I see all the pollution spewing out of the ships which empty their slops into this ocean, all the run-offs from rivers full of pesticides, and I groan." His voice was pensive, and his look abstracted.

Where does his vision come from? I see only the foam, the waves crashing on the beach, the gulls swooping overhead, the cormorants hovering, then diving. I am enthralled with the interplay of the forces of nature around me, and feel myself melting into the atmosphere. Ric's dark assessment of what we are looking at jars me.

"You don't know how we poison ourselves, and the world around us," he said. He lit a cigarette, absently offering me the pack. "Oh, I forgot. You don't smoke." He cupped his hand around the match, shielding it from the wind. Inhaling deeply, he dug the match into the sand. "When I was in Germany, I watched farmers walk their fields, spraying pesticides over their crops, not realizing that they were inhaling the poison they were spreading. What fools we are!" He wrapped his arms around his knees, and stared into the sea.

Baba bounded up to us, spread his legs and shook himself, spattering sand and brine, then lay flat, grinning with delight. I scratched his wet head, and then he was up again, chasing madly after a gull which had landed next to him. I laughed and turned to Ric. "Perhaps the sea knows how to cleanse itself," I said, "even if the farmers don't." He looked at me as if I were speaking in a foreign language.

"Don't you understand? We have the technology to kill or to cure ourselves! We can't do it with romantic mythology! Science and education are the only answers. There are answers to diseases that are killing us, if we only had the courage to accept them. Research! Research! That's the only answer!" He jumped up. "Let's run. Let's run on the beach!" He reached down and pulled me up. We ran along the shore, feeling the hard, wet sand between our toes, Baba keeping pace.

Finally we made it back to our sheltered spot among the rocks, and flopped down on our blanket. "Hey!" I said. "Time for some food!" I unpacked the picnic basket, filled with leftover roast beef, mustard, French bread, cheese, and a bottle of wine. The rocks were warm against our backs, the sunlight danced off the waves. I wriggled my toes in the sand, feeling caressed by the wind. I didn't realize how hungry I was until the first morsels of bread and meat slid down my throat. I opened the wine and offered Ric a glass. He was sitting a little bit away from me, once again with his knees drawn up, staring at the sea. He shook himself, as if shaking off a bad dream, turned and gave me his lovely Irish grin, his green-blue eyes softening. "Mmmm," he said. "This is the way to live!"

After polishing off the bread, meat, and wine, we snuggled down for a lovely nap, warmed by the sun and cooled by the breeze off the ocean. The change in the wind woke us up, and we packed our gear quickly, anxious to get back to the car before the evening fog came in. We drove back over the Golden Gate Bridge, the setting sun sparkling off San Francisco's windows, in a state of quiet happiness that only a day at the beach can bring.

Rhoda in 1952
(photo by Rondal Partridge)

Grant Avenue Street Fair

First Grant Avenue Street Fair (photo by Gene Wright)

Benny Bufano at the Street Fair

June 12, 1960   SAN   FRANCISCO   SUNDAY   CHR

EVENTS

Two Days of Art and Beards on the Beach

By J. L. Pimsleur

SEVEN SUMMERS AGO, the merchants along upper Grant avenue started something that was to become a San Francisco tradition. One Sunday morning, they blocked off Grant avenue between Union and Green for an all-day, outdoor festival—which evolved into a midget-sized Mardi Gras. The first Left Bankish exhibits of Bay Area artists and craftsmen were accompanied by plenty of singing, dancing and the offbeat humor of a bright new local comic, named Mort Sahl.

☆ ☆ ☆

Next week end, San Francisco will hold its seventh annual North Beach Arts Festival, sponsored this year by the Upper Grant Avenue Art Association (UGAAA). According to UGAAA President Jay Hoppe (the wily proprietor of the Coexistence Bagel Shop), this year's festival figures to be the biggest of them all. For the first time, two streets will be blocked off: Grant avenue from Vallejo north to Union. Commencing at 10 a. m. Saturday, the jubilee will run through the entire Father's Day week end, winding up a 8 p. m. Sunday, Hoppe estimates that with

Chronicle publicity

Chapter Twenty-Eight:
Grant Avenue Street Fair

⁓

R IC SKAHEN WAS A DETERMINED SUITOR, and I was wooed in a way I had never experienced before. There were daily telephone calls, flowers, and clever messages slipped under the door of the shop. Ric discovered that the radio in my shop was always tuned to the local classical radio station and that I loved classical music. When we talked about music, I found out that he liked baroque as well as twentieth century music in general.

Ric asked me about which composers and performers I liked, and then he turned up with recordings of those artists and those compositions. This man did his homework, and it paid off. In no time at all, I found a corner of my living room filled with a gigantic loudspeaker cabinet, consisting of six speakers and a complicated high-fidelity mechanism that stacked several seventy-eight rpm records at once. I was very impressed by the wonderful sound that came out of that Stephens speaker, which, I was told, was made by a very famous man. That was how he moved in. First the huge speaker cabinet, then his shaving kit, and gradually his clothes.

I gave Ric a key to my apartment, and he gave me a key to his apartment as well. Our dates usually ended up with us in bed in my flat above the shop, although sometimes we went to his place on Steiner Street after a symphony concert or the opera. I managed to overlook the fact that Ric consumed an enormous amount of alcohol, and was a chain-smoker. He never seemed drunk, and everyone I knew smoked, even if I didn't. Smoking made me cough, and gave me a headache.

We had lots of parties in the Grant Avenue apartment, and I met Ric's famous friends. There was Dr. Salvatore Pablo Lucia, chairman of the local Gourmet Society; Dr. Stuart Lindsay, a pathologist with his own practice in Redwood City; Dr. Henry Kaplan, radiologist at Stanford Hospital in Palo Alto; and many other scientists and researchers. They all regarded Ric fondly, and let me know that they thought I was a stabilizing influence on him.

In fact, Ric arranged for Dr. Lucia to take me dancing at the Fairmont Hotel, claiming that he had to work nights at the Veterans Hospital in Oakland, where he was the resident pathologist, but actually it was because he didn't dance very well. Sal was a wonderful dancer, and during all the evenings we went dinner dancing, he kept up a running commentary on how wonderful Ric was, how intuitive he was when looking through the microscope, and how brilliant he was.

Then there was Stuart Lindsay. Dr. Lindsay was a professor at UCSF, and Stu took me to UCSF faculty parties, where there was lots of music and dancing. I began to realize how carefully Ric had planned his courtship. All of Ric's friends seemed to be anxious to impress me with Ric's accomplishments. They were solicitous and almost paternally fond of Ric. They were sure Ric wanted to marry me, and were persuading me to accept him.

This kind of courtship was completely new to me, and I was flattered. My relationship with Ric was getting serious, and I kept expecting him to say something about marriage. We had been seeing each other several times a week, as well as every weekend, for about six months. I decided to bring up the subject directly, and one evening after dinner, when we were listening to music in the living room, I asked him how he felt about having children. I said that since I was in my late thirties, I wanted to have a child before I was forty, and that I really mourned the loss of my first child.

Ric became very agitated, and began to pace up and down the room. Finally, he sat down beside me and, with less than his usual composure, told me that his divorce from his wife in Seattle was not final. I rose, turned off the hi-fi, and in icy tones, told Ric to leave. There was something so forbidding in my voice that Baba stood up suddenly from his comfortable pillow near the stove, and came to my side, ears alert. I went to my handbag, fished out the key to his apartment, thrust it at him, and demanded the key to my flat. I told him to come back when he had clarified his status. Then I marched to the door and opened it. I could barely contain my rage.

Ric was absolutely stunned. He handed me my key and went out, without a word. After he left, I fell apart. I flailed around the apartment, picking things up and throwing them down, Baba following at my heels, looking anxious. I was too pragmatic to break anything, although I wanted to. I wanted to smash dishes, glasses, but I didn't. I didn't weep; I jumped up and down and screamed. I was so angry. I felt betrayed. Grabbing my coat and Baba's leash, I fled down the stairs and ran with Baba to the park. Only there did I sit down and try to collect myself.

All sorts of random thoughts ran through my mind. *Should I pack up his clothes, shaving stuff, and pajamas and mail them to him? Would he go to Seattle and settle things? Would he come back? What about the hi-fi and the Stephens speaker system? Why and how did I get myself into such a mess?* On and on my mind raced, around and around. Baba came back to me and put his head on my lap. I gave him a hug, and took a big breath. We went back to the flat. I fixed myself a strong Scotch on the rocks, drank it down, and went to bed. I figured, like Scarlett O'Hara, that I would figure things out tomorrow.

The alarm woke me at seven-thirty, and I groaned. Remembering the anguish of the previous night, I pulled the covers over my head, reluctant to get up. But the alarm woke Baba also, and his cold nose pushed under the covers. Sitting on the edge of the bed, my head in my hands, I concentrated on the day's chores, and tried to put Ric out of my mind. After a quick breakfast, I took Baba to the park, came back to the shop, and unlocked the door. It was only eight-thirty, and I knew I would have half an hour to further collect myself.

The phone rang, and I heard Ric's voice. Just as I was hanging up, without speaking, I heard him say, "I'm off to Seattle. I'll call you when I get back." I said goodbye and hung up. By this time, I was limp, and decided that when my staff of workers arrived at nine, I would go back upstairs and try to recover some equilibrium. I left Baba downstairs, and went up the back steps to the flat. I don't remember much about the rest of the day.

Boris called, and as soon as I heard his voice, I began to cry. He said he'd be over at six, right after work, and I felt better. Boris, my good friend and steady, calming spirit, was an insurance executive, a refugee from China via Germany, whom I had met at the same time I met Bill. Boris had helped re-design the flat, and throughout the reconstruction, had been a voice of pragmatism. "How much time will this take?" had been Boris's steady question. And "Let's do it now," had been another of his themes. He rang my bell, carrying Chinese food, a bottle of excellent wine, and after a tearful greeting on my part, we settled down to some serious talk.

Boris insisted that I make a "Pro/Con" list of my feelings about Ric, goals, alternatives, and myself. When we got to the alternatives, Boris was eminently pragmatic. He wanted to know how I felt if Ric were to show up in a few days with solid evidence of a clear break with his former wife. "Did I love Ric?" Boris wanted to know. "Did I love him as much as I loved Jim?"

That was a hard question. At thirty-six, I was not the woman I was at twenty-one. Too much had happened in between. I didn't realize that I had succeeded in creating a shell around myself, a carapace constructed to shield me from unexpected blows. I was not as trusting or as open as I had been. I told Boris that I didn't think I would ever be able to love as openly or as completely as I had once done. Boris was important to me; he was a good confidante and counselor.

I told Boris that I wanted security, and the fact that Ric was a physician, studying to be a Board-certified pathologist, meant that his future was solid. He had a good job at the Veterans Administration Hospital, and he had a lot of solid friends who believed in him. He was interesting; I liked him, and he was a moderately good lover. I had to admit that I did not love him as deeply as I had loved Jim, but I believed that the depth of a first love couldn't be replicated. I was uneasy about his chain-smoking and his drinking, but all of my friends drank, including me. Boris listened and nodded thoughtfully.

As we finished the bottle of wine, I lifted my glass and said to Boris, "If Ric comes back with solid evidence that he has divorced his wife, I'll probably see him again." I paused. "I may even marry him." Boris leaned over and kissed me on the cheek. "Let's see how it works out," was all he said.

By the time Ric called, about a month later, the pros had begun to outweigh the cons. I remembered his concern about the environment when we sat on the beach at Drake's Bay; I remembered his willingness to testify against Standard Oil by doing autopsies on fish poisoned by an outflow from a Standard Oil refinery. I remembered his comments about discovering abnormalities in microscopic sections of cells he had looked at under his microscope. He kept finding abnormalities overlooked by other pathologists. I realized why his scientist friends held him in such regard. I decided to see him again.

Ric rang my bell at seven o'clock on a Saturday night, and I greeted him warily, deliberately holding back an impulse to embrace him. We sat down in the living room with Scotch, cheese, and crackers, and I waited for him to start talking. After a long pull on his drink, he reminded me that his wife was a professor of biology at the University of Washington, and he had two children by her, a boy and a girl. *That was news—that Ric had two children!*

He told me that his wife did not want the divorce, and he had been reluctant to push for final papers. He said that until he met me, he hadn't intended to marry again. He said he hadn't felt married for a long time.

When I didn't say anything, he pressed on, saying he wasn't sure whether he could afford alimony and take on the responsibility of marrying again. I wanted to hear details, not explanations, and finally I asked him to tell me directly what happened. Had he filed the final papers? Did they agree on alimony? What, exactly, had happened? It was hard to get straight answers from Ric. He was great at spinning stories, but short on details.

Finally, he said that he had filed the necessary papers, and that his divorce would be final in another year. They had agreed that he would establish a trust fund for the children at that time, and that she did not want any alimony. The date of that conversation is burned into my brain; it was December 15, 1954. I felt as if a clear, fresh breeze swept through the apartment, even though the windows were closed, and rain was beating on the windows. I took a deep breath, and opened my arms.

Ric was different after he came back from Seattle, softer somehow, and more attentive to my physical needs when we made love. We continued to give parties at the flat, and soon our place became a haven for friends and acquaintances of Ric's who happened to be in North Beach in the wee hours of the morning. We learned not to answer the doorbell after one a.m.

Our salons became a magnet for artists, musicians, poets, writers, and painters as well as for their audience: the doctors, lawyers, architects, designers, and businessmen who were also our friends. All together they created a dynamic, electric environment that made every party we gave something special to remember. This kind of interaction happens in every generation anywhere in the world where artists and the people who care about them get together.

Beniamino (Benny) Bufano was a friend of Ric's, who rapidly became a friend of mine, too. Benny was a sculptor who worked in granite, steel, marble, and mosaic tile. His statues were large and dramatic, and Benny himself had a dramatic approach to life. He said he wanted his work to be available to everyone, not just to people who could afford to buy it. All he required was a studio to work in, and somebody to supply the materials. He would do the work, and offer it to the public, free. Benny was a small man, five feet tall, with a large head, a Roman nose, and deep set eyes which crinkled at the corners. He always looked as if he was privy to some private joke, and was simply waiting for you to invite him to tell the story.

Benny was an intense pacifist, and he cut off the index finger of his right hand at the knuckle (he called it his trigger finger), which he sent to President Woodrow Wilson, to protest the American entry into World War I. Benny was the darling of the San Francisco Press Corps, and someone from the San Francisco Chronicle introduced him to the owner of Moar's Cafeteria. Benny created three magnificent mosaic murals on the walls of the cafeteria, and instead of payment, he accepted free meals for the rest of his life. Unfortunately, Moar sold to a chain of restaurants in the 1950s, and the murals disappeared. Also, unfortunately, Moar's ceased to exist before Benny died, in 1970, so Benny lost his permanent meal ticket.

I introduced Benny to Nobuo Kitagaki, who had opened a shop next door to mine, on the corner of Grant and Union. Kit and his father, a master carpenter who had learned his trade in Japan, worked together making screens and cabinets. The Kitagaki family had been sent to special camps for

Japanese Americans in 1941, after Japan attacked Pearl Harbor. They went first to Arizona, and then to Illinois. After the war, Kit managed to go to the Art Institute in Chicago, and became a designer and an artist; his parents went back to Oakland. Kit had designed and made the screens for the dining room in my upstairs flat, and he became one of my closest friends.

Benny and Kit liked each other immediately; they both felt a kinship in their sense of being on the fringe of society's mainstream. Benny got most of his mosaic materials from Italy, especially the gold tiles, and he managed to acquire the materials he needed through his many connections. Benny had created a group of bas-relief sculptures that he wanted to exhibit, and I could see that they needed to be mounted on wood in order to be properly displayed, so I asked Benny to bring his sculptures around for Kit to look at. The three of us, Kit, Benny, and I, decided on some beautiful pieces of redwood that Kit had in his shop, and Kit mounted Benny's sculptures.

Then, of course, we had to have an "Opening!" Ric loved parties, and he shared my love for art and artists, so we planned the opening for a Saturday night, and invited our friends. I told Benny he could invite a few friends, but Benny invited the entire Press Corps, plus Mayor Christopher, and they all came! Ric provided hundred-proof alcohol from his laboratory and I mixed it with grapefruit juice. We served salami, French bread, and cheese, but the hungry reporters who came inhaled everything, and after the food ran out, settled on just the drinks. It was a great party and since the mayor was one of the revelers, the police left us alone. The street quieted down around three a.m. Benny did manage to get a lot of publicity, plus a few commissions for additional work. Kitagaki also made some important contacts, so I felt satisfied. I had an awful headache the next day, but the excitement of the evening made up for it.

One of Benny's friends was a jovial giant of a man, Placido Melchior. Placido was six feet two inches tall, and he worked in the marble yards in South San Francisco. Placido used his connections at the marble yards to get Benny a lot of the marble he needed. Placido also enjoyed polishing the nude female torsos Benny produced, as well as helping to finish Benny's granite animal sculptures, which were exhibited at different places in Golden Gate

Park and elsewhere in San Francisco.

One evening at dinner, Ric was telling a story about his time in Germany, and about the wonderful street fairs he had been to in Munich, Heidelberg, and Strasbourg. Benny said, "Let's have a Grant Avenue Street Fair!" and the idea took root. I went over to see Peter Macchiarini, who had been the first craftsman on Grant Avenue. His shop was located close to Green Street; my shop was at the other end, closer to Union Street. Peter was an established jeweler, whose beautiful work drew San Franciscans from all over the city. Peter liked the idea of a street fair, and we began to make plans.

We agreed that all the artists on the block at that time, Gretchen McAllister, a maker of small delicate paintings, Gene Wright, a photographer, and I would be the committee to create the rules of the Fair and do all the planning. We decided that only artists who made their living by their art, or who had participated in a group exhibition, or had a one-person show anywhere, would be invited. We didn't want amateur painters, and we didn't want entrepreneurs who would be selling other people's work. We felt very strongly that artists should be able to reach their public directly, without going through a middleman. We also believed that good art and crafts would crowd out amateurish art and cheaply made crafts. We were all deeply committed to our work, and we wanted to get our ideas across to the general public.

I offered to apply for permission to close the street from Green to Union for one Sunday, and I went to the police department to get the permits. Since this was the first street fair in San Francisco, it took all of my powers of persuasion to get them to even consider it. Two policemen and a City Hall representative came to inspect the street, and luckily, Benny was in my shop the day they came. The City Hall rep knew Benny, and from the way they greeted each other, I knew we would get our permit. The main thing they worried about was getting a fire engine through the street in case of an emergency.

We promised to keep the center of the street clear, and to make sure that the artists' exhibits would stay close to the curb. Once the permit was assured, we could work on publicity. Through my connections with Herb Caen and other reporters on the Chronicle, we managed to get good newspaper coverage. I also got free air-time on the radio and an appearance on KCBS TV. We got the word out.

We met regularly in the upstairs banquet room of Finocchio's New Tivoli restaurant, and gradually invited other people to assist in the planning. Felix Rosenthal came, and since he had participated in the street fairs Ric described, we had a first-hand idea of what some of those village fairs looked like. Felix suggested that we make big paper chains, like the ones children make in kindergarten, and stretch them across the street, from apartment rooftop to apartment rooftop. I pointed out that we would have to get permission from the landlords on the block to get up on the roofs, but Felix said he would take care of that, and he did. I wasn't sure how he was going to fling a paper chain across the street from one roof to another, but Felix was an engineer as well as an architect, and I figured he would work it out.

On the day of the Fair, we got up at dawn and Kitagaki, Benny, and Placido arrived to move Ric's huge Stephens speaker cabinet down the narrow steps from my flat to the street. Then they lifted it onto a flatbed truck at the corner of Grant and Union. Everybody was out in the bracing air of a San Francisco summer morning. Felix and his crew were up on the rooftops, flinging the weighted paper chains across the street; people were arriving with their tables and artwork; the entire street was humming.

We moved the sound system, seventy-eight-inch vinyl records and all, down to the truck, connected everything, and at nine a.m. we blasted the street with "The Prospect Before Us," by William Boyce, which is a beautiful eighteenth century baroque piece of music. The first Grant Avenue Street Fair was officially open. Bruno Iacopi had made room in his shopwindow for paintings by Emmy Lou Packard, and other merchants on the block had also contributed window space. Painters, craftsmen, graphic artists, cabinet-makers, weavers, photographers, all came. Most of the artists who came to the first Grant Avenue Street Fair are now famous.* (See Appendix)

In the middle of the day, Ric was called to the Veterans Hospital in Oakland, where he was the resident pathologist, to do an autopsy, and no one was really in charge of the music. He had stacked up a bunch of records before he left, at eleven-thirty, and when I looked at the stack at noon, I noticed that half of the records had melted. Kit and Placido immediately rigged up a tent cover for the sound system, and by one-thirty we had the music going again. We found out later that the Sunday of the Fair in July 1954 set a record for heat.

My cutter at that time was a large Italian woman, Felicia, who decided that we should invite our committee to the flat for a spaghetti dinner, to celebrate the day. She brought her own large aluminum pot for the pasta, another for the sauce, and spent several hours preparing a fantastic sauce. I don't remember where the bread, wine, and cheese came from, but it was all there by six o'clock. Ric came home about that time, and we had the first celebration of the first Grant Avenue Street Fair.

It was like a family party. We sat at the open windows of my flat, looking down with satisfaction, waving to the Italian families across the street, who were also at their windows. We had asked the artists to let us know their reaction to the day, and whether or not it was economically successful. All the reports were positive, and my belief that good art would crowd out bad art was vindicated. Our artists reported that their best pieces went first, and all of them had sold well. We toasted each other, and declared that we had established a tradition. From now on there would be an annual Grant Avenue Street Fair.

The Fair is still going on. The principles we established eroded over the years, and commercial exhibits have crept in. However, I still feel a deep sense of satisfaction at having helped to create it.

A lot was happening in North Beach during those years. Felix Rosenthal was a friend of Enrico Banducci, the owner of the "hungry i," which was a nightclub located in a brickwalled cellar at 599 Jackson Street near Pacific. Felix helped to design the interior before the "hungry i" opened, and Felix asked his friends to help create the lighting he had designed. This required collecting tin cans, stripping off the paper, and cutting holes in the tins, using the patterns Felix had created. Then we placed the tins over candles in small glass containers, and when the candles were lit, the light through the star and diamond shapes in the tins created a wonderful effect. Enrico was delighted, and so were we.

The hungry i was on the Greyhound Tour, and Luba, Enrico's wife, decided that the tourists should be offered some snacks. That idea lasted just one evening. The tourists inhaled the small sandwiches of salami and cheese she laboriously produced, and Enrico decided that the entertainment would have to be enough of a draw. He was right. The hungry i became more popular, and tourists didn't have to be lured with free food.

Enrico brought Mort Sahl, Jonathan Winters, Lenny Bruce and Harry Belafonte, to name a few performers who got their start at the hungry i. It was a heady time. Mort Sahl's barbed political satire had never been done before. This was 1952, in the middle of the Joe McCarthy period, and everyone was afraid to talk to anyone about anything. Hollywood writers were accused of being Communists, and were blacklisted if they refused to name any of their friends whom McCarthy had accused.

I was entranced by Harry Belafonte and never missed one of his performances. Talking to him after one of his shows, I offered to make him a shirt out of cream-colored leather, if he wanted one. He wore it every time he was at the i.

Marriage to Ric Skahen, 1955

Leaving for Mexico on honeymoon

Baba

Chapter Twenty-Nine:
Marriage #2, Mexico; Diego Rivera

⤳

WE LIVED AT AN INTENSE PACE, that year of 1954. Something seemed to be happening every evening. When we went to the Basque restaurant on Broadway, we ended up inviting the guitarist back to the flat for after-dinner drinks and an impromptu performance lasting into early morning. Jean Varda also became a frequent guest, and one of his favorite subjects for discourse was his theory of how the history of humans should be written. According to Varda, that history should be based on how humans got rid of their garbage. That led to lengthy discussions about waste recycling, water purification, cultural reeducation (how to teach people to dig their latrines downriver, away from the input of the stream), and the use of microbes to break down industrial waste. The discussions ranged far and wide, from the practice of Japanese waste management, which compacted its waste and used it for fill to build housing projects, to Swedish projects for recycling excrement for energy. All the discussions were invigorating, aided and lubricated by plenty of alcoholic beverages.

The intensity of our social life matched the intensity of the work in the shop. We were getting more and more retail customers, and more and more orders were coming in from the few stores we were selling to on a wholesale basis. I hired a pattern maker, and a bookkeeper/secretary. The staff had grown to seven.

Ric went to Seattle in November, and when he returned, on November

15, he had the final papers for his divorce. He was exuberant. "Okay," he said. "Now we can get married!" That was how he proposed. He just took everything for granted.

All of my friends also took it for granted that we would formally marry some day, although I don't think anyone cared much about whether we were married or not. Everyone knew we were a couple.

We decided on December 31 for our wedding day, which meant we would have a combination wedding reception and New Year's Eve party. Ric had friends in Ajijic, Mexico, which was a small village on Lake Chapala, near Guadalajara. When Benny Bufano heard we were planning on going to Mexico for our honeymoon, he gave us a letter to Diego Rivera, who was an old friend of his. We would leave for Mexico on New Year's Day. It all seemed like an auspicious plan.

Ric was taking his final Board certification exams as a Clinical Pathologist in early December, and I intended to clean up all the work from the Christmas holidays by the end of the month.

When I told Eileen about the plans, she immediately said that she and Rossi would plan to stay overnight, and clean up the flat on New Year's Day. She said she wanted me to go off to Mexico without worrying about anything. What a friend! I loved planning parties, and this was no exception. The guest list grew and grew, and we ended up with about three hundred people stuffed into my tiny flat.

I packed our bags before we left for the marriage ceremony, which was conducted by a nondenominational minister at the Swedenborgian Church in San Francisco. He was a friend of Ric's, and I liked him. Since Ric had been brought up as a Catholic and I was a Jew, we decided that a neutral wedding ceremony, conducted by a philosopher, would suit us just fine.

I remember sitting in the flat alone, the day before the wedding, deciding to let in all the ghosts that had been whispering in my ears since the day I agreed to marry Ric. There was Jim, gazing at me mournfully from the corner of the room. "I'll never love him the way I loved you," I said to the ghost. "But he has a steady job, and maybe I'll be able to work at the shop part-time, and be a full-time mother. I'd like that." My father was in the other corner, wagging his finger at me. "You're not marrying a Jew!" he said. "I'm a citizen of the world,"

I replied. "Religion doesn't mean anything to me, and it doesn't mean anything to Ric, either." My father wasn't convinced, and scowled as he faded away. "I'm free!" I thought. I remember standing up and twirling around the room, defiantly, shooing away the ghosts.

Boris, Jean Coria, Eileen, and Rossi were waiting for us when we got back to the flat, after the ceremony at the Swedenborgian chapel, and people began pouring up the stairs. I didn't recognize everybody, and I asked Boris if he knew any of the newcomers. He didn't recognize many of them, either, and he volunteered to act as an unofficial bouncer. He managed to get the ones we didn't know to leave (they confessed to being party crashers, and were quite good-natured about it). After that, Boris stationed himself at the head of the stairs, checking politely on who had invitations and who didn't.

It was a wonderful party. People came carrying food and drink; all of my artist and designer friends were there, as well as Ric's scientific and physician friends. Bufano was there, and Ginny and Jerry Stoll came with their cameras. It was a kind of open house with people coming and going all evening. I don't remember when we fell into bed, but we woke to find not only Eileen and Rossi in the living room, but Boris on a sleeping bag. They had decided we needed some support, like breakfast and a ride to the airport.

I wore a red goatskin wrap skirt, with a short bolero jacket, and carried my cream-colored leather coat over my arm. I was dazed with happiness, and got on the plane feeling that I was truly launched into a new and exciting period of my life.

We were high over Southern California when lunch and drinks arrived, and as we toasted each other, I said, "Here's to our first child." Ric looked at me, and didn't drink. He mumbled something about wasn't it too soon to think about that, and then looked squarely at me, saying something like, "I can't drink to that."

I felt as if he had punched me in the stomach, and put down my own drink. How could I have made such a mistake? I looked out of the window and contemplated jumping out of the plane. Swallowing hard, I decided to make sure that I had not misheard him. Did he have other plans for our marriage?

"I'm not sure what you mean. You know how important it is for me to have a child. You have a good job at the Veterans Administration, why can't we have children right away?"

Ric then launched into a long discourse about how he wanted to leave the Veterans Administration as soon as possible, and find a partner with a hospital connection, so that he could set up his own pathology practice. Failing that, he said, he thought he could supervise the running of my business, and he had visions about how it could be expanded.

I was horrified. Ric supervising the leather business? Planning to work with me as my business manager? No, no, no! My own plans were to quit the leather business, and become a stay-at-home mom and homemaker. I wanted to lean on someone else for a change, feeling tired, at thirty-seven, from taking care of myself for so many years. We were obviously on two different paths. We had different expectations, different goals.

Suddenly I remembered a passage from The Crock of Gold *by James Stephens, an Irish poet, who wrote this prose poem in 1919. In the story, Angus Og, one of the two verbal gods, is speaking about happiness and common sense and love. He says, "since time began, men have but coupled with their own shadows. The desire that sprang from their heads they pursued—and women have mated with the shadows of their own hearts, thinking fondly that the arms of men were about them." He continues, "I saw my son dancing with an Idea, and I said to him, 'With whom do you dance, my son?' and he replied, 'I make merry with the wife of my affection,' but it was an Idea he danced with and not a woman."*

Had I mated with a shadow, and had Ric been making merry with an Idea? Was there a gulf between us which neither one of us recognized? I felt an icy hand grip my heart. I stared out of the window at the clouds below us, and began to take long, deep breaths. Standing up, I made my way to the back of the cabin, and stood with my back against the bulkhead, collecting my thoughts. *What were my alternatives? After we landed, should I go to the ticket office and buy a return ticket to San Francisco? Why should I do that? That would mean I would give up meeting Ric's friends in Ajijic, and give up meeting Diego Rivera in Mexico City. I was carrying Benny Bufano's letter of introduction to Diego, and was looking forward to meeting him. Maybe Ric didn't mean he never wanted any children, maybe he meant he just wasn't ready right now. Maybe I was overreacting. And so I argued with myself, and talked myself into lowering or at least changing my expectations.*

In the end, I'm glad I chose to compromise. We landed in Mazatlan, and stepped off the plane into warm, wet, tropical weather. We stayed in a small beachfront hotel, and swam every day. Oyster sellers woke us in the morning with their cries of "Ostiones! Ostiones!" I would slip out of bed, not waking Ric, and go down to the boardwalk, where I ate fresh oysters in the shell, sprinkled with fresh lemon. The hot Mexican sauce was too hot, but the lemon was just right. Ric was horrified when he found out what I'd done, sure that I would get sick. But I didn't. We flew from Mazatlan to Guadalajara after a few days, and then took a bus down a four-lane paved highway, which ended at Chapala. We found out that the governor of the province kept a residence in Chapala, and that was why there was such a good road. Our destination was Ajijic, a small village on Lake Chapala, which we reached by taxi, driving on a dirt unpaved road, full of potholes. Ric had two artist friends living in Ajijic, and that was how we ended up there. Ajijic was full of displaced neurotics, many of them alcoholics, and all of them enthusiastic party givers. We felt right at home.

Every evening at nine o'clock, the lights in the village went out, and candles began to burn brightly in all the foreigners' houses. Our friends told us that every evening different people were hosts, and it was possible to drift from house to house if the conversation got too boring. We stayed about ten days in Ajijic, and then flew to Mexico City to look up Diego Rivera.

We had the letter from Bufano to Diego, and we wanted to deliver it. I had the address in my handbag; it was somewhere near the University of Mexico, and I was full of confidence in my ability to speak Spanish. When we got into the taxi, I gave the driver the address, and he nodded. I had a map, and I showed the driver the map, pointing to the area. He nodded again, but I didn't know that he couldn't read a map, and that he would have nodded his head, no matter whether he understood me or not. I didn't help, either, because I thought I was saying, "Go straight ahead (derecho)," but I was really saying "a derecha," which meant "go to the right," and we kept going around and around a particular block. Finally the taxi driver pulled over to the curb, jumped out, and ran away!

We happened to be in front of a small shop, and I went in to use the telephone. I called Diego, and a woman speaking perfect English answered. When she heard where we were, she laughed, said we were only about three blocks away, and she gave me directions. I was relieved. *That poor taxi driver!*

Diego's house was soft pink stucco behind a low wall, which was covered with bougainvillea, and as we walked through the gate, down a flagstone path, we inhaled with pleasure a mixture of the scent of jasmine, roses and a pungent scent I couldn't identify.

A handsome woman opened the massive wood door and we entered a high-ceilinged room filled with lovely young women, and several huge easels on which stood partially finished portraits of elegant Mexican women. The young women, all painters, were putting finishing touches on the paintings, on the gowns, and on the lush backgrounds of jungle-looking leaves. I noticed that there was also a half finished portrait of a Mexican hairless dog on the lower right half of one of the portraits.

Diego came forward, and I found my hand disappearing into his. He was a tall man, well over six feet, and everything about him was massive; his hands, his head, his bearing, his voice. We followed him and his companion to the covered veranda surrounding the house. We sat on rattan curved chairs in front of a low table, already laden with food and drinks. Diego wanted to know all about Benny, what he was doing, and all about our connection with him. Diego was gently probing us as to who we were, and why we had come to see him.

I produced Benny's letter, along with a print of Benny's "Black Cat," which had become a collector's item in San Francisco. Diego looked at the print a moment, then wrote on the bottom, "With thanks to Dr. Richard and his wife Rhoda," the date and his signature. He handed the print back to us, saying something about the print being worth more to us than to him.

I asked Diego about the paintings that the women in the studio were working on, and he said he would tell us about his current work after we had finished eating. The lunch was different from any Mexican food I have ever eaten. There was barbecued goat, a delicious Spanish rice with shrimp, green beans, delicate tortillas with a distinctive flavor, and cool rum drinks flavored with lime. Dessert was flan with fresh sliced peaches. Ric and Diego did all the talking, while the woman to whom I'd not been introduced and I sat quietly. From time to time, she leaned forward and laid her hand on mine, giving me a sympathetic smile, but she never volunteered her name. I knew that Frida Kahlo had died the year before, and I assumed that Diego had chosen another woman to take her place.

After lunch, Diego led us back into the studio, and told us about the portrait I had noticed with the dog. He told us that he had accepted commissions from upper- class members of Mexican society, and that the young women in the studio were his students. They were learning how to mix paints, and how to acquire the nuances of layered color. Then he scraped away some new paint on the dog in the lower right hand corner, and part of a face appeared. He laughed, and told us that the real portrait of the woman he was painting was underneath the painting of the dog. If the painting was ever cleaned, he said, his opinion of that woman would appear, and it would be an expression of his own contemptuous attitude toward her and her class.

We talked about his mural at Rockefeller Center, and of his stormy relationship with Rockefeller. Diego shrugged, as if to say that all that silly business was behind him, and it didn't really matter. He did say that it was New York's and Rockefeller's loss, not his.

The story goes that while Rivera was working on his mural at Rockefeller Center, Abby and Nelson Rockefeller came by frequently to check on how the work was going. On one of those visits, Rockefeller noticed that Rivera had included a portrait of Lenin in one corner, a portrait that had not appeared before. Rockefeller objected to the portrait and wanted Rivera to remove it, but Rivera refused.

The Rockefeller management team immediately ordered Rivera to stop work and paid him in full. The Rockefellers tried to get the mural moved to the Museum of Modern Art, but the mural was vandalized before it could be moved. According to a KQED program on Diego Rivera, "one night in February of 1934, two of Rivera's assistants, strolling around midtown Manhattan, noticed a dozen fifty-gallon oil drums near the entrance of the RCA building. When they looked inside, they recognized the smashed-up shards of Rivera's mural. The piece had been hammered off the walls—Rivera—returned home, and retaliated by painting a replica of the mural at the Palacio de Bellas Artes in Mexico City."

I looked around the room once more, fixing it in my memory. We embraced, and Diego once more swallowed my hand in his. We left, and as we walked down the stone path to the gate, I kept thinking about the hidden caricature in the corner of the portrait of that elegant Mexican lady. Diego's style of painting, particularly in the portraits, had changed. It was softer somehow, with a subtler hint of the power that infused his mural painting. Those portraits were more traditional, more stylistic.

We hailed a taxi at the corner, and I simply handed the driver the card from the hotel, complete with photograph and address. I didn't trust my Spanish anymore. Our honeymoon was over, and we flew back to San Francisco the next day.

On the airplane, I dipped once more into a familiar inner dialogue. *Of all the comings and goings of the past ten years, how was this return different? Once more I felt uncertain and uneasy. I had a familiar feeling of panic, a hollow in the pit of my stomach, followed almost immediately by a physical straightening of my spine. Once more I realized with cold certainty that I had embarked on a voyage into unexplored territory without adequate preparation. How did I manage to disregard hints and messages, warnings and portents? Maybe I liked living on the edge of a precipice.*

At this point in my gloomy musings, a different part of my brain took over; I scolded myself for indulging in circular retrospection, and forced myself to think rationally about the immediate future. My responsibility was to my employees, and to my career. That was really my life. *Yes, I was married, but evidently my life would not change all that much. I had added a companion for the hours I wasn't working, and it was my working life that was my priority.*

I took out a sketch pad, and began to think about new shapes and new combinations of colors and textures. I didn't know how the colors and textures of Mexican fabrics would affect me, but I knew that Mexico itself, the people, the light, the smells, and sounds had become part of me. That first visit to Mexico stayed with me for a long time.

Running the business meant having several jobs. First, I had to decide about priorities. I had to decide which order needed to be cut first, so I had to sort the orders. So many jackets of such and such a design in the same color. How many sizes in each color? How many hides of one particular color? Sort them out for variations in tone and texture. How many linings, and what sizes? Figure out if we had enough leather on hand to fill the orders we had. I had checked Arturo's selection of the hides he would cut while I was gone, and now I needed to work double-time to catch up on orders that had accumulated. Then came a list of linings to be cut, inventory to check, and of course the bills, always the bills. My bookkeeper called, and we made a date for the following day, so that I could see exactly where we were. I took no salary. That's one of the hazards of a one-woman business. The proprietor ends up working for the employees.

I didn't enjoy the mundane part of running the business, and wished I could delegate that part of it to someone else, but it wasn't possible. Looking forward to future quiet evenings poring over fashion magazines, I doggedly plowed through the accumulated correspondence. Feverish impatience drove me that first day. My hands itched to start draping muslin, and then leather, on my dress form.

We had a steady stream of visitors, people who wanted to hear all about our trip to Mexico, and our social life continued at the same frantic pace as before. Eileen and Rossi Reynolds were the first to arrive, then Boris and Jean, George Kosmak and Kit, Felix and his new friend. We were in a heightened state of euphoria. Baba followed me wherever I went, lying down on my feet, demanding attention.

Then, a couple of weeks after our return, Ric announced that he was leaving the VA Administration, and would be joining his friend, Stuart Lindsay, in Lindsay's laboratory at Sequoia Hospital in Redwood City. I was so deeply immersed in the daily running of my business that his decision didn't make much of an effect on me. Ric hadn't asked for my opinion, he had simply announced it. However, after a few weeks of arduous commuting to Redwood

City from San Francisco early in the morning, and returning late at night, Ric suggested that we take an apartment in San Carlos. It would be easier for him to be at the hospital early in the morning, and since I was self-employed, he said, I could manage my time more flexibly than he could.

We did move to San Carlos, and I commuted to San Francisco, driving an Oldsmobile convertible, with Baba sitting upright in the backseat. I caught amused glances from buses that passed us; it looked as if I was Baba's chauffeur. I kept the flat above the shop, of course.

LET'S EAT WITH CHOPSTICKS

Celebrities enjoy eating Chinese food the Chinese way. A few of those seen in San Francisco Chinatown restaurants are Dinah Shore, Lucille Ball and Nat King Cole. How many others can you identify in the photos above?

44

45

Naming ceremony at Johnny Kan's restaurant published in center fold of Herb Caen's Guide to San Francisco: Helen Colcord, Benny Bufano, (Ricky's godfather) Rhoda, Ricky, Chingwah Lee (second godfather)

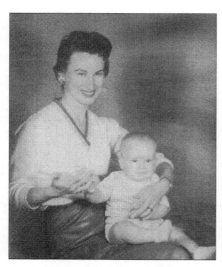

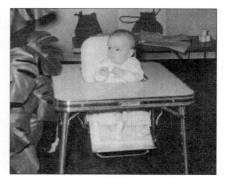

Photo of Rhoda and Ricky by Gene Wright

Ricky in the Shop

Chapter Thirty:
Birth of My Son: Changing Priorities

⁓

THOSE YEARS BETWEEN 1955 AND 1957 WERE A BLUR. This was a period in my life of intense creative activity. I buried myself in research; spent hours at the library, working out new designs for handbags and belt bags, as well as for jackets and coats. With all of the research, I was nagged by an internal doubt. I had not gone to design school; what did I really know? I did not credit my inventiveness; I doubted it, and felt that I was cheating when I adapted a Balenciaga sleeve or a Gres bias cut. Of course, I discovered early on that leather was all bias, and that I could achieve a drape in leather that Gres and Chanel had to work very hard to get in fabric. Any drape in leather had to be accommodated in lining on the bias, or the garment would fight itself. This was all very challenging, and I was totally absorbed.

However, I was thirty-nine in 1957, and I felt the pressure of having a child before I was forty. With all of the intense creative energy I was expending at the shop, the excitement of new designs, and an expanding list of stores that wanted to carry my designs, I experienced a surge in sexual energy. But Ric was not interested in being a father again, certainly not as interested as I was in being a mother. He was disappointed that his partnership with Stuart wasn't working out. I spent long hours weeping in frustration.

Finally, we moved back to the apartment above the shop, and Ric looked around for another association at a different hospital. Luckily, his reputation as a brilliant diagnostic pathologist was solid, and doctors don't often gossip about personal disagreements. Ric and Stuart remained close friends and trusted colleagues; they just couldn't adjust their different approaches to work habits.

After we moved back to San Francisco, Ric began to pressure me to put more emphasis on the wholesale business than on the retail business of the shop. The various buyers whose stores carried my line also began to pressure me to give up the custom business. The buyers at I. Magnin, Joseph Magnin, and Roos Brothers all wanted me to design lines that were exclusive with them. The buyer at I. Magnin in particular complained that my custom clients were the same as theirs, and that what I was doing was called "cross-trading." I resisted, primarily because I liked doing custom business, and also because I was worried about the difference in price and in gross profits.

So there we were. I didn't want to focus on changes in the business; I wanted to get pregnant, and I wanted Ric to maintain his own pathology business. I saw Ric as a steady provider, eventually allowing me to quit the business and become a mother. Ric wanted to make changes in the business, thinking it would provide him with a backup career. At the same time he was exploring a connection with Dr. Dave Singman in Berkeley, at Alta Bates Hospital. All those emotional currents were swirling around us.

Ric did make a connection with Dr. Singman, and I began to concentrate on getting pregnant, no matter what Ric thought about the time not being right. I decided to consult my gynecologist, and was advised to take my temperature every morning. When the temperature dropped, I was to make sure that I had intercourse with my husband, then I would have a good chance of getting pregnant.

One evening in February, Ric told me that he had to go to Seattle, to settle some business with his ex-wife, and he would be gone for two days. I took my temperature that morning, and to my despair, discovered that it had dropped. Would it stay down until he returned? I held my fingers crossed. When Ric returned two days later, I grabbed him passionately and insisted on having sex almost as soon as he came in the door. He was astonished, but pleased, and we had the best experience we'd had for a long time.

It worked! Six weeks later, I verified my feeling of nausea. I was pregnant.

It was not an easy three months. The only thing I wanted to eat was plain, unsalted crackers, but eventually that passed, and I began to feel wonderful. I began to eat everything in sight. However, the population of the neighborhood had begun to change, and more Chinese shopkeepers opened businesses. Next door to my shop, the Italian neighbors left, and a Chinese family moved in, establishing a laundry service in the front, living in the rear. The window of my bedroom opened onto an airshaft in the space between our two buildings, and the cooking fumes from our neighbor drifted into my bedroom.

I was in the habit of coming upstairs in the afternoon to take a nap, and one afternoon, shortly after the new neighbors moved in, I experienced a violent allergic reaction. Welts appeared all over my body, and I began to choke. I knew that I was allergic to peanuts, but I didn't know why I would be having an allergic attack when I hadn't eaten any nuts. Luckily Ric came home early that afternoon, and, taking one look at me, he grabbed his medical kit and gave me a shot of adrenaline.

He inhaled deeply, and immediately closed the window. "They're cooking in peanut oil!" he exclaimed. "We have to get you out of here!" He ran downstairs to the shop, told everybody what had happened, and asked Virginia, my secretary, to come upstairs and help me pack. We left for Berkeley that afternoon, and booked a motel. I'm sure that Ric's quick analysis and quick action saved my life.

The move to Berkeley was a good one. The people at Alta Bates were wonderful. The secretary in Dr. Singman's lab helped us find a house to rent on Spruce Street, and I met the doctors Borson; Harry, an internist, and his wife, Josephine, a gynecologist. I loved them, and Josephine became the godmother of our child. Harry's warning was explicit, the first time I saw him. He said, "Remember, Rhoda, all nuts are cyanide, as far as you're concerned." I never forgot his admonition.

I didn't gain much weight, and continued to work as hard as ever on the various collections I was now turning out. Finally, Josephine ordered bed rest in the hospital, and I reluctantly complied. I had a room in a ward which also boasted a small sun-room, and often left my bed to spread out pattern making paper to draft designs that had been in my head for a while. A nurse caught me on the floor, going over a design with my pattern maker, and sternly ordered me back to bed, sedating me with phenobarbital. I hated it, and kept trying to spit it out, but finally followed orders, and was rewarded by being released. I promised to rest every day.

We rented a lovely Berkeley house with an enclosed porch off the bedroom on the second floor. The house faced west and was flooded with sunshine. It was nestled in a depression in the hillside, and was at the bottom of a flight of steps from the street. It was quiet, secluded, and boasted a small garden with an apple tree. Baba was ecstatic, and ran around and around the front and back yards, exploring everything. The light that came in the casement windows on the north side helped our orchids grow, and Ric bought us a huge tropical aquarium. The owners of the house were on sabbatical, and had left the house furnished. I felt as if an angel had alighted on my shoulder. A Catholic family with eleven children lived two doors away; Peggy and her two daughters lived to our left; and a ninety-year-old man lived to our right. It was a peaceful, settled neighborhood.

Josephine told me that she didn't think I would be able to deliver my child normally, because the scar from the previous caesarean might rupture, and I'd better plan on having another caesarean. She and Ric thought it would be a good idea to have the baby in San Francisco, under the supervision of the chief of surgery, who happened to be a friend of Ric's. I still wanted to try for a normal delivery, but as soon as labor pains started, Ric rushed me over to Stanford Hospital, which was on Webster Street in San Francisco at that time. Ricky was born on October 1, 1957, weighing just five and a half pounds. But he was alive, and I nursed him. I couldn't believe my good fortune, and wanted him to sleep in a crib beside my bed. But he had to spend a few days in an incubator until he gained more weight. We spent ten days in the hospital, and each day I woke up in an apprehensive sweat, which didn't subside until I held Ricky in my arms.

The next three months were heaven. I was still pretty fragile, so I put an ad in the local papers for a "grandmother, to care for a new mother, age forty," and a wonderful woman answered the ad. She was Mrs. Baird, a matronly woman from Utah, in her sixties, who had come to Berkeley to take care of a daughter who had been in an accident. She lived in a trailer home in Richmond, and now that her daughter was well, said that she had been on the verge of buying a ticket home to Provo when she saw my ad. She decided to check me out.

What a lucky impulse that was for me! We liked each other immediately, and Ricky nestled quickly in her capacious arms. She stayed with us for four years. Mrs. Baird told me that she had raised four daughters and three sons, that she had three grandchildren, and that she was not a fancy cook. I loved her matter-of-fact directness, and the fact that she had specific boundaries. She said she was a Quaker by choice, a Mormon by birth, and she wanted permission to walk Ricky, in his carriage, to the Quaker church at the bottom of the Vine Street hill.

I sat listening to her calm, mid-western voice and felt a great peace descend upon me. We agreed that she would come early in the morning; she was willing to do light housekeeping, and she would leave at five-thirty. I was very tired, and I wanted to nurse Ricky as long as I could. When I told her that, Mrs. Baird patted me maternally on the head, picked up Ricky, and took him off to change his diaper. She was just what I needed.

Dr. Josephine Borson had warned me to be prepared to supplement Ricky's nourishment with solid food as soon as he showed signs of being able to tolerate it. By the time he was three months old, he was eating pureed vegetables, and draining both breasts. It seemed to be the right time for a ritual baptism. Ricky had already been circumcised, and both Chingwah Lee and Benny Bufano had expressed their desire to be godfathers. Neither Ric nor I saw any reason not to have as many prayers and good wishes for our child as we could, so we decided to have a big celebration. Dr. Josephine Borson agreed to be his godmother.

Chingwah and Ric talked to Johnny Kan, a famous restaurateur in San Francisco, and Johnny agreed to close his restaurant in honor of Ricky's naming ceremony. I hadn't known that Chingwah had appeared in *The Good Earth,* with Paul Muni during a brief stint in Hollywood, and that he was a very good actor. We had a marvelous celebration; Mason Weymouth took photographs, which appeared in Herb Caen's book, *San Francisco, A Guide.*

I fed Ricky some oatmeal before our dinner, and he went peacefully to sleep in his crib. Johnny Kan presented us with a framed rendition of Ricky's name in Chinese calligraphy, and Chingwah pretended to shave a small part of Ricky's head, near where a pigtail should be. The Borsons were there, as was Benny Bufano, Helen Colson, Chingwah's lover, and Peggy, our next-door neighbor. It was a beautiful evening, and Ricky slept through it all, waking up at an appropriate time during dessert. He was a remarkably happy child.

Ric and I had a serious talk in January. I asked him how he felt about my closing the business altogether, and becoming a stay-at-home mom. He was appalled, and launched into a long dissertation about how I was not that kind of person; that I would be bored, that I had a reputation to uphold, and why quit now, when my career was just about to take off? He argued persuasively that Mrs. Baird was absolutely capable of taking care of Ricky, and that I should pursue my career.

His argument fell on receptive ears. I had been working in leather since 1945, and was just on the edge, I felt, of understanding my medium. So I left Ricky in Mrs. Baird's care and went to work every morning, crying all the way across the bridge. Ricky began to howl as soon as I walked out the door, but Mrs. Baird told me that he stopped crying the moment I got to the top of the stairs and disappeared. She said that he looked at her, ready for the next bit of excitement, and gave her one of his dazzling smiles. I tried taking Ricky to work a couple of days, but found that I absolutely couldn't concentrate on anything.

The routine established itself, and gradually Ricky accepted my leaving, hardly looking up from his concentration on whatever contraption he was building. *Could there have been an unconscious push that allowed me to go back to work so soon? I was in the middle of tumultuous change. I had just become a mother, my marriage to Ric was only two years old; I was beginning to get some real recognition in the fashion world for my work. Was I really ready to give up my career? Could I do both? Maybe I could do both. Maybe I could be a mother and a creative designer; maybe I could be the person my mother never managed—an owner of my own shop. Maybe an unconscious wish to fulfill my mother's dreams was propelling me onward.*

I had joined the Fashion Group, an organization of women in the fashion business, designers, owners, and manufacturers, and had begun to win prizes for my designs. Yet I still felt I was not worthy of the prizes, because I hadn't been to design school. I felt like disowning the honors, while at the same time enjoying them. I didn't feel that I was as original in my concepts as other designers I knew, because I got so many ideas from the French designers in the magazines I studied so carefully. I didn't realize that everybody copies from everybody else.

The wholesale business was expanding rapidly, and for that reason I moved to a loft on Mission Street, behind the Emporium Department Store. With much misgiving, I gave up the retail business, the shop, and the apartment on Grant Avenue. I acquired three salesmen, and began to design three collections a year. By 1960, top retail stores carried the Rhoda Pack line, and there was great pressure on me to do special fashion shows. Retailers squeeze small manufacturers in many ways.

For instance, I was asked to design an exclusive line for Joseph Magnin, one for I. Magnin, and one for Roos Brothers. In addition, Goldwaters in Phoenix, Arizona, Marshall Field's in Chicago, Neiman Marcus in Texas, and Lord & Taylor in New York all carried parts of the Rhoda Pack collection. However, buyers at each store wanted me to do fashion shows of the entire collection, so they could offer custom orders to their special customers. As an incentive, they took out ads in newspapers featuring me and my designs. Bullock's Wilshire, in Hollywood, created a special corner for Rhoda Pack Leathers, and devoted all the windows on Wilshire for a display.

It was exciting, and the stimulation showed in the range of designs we produced. I designed a beautiful coat called "Le Fleur," all soft curves and a seamless collar. It won several prizes and was featured in most of the ads by my retail stores. Ten designers, including me, were invited to design a garment with Japanese fabrics as part of a special promotion. I did a dress of silk brocade, and lined a white leather coat with the same brocade. The outfit became part of a traveling exhibit, owned by the fabric makers, and finally ended up as a permanent exhibition in their showrooms in Tokyo.

I did a lot of traveling in those days. Joseph Magnin had branches in San Francisco, Palo Alto, and Reno, Nevada, and I did fashion shows in all those places. I traveled to Goldwater's in Phoenix, and to Marshall Field's in Chicago. In response to many requests, I added a holiday collection in which I used hand-embroidered sequins and beads on leather evening jackets, and black French lace laid over white or pink leather for evening skirts and tops. I branched out into fabric, doing a collection of simple dresses in knits and jersey, with leather jackets and coats lined with the matching fabrics. I became a huge fashion success, but the only year I broke even was 1960.

Small manufacturers like me, with limited financial reserves, have to borrow money to keep their factories going, and profit margins shrink. For instance, my leather came from Gloversville, New York, shipped "f.o.b.," meaning "freight on board," and the bill becomes due the date the raw material is shipped. By the time I got my leather, ten days after shipping, I would have about two weeks to fill the order and ship it before the end of the month. Retailers are supposed to pay their bills "E.O.M. eight percent," meaning that if they receive their goods before the end of the previous month, and pay their bills by the tenth of the following month, they can deduct eight percent from the gross amount. However, most retailers hold onto their invoices until the tenth of the following month, which gives them anywhere from forty-five to sixty days to pay their bills. That means that the small manufacturer has to have enough cash reserves to pay the employees, the taxes, and the overhead, while waiting for the invoices to be paid.

Of course, I didn't have enough cash reserves, and Ric was not bringing in enough money to support the business. I had to borrow money from the bank, and although I had established good credit, I still had to have Ric co-sign my loans. Also, there were all sorts of unexpected costs. If there was a rush order for a special store, I would sometimes order the leather shipped air freight, and sometimes we would work overtime. That meant an extra cost for raw materials, and extra money for employees. I could see the profit per item shrinking, and the cushion that retail trade gave me didn't exist anymore. Ric's income took care of our household expenses, and his liquor bill, but I had to make the business pay for itself, and increased orders did not mean increased profits.

I had a pattern of ignoring warning signs, and simply incurred more debt rather than cutting back on expenses. Joseph Magnin, Incorporated had gone into the invoice factoring business. That meant that this branch of the company bought a manufacturer's invoices for a ten-percent discount, and paid the manufacturer the net amount of the invoice (minus their discount, plus the eight percent that the retailer took) immediately when the manufacturer shipped their orders. Cyril Magnin knew I was struggling, because I had asked him to make sure his bookkeeper paid me on time, and he suggested that I use invoice factoring to provide needed cash flow. This is the same reasoning that politicians use when they borrow money to pay for public programs instead of raising taxes. I could have raised my prices, but I was afraid I would lose business. There's an old joke in the garment business that goes like this:

Two manufacturers meet on Seventh Avenue in New York, and one says to the other, "So, how's it going?" And the other one answers, "Oh, I lose money on every dress, but I make it up on the volume!"

It was that kind of silly reasoning that kept me going. By 1963, I realized I was practically broke. In San Francisco at that time, there was a way of going out of business that did not entail formal bankruptcy proceedings. It was possible to turn a business over to the Board of Trade. That Board would padlock the factory and sell off the inventory and all the machinery for whatever the sale would bring, and distribute the proceeds to the debtors. The manufacturer had to agree not to use the trade name for five years.

I liked the idea. I was tired of the strain of running an expanding business. I was doing four collections a year (including the holiday collection), traveling a lot, and struggling to meet the payroll and the overhead. Rhoda Pack Leathers was becoming too much of a business, and I was delegating more and more of the creative part of it to my sample maker. My four-year-old son was showing signs of unhappiness, and I decided the time had come to quit.

Mr. Hyde, of the Wood & Hyde Leather Company in Gloversville, New York, was my chief supplier of leather, and I had worked with him since 1950. He contacted some Montgomery Street brokers and businessmen, and they offered to buy me out. This group offered me forty-nine percent of the business, plus a salary, provided I would remain as the designer for the business. They would get fifty-one percent. That didn't appeal to me at all. I had a hunch that they would pressure me to design a less expensive line of leather clothing, and that there would be pressure to cut labor costs as well.

I remember that meeting very well. We met in my office, in the second-floor loft at 845 Mission Street, five men and me. I listened politely to their offer, and asked them to tell me what their vision of the business was. I asked them how soon they expected to recoup their investment, and what the budget would be for new designs. From the haziness of their answers, I had a pretty clear idea of what their bottom line was, and I said no.

Why should I give up control after all this time? Do I really want to continue this rat race? Finally, perhaps I can quit, and spend some time with my son. I think this part of my life is over. I'm tired, I want to get out.

Mr. Hyde looked sad and disappointed, but I knew I had helped him establish himself as a top purveyor of smooth leather that could be sponged off with soap and water, and he knew exactly what my contribution had been. He took my hand in both of his, and wished me well. After Mr. Hyde and the businessmen left, I called the staff together and told them what I had decided to do. We had about a week before the people from the Board of Trade came in to lock the shop. The cutter and the finisher told me that they would like to set up a business for themselves and wanted to know about the patterns. I told them they could come in during the evenings to copy the patterns, because the brass-bound patterns were part of the inventory, and were part of the assets. They couldn't take those, but they could copy the leather and lining patterns. If they wanted to go into business on their own, they would have a head start. I gave them the names of all the buyers in the stores we did business with. It was a validating feeling, knowing that the designs would live on, with other hands producing them.

Chapter Thirty-One:
San Leandro; Puerto Rico

A BOUT THE TIME I QUIT THE LEATHER BUSINESS IN 1963, other major changes in our lives occurred. Ric didn't get along well with Dave Singman at Alta Bates Hospital either, and we moved to San Leandro, where Ric had won the position of chief pathologist at Doctors Hospital. He now had his own business, and I thought that finally I would be able to assume the role of supportive housewife and mother.

We bought a house with a swimming pool on a hill in San Leandro, and Ricky attended a nearby elementary school. He was six, and he liked playing the trumpet. He quickly organized a small band of children who marched around the neighborhood, banging on pot lids and tambourines, leading them with his trumpet. I became the den mother of the neighborhood, supervising swimming pool activities.

Since I was accustomed to doing many things at once, I began to make braided bread (challah) on Fridays, took lessons on the piano, and re-upholstered our secondhand Mercedes in red goatskin. I had salvaged my special leather sewing machine (the Board of Trade allowed me to take the "tools of my trade"), and a few selected hides. I set up my machine and worktable in the downstairs room of our house, which looked out on the swimming pool and patio. I also joined the local League of Women Voters and the Ladies Auxiliary of Doctors Hospital.

Remembering that Elise and Robert de Boton at Alta Bates had been instrumental in getting local artists to display their work on the walls of the hospital, I decided to do the same at Doctors Hospital. Accordingly, I contacted all my friends at the San Francisco Art Institute, including Robert Holdeman, who had exhibited at the Grant Avenue Street Fair. Bob Holdeman had been president of the Western Artists Association, and he had many connections. His wife, Liz, had been my secretary for a short time, and both Bob and Liz were friends of long standing. I arranged an exhibit with Bob's help and with the consent of the hospital administrators. We had a gala opening, which was covered in the local press. Several pieces sold, and we all considered the show a success. I didn't succeed in raising enough money for the hospital to buy a few pieces for a permanent collection, but I considered the entire venture to be a good start.

I was on my way home, in my car on November 22, 1963, when I heard on the car radio that Kennedy had been shot. I pulled over to the side of the road and sat there, stunned. I felt as if a member of my family had died. When I got home, I turned on the television set and mourned with the rest of the nation.

Within the next few months Ric began talking about Puerto Rico, about how he might be able to connect with a hospital in that country, and do some really interesting research. Ric was a restless person, and was driven by many demons, which I never fully understood. One of them was his need to do what he could to improve the health of people in poor countries. This was one of the things that drew me to him at the very beginning of our relationship. He also was driven by a need to combat the exploitation of the environment by big business. He was the medical expert in cases against Standard Oil, when that company was accused of polluting the water in the East Bay near Richmond. I welcomed his involvement in all of these causes, but didn't realize how deep his obsession to leave a lasting legacy was. It almost amounted to a crusade. I didn't pay much attention to that talk; I was too busy adjusting to my new role of community mom. However, Ric was serious, and we went to Puerto Rico for a month in July of 1964. I didn't question Ric's decision; I assumed he knew what he was doing.

When we arrived after a long, exhausting flight, Ric and I took a nap, and Ricky explored the hotel. He rode up and down the elevators, and finally made his way to the pool and to the restaurant near the pool. I found out later that he had walked into the restaurant, sat down at a table in the middle, and waited. When he was told that the dining room was closed, and that he could be served at the counter, he marched to the counter and hoisted himself up onto a stool. He ordered a hamburger and milk shake, and proceeded to talk to the man next to him, who turned out to be the hotel manager.

I found out about that episode from the manager himself, when I went to see him Sunday afternoon. I had sent a letter of credit to an account I set up at a local Puerto Rican bank, but the money wouldn't be available until Monday. We arrived early on Sunday morning, and when I woke up and checked our reserves, I realized we needed cash. I wanted to rent an apartment for the month we would be on the island, and had located a possible rental in the local paper. Consequently, I went to see the manager, to see if I could arrange for a loan against our letter of credit. I'll never forget that conversation.

The manager, a handsome man in his fifties, listened politely to me, and then asked, "Are you the mother of that little boy in the black swimming suit, who jumped off the high diving board, and then came into the restaurant to buy lunch?"

Momentarily panicked, wondering whether we'd be thrown out of the hotel for something Ricky had done, I said, "Yes, why? Has Ricky broken any hotel rules?"

The manager laughed. "Oh, no. I just want you to know that any mother who raises a son who is that independent at six years old can borrow any amount she wants from me! He is the best evidence of reliability you could have!"

I was stunned and embarrassed, and told him that I didn't think Ricky was particularly remarkable, that in fact I considered him a bit too independent at times. Then he told me about how Puerto Rican mothers are overly protective of their sons. He said he had a twenty-two-year-old son who was less independent than Ricky! He despaired of his son ever breaking away from his mother's protection.

"My son still lives at home, while he attends the local university. He doesn't take responsibility for anything. If he wrecks his car, my wife gets it repaired, or even buys him another one. He is becoming a playboy, but he is my wife's darling, and I can't do anything about it." He shook his head. "I wish he could learn from your son." Then he became serious. "How much money do you want, dear lady? Just name it, and it's yours."

I told him I wanted to borrow three hundred and fifty dollars for just one week. I had found an apartment, and showed him the listing in the newspaper. He approved of the neighborhood, and said that if there was any difficulty with the letter of credit, I should come to him; he would vouch for me in anything I wanted to do in Puerto Rico. We shook hands, and he invited us to a special banquet they were having that evening for some visiting celebrities. "Eight o'clock," he said. "And bring your son!"

When I got back to our room, Ric had gotten up, showered, and was sitting on our little balcony. I told him briefly about my interview with the manager, and that I was going out to look at the apartment. I asked him if he wanted to come along, and he said he'd meet me in the bar downstairs when I came back. Ricky and I went off to check out our new apartment. It was a pleasant, breezy place, walking distance from the beach, with a view of the ocean, and a palm tree in the small backyard. My Spanish came back; the Puerto Ricans spoke the language more slowly than the Mexicans, and it was closer to the kind of Spanish I had learned.

The manager's party included the local chief of police, the fire chief, and other officials of the local government. Fresh shrimp, oysters, and other seafood was part of an elaborate buffet, and we had a lovely time. The fire chief invited us to a parade the following weekend, and when Ricky heard about the parade, he immediately wanted to know if we could visit the firehouse ahead of time. The fire chief looked at him, and said, "Would you like to ride in the parade with me?" I thought Ricky would fly up to the ceiling. He looked at me, and of course I said yes. We made a date to go to the firehouse at the end of the following week.

After we moved into our apartment the next day, we fell into a relaxed routine. Ric loved the local rum to such an extent that he drank himself into a stupor every night, slept until noon, and spent only a couple of sober hours with us. Ricky and I went to the beach every day; we raced up and down the beach, and dug for clams. We made the acquaintance of a wonderful Puerto

Rican man named Enrique, who made his living driving tourists around the island. He saw us at the beach, and came over to talk to us. His English was pretty good, and when he told us that he had a car for hire, I decided to make an arrangement with him. Enrique had two cars, one of which he used to drive tourists around the island, and the other an experimental model, which became a motorboat, folding the wheels underneath the chassis when it went into the water. We watched him demonstrate it, and he didn't sink! Enrique invited us to go deep-sea fishing on his experimental boat, but I decided to wait until he made sure it really worked. He became a solid friend, and took us fishing in special places all over the island.

Ricky loved rice and beans, the local standard fare, and we ate in small restaurants with Enrique, becoming part of the neighborhood. There were plenty of children around who accepted Ricky immediately; he made friends easily. With all the positive experiences around us, I didn't pay much attention to Ric's behavior. I just let him sleep half the day away, drink what he seemed to need, share dinner with us. Ricky and I were on our own.

Ric wanted to visit a hospital located in the southern part of the island, and we drove there with Enrique, stopping on the way to visit a deep mountain lake, hidden by lush foliage. Ricky and I plunged into the deep, cold pool, while Ric sat on the bank with Enrique. I can still smell the rainforest flowers, see the deep green of the forest surrounding us, and feel the smooth, cold water on my skin, after all these years. I swam, floated on my back, and kept a close eye on Ricky, who swam like a fish.

We continued south, and Ric spent a day at the hospital, exploring possibilities working there as a pathologist, but he wasn't offered a job. I never understood the depth of his desire to escape his life.

When we returned to San Juan, I contacted the fire chief, and he fulfilled his promise. When the time came for the annual parade, Ricky sat in the front seat with the fire captain, and Ric and I sat in the governor's box, along with the fire chief. What fun!

It's amazing to me, looking back on those years, how I managed to look past the fact that Ric was falling down drunk every night. I was so happy to be playing, free from the heavy responsibilities of running a business and a household that I concentrated on the immediacy of the present, fearful, perhaps, that if I challenged any part of it, it would disappear. *I wonder if other women do that too.*

When we returned to San Leandro, I decided to enroll Ricky in Sunday school at the local synagogue, and I sat in the rabbi's office during his two-hour classes, reading the Talmud and the Commentaries on the Talmud (called "Midrash"). Thus I acquired the religious education I'd never been exposed to. I got a firm understanding of the ethical basis of Judaism, as well as insight into the origins of the rituals that preserve religion.

Bob and Liz Holdeman were frequent visitors, and I found myself deeply attracted to Bob. He was, in many respects, a Renaissance man. He did many things well. Bob was a founding member of the Western Artists Association; he was active in political struggles for artists' rights in competing for low-income housing, and in pressing for city and state-sponsored exhibits, run by artists. He was articulate, a licensed landscape architect, and knowledgeable about the theory and philosophy of aesthetics. We had a lot to talk about.

Looking back, I realize that all of my three husbands, Jim Pack, Richard Skahen, Robert Holdeman, were genius intellects. I wonder if they were the same man in different bodies, with different names and backgrounds. They all had IQs well above one hundred and fifty; they were all articulate, interested in words and their origins, and they were well-read. They had other things in common too; they liked to drink, and they didn't have what Daniel Goleman, in 1995, called "emotional intelligence." They were all brilliant, but they couldn't manage their emotions, nor respond to the emotions of others particularly well. They had essentially the same problems. None of them got along with their mothers. That makes me wonder what there was in me that made us mutually attractive. Was it my nurturing nature that was the mutual attraction?

At Doctors Hospital, Ric was running into some of the same problems that had disrupted his association at Alta Bates and at Sequoia. A few doctors had caught Ric drinking absolute alcohol while he was studying slides under the microscope and started a campaign to revoke his contract. We hired a friend and an outstanding attorney, to represent Ric. I went around

San Leandro; Puerto Rico

to see various physicians in the area, whom I had met at different medical conferences, to plead Ric's case as a superb diagnostician (which he was), but I was scolded for my efforts. The doctors told me, in effect, to dump Ric, that he was a lost cause. I felt shamed and ridiculed.

Chapter Thirty-Two:
The Gun

⌐

I HAD NEVER LIKED SAN LEANDRO as a place to live. Their real estate
agents had created a barrier around their town excluding blacks, and I felt
that most of the residents were rednecks. I wanted to go back to Berkeley, so
I contacted the old man who lived next to us when we rented our first house
on Spruce Street, the house where Ricky was born. We negotiated for about
a year, while Richard Kaplan, our lawyer, pursued Ric's settlement with Doctors Hospital. It was a pretty good one, and enabled us to buy the house at
818 Spruce Street. Ric persuaded me to sign a quitclaim deed for the house
on the grounds that since I turned my business over to the Board of Trade,
that meant I had gone into a form of bankruptcy. He said that would go
against him when he tried to set himself up again in the pathology business. I
agreed. Ric then entered into a limited partnership with a friend in Hayward,
a fellow pathologist with his own laboratory, and Bob Holdeman agreed to
design the remodeling of the Berkeley house. Ric was gone most of the time,
and my relationship with Bob developed into a deep love affair. Bob and I
had a deep intellectual as well as physical connection while we were working
on the redesign of 818 Spruce Street, and those connections saved my sanity. I
found myself deeply attracted to Bob. He was tall and athletic. He had been
a gymnast in his youth, and he loved the outdoors. He had bought an old
Sicilian motorized deep-sea fishing boat and had remodeled it so that it slept
four people. He was gentle with Ricky and with me.

I liked Bob's ideas for remodeling the Spruce Street house, and for the attention he paid to wallpaper and colors of paint. We spent many happy hours redesigning the kitchen, the dining room, and the living room. The house at 818 Spruce Street had been dark and gloomy; with Bob's help it became a light and open space. Bob paid attention to everything I said; he really listened to me, and made me feel strong and competent. *I was still grieving, in a way, over the demise of my business, and I was full of doubt about the way I made decisions. Was I right in signing a quit claim deed for the house? Was I bringing Ricky up properly? Was I properly supportive of Ric?* I was full of anxiety, and Bob's gentleness soothed my spirit.

It may seem odd, but both Bob and I loved Ric, and we cared about him. Ric found many people to help him. He was brilliant and perceptive, and his friends respected him, as did we, for his dedication to research, and to his search for answers to difficult medical problems. We all tried to get Ric to go to Alcoholics Anonymous, but Ric refused, saying it was hocus-pocus religiosity and he would have none of it. He got cited for drunken driving, but he drank and drove anyway. He politely declined the carefully prepared meals I created, and night after night, Ricky and I would eat while Ric sat glumly at our beautiful Chinese rosewood table and drank. *As far as I'm concerned, there is nothing like rejection of food prepared with love to destroy a relationship.*

Slowly, like water eroding a riverbank, our connection with each other deteriorated into polite hellos and goodnights. Silent avoidance became a pattern, and I began to look forward more and more to the days when Bob came over to work on the house.

By 1965, I decided to go to work, and got a job at the Berkeley Adult School, teaching English as a Second Language to immigrants. Ricky was eight years old, in second grade. Since my job would be part-time, I could still volunteer in Ricky's class, and prepare lunch for him every day.

One evening, while I was reading in bed, I heard Ric fussing around in his dresser in the opposite corner of our wood-paneled bedroom in the Berkeley Hills. The evening was warm for early June, and the air was clear. Looking up from my book, I saw Ric's small body tense with concentration. I heard a drawer opening, the swish of fabric on fabric, then a click and then another click.

"What are you doing?" I asked.

"I'm loading my gun," was his laconic response.

A gun? What was he doing with a gun?

I continued, "Why?" And his answer was even more stunning. "What's the point of having a gun in the house if it isn't loaded?"

"When did you get it?" I asked, my voice carefully calm.

"Oh, I've had it ever since I came back from Germany."

What? This was 1965. He had come back from Germany in 1950, before we met in 1952, before we married in 1955, before Ricky's birth in 1957. I was thirty-nine, going on forty when Ricky was born. Ric had carried that gun around all those years?—hiding it in each move, from San Francisco to San Carlos, from San Carlos back to San Francisco, from San Francisco to Berkeley. He had hidden that gun all those years? Where had he managed to hide it? In his lab? Packing it among his medical stuff as he moved from hospital to hospital? Had he hidden it somehow among his clothes? What did I really know about this man to whom I had been married for twelve years? Why did he take it out and decide to load it now? Who would he aim at? Me? Our son Ricky? Himself? I scrunched over in the bed, as far over to one side that I could get. My body was tense as I waited for Ric to quit fussing with his gun.

Finally, he left the dresser, fell into bed and into snoring deep sleep. I slid out of bed and tiptoed over to the dresser in the corner. Opening the drawer as softly as I could, I lifted the gun from its place under the neatly folded shorts and balled-up socks. I held it gingerly by the barrel as I crept down the stairs, the pulses in my throat throbbing. Going down to the cellar, I crawled into the soft dirt in the crawl space under the house. Digging with my hands like a dog, scratching the dirt with my fingernails, I buried the gun deep. *As I smoothed the dirt over the gun, patting it down, I felt I was burying death itself.*

The next morning my eyes flew open as Ric rose to go to the bathroom. *Would he check up on the gun?* I had laid out his shorts, undershirt and trousers on the special stand next to his side of the bed, a chore he had taught me to do. I realized that that simple chore kept him out of the now empty drawer. I sighed with relief.

Ric waved goodbye from the bedroom door, and I called a cautiously cheery, "Have a good day." I rolled into a ball, shaking with fear and anger, mixed with relief and confusion. *Get a grip on yourself, Rhoda. Think! Think! I leaped out of bed, and began to talk to myself. Okay. First things first, wake Ricky.*

Walking into Ricky's room, I woke him gently, gave him breakfast, and sent him off to school, which was just two blocks away. Giving him his lunchbox, plus money for milk, I told him I'd see him after school. Then I called the school where I was teaching, told the secretary that I was ill, and would be out for a few days, making my voice harsh and croaky. I packed Ricky's clothes, bedding, stuffed animals, books, personal stuff, as much as I could fit into my car. Then I called a local realtor, a friend of mine, and made an appointment for later in the morning. Sitting down with a cup of tea, I considered my options. I would take Ricky out of school of course; it was close to the end of school anyway. We could go to the country for a few days, or, if I found an apartment or house in Berkeley, preferably partly furnished, I could move Ricky and me right away.

A cold rage enveloped me. I moved silently, as if in a daze, in a deliberately rational manner. I had to concentrate. I had to be efficient. I couldn't afford to panic. I was choking on fear, anger, and a sense of deep betrayal.

Helen, my realtor friend, was very helpful. June 1965 in Berkeley was a perfect time to be looking for a partly furnished house to let, especially if I was willing to sublet for three months or so. I found a house up the hill from the house on Spruce Street, within Ricky's school district. It had two bedrooms, a full bath, and a sunken living room with a fireplace. There was a small yard in the back, and a decent if old-fashioned kitchen. It was clean, the price was right, and I signed a three-month lease. Even though the lease was for a short time, I knew my move was final.

Still moving in a trance-like state, like traumatic shock following a serious accident, I found a rent-a-trailer place in the flatlands of Berkeley, and an obliging young man in the office who offered to help me move.

I packed kitchen equipment first; pots and pans, dishes, glasses, cups, just what I thought Ricky and I would need. I packed my candlesticks and a few good tablecloths. I thought of my mother, fleeing a pogrom in Romania, wrapping her candlesticks and kiddush cup in a linen tablecloth, but I banished the image. No one was chasing me.

I talked to myself again. *You're not your mother, Rhoda. You got yourself into this mess, now get yourself out. Pack up Ricky's clothes, shoes, books, and check his room carefully, making sure you don't leave anything behind. Ric will not be forgiving; he will feel I deserted him.*

I didn't take any of the paintings or artifacts that had been gifts to both of us over the years. I did take my sewing machine, and all the precious fabric I had collected. I left Ric a note, telling him that I had decided to take a few days off, and had taken Ricky with me. I told him I'd call him that evening, around nine.

Since Ricky was enrolled in an afterschool program, he wasn't too surprised to see me when I showed up around four o'clock. His second-grade teacher was still packing up her room, preparing for the end of school cleanup, and I spoke to her.

"I'd like to take Ricky out of school early. Will that be all right with you?"

"Oh, sure," she said. "We're not going to be doing much in the next few days. What are your plans for the summer?"

"I think Ricky will go to camp. Maybe the YMCA; maybe the Berkeley City Camp; I haven't decided. I'll be teaching summer school, but I don't know what the schedule is yet."

"Have a good summer, Rhoda!"

"Thanks," I said. "You, too. See you in the fall." *She doesn't know the half of it. Well, neither do I.*

I arranged for Ricky to play with a friend after school and went back to the new house I had rented. Walking into the house, I began to cry silently, the tears sliding down my face, into my mouth. I opened the door, looked around, not seeing anything through the tears, and tumbled into the bedroom, lying down on the bare mattress. I fell into a fitful sleep, dreaming that I was wandering down an unfamiliar street, lost, calling out for help, and hearing nothing but an echo. I woke with a shudder, and saw that it was nearly six o'clock. It was time to make up Ricky's bed, put things in order, straighten up the kitchen, and unpack a few things. Leaving the house at six forty-five, I went down the hill to a pay phone, and called my sister Fay in Palo Alto. Fay and Henry had moved from their suburban home north of Chicago and were now living near their daughter, Alice, in an apartment complex.

"I've left Ric," I said. "Can Ricky and I come and stay with you for a few days?" I knew that there was a swimming pool in this particular complex, and that there were other kids around Ricky could play with.

"Are you sure you know what you're doing?" Fay asked.

"Yes, I'm sure. I'll give you the details when I see you."

"When do you want to come?"

Suddenly I knew I didn't want to be in the same city with Ric that night. "Can we come tonight? We'll leave about seven-thirty, and we can be in Palo Alto by eight-thirty."

"Are you all right?" Fay was a sensitive listener.

"Yes, I'm just a bit uptight. See you later."

I dashed home and repacked for Palo Alto. Stuffing the suitcases into the car, I drove over to my friend's house to pick up Ricky. He and his friend were just finishing a hot game of checkers.

"Is the game almost over?" I asked him. "We're going to Palo Alto tonight. We're going to visit Aunt Fay and Uncle Henry."

"Tonight? Oh, boy! We're almost done." He jumped his king triumphantly over the few pieces left on the board, and sat back with a grin. We drove south to Palo Alto in the fading light of a summer night, and I couldn't believe that I was not in a dream. My mind whirled with disconnected thoughts. Ricky went calmly to sleep in the backseat, perfectly comfortable, trusting that his world was as he'd always known it. *How long would I be able to maintain that fiction? When and how would I be able to tell him how his life would be different now?*

I tried to think clearly, and to make some sort of plan. I couldn't. It was all I could do to keep the tears from clouding my vision. I turned on the radio softly and began to sing along with the music, concentrating on remembering the words. I got to Palo Alto in record time, and after parking the car, went into the apartment to get Henry.

"Hi," I said. "Ricky's asleep. Would you carry him in for me?"

"Sure." Henry lifted Ricky and kissed him gently as he stirred. Inside the apartment, Henry carried Ricky into the spare bedroom and laid him carefully on the bed. I covered him with a blanket, deciding to undress him later. I followed Henry into the living room and collapsed thankfully onto the couch. Henry went out to the car to bring in the luggage.

"How long do you want to stay?" Fay asked.

"I don't know, a few days, maybe a week. I have to collect my thoughts and do some heavy-duty planning. That's one reason I came—to get some clear-headed input from you two. I need some advice," I said, looking at Henry. "You're an accountant; you know how to analyze situations from a pragmatic point of view."

Fay and Henry sat side by side on the upholstered couch. They spoke together.

"Would you like some tea? Are you hungry?"

"I'd love some tea, and a sandwich of something or other. I didn't have dinner. It's a long story. Let's go into the kitchen, I'll tell you both while I eat."

We trooped into the kitchen, and I sat down heavily. "Ric has a gun."

"What?" Fay dropped the knife she was using to butter the bread.

"Yes, and last night he stood at his dresser, loading it. I was reading, and when I looked up from my book, I saw him."

They were silent for a moment, and then Henry said, "What did you do?"

"I waited until he was asleep, then got the gun and buried it in the dirt in the crawl space in the basement." I took a deep breath, trying to be calm and controlled. "I moved out, left him a note, found a sublet, called you, and here I am. Oops, what time is it? My note said I would call him at nine. Ah, it's only nine-twenty. Where's the phone?"

I dialed and Ric answered on the first ring. "Where are you? Are you coming home tonight?"

"I'm not in Berkeley, and I'm not coming back."

"What did you do with the gun?"

"It's gone, and you'll never find it. By the way, did you have a license for it? If the police ever find it, they'll want to know."

There was silence on the line for a moment, then, "You had no right to take it," he said angrily. "What are you going to do? Where are you?"

"I haven't decided yet what I'm going to do, and I don't intend to tell you where I am."

"Don't worry," he answered. "If I decide to find you, I'll find you. You're making a mountain out of a molehill."

"I'll let you know what I decide when I decide. You haven't asked, but Ricky is fine. Goodbye, Ric." Shaking, I hung up the phone and put my head on my arms on the table. Fay came over to me and put her arms around me.

"Come on. Let's go in the living room."

She steered me to the couch. Henry followed with the tea and the sandwich. When we were settled again, Henry asked, "Do you want to talk any more? Or do you want to go to bed, and we'll talk tomorrow?" *He was so damned reasonable! Steady, steady, my inner voice cautioned.*

"I'd rather talk a bit. I'm not ready to sleep yet. I'm still in shock."

"Okay," said Henry. "So you buried the gun, found a sublet and moved out. Are you going to file for divorce?"

At that moment I decided. "Yes, and the problem is that I don't have much money. I have a separate account, but there's not much in it. I haven't been teaching that long. I'll have to find a lawyer, but I don't know where to begin."

"How about the house? Is your name on the deed?"

"No. When the business was taken over by the Board of Trade, Ric insisted that I give him a quitclaim deed to the house because he said that my action was a kind of bankruptcy, and that would be a black mark against him, which would hurt his credit rating."

Henry groaned. "I could ask some of the people at the office; find out if anyone of them knows a lawyer who wouldn't charge too much."

"Wait a minute. First off, I want a lawyer who lives in Berkeley or Oakland, and secondly, I don't want gossip. Ric has a lot of clients in this area at different hospitals in the Bay Area, and he has enough trouble with referrals as it is."

Fay reacted sharply. "Are you still trying to protect him? After his behavior?"

"What difference does it make?" I said, wearily. "There's no point in trying to destroy him. I just want out."

Fay looked at Henry, then at me. "You look exhausted. Let's get Ricky undressed and put to bed, then I'll make up the couch for you here. We'll leave the door to the spare bedroom open, in case you want to check up on Ricky during the night."

I looked at her, my eyes filling with tears again. Fay put her arm around me and we went into the spare bedroom together. Henry made up the couch. We got Ricky undressed, managed a trip to the toilet, put his favorite stuffed toy into his arms, and guided him back to bed. He went through all these maneuvers with his eyes half open, then sighed happily and closed his eyes.

"Do you have any aspirin?" I asked my sister.

"I have something mild that's also calming," she answered. "Things will work out. I'm glad you're here."

As I drifted off to sleep, I saw myself crossing a bridge that fell to pieces behind me, the jagged pieces falling into a deep canyon. Nothing would ever be the same. A drugged calm settled over me, as I let go of a heavy weight I'd been carrying for a long time.

Chapter Thirty-Three:
Third Marriage

⊸

O N THE WAY BACK TO BERKELEY, I told Ricky that we would be going back to a different house; we would not be going back to 818 Spruce Street. He received this news in silence. Then he wanted to know if he would be going to the same school. I said he would, that our new house was just as close to his school as our other one. I decided to be as open with him as I could. I said, "I've moved us out of the house on Spruce Street, and we are not going to be living with Dad anymore. I'm sorry, but it just isn't working out." The silence was heavy in the car, as Ricky digested this information.

Arriving at the house on Ridge Road in the early afternoon, we unpacked the car, with silence still hanging heavily between us. Ricky liked the sunken living room with its high ceilings, bay windows, and fireplace, and said he also liked his bedroom, which looked out on the small yard in the back. I led him into the living room, and we sat down on the couch.

"Your father and I aren't getting along well," I said. "We are separating for the time being." Ricky wanted to know if we would visit Dad, and if Dad would visit us. I didn't know what to say. I hugged him close to me and said I wasn't sure. We'd have to see how things worked out. Then he wanted to know if he could go over to Jimmy's house to play. I called Jimmy's mom, and got an enthusiastic "yes." Both of us were relieved. Ricky was only eight years old.

It was Monday, and I called a lawyer Henry had recommended. We set up a date for later in the week, and he told me to put together as many legal papers as I had; proof of income tax filings, joint assets, and so on. When I saw him, I told him I wanted to file divorce proceedings immediately. I didn't say anything about the gun, knowing that if I did, I would have to produce it.

Ric countersued, claiming desertion. He must have been furious. I have no way of knowing exactly what his state of mind was, but he behaved as if he wanted revenge. He hired one of the most aggressive divorce lawyers in Oakland, a clever attorney with a reputation for sharp bargaining.

The court appearance was very painful. Ric showed up in his usual tense, alcohol-fueled state, angry and belligerent. I didn't ask for alimony, but I asked for child support, which was granted, and set at one hundred and fifty dollars per month. I asked for various artifacts in the house, but was refused, on the basis of Ric's counter-suit, and because of my signature on the quit-claim deed. Perhaps if I'd had a more knowledgeable attorney, I might have gotten a better deal, but I settled for what I was told I could get. Remorse haunted me.

Had I failed Ric? Had I failed myself? We had had a fascinating life together. What would happen now? How could I ensure Ricky's stability and happiness? Did I really know what I was doing?

There weren't many single mothers among the women I knew in 1965. My friends were kind to widows; there was a widows' group at the local Jewish Community Center, but there were no divorcees in that group.

One thing was clear to me. I would not have been able to make this move if I hadn't had a job. As Virginia Woolf made so clear in her book, *A Room of One's Own,* independence is impossible for a woman without money. *How many women stay trapped in an unhappy marriage because they have no means to survive without an independent income? How many women remain in an unhappy marriage "for the sake of the children?" I remembered my mother. If she had had her own shop, would she have stayed with Pa? I don't know. Perhaps the shop or the business she wanted would have given her enough outside stimulation to satisfy her restless nature.*

When I went to the Berkeley Adult School to apply for a job, I was asked what kind of job I was looking for by the principal. I told him that I could teach creative fashion design, especially in leather clothing.

He looked perplexed. "We don't have an opening in the crafts area," he said, and then he wanted to know if I had a California teaching credential. When I told him that I had a credential in elementary education, and that I had taught in both Berkeley and in Oakland, his face lit up.

"Ah," he said. "Excuse me." He disappeared for about ten minutes and returned with a piece of paper. "Yes," he said, "your certificate is still valid. Would you like to teach English as a Second Language?"

His question stunned me. I had been trained as an elementary school teacher, yet I had never taught English as a Second Language. However, it was June 30, 1965, and I thought I was applying for a job in September. I figured I would have time to get ready for anything, so I told him that while I didn't know anything about teaching English as a Second Language, I guessed I could learn.

The principal leaned back in his chair, putting his fingertips together in a pyramid, and said, "I have a job opening next Tuesday. The teacher in the English as a Second Language program has received an offer of a permanent job in Contra Costa County, and I don't feel I can stand in her way. You have a valid certificate in teaching in the State of California and in Alameda County, and you would be eligible for that job. Are you interested?"

I gulped. "Yes, but—I don't know anything about—"

He interrupted me. "You could take a course this weekend, in the Laubach Literacy Method, and that would prepare you for the classes on Tuesday. This is the Fourth of July weekend. The classes meet in the Women's Community Center on University Avenue near Tenth Street." He leaned across his desk and smiled, confident he'd made me an offer I couldn't refuse.

Stunned, I thought, *why not?* "Two things," I said. "Where is the Laubach Method being taught, and two, will I be able to talk to the teacher who is leaving, and get an idea of how she runs her program?"

The principal reached across his desk to shake my hand. "Sure." He pulled out a file and copied out a name, address, and phone number. Handing it to me, he said, "I'm sure she'll be glad to talk to you. And here is the information on the Laubach course. It starts tomorrow morning at nine o'clock, here at the Adult School. You'll find the flyer posted in the lobby." He stood up, very pleased with himself, and ushered me out.

Looking at the flyer, I noticed that the class would be held on Saturday,

Sunday, and Monday from nine till three, and I knew Ricky would be happy to play with his friends either at their homes or at the playground just across the street. I got into my car feeling exuberant.

I called Gerry Davis, the teacher I was replacing, and asked her if we could meet. She lived in Walnut Creek, but she suggested coming to Berkeley, saying, "I keep most of my materials in my car, so it'll be easier to transfer them if I come to your place."

When she arrived, Gerry told me that she was the only credentialed teacher in the program, and that she had five retired English teachers working with her as volunteers. The class met in the gymnasium at the Women's Community Center, and there were six levels. "I teach the sixth, and most advanced level," she said. "They're darlings; most of them are elderly Chinese and Japanese ladies; recent immigrants from Mexico are in the lower levels. We have a coffee break every day, and most of the students bring snacks. You'll see, they're a very congenial group."

She paused, and then said, "My volunteers are very set in their ways, so I let them do their thing, and I do mine. I supply the textbooks and keep track of the attendance, and do whatever paperwork is required. It works out."

We transferred her books to my car, and I went to the Adult School to learn the Laubach Method of teaching English as a second language. The instructor taught the class Hebrew in order to give us a sense of how difficult it was to learn a language with a different alphabetical system, a different phonetic system, and a totally different syntax. She wanted us to sympathize with our Asian students, and she kept telling us how well her system worked. However, after leaving the class, I went over to the University of California and picked up a brochure from Extension, looking for a course on teaching English as a Second Language, determining to get as much information as I could. There was only one class offered at that time, taught by George Rothmell. I signed up immediately.

Bob Holdeman began coming over to our new house frequently. He had asked Liz for a divorce, and they had come to an amicable agreement. They had been together for almost ten years, and had had no children. Bob held onto the house on Potrero Hill, and Liz moved out. Bob said that his relationship with Liz had deteriorated over the years, and that they had agreed to separate, amicably. I decided to talk to Liz. She had worked for me as my secretary for a short time, and I wanted to make sure that she didn't hold me responsible for their breakup.

That conversation was another eye-opener. It turned out that Ric had had an affair with Liz, years ago, when he was a medical student! Liz was a laboratory assistant in the hospital where Ric was doing his internship, and they had had a brief affair. I looked at her, not able to respond to this bit of information. There was an awkward pause in our conversation. However, Liz assured me that I did not "cause" the breakup of their marriage, but that Bob's genuine love for me probably gave him the courage to speak up. I asked her if she would have initiated the separation, and she said no, but that she felt relieved. She said she tended to resist change. She did warn me that Bob was not an easy person to live with, but she refused to elaborate. I told her that I was probably not easy to live with, either, but that I was in no hurry to marry again, anyway. We parted politely, on guard with each other, but certainly not as enemies.

Six months after my separation from Ric, Bob moved in to the Ridge Road house, and Ricky accepted him as part of our family. Bob helped Ricky with his homework, played ball with him, and taught him to sail. Bob had rigged a sail on his Italian fishing boat, and he also had a small dinghy, called an "El Toro," a single sailboat, suitable for one person. The cabin cruiser, as I liked to call it, was outfitted with bunks, a small kitchen, and a toilet. We all loved the boat, and took frequent trips to the San Joaquin Delta, and to the dock near Sebastopol, across the Bay. Ricky and I took sailing lessons at the Berkeley Marina, and we both earned international small boat sailing certificates. It was a time of personal expansion, mutual respect, security, and love.

Bob had been an Eagle Scout, and he was an expert in outdoor camping. We went camping in the Redwoods, in Yosemite, and along rivers in the northern part of California. We had a lot of fun during the years between 1965 and 1968. We agreed that children should be treated as "little professors," in the words of Dr. Spock, and that adults should respect their opinions and feelings. We also agreed that children needed to be held responsible for their actions.

My divorce was final in 1967, and Ric had not attempted to contact me since the final papers were filed. He was spending most of his time in Hayward, where he had made a connection with a pathologist who had an independent laboratory. His payments of child support were sporadic, but I was making enough money teaching to support Ricky and myself, and just ignored the non-payments.

By 1968, Bob and I were thinking about marriage. We needed a house, of course, and the one we were living in was not for sale. We found a house on Eunice Street, 2324, which was on the market for thirty-three thousand dollars. It was a big house, with four bedrooms, a bath and a half, a full basement, and a big garden. The plot was fifty feet by one hundred and fifty feet, and there was a view of the Golden Gate Bridge from the master bedroom. Bob would have one room for his painting studio; we would have the master bedroom overlooking the garden; and Ricky could have the room with the slanting ceiling overlooking the garden, or he could have the front room overlooking the street. There was only one problem. The house was sliding down the hill. Looking down into the basement from the kitchen, we could see the wall curving at a thirty-degree angle. Bob was a landscape architect, among his other accomplishments, and he was a little uneasy about the foundation. He said he thought we ought to offer twenty-seven five for the house, especially since it had been on the market for five years.

We were married in February 1968 in the living room of 2324 Eunice, by a reform rabbi, under a canopy. Ricky played the wedding march on his trumpet, and the party was a gala affair. All of our artist friends came, as well as Fay and Henry, and we felt that the house was blessed.

1968 was a year of tremendous social change. Students all over the world erupted that summer. There were riots in Paris, in Tokyo, as well as in the United States. Students staged sit-ins and teach-ins at Columbia University in New York, in Wisconsin, and at the University of California at Berkeley. I remember a closing of Telegraph Avenue for a demonstration that resulted in a riot when police declared the demonstration illegal, even though a permit had been issued.

I had been directing traffic at the corner of Dwight Way and Telegraph, and had gone down to Cody's to listen to a speaker when the police appeared and declared the meeting illegal. I remember feeling trapped as I looked around, seeking a way to leave, and found myself and others surrounded by police. We ran, up and down alleys; the police opened fire on demonstrators standing on roofs, and one person died. Ordinary, law-abiding citizens became radicalized that year.

The uprising in Berkeley in 1968 was not sudden. The Free Speech movement began in Berkeley in 1964, but it was not until 1968 that the general public became involved. That summer, members of the religious community, Jews, Catholics, and Protestants gathered together in support of students and young people demonstrating for change in the way classes were organized and taught. I was a member of Beth El Synagogue, and also a member of its Political Action Committee, so that was why I was directing traffic that fateful day when Reagan ordered out the National Guard. Reagan sent National Guardsmen to set up a base in the Marina; he ordered a curfew of ten p.m., and he had armed soldiers ride up University Avenue in their jeeps, carrying fixed bayonets.

The young guardsmen took up their posts on Telegraph Avenue, and pretty soon, young women arrived on the scene, carrying flowers and homemade cookies. The cookies were called "Maryjanes," since they were not regular brownies. They were laced with marijuana. In a very short time, the soldiers were laughing and joking with the coeds, and flowers sprouted from the tips of their bayonets. That peaceful scene didn't last, however. The sergeants replaced the young soldiers with older men, who were warned not to accept blandishments from pretty young girls.

Then Reagan ordered the Guard to drop tear gas on the campus; only the prevailing winds spread the gas all over Berkeley, and Ricky, then eleven years old, came home from school with his eyes burning, and tears running down his face. I still seethe with anger when I remember those days.

Before our marriage, Bob had taken an active role in Ricky's life. He helped him get a paper route, and worked with him in designing a science model for his fifth grade class. Both Ricky and I liked Bob's way of taking charge. We knew him as a kind person, genuinely interested in the well-being of people around him, and we forgave his bossy manners. However, with the legal document of marriage came a kind of possessiveness I had not encountered in Bob before. In his zeal to be an active father, he sometimes became his own grandfather, who had been a bible-thumping traveling minister of the Gospel, an authoritarian figure in both his father's and his life. Ricky and I ignored this change in him.

I asked Ricky, now twelve, if he wanted to have a bar mitzvah, and he said he did. So he enrolled in the Hebrew class at Beth El, and Bob undertook the supervision of his studies. In the process, Bob also became interested in Jewish studies, and considered converting.

Bob continued to paint, and the work he turned out in this period was truly beautiful. I turned the living and dining rooms of the house into an informal gallery, and invited friends to special showings. Those were good years. I got tenure in the Berkeley Public Schools system, and built a solid career at the Berkeley Adult School. I joined the California Federation of Teachers, which was part of the AFL/CIO union. Ricky did well at Oxford school, and went on to middle school, which was called Garfield at that time.

It's hard to pinpoint the exact time when a relationship starts to decline. Several things converged. Ricky was now thirteen, and after his bar mitzvah, he began to flex his adolescent muscles. I remembered my own rebellious adolescence, and was sympathetic, but I was also fearful of the consequences for my son. I was appalled at the ease with which Ricky and his friends had access to marijuana.

In 1969 Berkeley was in the throes of integrating its school population, and students were bused to and from the flatland schools of Berkeley to the hill schools, and vice versa. Garfield became an integrated school, and there was a lot of friction. The impact of drugs on young students was frightening. Some students would simply flip out, jump up and dash wildly around the classroom, or fall down in a drugged stupor. Ricky became part of a task force going to different schools to talk about the effect of drugs on the mind. The information they were dispensing didn't mean that his task force stopped smoking cigarettes, as well as marijuana.

At the same time, almost overnight, it seemed, Ricky no longer acquiesced in anything I asked of him. I felt I was losing control, and yet I wanted his respect. Bob didn't have those conflicting feelings. One day at lunch there was a disagreement about something, and Bob bellowed, "Who's in charge here? Who makes the decisions?"

I looked at Ricky, and he looked at me. "We all do," I said. "This is a democratic household. We all participate in the decisions."

"I don't think so," shouted Bob, as he threw down his napkin. "What I say goes," and he stormed out of the room.

Now that I look back on that moment, I think it signaled a significant change. Ricky may have felt he had scored a point, and I suddenly felt torn between my husband and my son. Uneasiness settled down upon us.

One afternoon, when I returned from teaching, I found a note from Ricky.

"I've run away," the note said. "Please meet me at the Runaway Center at six p.m. for a conference." The Runaway Center had been set up in 1968, during the "Summer of Love," and it functioned for several years as a place where parents and teenagers could get counseling.

Bob and I showed up promptly at six p.m., and a young psychologist, a volunteer at the Center, was with Ricky, waiting for us. During the course of the conversation, it turned out that Ricky wanted to go and live with his father, even though his father had been absent from his life for many years. I pointed out that Ricky's father was an alcoholic, and that that was one of the reasons we had divorced. I remember the psychologist's private comments to me.

"Ricky will go to live with his father, no matter what you do," he said. "He needs to do this; he needs to find out who his father is." The young man paused. "Actually," he said, "some day he will need to become his own father." I wasn't sure exactly what he meant, but I realized he was right about Ricky's need to live with his father. "Have you contacted Ric?" I wanted to know. "Maybe he doesn't want him to come."

The counselor had already contacted Ric, who was on his way over. Ric arrived soon after we finished our conference, looking thin and haggard. He and Ricky left together. Ricky had already packed a bag and had it with him; he was so confident of the outcome.

The early seventies were difficult years for parents with adolescents. There were classes called Parent Effectiveness Training, where parents were encouraged to use strategies with their children which were outlined in a book called I'm O.K. You're O.K. There were frequent parent meetings where we all held our heads in despair. I felt somewhat comforted when I realized that even in two-parent families, the children were acting out, and the parents felt just as confused as I was. We all felt guilty about something, but we weren't sure what it was we had done or not done to produce the kind of behavior our kids were exhibiting. We were all frightened of the effects of marijuana. None of the parents I knew at that time smoked dope, but many of them smoked cigarettes, and we all drank alcohol.

Bob didn't attend the parent meetings with me, since he didn't approve of any kind of what he called "permissive behavior" on the part of parents. He was in favor of tight control, strict rules, strictly enforced. Perhaps Bob was determined to be the dominant father figure in his new life with me, because his own mother was the dominant force in his family, and he always felt his father had been put down by his mother.

Shortly after Ricky moved to his father's house, we went to Guatemala for three weeks to visit a student who had invited us. I told Ric and Ricky where we were going, and where we could be reached in any kind of emergency, and Ric reacted haughtily to my information, as if I were impugning his ability to take care of everything adequately. That wasn't my intent, but we often send messages that are received differently from the way we expect.

When we returned from Guatemala, I found a message from Ricky on the answering machine. When I called, he said that he wanted to come home. I asked him when he wanted me to pick him up, and he said, "Right away." So I didn't bother to unpack, left my bags in the middle of the living room, and went over to the house on Spruce Street to pick him up.

He was waiting outside, on the curb, with his bags. He got into the car without a word, and didn't speak until we arrived at home. Before getting out of the car, I turned to him and said, "What happened?" He looked so sad. He said, "I can't save him. I tried to get him to switch from alcohol to marijuana, because I thought it would save his liver, but he wouldn't do it." Without another word, he opened the car door and went into the house.

Chapter Thirty-Four:
Changes, 1965–1974

⌐

URING THE YEARS I WORKED FOR THE BERKELEY ADULT SCHOOL, between 1965 and 1981, I discovered that the Berkeley Adult School was the repository and last resting place for failed administrators. By failed administrators I mean those men who were so incompetent that they had been asked to leave other schools or departments in the District. They had tenure, and couldn't be fired. Therefore, as is common in large governmental agencies, they were promoted to their level of incompetence and placed where, it was figured, they would do the least harm.

That's how the system seemed to work during the years I taught there. The prevailing idea was that adults could cope with inefficiency, laziness, and drink better than children. One might think that this was a highly illogical rationale, but it offered protection for the Old Boys' Club.

Angus McPherson (not his real name), ended up at the Berkeley Adult School as the Director of the Adult Basic Education Program. The English as a Second Language program fell under his jurisdiction, and it was to his office that I went, one day in 1971, to sign a contract for part-time teaching in the summer session.

As I walked into his office, Mr. McPherson, a big man, six-feet-two, weighing close to two hundred pounds, was teetering dangerously in his executive swivel chair. I noticed a half-open drawer on the right side of his desk from which something in a brown paper bag was visible.

Suddenly, without warning, Mr. McPherson toppled sidewise. I screamed, "Mr. McPherson has fallen out of his chair! Help!" and ran into the outer office. Thelma, the only black secretary in the office, leaped up and followed me. We ran to Angus, and the two of us hoisted him into his chair.

"This has happened before," Thelma said, calmly. "Hang on to him, I'll get the principal and the vice-principal. Just keep him propped up in the chair."

Mr. McPherson, red-faced, breathing heavily, looked comatose, but he was alive. The chair kept swiveling, and it took all of my strength to keep him from sliding to the floor. When Pedersen and Harris arrived, they hoisted him out of the chair and walked him down the stairs. "He's ill," said Pedersen, over his shoulder, "he'll be in the hospital for a while, but he'll be all right."

"Yeah," muttered Thelma, behind me. "He's off to the Catholic drying out retreat. We'll see him in about six weeks."

"How about my contract?" *First things first.* "And my paycheck?"

"Don't worry," Thelma assured me. "Harris takes over for McPherson when he goes on these little vacations. I put the papers on his desk and he signs them. Relax, your papers will be on top of the pile." She gave me a friendly pat on the shoulder, and a conspiratorial wink. Right then and there we forged a close and lasting relationship.

I felt secure in my job in 1972. But it was a difficult year for my relationship with Bob. The interior design company that Bob worked for was taken over by another company, and Bob was laid off. I had thought that Bob would welcome the extra time he had for painting, and would also look for a gallery to exhibit his work, but I was wrong. His pride was hurt; he rejected my statement that I was now making enough money to support the family, and he could therefore devote his energies to painting. He was close to sixty years old, and he felt rejected by society. He went into a deep depression and started to drink heavily.

Caught as I was in the Rescuer-Victim-Persecutor syndrome described by Eric Berne in *Games People Play,* I tried to break the pattern by enrolling both of us in a Transactional Analysis program in Berkeley. Transactional Analysis is a psychotherapeutic system created by Eric Berne, and the psychoanalyst I contacted said he thought the program would help both of us. Bob was not enthusiastic about the idea, but he agreed to go along for a few meetings.

The theory of Transactional Analysis is that we interact with other people on any of several levels. The levels are divided into Parent, Adult, and Child. The Parent level is divided into two parts, Nurturing Parent and Punitive Parent, and the Child level is also divided into two parts, Natural Child and Adaptive Child. The Adult level has only one part. The therapeutic environment consists of eight or ten people who sit in a circle and talk.

If someone makes a remark with an attitude similar to that of a Punitive Parent (that is, a remark carrying the implication "you do as I say or else"), the remark may provoke a response like "Oh, yeah? Who says?" or something similar. The interaction becomes immediately obvious to everyone in the room, and the psychiatrist can intervene, pointing out that it's possible to respond to an aggressive remark on an Adult level, defusing a conflict situation. This would be a cross-transaction, leading to positive change.

I found the sessions fascinating and helpful, but frustrating at the same time. That was because Bob sulked. He sat in the circle with his eyes closed and refused to participate. Finally, the other people in the group insisted that he either take part or leave, so he left.

Those sessions took place in the winter of 1972, and in the spring of that year, Ricky decided to use a three hundred-dollar bond his aunt Sara had given him on the occasion of his bar mitzvah to go to Israel. He didn't want to go with a group, he wanted to go alone, and I agreed. I contacted Pierre and Britta in Belgium, and another former student now in Israel. Pierre and Britta agreed to meet Ricky at the airport in Belgium; he would stay with them for a few days, and they would make sure he got on the right plane for Tel Aviv. I arranged for him to stay at a kibbutz, and to spend time with a family in Jerusalem.

But just before Ricky was to leave, in June, we got a call from a friend of Ric's. Being unable to reach him by phone, this friend went over to the house, and finding the door unlocked, went in and found Ric dead from an overdose of drugs. He had left a note stating that he didn't want any funeral orations or any kind of final rituals. Shaken, I asked Ricky if he wanted to cancel his trip.

"You don't have to go, you know. I can cancel the ticket."

"What difference does it make?" was his response.

I didn't know how to respond to his feeling of disconnectedness, and I was too stunned to think clearly. I immediately felt overcome by guilt, because I had put pressure on Ric, asking him to renew the child support payments which he hadn't made for three years. Money was tight at that time, since Bob was no longer working. I had called Ric and left several messages on his answering machine. He didn't respond to any of them. I called him at home and at his lab, but got no response. Deciding to take legal action, I contacted a lawyer (not the one who botched the divorce proceedings), and she advised me that even though I had re-married, Ric was still liable for child support payments. The day before Ric was due to appear in court to show cause as to why he hadn't fulfilled his obligations, he took an overdose of pills.

His will reinforced the statements in his final note. The will stated explicitly that he wanted absolutely no funeral ceremonies, forbade any kind of orations, and authorized his cremated remains to be scattered. I contacted his mother, Marion, who came to Berkeley, and we both went to the coroner's office to identify him. She was very upset that there wouldn't be any ceremonies, and when I told her she could always have a Mass said for him at a Catholic church in Berkeley, she said she preferred having Mass said for him in her own community with friends, not strangers, around her. She insisted on taking his ashes back with her to Minneapolis. I wrote a brief obituary, which she approved; it was published in the *San Francisco Chronicle*, and Marion left for Minneapolis without even seeing Ricky. Since suicide is a sin in the eyes of devout Catholics, Marion seemed uncertain, even embarrassed, by Ric's death.

When my mother died in Chicago of a heart attack, my brother and sisters made all the arrangements. The entire ritual was a kind of performance. Rituals are soothing. There is a prescribed way of behaving. We don't have to choose. We don't have to decide anything. We choose the people who will perform the ritual, and we happily follow the rules. Ric's death was different. Our society regards suicide as a shameful act, and the coroner acted as if it were somehow criminal. There were no accepted rituals that I knew of, and instead of looking for help, I simply chose to do what was absolutely necessary. Going through the legal motions meant identifying the body, and allowing the coroner to follow Ric's last wishes. The Internal Revenue Service locked the house at 818 Spruce Street, impounding its entire contents, putting everything up for auction. It turned out that Ric hadn't paid withholding taxes on his employees for several years, and there may have been other defaults on taxes I didn't know about.

After Ricky left for Israel, I took time out to grieve over Ric's death. I went to Drake's Bay alone. Baba had died in 1964, shortly after we moved to Berkeley, so I didn't even have my dog's company as I mourned. Gazing at the sea, my back against the sun-warmed rocks, I thought about Ric.

What were his demons? He felt that his mother had betrayed him. His mother sent him off to military school when he was five. She was nineteen when he was born, a Polish floor cleaner in the office building where his father, a lawyer, still practicing at age seventy-five, spotted her one night when he worked late.

Marion was poor; Richard Skahen senior was rich and old. He died the year Ric was born, and Marion deposited the money she inherited in a widows and orphans fund at a local bank in Minneapolis. The bank mishandled the money; Ric's mother was cheated, and therefore Ric was cheated, too. Marion went to secretarial school and became a secretary to a firm in the same building where she had worked as a floor cleaner. As a widow with a child in 1920, she must have been frantic about trying to care for him, and sent him away.

Who was Ric Skahen? What did I know about him? Richard Skahen, M.D., who committed suicide at the age of fifty-seven, in the sixth year following our divorce, did research on the effect of drugs absorbed through the skin. He was a brilliant dermatological pathologist, passionately interested in solving problems. He described the skin as the most important organ of the body—the envelope in which the body, and the person, lives. Ric felt that many physicians ignored the importance of the skin. He kept reiterating this point at countless medical conventions, to which his audience, half-or-all-the-way-drunk, turned their deafened ears. Even though Ric, also in a state of semi-numbness induced by alcohol, functioned beautifully in those days, his wit and erudition didn't get through.

Ric was interested in the intradermal administration of drugs, which goes back thousands of years. I remember journals of Chinese medical research scattered all over the house, plus journals from Egypt and Morocco, dealing with articles on the subject, including North American, Central, and South American Indians. All of the research spoke of the use of "rags" soaked in herbal potions, to be applied to certain parts of the body depending on the symptoms.

Ric was also an etymologist, loving words and their origin. We had the unabridged Oxford English Dictionary, to which we both constantly referred in our loving arguments about which words originated when, and what did they *really* mean? One of the words I remember we talked about was *pudendum*. When Ric told me it was a wig worn by women in the Middle Ages to cover their pubic areas, I accused him of making it up. So we made a substantial bet (dinner at Trader Vic's—on me—if I lost, or a pearl necklace, if I won. We looked the word up in the Oxford dictionary, and he was right. I lost, so we had the dinner, and I got the pearl necklace anyway.

I'm not sure what compelling impulse led me to deny the bells ringing in my head when Ric and I first met. At thirty-four, in 1952, I was desperate to have a child, probably to prove something to myself. I remember thinking that pathologists make a good living, and maybe I would be able to quit the leather business and become an acceptable member of society, a housewife. After all, this was the fifties, the age of Ozzie and Harriet on television as well as Leave it to Beaver. Hollywood movies all portrayed normal families, defined as including a stay-at-home mom, a working dad, happy, obedient, white, middle-class children. I felt outside of the mainstream, and I felt the push to belong. I wanted to be a stay-at-home mom.

Remembering that after Ricky was born in 1957, Ric began to drink more and more heavily, I had to tell myself again that Ric's problems at various hospitals he was connected with had something to do with his drinking. I thought back to our move to San Leandro after I quit my leather business, when I realized that his falling out with Stuart Lindsay in San Carlos and with Dave Singman in Berkeley had begun to bother him. Unfortunately he felt persecuted by administrative personnel, and the more victimized he felt, the more he drank. It was a vicious circle.

What bothered me was a haunting, familiar feeling that I had somehow contributed to his inability to control his drinking by my passivity.

I walked for a while, allowing the wind and the air to soothe my troubled spirit, and after the wind came up, drove back to Berkeley feeling calmer.

By 1973 Bob and I had moved far apart on the question of the amount of freedom that Ricky should have. However, as usual, most of our discussions ended with Bob's silence and a prolonged sulk. I could never get anything firmly resolved. Meanwhile, Ricky took up Kung Fu, a form of Chinese martial arts, and got up early every morning to get to special classes at eight a.m. I was impressed with his dedication. Whatever he decided to do, he did with intense concentration and with his whole being. I knew that Bob appreciated these traits in Ricky, but he felt challenged by Ricky's independence.

With all that was going on in my personal life, I was still involved in politics. 1972 was not only the year of Women's Liberation, it was the year that Shirley Chisholm ran for the Democratic nomination for President, and activists in Berkeley were sharply divided over whether to support Chisholm or go for a man they thought could win—McGovern. Looking back, the arguments were similar to those that racked the Democratic Party when Nader ran for President against George Bush. The progressives argued that Chisholm would pull votes from McGovern, just as they argued that Nader would pull votes from Gore. I supported McGovern.

Jeanne

My sister Jeanne moved to Palo Alto from Philadelphia in 1973, after her husband Arthur died. I hadn't seen Jeanne since 1945 in Washington, D.C., and I began to go to Palo Alto fairly regularly, to get acquainted with her again. She was in a deep depression, and I decided to ask her to go to Europe with me, to lay down some different memories. Fay and Henry, Jeanne and Arthur had gone to Europe together regularly every summer for several years, always first class. I had never been to Europe, and I thought that if we spent some time together, it would be helpful and healing for both of us. I was still reeling from Ric's death, a year earlier; from Bob's silent withdrawal, and Ricky's changed behavior. I needed a break, and I figured Jeanne did too. I told her we would be traveling on a budget, probably second class and she agreed.

Ricky and Bob were fighting all the time now and Ricky came to me with a plan. He and several friends were going to sublet an apartment on Virginia Street (near our house), and he wanted to know if I would let him try living on his own for the summer. I remembered my own desire to leave home when I was fifteen, to get an apartment in downtown Chicago with my friend Sima, and I sympathized with him. He said he would get a job as a gardener and play music. He invited me to come over and check out the apartment. I already knew the boys he would be living with, and I talked to their parents. They all seemed to think it would be an interesting experiment for the summer.

I asked Bob if he would be willing to check in on Ricky from time to time, and if he would be willing to take care of the garden while I was gone. He said he thought that I was out of my mind, but that he would take care of things. Everything looked possible on the surface.

Jeanne agreed to travel with me on a special teachers' discount fare, and I contacted former students all over Europe who were constantly inviting me to visit. Jeanne had always traveled first class, but this trip would be different. If we couldn't stay with students, we would be staying in second-class hotels.

We had a marvelous trip, traveling from Belgium to Portugal, from Portugal to Spain, through Spain to France, then home from Belgium. We visited Philippe de Naeyer and his wife Birgitta in Berchem, near Antwerp, who lived on a famous street, Cogels Osylei. They were generous hosts, and we felt privileged to be accepted so readily by their children and by their friends. From Belgium we flew to Lisbon, and then traveled by train through Portugal to the south of Spain, where we stayed with other students on the coast. Traveling by train up the middle of Spain, we felt connected to the land of Cervantes, and Don Quixote seemed to be riding alongside the train.

In Madrid we connected with Victoria Parraga, whose father was still imprisoned by Franco. Victoria was very cautious when she visited us in our hotel room. We sat on the floor with our backs against the wall after she checked all the lamps and under the beds for hidden microphones. We turned on the radio and talked in low voices while Victoria told us stories of persecution by Franco and his men. Her father and mother were members of the Communist Party, and Victoria had been spirited away to the countryside by an aunt when she was eleven. Victoria's father had died in prison, but her mother was released.

The streets of Madrid were full of policemen in those days, and we understood Victoria's caution. When we went to visit the Basque country, Victoria met us in Bilbao, and introduced us to her aunt. The two women, Victoria's aunt and my sister Jeanne, had immediate rapport. They chattered away amiably, Jeanne in English and Victoria's aunt in Spanish. At one point, Jeanne admired a ring with a green stone on the aunt's hand, and she immediately took it off and placed it on Jeanne's finger.

We traveled through France by train, and arrived in Paris in August. One of my students had invited us to stay in her apartment for ten days while she was off on vacation, and had arranged for the concierge to give us a key. We had been traveling together for a month in very close quarters, and when we walked into the apartment, noticing the bedrooms opening off a hall, we fled into our separate rooms, and didn't emerge for several hours. What a relief to be alone for a while!

The ten days in Paris were a real joy, especially since the city was relatively quiet in August. We had made an agreement to pool our money every day and to be frugal with where we stayed and where we ate. We used to peruse the menus posted outside restaurants, checking prices carefully before we ventured inside. One evening we had chosen a restaurant in our neighborhood whose fare was within our limited budget, but as we went in, I noticed the dessert table. There were fraises de bois (fresh raspberries) and the price was the same as the entire main course. I shocked Jeanne by ordering them anyway, squandering part of my budget for the following day. She never got over that and often referred to my action as indicative of how impulsive I was. I didn't mind. I had already adjusted to myself. We came back home from Belgium after our six-week trip together, and that trip cemented our relationship until her death in 1992.

When I returned to Berkeley, I discovered that Bob had really gone into a funk. The garden was full of weeds, the house was a mess, and he was in a drunken stupor. I called Ricky, who said that he hadn't seen Bob since I left, and he confessed that living on his own wasn't all he thought it would be. So once again he came home. But Bob's hot temper flared higher and wilder, disagreements escalated, and soon neither Bob nor Ricky would talk to each other.

Once again I tried to connect with the Bob I thought I knew. I asked him to go with me to a psychologist known for helping married couples work out their problems.

"I don't have any problems," he said. "I just need a job."

"Well, I have problems," I replied. "And I'd like your help in solving them."

He shrugged, and agreed to go to a few sessions. It didn't work. Once again, Bob sat in the sessions with the psychologist and me with his eyes closed, occasionally making a cryptic comment like, "Discipline is the source of true creativity," just to demonstrate that he wasn't really asleep. We gave up, and once again, I had to decide whether to go on living in this antagonistic environment, or to separate from Bob. I felt I had to choose between my son and my husband.

Bob and I had a long conversation, and this time Bob's eyes stayed open. I told him that I was truly unhappy in our present environment, and that I thought we had better divorce. I pointed out that he still had his house on Potrero Hill, and that we would figure out how to divide the equity in the house on Eunice Street. It was a long speech, and Bob was silent after I finished. He began to weep, and I brought him a glass of water, resisting the impulse to take him in my arms and comfort him. I waited, and finally he looked up and said, "The hell of it is, I know you're right, but I'm miserable."

I was also miserable, and went outside into the garden to weep. I wanted to take him in my arms, to love him and to comfort him. Yet my mind told me that this was the wrong path to take. I didn't want to lose Ricky, who was more vulnerable than Bob, and I was dismayed over Bob's uncontrolled drinking. It triggered a familiar fear. I had to make the separation before it was too late.

We went to bed in separate rooms that night, and when I came home from school the next afternoon, I found Bob lying on the couch in the living room.

"Are you all right?" I asked.

"As all right as I'll ever be," he answered in a mournful tone.

I sat down beside him, and showed him a book I'd picked up at the library, specifying the procedure for do-it-yourself divorces. Determined to be as matter-of-fact as possible, I said, "It seems to me that if we agree on the way we divide our assets, we'll save a lot of money. I think we can do the whole thing for five hundred dollars. If you agree to allow me to buy your share of the equity in the house, it will make things a lot easier."

"Oh, god," he moaned. "Of course you will keep the house. And you can pay me off so much a month with interest. Where will I go? I don't want to lose contact with you or Ricky. I love you both." He held his head in his hands. I waited. Then he sighed deeply, sat up, and gave me a long, steady look. "I'll get the files on the house and the income tax returns," he said. "We might as well sit down and start figuring everything out."

That was a hopeful sign. If he could only stay sober! We found an attorney in Berkeley who turned out to be a gentle, sensible, intelligent man. He listened to both of us, helped us draw up the papers, and did his best to make the whole separation as painless as possible. I took over the mortgage on the house, and signed a loan agreement whereby I agreed to pay Bob his share of the equity over the next three years.

No matter how sensibly we thought we were behaving, the dissolution of our marriage was painful. I helped Bob pack, and it was wrenching for both of us. My sisters and friends had bought many of Bob's paintings, and Bob knew I loved his work, so he asked me to choose two or three paintings that meant a lot to me.

When Bob found a small studio apartment on Alcatraz near Shattuck, he asked me to drive him there one rainy night in December. He said he felt too ill to drive himself. Ricky and I helped him unload some of his stuff, and he said he'd come by to move the rest of his things in a few weeks. It took three months for Bob to finally move out.

In 1974 Ricky met a group of musicians from Philadelphia, and he began to take conga drum lessons from one of the members of the band. Ricky had been playing an instrument of one kind or another most of his life. He had made music on a bugle at the age of three; he played both trumpet and guitar, but he always wanted to play drums, and now was his chance. Coincidentally, he decided that he wanted to drop out of high school, so that he could play music on a more professional level. We had several conferences with his math teacher and other counselors, who all advised me that if this was what he wanted to do, I might as well encourage him to do it. This was the seventies, and the counselors at Berkeley High School realized they couldn't hold reluctant students.

I told Ricky that if he wanted to be a drummer, he should be the best drummer he could possibly be. He looked at me in disbelief, and said, "Oh, come on. You know you want me to be a doctor or a lawyer. You're just saying that."

I really believed what I said, but I don't think he ever accepted it, until one day he heard me refer to "my son, the drummer." Then I think he believed me.

I also told Ricky that if he wanted to move out, he would have to get a job to pay for his room and board, wherever he went. And he said that he would get a job as a gardener during the day, since he had done that before; then he could play music at night. So he left, and this time it was more serious. I told him I would have to rent the other three bedrooms in the house in order to pay all the loans I had taken out, and that would include his bedroom. Ricky knew this move had finality about it that he couldn't ignore, and he accepted.

Renting out the bedrooms meant that I was setting up a cooperative household. I didn't know how this would work out, but I knew that some of my friends were living in cooperative households and I felt it was worth a try. I decided there would have to be agreed-upon rules. I told prospective renters that we would divide the cooking chores, and whoever cooked wouldn't have to clean up. We would meet once a week on a designated day to calculate the sharing of household expenses, including food. Whoever cooked could post the shopping list on the refrigerator, and someone else would shop. I would post a list for soap, toilet paper, and paper towels, which would be included in the food shopping. We would post the cooking schedule on the refrigerator, and if something unexpected came up, the cook for that day would have to find a substitute. Saturdays and Sundays were open days, but on Mondays through Fridays, meals would be shared. We could label special food for ourselves in the refrigerator, but we couldn't have individual shelves; the refrigerator was too small.

I ended up with some very interesting graduate students. One was a tall Chinese man in the School of Architecture, who had grown up working for his uncle in a Chinese restaurant in Chicago. What fabulous meals we had! Another was an Iranian man who cooked delicious Persian food, and a third was an MBA candidate from India who wasn't a very good cook. I did what I was good at: meat loaf, baked fish, and chicken soup. It was a good arrangement, and it worked well for three semesters. But graduate students move on, and every time there was a change in personnel in the household, new adjustments had to be made.

In the fall of 1974, McGovern went up against Nixon and lost. I had campaigned for McGovern in my car, which had a loudspeaker mounted on its roof. I drove slowly through San Francisco's Financial District, declaring, "A vote for McGovern is an investment in the future," which made me feel good, even though we lost.

By this time, I had joined two professional organizations, and I began to go to conferences. I took every UC Berkeley Extension class I could find that dealt with teaching English to non-native speakers, and I began to acquire a reputation for innovative teaching. By observing closely the different learning styles of my students at the Berkeley Adult School, I found myself more and more eager to try out different methodologies. I did a lot of experimenting.

Under the urging of my colleagues, I began to give presentations, first at California Teachers of English to Speakers of Other Languages (CATE-SOL), and then at national TESOL conferences. The International Association beckoned, and since my foreign students at the Berkeley Adult School kept encouraging me to visit them, I decided to go to Europe every other year. I worked through the year, saved my money, and traveled abroad every other year for at least two months or more, managing to include a conference somewhere. It didn't matter that I emptied my savings account each time; I knew I had a steady job to come back to. My renters took care of the house; Ricky seemed to be all right with the band he had connected with; and that was how I embarked on a new phase of my life. I looked forward to new adventures with zest and enthusiasm.

Chapter Thirty-Five:
A Fourth Career

⟨⟩

RICKY HAD MOVED OUT, and he was now part of a band called "Raw Soul." He seemed to be doing all right, and with my cooperative household established, I felt free to explore challenges that were coming up in the field of ESL. When I read an announcement inviting teachers to submit applications for creating videotapes to teach ESL, I decided to apply. Janet Hafner, a professor at Palomar University, near San Diego, had received a grant from the State of California to create an archive of videotapes that could be used for training teachers of ESL in public adult schools throughout California.

I had always been interested in film, and had taken a course in filmmaking. In fact, I had worked with Michael Chu, my Chinese housemate, on an antiwar movie he was making, and he had worked with me on a movie I had tried to make. My movie was going to be sort of a black musicians' *The Music Man,* based on the group Ricky was playing with. My movie was still in the can, but Michael finished his.

The application specified that I submit an outline, a storyboard, and a shooting script, plus an analytical essay describing the methodology I wanted to portray in the film. I was so anxious to be accepted that I submitted two scripts.

One of the scripts dealt with a methodology called "The Silent Way," created by Caleb Gattegno, whose idea challenged teacher-directed and teacher-centered methodologies. Gattegno had written several books, which I had read, and I was trying to use his philosophy in my own teaching. He said, "The job of the teacher is to observe the student; the job of the student is to learn." In practice, this means that the teacher presents the stimulus, and the students produce the response. This is quite a different approach from the "Audiolingual Method," which I call "listen and repeat." In the Audiolingual Method, which seems to be an accepted methodology worldwide, the teacher says something and the students repeat, like monkeys, what they think they heard.

The main point of Gattegno's philosophy is that teaching is subordinate to learning. The teacher is a facilitator, not a military commander. One of the effects of using this philosophy in everyday teaching is that the teacher has to let go of her ego, and this approach appealed to me. I had absorbed this idea gradually into my own teaching, and it wasn't easy. I found that it took me ten years to back my way into it. I developed many strategies to teach grammatical structures, reading and writing, as well as pronunciation, and it was those strategies that I wanted to demonstrate on my videotape.

The other strategy I was interested in was a communicative exercise, which I called "Situational Dialogues." This was a teaching strategy that involved a scenario requiring the use of advanced grammatical structures, and was designed for upper intermediate or advanced classes. I encouraged the students to create their own situations and their own dialogues. The students then performed their scripts in front of the class. They created different situations around bus stops, movie theaters, the library, conversations on an airplane, or in a supermarket.

Both ideas for videotapes were accepted, and I found myself writing two storyboards and two shooting scripts. Janet Hafner and her crew came to Berkeley, inspected my classroom, checked out the electrical outlets, and after getting permission from various bureaucrats, as well as permission slips from the students, we shot the films. Then I went to Palomar College for a studio-taped interview, and the tapes became part of the Palomar Tapes for Teaching English to Adult Learners. Those tapes are still in use in teacher-training programs throughout California.

Flushed with success, I decided to go to Europe that summer to attend a Teachers of English to Speakers of Other Languages (TESOL) conference in Dublin. This was an international conference, and I wanted to sit in on a special session presented by Gyorgy Lozanov, a psychologist and linguist from Bulgaria. Lozanov had published a theory and methodology called "Suggestopaedia," based on the idea that as we grow and mature, we are exposed to rings of negative suggestion around our inner core, restricting our ability to learn, especially foreign languages. His philosophical methodology embraced the use of music to penetrate to one's core, putting language on top of the music to facilitate learning. Having just seen a film called Clockwork Orange, by Stanley Kubrick, I was highly skeptical and dubious about how this methodology really worked. I was prejudiced against anything that resembled brainwashing in any way, but I wanted to find out how and whether Lozanov's method worked.

In Dublin, Lozanov was mesmerizing. In an audience composed mostly of women teachers from all over the world, Lozanov was a Pied Piper. If he had started walking toward the door, and said, "Follow me," I think most of the audience would have skipped along. I, too, found myself drawn to many of his ideas, and found them less threatening than I thought they would be. In a way, Lozanov's theories of stress and anxiety reduction fit in with other theories being launched at the time, including Gattegno's "Silent Way." Charles Curran's "Counseling Learning/Community Language Learning" methodology, James Asher's "Total Physical Response," Stephen Krashen's "Natural Approach," all embraced the idea that learning, especially language learning, was more effective if the psychological and emotional state of the learner became part of the teacher's strategies.

After the Dublin conference, I traveled through the Scandinavian countries, visiting continuing education programs in various places, and staying with former students when I could. I discovered that in most Scandinavian countries, "guest workers" were not expected to learn the language of the country to which they had emigrated. These were workers imported from other countries like Turkey or Algeria to do the kind of work the natives didn't want to do. The Swedes, Norwegians, Danes, and Finns all wanted their guest workers to go home after a few years, when they were no longer needed. No one wanted to pursue the question about what would happen if their non-native workers didn't go home. (Now, thirty years and more later, countries like Sweden, Denmark, and Holland are dealing with the anger that their non-assimilated workers are demonstrating.)

Before I left for Europe, a new superintendent had come to the Berkeley Public Schools. He had a reputation for being a tough bargainer with teachers' unions. By this time I was secretary of the BFT (Berkeley Federation of Teachers, an AFL/CIO union) and a member of the bargaining team. We had just finished a hard-fought battle to get the School Board to open its books, and allow us to make sure that federal money, in the form of grants, was being used properly. The contract was to take effect in August of 1975.

At the celebration party in June, I was the only one who was suspicious of the ease with which we had managed to get approval of that contentious issue and I tried to warn the president and other officers of the union to beware of the new superintendent's maneuvers. I warned them, "Be careful, this guy will find a way to break the contract. Watch out! Neither the superintendent nor the School Board wants to open their books to the union. There's something fishy about their agreement!" But no one wanted to hear anything negative. I took off for Europe two days after the last day of class.

I was in a hotel in Belgium, planning to leave for home in a few days when I received a telegram from Berkeley, asking that all union members be sure to return before Labor Day, because the superintendent had broken our contract, and we had to discuss a strike call. My prediction had been correct. There was intense discussion about how to respond to the superintendent's breaking of our contract, and after lengthy, often acrimonious arguments back and forth, a strike call was taken, and passed. I realized that the superintendent had set the trap and the bait, and we had swallowed it.

The strike of 1975 was a unifying experience for all teachers employed by the District. Ninety-eight percent of the teachers supported it, including part-time and home-school teachers. The AFL/CIO union leaders who came out to help us said they had never seen such overwhelmingly unified support. I was in charge of public relations, and in the course of arranging television appearances for Judy Bodenhausen, our president, I realized how media bias can frustrate amateur public relations people like me. I kept trying to present the teachers' point of view that we were striking for smaller classes and improved classrooms, and all I got was the response, "Well, you're really talking about money, aren't you? Smaller classrooms mean you have to hire more teachers, right? See? It's all about money." And the body language was dismissive.

The strike lasted three months, and many of us ran out of money. For the first time in my life, I obtained a credit card and borrowed money to live on. What a trap! It took years to escape. After all of our efforts, after all the help we received from professional union leaders, we lost the strike. We were outwitted, out-argued, pressured by parents to give up, and we did. With no support from any part of the mainstream media, we really had no choice. The tight bonds we developed with each other lasted for years, but we never recovered the ground we lost in that fight.

Chapter Thirty-Six:

Bolt

‿ɔ

WHEN I RETURNED FROM EUROPE in time for the union meeting in September, Ricky met me at the airport, and he was full of talk about the band. He wanted to know if I would come to the Fillmore venue where the band was playing that night; he was so anxious for me to hear them. I laughed, and told him I had just come off a seventeen-hour flight, and I didn't propose to go anywhere for at least twenty-four hours. He said that the band was playing the following night, and that there was someone he wanted me to meet. He kept talking about the wonderful man who was the manager of the band, and how he really wanted me to come to hear the group. He was totally absorbed in his current life; we didn't talk about my worries about the impending teacher strike, or about my trip. Our conversation was all about the band.

The following evening Ricky showed up at eight o'clock, ready to drive me to the city. He looked me over critically as I came down the stairs wearing black silk pants, flared at the bottom, a silk blouse, and hand-knit wool stole. He nodded, as if to say, "That's fine." I wondered why he was so interested in what I was wearing, but I figured he wanted me to make a good impression on his friends.

That was the evening I met Leon, the manager of the band, who became the next important figure in my life. Leon and I began a smoldering love affair that night, which lasted for years. I will call him "Bolt," short for "Thunderbolt." I was fifty-seven, and felt adventurous. Ricky and I walked into the small, smoky club, which had the intimacy of a neighborhood pub. The musicians were young, between nineteen and twenty-five. The lead singer, George, was about twenty-three, and he was singing when we walked in.

We stood at the entrance, and I looked tentatively over the scene. A lean, tall, six-foot-four, handsome black man rose from his seat against the wall and came over to us.

"This is Bolt," Ricky said, introducing him.

He smiled at Ricky, took my hand, and looked at me. "Ah, finally, here you are," he said. "Ricky has been telling me about you." Ricky drifted away, and Bolt led me to his table. He had a tall drink of something or other in front of him, and he asked me what I would like to drink. I said I'd have rye whisky on the rocks with a soda chaser.

"Good choice." He smiled. "The only rye whisky they have is Old Overholt, and they don't water it down."

He said he was the band's manager, and he spoke protectively about them.

"They're young," he said, "and they're good, but they're not as good as they're going to be."

Bolt had a deep voice and a commanding presence. There was a magnetism about him that struck me like a physical charge. We didn't spend much time in the pub. In fact, after I had my drink, Bolt invited me to come outside with him—he wanted to smoke a joint, he said. I learned that Bolt had brought the band west from New Jersey, and that he commuted between Los Angeles and San Francisco on business. We talked about music, rock bands, and the San Francisco scene. We sat in his vintage Cadillac, and while he smoked, I felt myself relax and laugh, free and childlike, a feeling I hadn't had for a long time. I didn't smoke because smoking made me cough. It seemed natural to invite Bolt to come back to my house in Berkeley.

At home, in bed, we talked and talked, and I discovered a new kind of seduction. Bolt fucked my mind before we made love. He got into me with his talk, opened me up, and got me to think, to reveal myself, to loosen up and let go.

"Relax, baby," he said. "What kind of inhibitions do you have?"

"I feel that it's wrong to want you to keep probing my body with your gentle hands, and that I should repress the shivers of delight along my spine."

He chuckled. "Tell me where you are when I caress your breasts," he said.

"I can't."

"Try."

"All right," I said. I talked about dreams, ambitions, feelings, and disappointment.

"That's not what I mean," he said. "You are outside of your feelings. You don't have to edit for me, just talk." Then he laughed. "You've got a long way to go, kiddo, and I'm going to take you there. I've known lots of women, black, white, professionals, and music groupies. They all let go eventually. I know how to reach deep inside you, and get you to accept sheer physical delight. Relax, because when you let go, I can too. Here, take a small drag, maybe you won't cough," he said, passing me the joint.

I tried, but I coughed and sputtered; I gave up. I didn't need the pot. I needed someone to listen to me. That was the ultimate seduction, and I felt myself relaxing. Bolt's power and beauty entranced me.

"I have a sense that we have met before, in another life," I confessed. "Is that silly? Do you feel that too?"

"Of course," he said. "You belong in my life. I knew it the first time I saw you. When you walked into the club, in those long black silk slacks and that Picasso print shirt, with that shy what-am-I-doing-here-look, I decided exploring you would be fun."

"I feel like I'm floating," I said, "almost outside my body."

"Ssh. Don't talk now. Just let go."

His hands were all over me. I sighed and drifted off. We learned to move in rhythm; I could sense what he was thinking, and he knew when I was turned off. Through it all there was a dreamlike quality to our relationship. It was so different from anything else I had ever experienced with anyone. Bolt was always high on something, and he kept assuring me that being high was fine. He would smoke weed, drink brandy, snort coke, and yet always be in control. At least that's how it seemed to me. His enthusiasm for life was infectious, as was his love of living deeply, for the moment.

"Let's go for a walk," he'd say.

And off we would go, for a walk in the grass around Lake Merritt. He loved to walk barefoot, especially in the grass.

"I like to feel the earth beneath my feet," he said. "Don't you like that tickly feeling between your toes?"

"Oh, yes," I said, enjoying the sense of being so brazen, walking in the grass in the middle of the day, goofing off from work, being a kid again, playing hooky. There was a sense of dangerous excess about Bolt. He was passionate and extreme. He was expansive, mercurial. Sometimes he would pick me up and twirl me around in the air, exuberantly happy. He would launch into a song from The Music Man and act out the scene for me, letting his voice boom out across the lake, while I sat on the grass, entranced.

At home, in bed, we were in fantasyland. We could talk ourselves into a state of ecstasy. "Just imagine we're on an island in the Caribbean—Jamaica, maybe—it's warm and damp," his deep voice soothing and seductive, his large hands cupping my buttocks as he lifted and held me.

"Do you hear the waterfall?" He whispered as he nuzzled my ear.

I loved every part of the ceremony we established—the talk, the mental and physical exploration of each other—I was finally willing to accept what I'd always thought of as my hidden, unacknowledged, self. I learned to run my fingers up and down the inside of his thighs, relishing the moan of satisfaction that came from him. His skin was the color of milk chocolate. He was the most beautiful man I had ever known.

The important part of the talking—and the fucking—was how we made each other feel. I always felt like a Queen of the Nile, and he said he achieved a high with me that he'd never reached with any other woman, black or white. I really loved him for that. I loved Bolt in a way I'd never loved any man before. I accepted him in a way I'd never done before. I suspended judgment, thought I knew him for what he was, and walked around or passed over whatever offended me about his behavior. I had broken off relationships with men who drank too much, used foul language, and seemed to lose control when they became angry. With Bolt, I pushed away the things that made me want to cry or hit or spit. I looked past the cocaine, the drinking, the way he took me for granted. I don't know why. His strength and control mesmerized me. I remember a statement by the French physicist, Blaise Pascal, who wrote this about three hundred years ago: "The heart has reasons that reason cannot comprehend." I know that I envied Bolt's assurance. I was never that bold or assured. I had to know where I was going, all the time. I usually wanted to be in charge, but with Bolt, I let all that go. I didn't nurture him; he nurtured me.

Bolt encouraged me to be wild and silly. In the bath together, I would splash and tickle him, as if we were kids again. It was intoxicating. I didn't mind getting drunk, dancing around the apartment naked—Bolt made me feel that anything I did or said was all right with him. But sometimes the booze or the dope would take over, and he would rant and rave about "the white bastards in control of the music business"—swear he'd get even. I couldn't handle the intensity of his anger. I would become silent and turn away. He would look at me, take a deep breath, shake himself like a wet puppy, and tease me out of my withdrawal. He usually knew when his language or behavior offended me, and he would be able to switch off his smoldering anger.

When something in particular would set him off, his face would darken, his eyes would burn, and he would pace restlessly around my living room. Bolt never raised his hand to me, or threw the furniture around, but his deep, choking anger frightened me. When he was in that state, I felt outside, far away. He simply didn't "see" me. I would wonder at those times whether he gave himself to our relationship as fully as I did. Then I would shove the thought aside.

In my heart I knew our adventure couldn't last. Bolt took me into a world I had never known, a musician's world. It was a world of female groupies, flattery and deceit, suspicion and jealousy, free access to drugs I never knew existed. This was Bolt's world. He knew it was a game where the odds of winning were stacked against him and against his band; they all knew the stakes at risk in jockeying for power in that game. It was a world I would never know again.

My world was peopled with academics, writers, artists, and professionals, who defined themselves as liberal activists. We lived safely within the boundaries of the white, educated middle class. Now I found myself in the middle of the rock music world, divided as it was between rock and pop. Pop was the crossover world where the real money was to be made; rock at that time was the pigeonhole black groups were pushed into. That was the pigeonhole Bolt hated, the color line imposed on him; the barrier he was determined to break. I knew the intensity of the ambition that drove Bolt. I could identify with that. I thought I understood the game, but I didn't realize how quickly it could change.

George and the band members were living in a small apartment in Oakland, and Ricky stayed there too. Before Bolt met me, he would also stay in the apartment when he came up from Los Angeles. He ran a cleaning franchise business in Los Angeles, and used the income to support the band. In his spare time, he hustled the studios in Hollywood, trying to get a record deal for the group. He loved having my place to come back to instead of staying with George and the band. He liked having someone closer to his own age (sixty) to talk to. Whenever he returned from Los Angeles, he regaled me with stories of how the franchise business worked, but he avoided any specific information about record deals. He said it was bad luck to talk about something that hadn't happened yet.

One day, we were at the DeYoung Museum in San Francisco, and Bolt stopped suddenly in the West African Hall before an exhibit of an African compound. There was a statue of a man who could have been his ancestor. Bolt had a body like a Nigerian spear-thrower. He was tall, long in the body, lean, with long arms and large hands. As we gazed at the statue, we looked at one another, smiled, and nodded. We squeezed each other's hands as a current of recognition swept through us. He had told me about growing up in New Mexico and of his Cherokee Indian grandmother. I saw the traces in his chiseled aquiline nose, his high cheekbones and forehead. That night he talked about "what-might-have-been" and of how his life changed after he left home.

"I was born in Albuquerque, New Mexico. My mother was a music teacher, my father a tailor. We were middle class, two cuts above Mexican and Indian. I didn't think of myself as different from anybody else until I went east to study law." He stopped and took a long swallow of his drink. I stroked his neck, and gently massaged his shoulders. He reached around and kissed my hand. "Don't stop, baby. That feels good."

I gave him a squeeze and he kissed the top of my head. "You know, that was the first time I realized what it was to be black in the U.S.A." His voice hardened, and he shook his head as if trying to get rid of something unpleasant. "After two years at Princeton, I realized that a black lawyer in Philadelphia would end up in the bail bond business or be relegated to being a minor clerk in some second-rate law office. That wasn't for me, so I dropped out. I couldn't see myself pushing against those invisible walls, and that was why I quit, went to Philly and became a disk jockey. I was such a hotshot radio announcer and salesman that I got the nickname 'Thunderbolt.' Are you sure you want to hear all this stuff?"

I was fascinated. "Of course I do. What happened in Philadelphia? How did you happen to hook up with George?"

"Oh, I dropped into a small club one night in East Philly. George had a small band; all young black men, and the songs he was singing sounded different from anything I'd been hearing. We had a little talk, and it turned out that George had written his own material. Right then and there I decided that I could help George become a star, and I liked the idea. I figured that with my connections we might both make some money. George had cut a few forty-fives, and I contacted some buddies of mine in Chicago, who promised to play his records on their stations. I thought we could build up a reputation, then go to Chicago, cash in on that reputation through record sales, and then go to Los Angeles. That was my long-range plan. We worked hard in Philly the next two years and even played the Palladium. We were big, and decided to hit the road."

Bolt's eyes shone as he described the old bus he bought, and their trip to Chicago. He laughed ruefully. "The trouble was that the guys I thought were my pals double-crossed me. They said the owners of the station wouldn't let them play any unknowns—so there we were, stuck in Chicago—couldn't even get a gig. We loaded up the bus and headed west. Some day I'll tell you about a small town in Kansas where the bus broke down and we ended up spending six weeks there. What a kick! But let's go to bed now, baby."

During the long nights Bolt and I spent talking, I got all the stories about his life, which deepened my understanding of his complex personality. I finally heard about how their bus broke down in that small town in Kansas—a town whose citizens had never seen or known black people. He told me about how the townspeople elected him honorary mayor, and he showed me the newspaper clippings. He laughed as he described the band's reaction to fields and fields of hemp, being grown for rope.

"Wow!" they had cried. "Look at all that marijuana!"

Bolt talked about the music scene in Los Angeles, bitterly recounting the snubs and brush-offs he'd received, vowing to "show those bastards" some day. I heard the pride and bitterness in his voice.

"You can't imagine what it's like. I know how good George and the guys are. We had half a dozen forty-fives out, selling like hotcakes in the East, and those bastards wouldn't even listen to them! We had a recording date all set up, but when the van broke down, we were delayed, and missed the date. Do you think anybody in that fucking music business would cut us any slack for that? Nah, they're so damn superior, they love to stomp all over you. Ah, the hell with it."

Bolt's visits to Berkeley became a magical interlude in my everyday life. When I went out with him, I felt as if I was on parade, as if I was thumbing my nose at the careful middle-of-the-road person I had become. Bolt was a commanding figure; his height, his graying hair, and neatly trimmed beard poised above an elegantly cut suit and handmade shoes; he had a way of walking and looking a person in the eye that was at once arresting and appealing.

We went to an opera at the Civic Opera House in San Francisco one evening. I'd been given complimentary passes, which we exchanged for tickets at the box office. I expected to be stuck in the second balcony, but the cashier took one look at Bolt and gave us first-floor seats. As we walked down the aisle, it seemed to me that waves of people parted before us. Both Bolt and I were elegantly dressed. That night, I was wearing an off-the-shoulder iridescent gray taffeta long dress with a coral suede cummerbund and a coral suede and taffeta stole. My long dark brown hair, twisted into a French roll with a coral hair ornament, my long neck and dancer's walk added to the impressive appearance we made. I came to just under his shoulder, so he was always deferentially bowed over my head. His mellifluous voice and laugh created head-turnings at the bar at intermission. I enjoyed the sensation of being onstage, which was how I always felt when I was with him. We also enjoyed the rather shocked double take, as I would introduce him to friends in the lobby of the Opera House, at the theater or the ballet. We loved watching the surprised look change to interest and respect as Bolt began to talk, his law school-educated self emerging, his rough, swearing, music business-talk turned off for those occasions.

We both knew what a grand game it was; that the bottom line was having enough money for first-floor tickets and/or connections that put you in the right place at the right time. We were both cynics, really, and that was part of the strong connection between us.

Some time in October Bolt made a connection with a record company in Los Angeles that promised to listen to a tape of the band. That was the beginning of a furious period of rehearsals. Between October and December 1975 Bolt made his musicians rehearse constantly. When he thought they were ready, he scrounged up the money to get them into a recording studio, produced a tape and took it south. In January 1976, a prominent record company bought the tape, and Bolt signed the deal in February 1976. The white guitarist had to quit, and Ricky did, too, because the record company informed Bolt that they would not be able to tour the South as a mixed black and white band. This was 1976!

Ricky was devastated by his change in status, and had to come home. I had rented his room to a young man who refused to leave, and Ricky had to sleep on the couch in the living room. It was a terrible time. Ricky had accepted Bolt as my lover, and he had accepted Bolt's behavior as a surrogate father. They had a good relationship, and I appreciated both Bolt's support of Ricky, and Ricky's acceptance of him.

Bolt hated the band being pigeonholed as a rock band, rather than as pop, and he felt stigmatized. But he had no choice. He also hated being on the road, since he knew the kind of second-rate accommodations they would be offered. He hated the demeaning aspects of this part of the music business, yet he knew it was necessary. He would often call me from Atlanta, Memphis, Louisville, Nashville, as they traveled. I could hear the frustration and simmering anger in his voice; I could hear his not wanting to be where he was.

One night in the spring of 1976, I saw a side of Bolt I had only sensed before. If he felt betrayed, or if he felt anyone he was protecting at the time was betrayed or downgraded in any sense, I knew he would launch into a frightening diatribe. This time I was in its path. Bolt and the band were coming back from several weeks on the road. I drove to the airport to meet them as they got off the plane. They were tired and subdued, except for Bolt, who was high on something and feeling mean. I was the only one with any visible economic stability. I had an American Express card! The band members needed transportation—they would be in the Bay Area for a few days—just long enough to do a gig, and then move on. They needed to rent a car.

The band members were sitting around in the baggage claim area, stretched out on several seats. I walked over to George. "Better come with me, George," I said. "Do you have your driver's license with you? We have to go over to the Avis Rent-A-Car place."

Bolt was furious. "What are you talking about? Just get the fucking car!"

I looked at him, stunned. What did he expect me to do? Did he want me to conjure up the car without anyone connected with him assuming any kind of formal or legal responsibility? I wasn't aware at the time of the depth of his anger at what he perceived as humiliation. It took several years for me to fully comprehend Bolt's behavior. Bolt was behaving in the tradition of kings who could do no wrong. The only problem was that Bolt had anointed his protégé, George, prince, and no one else recognized Bolt as a king, or George as a prince.

George immediately went up to Bolt, and whatever he said to him worked, because Bolt subsided; George and I got the car registered to him, and we took off. Half the band went with George in the rental car—the others went with Bolt and me in my car. On the way home, Bolt began to lambast me with such a stream of abusive language that I suddenly pulled over to the side of the road, and in a tight, hard, clipped voice, said, "Look, you bastard, if you don't shut your mouth, you can just get the hell out." I don't even remember what he said, but words like "bitch" and "cunt" were probably part of his diatribe.

There was shocked silence in the car, as if how did I dare to question the King, the giver of all sustenance, the great Thunderbolt. Ben, the oldest member of the band, leaned over and stroked Bolt gently on the shoulder. We sat there. We waited. The silence grew. Finally, I put the car in gear, and in a thick, heavy, sullen silence, we continued on our way to Oakland.

His mood passed, and after a few days of rest, Bolt became the loving, caring person I connected with. One day, after a particularly stormy session on the telephone with somebody at the record company, he came into my bedroom in a rage, and said he was going to Los Angeles to live. He said that he needed to stay on top of the record deal and keep those fucking bastards in line. He took all his beautiful suits out of the closet and threw them on the floor, grabbed his shoes and began stuffing everything into his bags. I just sat on the bed and watched him, feeling numb. Finally, choosing my words carefully, I said, "Do you want me to pack for you?"

He looked at me, his eyes dark with anger, gave that familiar sigh, shook himself, said, "Yes, baby, would you?" and sat down heavily in the only chair in the room. "I'm tired."

I repacked his stuff, putting the suits and slacks and jackets on hangers in the garment bag, putting shoetrees in his shoes, and getting things squared away neatly in his suitcases.

"When are you leaving?" I asked, sitting on the floor with the entire luggage around me, managing to be very calm and not letting the tears show.

He gathered me in his arms, held me close and said, "Oh, hell, I have to go. Come with me."

I took a deep breath, and thought, "Oh, well. I'll just take sick leave. I haven't used any of it that's coming to me."

We drove south in Bolt's old cream-colored Cadillac, which he'd had someone hand-wash and hand-polish for him every week, even though the car was a good twenty years old. He really loved that car. When we got to Los Angeles, we went shopping for an apartment. We had to be a bit circumspect, because of the race thing. I looked pretty dignified, and I'd go in first and check the place out. If I liked it, and if the price was right, I'd say, "Excuse me, I'll just get my husband—he's in the car. If he likes it, we'll take it."

Since there was a law in L.A. against racial discrimination in housing, the landlords couldn't say anything when Bolt would saunter up in his three hundred dollar cream-colored slacks, his open-at-the-collar handmade shirt, and his bare feet. Although he had about ten pairs of shoes and handmade boots, he hated shoes and boots. He said they hurt his feet—and even if they didn't, he said he liked the feel of earth; said he could feel the earth beneath the concrete.

We looked at about five places, and finally chose one with a swimming pool. After we'd moved in—it was a partially furnished apartment—we sat down in the living room, bouncing on the hard cushions of the secondhand couch. Bolt put his arm around me, and as I snuggled up to him, he took a deep breath and told me there was another reason he'd decided to move permanently to Los Angeles. It seems that his wife of eight or ten years or so had decided to leave Philadelphia and come west to join him. Now that he was making money, and was in a position to make a lot more, she had decided it was time to leave her church groups and claim her rightful position. Bolt said it wasn't only his wife; it was that Los Angeles was where the action was, and he needed to be there. He swallowed hard.

What? A wife? I got coldly angry. Bolt had never mentioned a wife. I was prepared for the second part of his reason, but news about his wife stunned me. My body stiffened and my mind froze. His arm tightened around my shoulders in what he thought was a reassuring pressure. In the taut silence I shrugged myself out of his arms and went into the kitchen.

Damn it! Why hadn't I asked more questions? Why wasn't I more curious about those blank years in Philadelphia, even New Jersey? What kind of deluded fool am I anyway?

Struggling with fury, my hands shaking, I made myself a stiff drink. *"Calm down," I said to myself. "You knew it couldn't last. You just thought you would be able to decide when it was over. Well, here it is. It's over. Now what."*

I sat down at the plastic kitchen table. I picked up the phone, called the airport, and made a reservation for the next plane back to San Francisco. I took a deep breath and walked back into the living room. In that clipped voice I'd only used once before with him, I said, "Will you drive me to the airport, or shall I take a cab?"

He took my hand, pulled me down on the couch beside him, his face sad. "Listen, baby," his voice low, consoling. "That marriage was over long ago. She's a middle-class educated black woman, active in community affairs, wrapped up in church stuff. I have a responsibility to her. I left, sure. I was choking in that proper atmosphere, I had to get out. But I never stopped sending money, whatever I could spare. News gets around, she found out from somewhere, not from me, that I was beginning to make some real money, finally. She has a claim on me, I can't help it. Try to understand."

I sat rigid, my hands clenched. "You could have told me. You didn't trust me."

He looked at my face, sighed, got up, and we went downstairs to the car. He put my suitcase in the trunk and we drove in a weighted silence to the airport. The unspoken words trembled in the air. When we got to the airport, he said, in that teasing voice I knew so well, "We just got here, you know, do you really want to go back so soon? We haven't even tried the bed out yet!"

I sat silently in the car, listening to the voices that had been jabbering inside my head all the way to the airport. *Do I really want to give up this crazy, wild, unreal life just yet? What do I really have to lose? She's still in Philadelphia, isn't she? What the hell!*

Suddenly, something in me gave way. I laughed, threw my arms around his neck and said, "Of course not, you crazy bastard. You're right. We just got here."

We laughed, the tension spilling out of us. He said, "Shall we go home and fuck or eat first?"

I said, "Let's eat, I'm starving."

So we went to an oyster bar on the wharf, stuffed ourselves with oysters and martinis, went back to the apartment, and had a glorious time.

That's the way it went for the next six months. I went back to the Adult School in Berkeley, and on Friday afternoons I'd take the afternoon plane to Los Angeles. I'd fly back to Oakland on the seven a.m. flight to get to work by nine. Sometimes I'd be pretty sleepy, but it was worth it. Some weekends Bolt would come to me, and it was all right. I knew we were on borrowed time. I liked living on the edge.

During the long weekends and the long nights together Bolt talked about the world he lived in. "It's all bullshit, baby, you know that," he'd say, in a ruminating kind of voice, and then I knew he was moving into an area he usually kept closed off. In the romantic aura I had created around Bolt, I thought of him as altruistic. I thought his anger was directed at the treatment of blacks everywhere. Hell, no. He only cared about the band—and himself. He kept telling me that.

"Listen, I'm where I am because I want to make a lot of money fast—and get out. I don't give a shit for music—George's or anybody else's. I'm in this business for me, and don't you forget it!"

Somehow, I managed not to hear what he was saying. By this time, late 1977, the band was churning out one or two gold records a year, and Bolt was getting restless. He made sure that George and the other musicians in the band invested their money in real estate, as he did, and tried to make sure that they didn't blow away their windfall. He felt responsible for them. Bolt wanted to be successful in the white man's world on his own terms—and he was convinced that money would do it.

"Everyone has his price, baby, even you. I intend to get mine."

"Really? What's my price?"

"Not money, baby. Power and you love it. I make you feel powerful, and that's why you and I get along. You have more than money. You have class. I need money for people to recognize my class. Don't talk to me about 'black people.' I don't give a fuck for 'black people.' I'm here for all I can get. I'm here for me, and I aim to get what I want. Sure, I'm helping George, but that's only because George is my ticket to money and power. I use everybody."

The summer of 1977 I went to Japan to conduct a teacher-training workshop, and to recruit teachers for a special program at San Francisco State University. I was running away from the inevitable end of my and Bolt's relationship, and running toward an expanded part of my professional life. When I returned, I found out from George that Bolt's wife had indeed come to Los Angeles, and that Bolt had moved to a three-bedroom apartment, big enough for him to have his own breathing space. I never called him, or tried to contact him in any way. He never called me either. I knew that part of my life was really over now. A couple of months later I heard from George that

Bolt had cashed out some of his investments and gone to Louisiana. After that he really dropped out of my life, but never completely out of my mind.

Several years later, I got a phone call from someone who had stayed in touch with the band. I was sitting in my apartment, gazing out at the garden, thinking about Bolt, when the phone rang. "Did you know that Bolt died?" she said. "He was at a party somewhere in New Orleans, and just keeled over. Heart attack."

I felt as if someone had punched me in the stomach. "Ohh," I sighed. "Thanks." I hung up and sat there, numb. I wondered if he had finally "shown those bastards," and died with no regrets. I found myself back in that Los Angeles apartment, having just heard about his wife. I began to remember everything—the good things—and the bad. I remembered best how good I felt when we were fucking, especially the mind-fucking, how he got me to accept the daring part of me that said, "Why not? It's all right to lose control. You're safe. He'll catch you. Let go!" Was I sorry? Not really. I knew, thanks to Bolt, I was not the same person who walked into that nightclub on that rare night in San Francisco in 1975.

I learned something about myself during the affair with Bolt. I learned what fun and how satisfying it is to make physical love with a good partner at any age. At sixty, Bolt was three years older than I was; an experienced and careful lover. He knew how to bring out sensual enjoyment in me, engaging on an intellectual as well as an emotional level. He understood how important it is to use the mind in order to release the spirit. His childhood, with a loving, intelligent mother, and a responsible father who had his own tailoring business, must have had an effect on his personality. He was a nurturing man, who awakened my sexuality, enabling me to enjoy the act of sex without guilt.

Chapter Thirty-Seven:
Korea

⁌

IN THE YEARS BETWEEN 1976 AND 1978, Ricky did several things. He left the band, studied for, and got his G.E.D. (General Education Degree, the equivalent of a high school diploma). Then he entered Laney College, a community college in Oakland, and in three months was on the Dean's List, having achieved high honors in algebra, calculus, advanced chemistry and physics. He had decided to study for an engineering degree at the Maritime Academy in Vallejo, California, and join the Merchant Marines.

The other thing he did was to change his last name from Skahen to Lucien by petitioning the court in Alameda County to change his name. He chose Lucien because he idolized a Cuban musician by that name. He could do that because he was over eighteen. At that point I knew he would become his own father, as the counselor-psychologist had predicted when Ricky was thirteen.

In August 1978, I was teaching in a summer intensive teacher-training course for Japanese teachers of English at San Francisco State University, having spent several months in Japan prior to teaching the course. That was the year the California State Legislature passed Proposition 13, also known as the Gann Initiative, which reduced tax support for public education in California. That proposition was sold to the public as taxpayer relief, and what it did was to undercut a carefully built infrastructure for support of social and educational programs in the state.

One of the consequences of the passage of Proposition 13 was that the

Berkeley Board of Education abolished my job at the Berkeley Adult School as a cost-cutting measure. I was offered a job as a long-term substitute, since I had tenure, and couldn't be fired. They hoped I would quit, of course. I was incensed. I had created the curriculum for the ESL program, helped to train the teachers that were hired, and had built a strong, cooperative teaching cadre. Now I was out. I had been named "Outstanding Teacher of the Year" in 1976, had been active in the union, and had done professional presentations at conferences. The teaching videos I had produced for Palomar College were in wide use, and now I was being tossed aside like an old shoe.

That summer I was invited to participate in a three-week program at San Francisco State University for Japanese teachers of English. It was the first teacher-training institute in which I was invited to teach, even though I didn't have a master's degree in TESOL. Of course I shared my distress with my colleagues, and one of them, Suzanne Griffin, suggested that I apply for a teaching position at St. Mary's College in Moraga, which was just starting English as a Foreign Language program. I wasn't sure I had the qualifications to teach in a four-year college, but I went to St. Mary's anyway for an interview.

At that time, the Christian Brothers, a teaching branch of a Catholic brotherhood, were the directors of St. Mary's. Many of the priests were professors at the college, and I was interviewed by one of them. After looking over my resume, he asked me if I had a master's degree in teaching English as a second or foreign language. He noticed that I had written a thesis in the field of remedial reading in 1941, but that I had been one course short of completing the academic work leading to the M.A.

I said, "No, I don't have a master's degree in TESOL, but I'm really interested in teaching at St. Mary's. If I agree to get my degree in one year, will you hire me? I think I can do that while I'm teaching at St. Mary's."

He looked at me searchingly, and after a long pause said, "I think we can consider the possibility. You have a very impressive resume. I'll take it up with our Board of Directors, and we'll let you know."

Driving back to Berkeley through the leafy, pastoral roads of Moraga, I wondered how I would fit into the calm, peaceful world of that cloistered campus. I looked at all the lush estates behind their ornamental gates and wondered what I was doing in that atmosphere. Also, I had learned that most of my students would be from Saudi Arabia, the United Arab Emirates, and Iran. I would be teaching in a newly organized English language program for foreign students, and I would be teaching freshman writing, among other things. I felt very anxious about the prospect, and didn't think that I, a city girl, belonged in that atmosphere. I remembered my first job interview in Marin, and felt something of the same apprehension. Would I fit in that environment? Of course, I didn't know whether I would be offered the job, but there was something positive about the interview. I called Suzanne when I got home.

"Suzanne," I said, "I'm not sure I belong in that rarefied and bucolic atmosphere, teaching rich students from Arab countries."

Suzanne answered with a question, "Rhoda," she said, "Are you ambitious?"

That was a stunning question. I took a long breath. "Yes, I guess so."

Suzanne was emphatic. "Then go for it. If you don't, you will be a big frog in a small pond. You have a chance to be a big frog in a big pond. Take it."

St. Mary's offered me a job and I took a year's unpaid leave from the Berkeley Unified School District, not ready to retire from the system just yet. I was assigned fifteen hours of teaching at St. Mary's, and taking Suzanne's advice, began the most intensive year of my life. I registered at San Francisco State University in the master's program in English with an emphasis in TESOL in August of 1978, signing up for fifteen units in the fall and fifteen units in the spring. I intended to graduate in May 1979. I was sixty years old.

My schedule meant that I got up at seven every morning, drove to St. Mary's, taught my classes, and then took BART or drove to San Francisco for late afternoon and evening classes. I had not been in a formal university classroom for forty years, but all the habits of study came back. I knew that I would have to do a lot of reading in my courses, and although I read fairly rapidly, knew that I would have to increase that speed. So I signed up immediately for a laboratory course, and managed to double my reading speed in two months.

It was a heady experience; I lived in a tunnel. I didn't even have time to write letters. A letter took twenty minutes, and I never had a free twenty minutes. During the hours I spent studying in my room upstairs in the Eunice Street house, Ricky was studying in his room, working on his goal to enter the Maritime Academy the following year. I liked the academic atmosphere on the second floor of my house.

One evening, in one of my classes at San Francisco State, a student came up to me and said, "What are you doing in this class? I just saw you on video demonstrating the Silent Way."

I laughed and said, "I'm getting the mark on my forehead. I'm in the process of getting my M.A." *I realized that I needed this mark of validation, and suddenly understood why. I realized that when I was in the leather business, I was haunted by a sense of uncertainty. Yes, I had achieved international recognition of my skills in designing leather clothing, but had I gone to a reputable design institution and graduated? No. Therefore there was always a nagging sense of non-approval. I was self-taught in the fashion world, and apologetic. This time around, beginning a new career, I was going to do it right. I knew I was a good teacher, and a good researcher, but this time, I was going to be validated. I was going to be legitimate.*

I graduated in May 1979, having completed a thesis and two major papers. It was exciting, and I felt ten feet tall. Ricky completed his year at Laney, and was admitted to the Maritime Academy. We had both set ourselves important goals, and basked in each other's achievement.

I went back to the Berkeley Adult School, and continued to give presentations at various conferences, building on the research I had done at San Francisco State. In talking to teachers around the state, I realized that not many teacher-training courses offered any kind of survey course of our field. I knew that my thesis, a comparison of the six major methodologies then currently in vogue, offered a new approach. I took my idea to the Director of Education at the University of California, Berkeley Extension, and offered to teach a course called "Exploring the Process in TESOL." Marty Egan, the director, liked the idea, and said that they would offer the course if fifteen people signed up. Once the course was announced, registrations poured in, and the department accepted seventy-five people.

I called a friend of mine who was currently teaching English in a high school in Sacramento, and asked her if she would be willing to co-teach the course with me. Sharon was still in the TESOL program at San Francisco State, but I knew her abilities, and knew that we shared the same philosophy about the importance of student-oriented classroom teaching.

The course was extremely successful, and it became the basic course in the TESOL Certificate Program at UC Berkeley Extension. The program is still going on today.

In January 1981, I received a call from Father Norbert Tracy, a Jesuit priest and professor at Sogang University in Seoul, Korea. Father Tracy had been a professor at the University of San Francisco, and was now in charge of a special program at Sogang. He said he had been referred to me by Suzanne Griffin, and wanted to talk to me about teaching in South Korea. Suzanne had told him that I was the person he needed for his new teacher-training program.

We met at a small restaurant near the Claremont Hotel in Berkeley, and I listened politely while he told me of the project he had in mind for Sogang. He wanted to set up what he intended to call the Institute for English as an International Language, and he was working with the Korean Department of Education to retrain one hundred teachers of English, including high school and university teachers. He said the Peace Corps had started the process, and he wanted to continue it with the help of the Fulbright Commission. He had it all figured out. I would apply for a Fulbright; Sogang University would cosponsor the appointment and split the cost. He was a confident man, and seemed to be sure that all I had to do was to apply, and I would get the appointment.

While I listened to his proposition, I wondered, what did Suzanne tell him about me? He seems absolutely convinced that I am the right person for the job!

I asked Father Tracy how long the commitment would be, and he replied that it would be for two years. I hesitated. "I don't think you want to hire me," I said. "I am a political activist, and Korea is run by a dictator."

Tracy assured me that Chung Doo Hwan was a different sort of autocrat, that he had recently released many intellectuals from prison, and that at any rate, I would be teaching teachers and students of Korea, and I would be performing a needed service. He had the forms for applying for the Fulbright with him, and took them out.

I said, "Another reason I don't think you want me is that I'm a Jew. I have one God and you have three."

"Ah," he said, leaning back in his chair. "That's no problem. Ours is three-in-one. We agree."

How like a Jesuit! I can't argue with him on matters of theosophy. I'd better change the subject.

Aloud, I said, "Well, you are asking me to make a commitment of two years, to go to a country where I really don't know the language, don't know anything about the country, and to take part in the administration of a program that is not clearly defined. I'm not sure I'm ready to do that."

"Oh," he said, "Would you like to go to Korea? When would you like to go?"

Everything was moving pretty fast. I thought quickly. "We have a week in February that includes the two national holidays, Washington and Lincoln's birthdays. In Berkeley we call it 'ski week.' I could go then," I said.

He took out a small notebook. After I gave him the dates, he said. "I'll arrange it. In the meantime, fill out the forms and mail your application to Washington. There's a deadline. Then if everything goes well, and if the Fulbright committee accepts you, we'll be all set. I'm sure you will like Korea." He stood up. As far as he was concerned, the interview was over. We shook hands, and parted.

I walked in a daze to my car, never having been subjected to such an intense selling job. The ticket to Korea arrived in the mail the first week of February, along with a long, welcoming letter from Father Tracy, and I took off for Seoul.

Arriving at the airport in Seoul, I smelled the air—smells just like Chicago, even looks like Chicago, gray, dirty sky, smell of coal dust—cold penetrating damp of a Chicago winter—ugh.

Father Tracy was there with a welcoming committee, consisting of his secretary and some students to help carry my bags. Ushering me into a warm car, we drove off to the Lotte, an elegant hotel in the heart of downtown Seoul. That was the beginning of an intense ten-day selling job, which amounted to a kind of seduction. Seoul, Korea, is a busy, congested city in the northern part of a country with a first-world face and a third-world heart.

Norbert Tracy never looked or acted like a priest. He wore western suits, exquisitely tailored, and behaved like what he was, an urbane, sophisticated man of the world. He brought Professor of Psychology, Rose Kim, with him. Professor Kim came to Norbert's shoulder, an animated, bright, beautiful, accomplished conversationalist. Her English was excellent, and she, too, was beautifully dressed. They took me to a famous French restaurant for dinner.

Over dinner, Tracy casually mentioned the possibility of visiting the Hyundai Shipyards in Pusan, if I was interested. I had done some reading about South Korea, and knew that Pusan was on the southern coast. I thought this might be a good way to see something of the country, so of course I said yes. I caught a quick glance between Kim and Tracy, and suddenly the suggestion didn't seem all that casual. But I dismissed the idea. I asked him how long a trip it would be, and if we would travel by train.

It turned out that Koreans work six days a week, like the Japanese, and the suggestion was that we would travel the next day, Saturday, and spend Saturday night and Sunday in Pusan as the guests of Director Chung, the president of Hyundai Industries. It was about a four-hour trip, and we would travel by train through the center of Korea. I liked the idea, and I liked Rose Kim, who put me at ease.

During our trip to Pusan, Rose got me to talk rather extensively about myself, my son, my ideas about education; in fact, she managed to interview me rather thoroughly. I'm sure she learned more about me than I did about her. Now that I think about it, every time I tried to learn more about her and about her personal life, I ended up getting information about Sogang and about her education in a Catholic university in the Midwest.

We stayed at another elegant hotel in Pusan, and after a few hours of rest, we gathered for dinner in the hotel dining room. All the Hyundai executives were there, seated around a long banquet table with Director Chung at the head. Rose Kim and I were the only women guests. Everyone was drinking whisky, either Scotch or Bourbon, and whisky was the only alcoholic drink offered, all through dinner. I don't remember much about the dinner. However, being seated next to Director Chung, who had an interpreter at his side, I found myself being interrogated rather intensely as to my ideas about teaching English.

When dessert and brandy were served, Director Chung turned and asked me, through the interpreter, whether I would be willing to conduct an intensive training course for his engineers. It seems that he was planning to send a select group of engineers to Detroit to work with a particular General Motors plant. He was planning to expand his shipbuilding business to the making of automobiles in Korea, and he wanted to set up some sort of joint venture. I turned to Rose Kim for further explanation. But Chung, who stood, bowed, and left, interrupted our conversation. Everybody else stood also, and Rose told me, in a soft voice, that she would tell me all about it in my room.

It turned out that Chung was quite serious. The whole trip to Pusan had been planned. When Chung heard that I might come to Korea to do a program for Sogang, he had contacted Tracy, and told him about his own plan. Chung wanted someone to do a four-week intensive course for his engineers, and he thought it would be a good idea to meet me and see if I would do. I asked Rose when he might want a proposal, and she replied, "Tomorrow morning." I fell into a chair, stunned. She also said that the proposal should include a price tag.

It was now midnight; I had had a lot to drink, and it had been a long day. However, all my senses were on high alert, and the adrenaline was flowing. I asked Rose to get me a typewriter and a large pot of strong black coffee, and I started to work. I really didn't know whether or not I could do the kind of job Chung described, so I put what I thought would be a really high price for the course, five thousand dollars, including airfare and housing. My course outline included a "needs analysis" in the form of a questionnaire, and preliminary testing of the engineers, so that I would know what ability levels I would be dealing with. I agreed to provide testing and teaching materials. Rose had mentioned that a group of fifty engineers were to be tested, and maybe twenty-five students would have adequate skills for the kind of intensive course I proposed. I finished the proposal at about four-thirty a.m., and called the desk for a messenger. After sending the proposal off to Chung, I fell into a dreamless sleep, confident that I had risen to the challenge, and that nothing would happen.

I was wrong. Rose came to my door at eleven, all smiles. "Director Chung has accepted your proposal!" she announced, happily. "All you have to do is set the date! But first, he wants to know if you would like a tour of the ship-yards and of the facilities here."

I couldn't believe what I was hearing, but of course I went on the tour, feeling like Alice in Wonderland walking through a wall mirror into entirely new territory. As we wandered around the shipyards, I looked carefully at the men around me. No one spoke English, and I wondered if Hyundai Industries had any kind of English program. Oh, yes, Rose Kim told me, they had a regular English language program in place in Seoul, and that's where my course would take place. Everyone seemed to be taking it for granted that the only thing missing was for me to set a date.

I needed time to sort things out. I had no idea how or what I would do, but I decided to create some space for myself. I told Rose and Father Tracy that I needed to check out the facilities in Seoul, and that I would have to go back to Berkeley to do some research on appropriate materials. I said that I would check my teaching calendar, and send a formal contract once I got home. Privately I decided I needed some advice on how to write a proper contract, and some help in designing the course. There was a TESOL conference scheduled for Detroit in March, and I knew Joe Hambrook, my producer friend at BBC English by Radio and Television, would be there. I liked BBC's teaching materials, and I figured Joe could help me plan the course, maybe even write the contract.

Detroit in March was cold and rainy, but we were in a high-rise hotel with a controlled environment. I wanted to go for a walk around the hotel, which faced a river, but was warned off by security personnel, who were everywhere, that "it wasn't safe" to venture outside the hotel. We were also cautioned not to go into Detroit itself, as if we were inside a fort, surrounded by hostile Indians. I found out later that Detroit was indeed a segregated city, that white and black workers, lining up for public buses, would wait for the next bus if one came along full of either black or white people. Both blacks and whites enforced the segregation. Nobody mentioned other races.

I caught up with Joe at the plenary session, and unloaded all my fear and trepidation about the assignment in Korea. I had set a date for the middle of June, to be completed by the middle of July. I didn't have much time. Joe was reassuring.

"Don't worry," he said. "I have a friend who is an expert in designing diagnostic tests. He worked for the Council of Europe and for IBM, and he's a professor at Oxford. He's here at the conference. Name's Leo Jones; I'll introduce you at dinner. You're available for dinner, aren't you?"

That was Joe. He always came right to the point, whatever the point was. I had met him the previous year at the TESOL conference in San Francisco, and we had become good long-distance friends.

Leo Jones was a tall, thin man, slightly bent over from years of accommodating himself to shorter people, and he spoke in a soft voice with a diffident manner. But when we got onto the topic of diagnostic testing, he became quite animated. He had created something called "The Stages of Attainment Test" for the Council of Europe, which was picked up by IBM, and used extensively by large corporations in many countries. This was a comprehensive test that measured real abilities in using spoken, written, conversational, and technical English. It enabled an instructor or a personnel director to place a non-native English speaker in the area where that person needed instruction. For example, perhaps a student or employee could handle meeting someone at an airport and get that person to the office building, but couldn't carry on a conversation with the visitor in the car on the way. The test would show the exact ability of that person. In addition, the test could reveal a profile showing that that particular employee would be able to handle technical writing better than somebody who could carry on a conversation with a stranger. The test would show the instructor or the director exactly the strengths of his employees. I was fascinated, and made a date with Jones for breakfast. I wanted to see that test.

The Stages of Attainment Test turned out to be the most comprehensive, and the best indicator, of a person's ability in language usage I had ever seen. Not only that, Jones and his coworkers had tied the levels of the test to specific materials, so that the user could assign specific exercises in a particular set of materials designed to improve performance in specific areas.

Oxford Press published the materials, and I had to admire the genius that lay behind this particular design. I knew that Jones was the man I wanted to work with.

I described the task I had undertaken to Leo, and asked him if he would be willing to do the diagnostic testing of the Hyundai engineers. I would split the fee with him, and make sure that his travel expenses and living expenses would be paid while he was in Korea. I said that I would tell Chairman Chung that the deal was a no-go unless he agreed to use Leo Jones as part of my team, and that his expenses would be added on to the fee. Jones would get a net twenty-five hundred dollars (not Korean won) and I would get twenty-five hundred dollars, travel and living expenses paid.

Over the next few days, Leo and I drew up a contract between the two of us, and with Joe's help, a contract to present to Chairman Chung of Hyundai. We agreed that Leo would go to Korea some time in May or June, depending on his schedule at Oxford, would do the testing, then we would meet in the International Lounge at San Francisco Airport on his way home. We would discuss the results of the tests, and Leo would continue his flight to London. I would then have time to digest the test results and design a course that would fit our trainees. It sounded like a sensible plan to us, being the rational academics we believed ourselves to be, but we didn't know what fantasists we were.

I sent the contract on to Korea, having signed it, and left a space for Chairman Chung's signature. I received a letter from somebody at Hyundai Enterprises, but I didn't get a copy of the signed contract back. The letter said that Hyundai agreed to the training, and accepted the dates I had included. There was no mention of payment of airfare.

I called Father Tracy and told him about everything that had happened so far. I also sent him copies of all my correspondence, and told him of my confidence in Jones.

Tracy assured me that Chairman Chung was a man of his word, and that when a Korean pledges his word, that is his bond. I replied, "That's all very well, but who pays for the airline tickets and the hotel?" Tracy said he thought that I would be reimbursed. I thought about that for a few seconds, and then told Tracy to get in touch with whoever handled the payroll at

Hyundai. I said, "Tell the paymaster that unless Hyundai sends a roundtrip ticket to Leo and one to me, neither one of us will come. We don't have the resources to lay out any funds ahead of time." *I didn't know why, but I had a feeling that I had better not take anything for granted.*

The open tickets arrived, and Leo took off for Korea as planned. He called me from the Lotte Hotel, and told me that he intended to go to the Seoul offices of Hyundai the next day and he would let me know how the testing went. I didn't hear from him for a week, and got nervous. Calling him on the ninth day, I found out that he hadn't been able to do any testing at all; that the supervisors of the trainees refused to allow them to leave their jobs for the testing period! I asked him what he'd been doing all that time and he replied that he'd been having a ball, being wined and dined and treated like visiting royalty. He was having a fine time. I was livid, and called the project director at Hyundai immediately.

After listening to profuse apologies about how busy the engineers were, and lame excuses, including sly statements about was this testing really necessary, I told him that he needed to get all the engineers tested within the next two days. If he didn't, the entire project was off, and I would not come in June to do the teaching. I also told him that Hyundai was still liable for twenty-five hundred dollars, not Korean won, payable to Mr. Jones upon his departure. And then I called Father Tracy and told him what I had done. He listened with what I felt was disapproving silence.

I then called Leo, and told him to be prepared to test all the engineers within the next two days, and be prepared to meet me in San Francisco the following Saturday. I told him what had transpired, and suggested that he present his bill to the paymaster when he went to the training school to do the testing. Right here I'm reminded of Robert Burns's poem To a Mouse written in 1785: "The best laid schemes o' mice and men/Gang aft a-gley;/An' lea'e us nought but grief and pain,/For promis'd joy"—our plans were well laid, and left us with nought but grief and pain.

Leo met me as planned, with results of the testing of twenty-five, not fifty, engineers. Of those twenty-five, only two qualified for the level of English they would need to function at an entry level in any automobile plant in Detroit. None of them would be able to function at an executive level, which is where they were in Korea. Those engineers would definitely not be able to handle the English they would need in three to four weeks. Both Leo and I knew that even absolute beginners, under the best of circumstances, could advance only one or two levels within six months. These students had studied English in middle school and high school and had had some English training in special classes at Hyundai, but they had been taught by rote. They had learned to decode the language, but not to read with understanding. They couldn't write well, and they tested at the absolute bottom on the listening part of the test. They could fill in the blanks on standard grammar tests, but they couldn't communicate their ideas. They had no ability for analyzing a written problem and coming up with a coherent plan for solving it. Most of them were at Level Two, and they needed to be at Level Six.

I was devastated, and looked at Leo for some suggestions. He shrugged his shoulders, threw up his hands, and said, "Well, you didn't guarantee their level; you simply said you would teach them how to communicate more effectively in English. If they end up fifty percent better at the end of four weeks than they were at the beginning, you've done your job!" I laughed. We both knew that if a student does nothing at all but sit in a class for four weeks, five hours a day, he will improve his ability in language acquisition by fifty percent. That's not saying very much. I asked him if he'd collected his check. He hemmed and hawed a bit, hunched his shoulders, and finally confessed that he'd agreed to have them send the check to him in London. We said goodbye, and I went home with my test results, heavyhearted.

I had samples of all the materials designed to work with the Stages of Attainment Test, and I had to throw out everything above the lower intermediate level. I decided that was about as far as the most advanced of the engineers would be able to go. I wrote out a carefully detailed profile of each of the twenty-five engineers, stating exactly what their abilities were, using the examples in the tests. I created a class of five groups of five, with graded materials so that the students could work together. I knew they lived in dormitories... none of them was married... and that they would do their homework together, if they did it at all. I sent copies of everything to the director of the project and to Father Tracy. I thought that when they saw the dismal test results they would give up the project, and I wouldn't have to go to Korea in June. I don't know whether they read them, or understood them, but I received a thank-you letter that said they were looking forward to my visit.

I ordered the materials I thought I would need from Oxford Press, plus some supplemental remedial material, and left for Korea the middle of June, with a deep sense of foreboding. By the time I arrived, five more engineers had gotten cold feet, and I had a class of twenty. I discovered that Hyundai had established a private school within their offices in Seoul, staffed with two Americans, an Australian and a Scotswoman. The Americans had never had any English as a Second or Foreign Language training; the Australian had a degree in political science, and the Scotswoman had majored in English rhetoric. None of them had a master's degree in TESOL. They taught English as if it was a dead language, the way the Koreans taught English, but the teachers spoke English in class, and that was what mattered to their Korean bosses. They were totally incompetent, as far as I could see, but they were well paid and comfortable. They looked upon me with suspicion, and I probably came across as an opinionated, arrogant know-it-all. I certainly felt superior to them, and it probably showed.

I've never worked so hard, before or since. I prodded, pushed, cajoled, and spent hours designing different, challenging exercises. Most of the printed materials turned out to be too difficult, and the tapes had to be played over and over and over again before the students could understand the British accents. They all made some progress, and seven of the twenty did extremely well. I managed to take my meals with them, both lunch and dinner, and I think those times were the most effective.

I got those engineers to talk about their home lives, their loneliness, their hopes and dreams. Finally, I got some of them to keep a personal journal. They were worried about going to America, and plied me with questions. What were American girls like? Were all Americans rich? They had seen some American movies (all dubbed in Korean or with subtitles) and wondered if America was like the movies. I had the feeling that nothing I told them would change their fantasies. We did a lot of role-playing, which they enjoyed, and I encouraged them to learn American pop songs. Some of the engineers had guitars, and they brought them to class.

I was due to return to Berkeley on July 10, and went to see the paymaster at the end of June. I gave him a copy of my contract (which had never been signed by anybody but me), that said I was to receive a cashier's check for twenty-five hundred dollars by or before July 5. He took the contract from me without a word. I asked him if I should come back on the fifth of July to pick up my check. He said he would call me. Days went by with no word. I called him on the fifth of July; he was out of town, I was told.

Finally, I caught up with him on the eighth, and he said he wasn't sure that the Bank of Korea had that many dollars in reserve. I can still feel the rage that boiled up inside me.

My Minolta camera had been stolen in the first week on the job, having been removed from a drawer in my desk; I was frustrated, hot and tired. The weather in Seoul was hot and humid and I was fed up. I called Father Tracy in a fury, and said that I would contact the trade commission at the American Embassy and tell them how the Hyundai Corporation was reneging on its agreements. I told him that Jones hadn't been paid yet, and now they were trying to pull the same thing on me. He said he would see what he could do.

Saturday afternoon, July 10, was my departure date. Rose Kim called Saturday morning as I was packing. She said she would take me to the airport, and that we would stop at the Hyundai offices on our way. When we walked into the office, we were greeted with smiles by the entire staff, and the project director handed me the certified check. Then a clerk stepped up and handed me a brand new Minolta camera with a deep bow. I immediately handed the camera to Rose, who took a photo of me accepting the check. We all bowed, smiled, shook hands, and left in a cloud of phony goodwill. Jones also got his check shortly after I got back to Berkeley.

Chapter Thirty-Eight:
Korea and UCB Program

⌒

WHILE I WAS IN TO KOREA IN FEBRUARY 1981, Father Tracy had asked me whether I would be willing to recruit teachers for the special project he wanted me to direct. He was so sure that I would be granted the Fulbright Commission that he acted as if it was a fait accompli. *He was right; the fellowship was approved.* I had agreed, and when I went to the conference in Detroit, I had interviewed twelve teachers, using guidelines based on the Fulbright paradigm, in addition to working out the program for Hyundai engineers.

After the three-week struggle with the Hyundai engineers, I met with Father Tracy and John Harvey in Seoul to discuss the new project that would begin in August. We met for dinner at an elegant French restaurant, and I showed them the questionnaire I had created as well as a tentative contract. John Harvey was a former American army man who had been in Korea for twenty years, fluent in Korean, who was working at Sogang, the sister university for the University of San Francisco. Father Tracy was one of the head administrators at Sogang. Both universities belonged to the Jesuit order, and instructor priests from USF taught at Sogang, on a rotation basis, in many departments.

Tracy wanted to expand the English department, and to establish an Institute for English as an International Language. To that end he was working on a contract with the government of Korea to retrain six hundred high school and university teachers of English, and, at the same time, he wanted to create classes for the general Korean public, especially businessmen. He thought that general public enrollment, plus money from the contract with the Korean government, would create the additional income he needed. Major support for Sogang came from headquarters in Minneapolis.

There would be three of us in the administration, he said; I would be in charge of curriculum and would oversee ten teachers with master's degrees in TESOL, while he and John Harvey would take care of recruiting students and other administrative details, like housing and classrooms. We would be a triumvirate, he said, but would act as one. How Jesuitical!

I brought out the questionnaire I had distributed at the TESOL conference and the tentative contract I had written up. The teachers I interviewed wanted round-trip airfare, paid housing, and at least four weeks paid vacation. I decided to offer seven weeks, four in one chunk, and three taken at different times during the year. I knew that the Korean educational system provided at least three weeks vacation or more every year. I hoped Tracy and the Sogang administration would recognize the advantage of the wording. Father Tracy said he thought the contract was acceptable, and he added a paid two-bedroom apartment for two occupants.

I had asked the twelve teachers I interviewed in Detroit to send their resumes directly to Father Tracy. We agreed to meet in Berkeley in August, sift through the applications, arrange to talk to them by phone, and decide on our staff of ten. John Harvey would have interviewed two former Peace Corps volunteers who still lived in Korea, and I wanted them to consider Kang Hee Won, a woman I had met at San Francisco State, who was getting her master's degree at the same time I was. I argued that she would be a good role model, as a teacher. Tracy was extremely prejudiced against her, but I told him that if Hee Won wasn't accepted as a teacher, I wanted her on the staff as my administrative aide.

After I came back to Berkeley in July, I realized I had to do something about the house. Ricky had moved out and was now living in his own apartment in Berkeley, and I decided to create a small place for myself on what was now the patio in the back of the house. I figured I could rent the house and use the income to pay the mortgage while I was gone, and I would have a place to stay during vacation times.

I contacted two young men who were in the business of installing solar panels on houses in Berkeley. A special tax advantage was offered by the state of California that year, and the idea was intriguing. Paul Cooper and his partner suggested that we build a "solar greenhouse" on my patio as a space for me to live in. It would be a rectangle that was four hundred square feet, with floor to ceiling windows looking out on my deep, lush garden. I loved the idea and, using the money I had earned on the Hyundai project, we drew up the plans. The space was partially built when Harvey and Tracy arrived.

Our conferences went pretty well. Since I had an extension telephone, two of us could listen in on any call we made to prospective teachers. We didn't have the option of a conference call in 1981. We got to know each other pretty well in the relaxed atmosphere of Berkeley, and some of my doubts about how our triumvirate would work began to dissipate. At first I wondered how two men with Korean mind-sets would be able to work with an activist Jewish woman, but they were so courteous and so considerate, I shoved my doubts aside. We got verbal commitments from eight teachers, and Harvey and Tracy said they would follow through on the other two from Korea. Kang Hee Won was also accepted as a teacher in the program.

After Tracy and Harvey left, I began to deal with all the other problems connected with leaving the country for two years. For one thing, there was the new course I had started at UC Berkeley Extension. As I mentioned, that course was called "Exploring the Process in ESL Teaching," and while it had attracted seventy-five students at first, I insisted on limiting enrollment to thirty students. I planned to teach the course twice a year, once in the spring semester and once in the fall. I knew my program filled a need, and I didn't want to give it up. How would I do it? I called Marty Egan, Director of the Educational Department at UC Berkeley Extension.

"Listen, Marty," I said. "I'm going to Seoul, Korea, for two years, starting at the end of August, but I still want to do the TESOL course. This is how I've worked it out. I'll fly in from Korea in February, do the course on two weekends, Friday night, Saturday, and Sunday, read the students' papers in the third week, grade them and turn in the grades on the third weekend.

Then I'll fly back to Korea. I'll be able to do the course twice a year, once in February and once in September, if you agree."

Marty didn't say anything for a while. Then she said, "Are you sure you want to do this? Maybe we could get a substitute."

I was firm. This was my course, and I didn't trust anybody else to do it. "Yes, I do. I love teaching that course; it's my chance to test all the theories I've accumulated over the years, and flying back and forth doesn't bother me. I'll get the grades in on time, don't worry."

Marty agreed, and I turned my attention to cleaning out the big house, finding tenants, and getting ready to leave. I sent two stuffed mailbags to Korea by sea, which included all kinds of books and materials, plus a wideband radio/tape player. I packed prints and tapes I didn't want to live without, and clothes for two seasons. I was full of hope and enthusiasm when I boarded the plane in San Francisco.

Arriving at the airport in Seoul, I was met by Father Tracy, his secretary, Mrs. Gill, and two young men to carry my bags. However, when I heard that I was to share a large, elegant house with four women teachers, one of whom had brought her ten-year-old daughter, I felt a stab of betrayal. *Wasn't I supposed to be an administrator? Didn't I deserve an apartment of my own? As usual, I registered my feeling and set it aside.*

We all assembled for our first orientation meeting on Monday morning in Father Tracy's conference room at Sogang University. We introduced ourselves, spoke about our teaching experiences, and what we hoped to achieve in Korea. Tracy talked about the main project, a contract with the Korea Department of Education, to train six hundred teachers of English, drawn from high schools throughout Korea, and to create an English as an International Language Institute to attract nonacademics who wanted to improve their English. He spoke in broad, general terms, and I sensed uneasiness among the teachers.

"When do we start?" Alan, one of the teachers, asked. We all nodded; that was the question on our minds, also.

Tracy was vague, and I got the first of many sinking feelings in my stomach. He said the final contract had not come through yet, and he was expecting it any day. In the meantime, he said, we would have an opportunity to learn Korean with the help of John Harvey, and we would have time to plan our curricula. Then he asked the teachers if they were satisfied with their housing, and introduced Mr. Hagen, the business manager. He said that if we had any problems with housing or other matters, we should see Mr. Hagen. He invited us all to lunch in an hour, and closed the meeting.

After the teachers left, several of them with Mr. Hagen, I went up to Tracy and asked to meet with him privately. In the quiet of his office, I asked him to be explicit about when we might be expected to start teaching. He said he wasn't sure, but he thought it would be at least four weeks. Four weeks! He seemed surprised that I was upset, and when I asked him what he expected the teachers to do in that period of time, he said, "Oh, design curricula, and learn Korean."

I was appalled, and suggested that we hire a van and travel around Korea. "Give the teachers a chance to see the country," I suggested. "Can't we arrange a series of tours? They should be given an opportunity to visit schools, to see the difference in the way Koreans live in small towns, in villages, in cities. They need to discover, as much as possible, the background of the people they will be teaching. It would be an important part of orientation."

Tracy was adamant in his refusal. "We will have lectures and films," he said. "We cannot afford to go joy-riding around the country." There was no way to move him from his opinion that tours of the country would be frivolous, or "joy-riding," in his view. He seemed to feel that any travel should be on the teachers' own time. "I expect the teachers to come to the campus every day at nine a.m.," he said. "John Harvey will teach Korean for three hours, and teachers can plan curricula in the afternoon."

My argument that it would be difficult to plan curricula for a student body that we didn't know fell on deaf ears. He said that people write textbooks for the teaching of language without knowing the people they are writing for, and therefore we could set up a teaching program without knowing who would be attending the classes. *That's exactly the trouble with most textbooks!*

That evening my four roommates and I gathered in the large, elegant living room of our wood-paneled, hardwood-floored Korean mansion on a hill to get further acquainted. Doris's ten-year-old daughter sat in a corner, reading. There was a Canadian woman in her fifties, a twenty-two-year-old recent graduate, an Indian woman from Fiji in her early thirties, and Doris, a Californian single mother in her late thirties. I was sixty-three, embarked on my fourth career, given the title of Assistant Professor at Sogang University, with seventeen years of teaching ESL behind me.

I soon discovered that the Canadian thought we were going to be soul mates, and that she saw this assignment as an important step in her life. I wasn't sure about the soul mates business, but I knew we had to establish some ground rules for the use of the small kitchen. I wasn't sure whether or not we would share meals, and so on. I soon discovered that none of the four wanted to share anything, except for Martha, the Canadian woman. Doris and her child were vegetarians, as was Anya, and the young graduate from Indiana, Melissa, thought that a meal without meat and potatoes didn't qualify as a meal. None of them wanted to create a cooperative living arrangement, such as the one I had created in Berkeley. I said that I would ask Mr. Hagen to get us a larger refrigerator, so that we could each have a shelf for our own particular food. Then it would be up to us to check with each other as to when we wanted to use the stove.

Martha and I shared the largest of the three bedrooms; Anya and Melissa got the one nearest the kitchen; and Doris got the smallest one. We disbanded amid an aura of mutual wariness.

John Harvey's approach to teaching Korean was the methodology we all despised—the aural/oral method, which I called "listen and repeat." Then he did what we had all rejected during our first courses in TESOL—translation and grammar analysis. I couldn't believe it. Morale declined rapidly. The afternoon sessions were almost bedlam. I organized the ten teachers into two groups of five, and tried to get them to work together on setting up some paradigms for effective teaching methods and exercises for different levels. There was so much scrambling for authority that sometimes the sessions ended in shouting matches. When I tried rearranging the groups in twos and threes, things were a little better, but mainly these teachers resented having to do what they called "make-work." By the end of the third week, the atmosphere in our classrooms was heavy with antagonistic tension.

I had a theory that any experience taking a person out of a familiar and regular routine results in culture shock, and that there is a period of six weeks before the shock hits bottom. Let's say that someone moves from one coast to another in the United States, or goes abroad for a visit or for work. There is an inverted bell curve that occurs. At the top of the curve there is a sense of euphoria—things are so wonderful, so exotic, so surprising; the colors, the air, the people; everything is different. Over the next few weeks, as we become accustomed to the new place, the excitement dies down and reality sets in. At about the sixth week, no matter if we are visitors or immigrants or settlers in a new place, we wonder why we are where we are. If we're immigrants, we often have headaches or stomachaches; we often feel depressed, and we want to go home. If we're in a new job, we begin to question the capability of the administrators.

The teachers at Sogang had reached the bottom of the culture shock curve in three weeks, rather than six. They asked Father Tracy for a conference meeting on a cool afternoon in late September. We met in the empty second-floor offices of our projected Institute, in a building in downtown Seoul. It was a room with a long rectangular table, with the teachers arranged on either side of it, and Harvey, Tracy, and myself at one end. Alan, the outspoken teacher from Los Angeles, opened the meeting by calling for my resignation on the basis of incompetent leadership. He then asked all the teachers to vote by raising their hands. They all raised their hands, including Kang Hee Won.

Upon reflection, I have decided that there may have been a perception of me as a mother figure, since I was at least twenty years older than any of the oldest teachers, and they saw me as their closest, most vulnerable target. They were angry by the way they were being treated; their expectations were not being met, and they revolted.

I don't know where the strength came from that prompted my reply. I stood, looked at them all, and said, "If I have become the catalyst that brought you all together in one concerted action, then I have performed an important function." Then I turned and walked out. As I stood in the corridor, waiting for the slow elevator to arrive, I was joined by Harvey and Tracy. Father Tracy apologized profusely for allowing me to be "on the front lines," as he put it, stating that of course there would be no change in the administration. Harvey invited me to dinner, and we ended up going to a bar/restaurant he knew, a real dive, and I got thoroughly drunk on soju, the local Korean variant of potent rice wine. When I drink a lot, I have to move, and I usually dance. So there I was, dancing alone on an empty dance floor to recorded sixties jazz music, when the madam who owned the bar joined me on the floor. Then she asked me if I wanted to "go upstairs for a little fun." That jolted me, and I asked Harvey to take me home.

Two days after the mutiny, Tracy organized a trip to the countryside, to visit a model Korean village. As we were introduced to the village council (all men), we observed that the older men sat a little apart from the others. Our tour guide explained that every one on the council had an equal voice in deciding how the village would use its resources—to build a school or a road or a dam, whatever. I asked, "Who speaks first?" and our tour guide answered, "Oh, the oldest, of course." *So much for democratic voices.*

We were also treated to a tour of the DMZ (the Demilitarized Zone separating South Korea from North Korea) and were invited to observe a meeting of the South Korean delegation with the North Koreans, supervised by the U.S. Intelligence branch of the Army. Those meetings took place around a long narrow table that filled a long narrow room with windows high in one wall. South Korean soldiers pressed their faces against those windows, seemingly endlessly curious about what went on in the room below them.

I observed that there were several small flags on the table, representing the flags of South Korea, North Korea, and the United States. Each standard was perched on top of flat stones. How curious. We walked outside to look through binoculars at the fake village the North Koreans had erected on their side of the line, and I found myself looking at someone on the other side looking at me! Putting down the binoculars, I asked a young Intelligence officer standing next to me about the flags sitting on stones. "What was that all about?" He laughed and told me that at the first meetings of the two sides, the North Koreans had complained that their flag was at a lower level than the South Koreans' flag, and had put a stone under their standard. That raised the North Korean flag above the South Korean, so this little battle of the stones went on until the height of both flags was exactly even.

By the end of the following week, Tracy announced that the contract from the Department of Education had arrived, and we would begin teaching immediately. With morale restored, we gathered in Tracy's conference room, and began to choose our diagnostic materials. The mutiny of the previous week was apparently forgotten by the teachers, but not by me.

Before our sessions actually began, however, we had a fire in the boiler room of the big house on the hill. I was upstairs in my room, writing in my journal, when I heard a scream from the kitchen, and ran down the stairs to see Melissa throwing salt on an oil fire in the furnace room, which adjoined the kitchen. We all soon assembled in the kitchen and took turns throwing flour, sugar, and salt on the blaze, which soon subsided into a smoking, smoldering mess. Meanwhile, I dialed 119 (the Korean equivalent of 911) and, translation dictionary in hand, yelled, "Help! Fire!" in what I thought was acceptable Korean into the telephone. There was a stunned silence on the other end, then a click. I tried again and repeated my plea. Another click. So I called Mr. Hagen and told him of our situation. He said, "No problem. I live right across the street from the Fire Department. I'll go over there and tell them to come over." The weather had turned cold suddenly, and rain had become sleet, but I ran out onto our balcony, where I had a clear view of the approach from the bottom of the hill. Suddenly I didn't want the firemen dragging a dirty hose across the pristine hardwood floors. When I spied them coming up the hill, I waved my arms frantically, and motioned for them to come in through the garden and the back door.

They looked grimly at the mess we had made, threw more stuff on the still smoldering fire, and the sergeant spoke to me in halting English. He said we shouldn't try to light the boiler until the next day, when they could send a repairman to clean it up. I showed him my dictionary and asked him why the person who answered the emergency line had hung up on me. I repeated the phrase I had used. He turned purple with the effort to restrain his laughter, finally choked, waved his hand, and fled.

The next day I approached John Harvey in his office, and told him the story. When I repeated the two words I had used, he fell off his chair laughing. What had I said? Apparently I had said, "I'm hot, and I'm burning up!"

which can also translate into the lewdest interpretation you can imagine. Apparently it's not possible to say "Help!" in Korean. You have to be specific: "fire burning—ship sinking—thief running," and so on.

Shortly after that episode, I decided I needed a place of my own, and since we now had advance money coming in from our contract for teacher training, Father Tracy was willing to allow us to make other housing arrangements. Doris and Melissa teamed up, Anya and Martha shared an apartment, and I got my own place. We all settled in, and tensions between us eased off.

Since we had contracted to retrain six hundred Korean teachers of English over a period of two years, we decided to do three six-week sessions, one in the fall, one in the winter, and one in the summer. The high school teachers came from all over Korea and were paid; they lived in dormitories on the campus. In addition to weekly classes with the teachers, Father Tracy rented offices in downtown Seoul, which became his Institute for English as an International Language. We scheduled regular day and evening classes, hoping to attract Korean housewives during the day and businessmen at night. He was right. Registration for those classes began to grow, and we began to average twelve to fifteen students per class.

Harvey's job was to coordinate the schedule for the Institute, and I was to supervise the teacher training. The teachers attended classes from nine to noon and one to three p.m. five days a week, and then they had political indoctrination classes on Saturdays. It was a full schedule for them. They were polite, but stubborn. For every communication activity we taught, we got "yes, buts", and all the naysayers proclaimed that none of the communication activities would work because there were too many students in their classes. When we pointed out the success of the activities in large, unheated, concrete-floored classrooms with one hundred teachers participating, they smiled and said, "Well, yes, but that's because we're teachers."

We designed methodology classes with fifteen participants, but we had at least one large meeting once a week, in order to challenge their reluctance to accept new ideas for large classes. They didn't want to accept the idea that there really were other ways to teach English than the ones they were accustomed to using.

Frustration among the teachers in our original group resulted in many teachers leaving by 1982. They simply reneged on their contracts and left. We replaced them with former Peace Corps volunteers already in Korea, and I managed to recruit one from a conference in Hawaii that I attended. We were all pretty discouraged, and began to feel that we weren't making any progress at all.

About that time one of the teachers in the program, Kim Sung Ah, invited me to come with her to a monastery high in the mountains outside of Seoul. The monastery was invisible from the bus stop, nestled in the hills, and it was remarkable to come upon it suddenly in a bend in the road; it blended in so well with its environment. Not like the skyscrapers of Seoul, with its concrete and glass towers piercing the sky, its concrete streets teeming with people, cars, and buses.

This was to be a six-day retreat in the dead of winter, and it was a break for both Sung Ah and me from the hectic atmosphere of Sogang University. I learned to meditate before breakfast at six a.m. (other monks started their meditations at four a.m., which was announced by a bell-ringing nun walking around the compound), and to eat a bowl of rice with pickles and toasted grass quickly and silently in five minutes.

I shared a small room with Sung Ah, and she gave me the part of the floor over the heated pipe to sleep on. (This method of heating is called an "ondol floor" and it was invented by the Koreans thousands of years ago.) She also thoughtfully provided me with a commode, so that I wouldn't have to walk down a pebbly path to the common outdoor toilet at night. There was a sliding paper door between our room and that of an elder nun on the other side. I soon discovered that our neighbor was a designated "Special Person" and since I was a visitor from the outside world, an American teacher, I was given the privilege of being next door.

After our sparse vegetarian dinner, which included soup, rice, fried grass, and kimchee (Korean pickled spiced cabbage with lots of garlic), we went back to our room. There I discovered that the sliding door between our rooms was open, and we were invited to share the elder nun's establishment. Soon a few young acolytes arrived, and a cupboard was opened revealing peanut butter, crackers, and a small TV. Kim Sung Ah brought a large thermos pitcher of tea, and we all had a feast. There was much joking, giggling, and chatter, which I didn't understand. However, I noticed that the nun who took care of our Special Person walked with a limp, and that her ankle was badly swollen. I asked her (with gestures and raised eyebrows) why she was limping, and without a word she sat down beside me and unwrapped the rags around her leg. The leg was badly swollen just above the ankle, bluish, and obviously painful to the touch. It seemed to me that the best treatment at the moment was to soak it, preferably in hot salt water, but if no salt was available, we could start with hot water.

Sung Ah translated my suggestion, and immediately two young women disappeared. They came back with a basin and another thermos of hot water. Then I asked for some clean rags or bandages of some kind, and I lifted her foot gently into the hot water and began to bathe the injured area. I couldn't tell if the swelling was caused by an injury, a bite, or an infection of some sort, but cleaning and soaking couldn't hurt, I thought.

This became a nightly ritual. The next night, the young women students at the monastery had gotten hold of some rock salt, which I added to the hot water, and over the next couple of nights, I was happy to see that the swelling was going down, and her skin was resuming a normal color. She also seemed to be in less pain. As the swelling went down, I saw what looked to be an insect bite, and it turned out that she had gone foraging for edible grass in the woods the previous week. Whatever it was, it was definitely infected, and apparently the soaking was helping.

One morning after breakfast I went into the main temple shrine to meditate, and was kneeling on the floor in front of the altar when a nun came in behind me and shoved my head toward the floor. She said something in a scolding voice about the proper position for prayer, and my hackles rose. I turned around and asked her, in my halting Korean, how old she was. When she said she was fifty-eight, I said in a furious tone that I was sixty-three, and she had better not touch me again! I knew by this time how the Korean hierarchy worked, with the eldest at the top; I also knew how important it was to know a person's age. The cultural structure is vertical, and manners of speech are carefully regulated according to this hierarchy. There are, in fact, several different ways to say "hello," depending on the age of the person speaking, and that of the person being addressed.

I'm sure that the incident in the temple, and my care for the assistant to the Special Person, flew around the compound. I did notice that people bowed to me as I walked around the grounds, and I simply bowed back. I spent a lot of time by myself, sitting in secluded areas wrapped in woolen blankets, watching the mist rising between the mountains before sunrise, and the changing colors of the forest as the sun lit the trees.

Outside of Seoul, the Korean land is full of magic. There are spirits in the rocks and in the mountains that are everywhere in this land; even in the mountains that surround Seoul. I remember the chanting of the priests and shamans in the forest and hills above Seoul that soared above the rush of morning traffic. In the monastery I could forget that roar of traffic, so loud and heavy that I had to shout in order to carry on a conversation while I walked on the street; could forget the honking cars and taxis, the thousands of people moving through the city like the rush of water down the hillside below me. I could breathe clear air rather than the fumes belching from the buses lined up like herds of elephants on the streets of Seoul.

Now when I close my eyes and will myself to go back to those mountains, I can still smell the air and see the wildflowers around me; I can especially see the rocks around the special clearing in which I sat, and my body relaxes. The combination of calm and wildness of that particular place have stayed with me.

When it came time for Kim Sung Ah and me to leave the monastery, all the nuns walked down the hill with us to the bus stop, including the assistant whose leg I had bathed. She was walking quite normally by this time, and wept as she embraced me. She didn't speak any English, and I certainly couldn't converse in the exalted Korean she used, but we had already bonded without words.

Returning to Seoul, I found that Mr. Hagen had been apartment hunting for me, and I went with him to look at the place he had selected. It was perfect. It had two bedrooms with a balcony and a view of a wooded hill opposite, a kitchen and bathroom with shower, plus a small enclosed porch off the kitchen on which to hang laundry. It was in a section that housed foreigners, members of foreign embassies or trade offices, and the apartments had been modified to fit the needs of non-Koreans. However, I noticed that as soon as foreigners left, prosperous Koreans moved in.

We went furniture shopping, and within two days I was completely settled in. I came back to teaching lighter in heart and spirit. The six-day retreat had left its mark, and I felt calmer and more confident. I was able to raise morale among the teachers by showing them how important they were. I told them that if we could move one teacher in ten from "translation and grammar analysis" to "listen and repeat," that would be a plus. (The Korean way of teaching English was to translate from Korean to English and from English to Korean, and then to analyze the grammar in Korean. We had to lower our expectations, and we had to realize that each one of the teachers we worked with would eventually affect at least five hundred students.

One day as I got off the bus at my corner, and walked down the street to my apartment, I noticed an art exhibit in a storefront window. Looking through the glass door, I saw what appeared to be a setup for teaching art. There was a long, green cloth covered table with a pot of brushes at one end, and several chairs ranged along its length. I opened the door and walked in. Pointing to the brushes, the inkstands, and the table, I said in my clumsy Korean, "Paint teaching?" and waited. The artist, Mr. Lee, smiled and nodded. I pointed to myself and then to the calendar, showing him the days I wanted to come. He shook his head to them, and pointed to one specific day, writing down the time.

Then I looked carefully at the screens, the scrolls and the pottery, all, it seemed, the work of Mr. Lee. I was mightily impressed. I wasn't sure how to ask him how much the lessons would cost, but decided I would find out exactly how to ask that question when I came for my first lesson. By this time I had acquired a roommate. I had met Seong Ja Kim through Mrs. Gil, Father Tracy's secretary, and when I heard she was studying at the Buddhist College, and was an artist, I was delighted to have her move in. Her English was pretty good, and I asked her what she could afford. I agreed to anything she said, because I realized I really needed an interpreter. This arrangement turned out to be another positive shift in my adjustment to Korean life. Seong Ja helped me navigate the Korean markets and also became an interlocutor between Mr. Lee and me.

I took lessons once a week and painted every day. When I taught evening classes, I painted in the morning; when I taught morning classes, I painted in the evening. Grinding the ink for twenty minutes was a meditative experience; the whole process of sumi ink painting is concentrated meditating.

The retreat helped open my eyes to the Korean landscape, and through my lessons in brush painting with Mr. Lee, I learned how to look at Eastern art. The three of us, Seong Ja Kim, Mr. Lee, and I went to museums together, and I learned how important negative space is in the way objects are depicted. For instance, the space between bamboo branches or clusters of grapes is just as important as the bamboo or the grapes. The space is almost sculptural, and the Eastern artists know this. They have a different view of the world.

Western artists tend to fill the space on the canvas, creating the illusion of three dimensions with shading and rules of perspective relating to distance. Objects near the viewer are larger than those farther away, and that is one way they achieve perspective. In Eastern art distance is vertical and perspective is handled with shading. I studied and practiced sumi ink painting on fine rice paper. I learned that shading and perspective is achieved by the amount of ink in the brush and the way the brush is used. That is also how Eastern artists achieve three dimensions on a flat surface.

I learned to paint bamboo, although Mr. Lee wanted me to paint the other "three gentlemen" of Eastern art: cherry blossoms, pine, and chrysanthemum. I told him I would paint bamboo in the winter, bamboo in the summer, bamboo with rocks, and bamboo with water. I said I would paint bamboo for ten years, and then I might tackle other subjects! He was satisfied with that explanation, and I was happy to stick with something I was able to do.

Seong Ja also provided me with inside information on the social and political life of ordinary Koreans. Her mother was a shaman, and I was invited to many shamanic ceremonies. I remember participating in a special ceremony on the shore of the Han River. We assembled there on a chilly evening in January, several Korean women and me, the only stranger, each with her own piece of underwear. We built a huge bonfire on the narrow beach, and accompanied by harmonic chanting, we threw our underwear onto the fire. It was a cleansing ritual, a spring-cleaning of part of our selves. Then we took a Korean piece of paper money, a hundred won bill, threaded a stick through it and floated it down the river, along with other little paper boats carrying small candles. It was a lovely ritual.

Through Seong Ja, I met young poets and moviemakers in the underground world of writers, singers, and dancers, artists who function outside of any mainstream culture. We went to masked dance programs in the fields outside of Seoul, to art show openings, to symphony concerts, and to bars and nightclubs where I was often the only foreigner.

My tour of duty in Seoul was over in August 1983, but Father Tracy asked me to stay on for two more months, to help him with his expanding Institute. Our contract with the Department of Education was completed, and now Korean students in the business world would be the main source of income.

In Korea I lived in a kind of cocoon. I didn't have to make many choices. I had a regular routine; my living space was paid for by the university; I took buses to work or to any place I wanted to go. If I needed medical attention, I went to the Catholic Hospital, and everything was paid for. I have thought deeply about what I learned from my stay in Korea, and I realize how much I was changed by that experience. I learned that social equations cannot be measured by mathematical criteria, nor can they be compared on any kind of mathematical scale or statistics. I was reassured that risks are worth taking, and uncertainty is a way of life.

I also learned that I was able to make connections on all levels of personal communication, whether or not that communication took place in Korean or English. In addition to all those positive, life-affirming things, I was lucky to be detached from the political, social, and economic struggles of the people around me. I was, after all, a visitor in a different country and not one of their responsible citizens.

When I returned to the United States, I realized that in my culture I had to make choices about everything. What was my budget? Which bills should I pay first? Which of the many charities soliciting my help could I afford to support? I had to create priorities. What to do first? How would I organize my time? What did I have to do to secure my job at UC Berkeley Extension? Was it really secure?

I had never realized before how burdened I was by all the societal and professional obligations I carried. In Korea I exchanged individual choice for security and comfort. My choices were limited in Korea, and I didn't mind that a bit. *Is that why so many of us are nostalgic for our childhood when our choices were limited by our parents? Is it why some of us choose dictators?*

Chapter Thirty-Nine:
China, Part I

‿

IRETURNED TO BERKELEY IN JANUARY 1984 from Korea, and missed my son's engagement party to Remi Omodele in December of 1983. Ric (at 27 no longer "Ricky") told me that they planned to marry on the first day of May by a Justice of the Peace, because they were both in school, and didn't have time for a formal wedding ceremony. Ric was completing his degree in Accounting, and Remi was writing her Ph.D. thesis on the Music, Drama and Literature of West Africa at the University of California, Los Angeles.

By January 1985, the Certificate program in TESOL at Berkeley had grown by leaps and bounds. I found myself teaching at least three different courses. Between that and giving presentations at conferences, I felt at the top of my energy. Then I received an invitation to teach English in Lanzhou, China in the fall, on the basis of a recommendation from a friend of mine, a professor at the University of California at Davis, and an invitation to do an ESL teacher-training course in West Germany for the Department of Defense Dependent Schools in June 1985. I felt a little giddy at these prospects, and happily signed a twenty-five-hundred-dollar contract with the Defense Department. The contract was for three weeks, beginning the second week in June.

After I sent off the contract to the U.S. Department of Education, Remi told me that she and Ric were expecting their first child, who would be born the first week in June. I realized with a shock that I would have to leave for

Germany shortly after their baby was born. Here I was, sixty-seven years old, rushing off to Germany the same month my son, at age twenty-seven, would become a father. I would miss being around that first month, but at least I would be earning enough money to help them with their expenses. I didn't think much about becoming a grandmother; working at what I knew best was far more intriguing. I was strong and healthy; working was not only a habit, teaching was my passion.

So I decided to clean out my bookshelves from the big house upstairs and I also went to various secondhand bookshops in Berkeley to fill out the gaps in my own collection. I was asked to teach American and British Literature of the Twentieth Century and Methods of Teaching English to students in a master's degree program. By the time I finished assembling the books I thought I might need, I had seven cartons of books, which I shipped off to China around June first. I fully expected the books to arrive in Lanzhou by the time I got there in September, having arranged for shipment by sea from San Francisco to Tianjin and by train from there to Lanzhou. However, it didn't work out as planned.

I left for China on August 25, 1985, on China Airlines for a twelve-hour flight to Shanghai. There would be a one-hour layover at Shanghai, and then I would go on to Beijing. I figured that I would arrive at Shanghai at three-thirty a.m. and at Beijing at five-thirty a.m. It was three-forty-five in the afternoon when we left, but I tried not to think about the arrival time.

When I finally arrived at the airport in Beijing, there was no one at the gate to meet me, and no one answered the page for Mr. Zhang, who was supposed to be waiting for me. I made my way to the Friendship Hotel, and when I checked in at the desk, I was informed that there was no room. It was now nine-forty a.m. California time, and I was numb. I curled up in a narrow seat and fell asleep. Three hours later I woke up and saw another foreign woman in an adjoining chair.

"Was someone supposed to meet you?" I asked her. "A representative from Lanzhou University was supposed to meet me, but no one has appeared."

She extended her hand. "I'm Mary Pat Rouse," she said, "I'm at the Chengdu University of Science and Industry. That's in Chengdu, Sichuan Province. My contact person booked a room for me, but it was given to someone else. I expect I'll get one eventually. Would you like to share my room?" *Her casual acceptance of the entire situation told me that she was familiar with Chinese bureaucracy.*

"Boy, would I! Thanks. I really need some sleep."

Finally, by one-thirty, we got a room, and we were in bed by two. We woke up about six p.m., and went out for noodles. Mary Pat was a very interesting woman from Cornell. She was an Olympic Judo contestant and worked out with weights. She had lived all over Europe, and at one of the competitions had made a connection with a Chinese athlete. That connection led to an invitation to go to Chengdu to help them set up an athletic program, and she had decided that might be fun. We went to bed early and Mary Pat said she would try to call Lanzhou for me the next day.

It wasn't easy to make long-distance calls in 1985, but Mary Pat was persistent, and after about an hour, she finally got through to the Foreign Affairs Office in Lanzhou. It seems that the representative, Zhang Xilong, was in Beijing and had been in town for ten days. He had already "collected" five foreign experts, and the only one he was having trouble with was "Mrs." Curtis. Mary Pat was told that Mr. Zhang was in the Friendship Hotel also. So of course we tried to locate him, and finally found him in the lobby at noon. It seems that my letter stating that I would be arriving on Flight 982 on the twenty-sixth of August never reached him. He thought I was coming in on Flight 986 on the twenty-seventh. The other two Americans, from Southern California, had arrived several days earlier. Nobody in the Foreign Affairs office or at China Airlines had thought to coordinate our flights from California.

Mr. Zhang had already put Samia and Bob, the two Americans, along with three Australians, Jennifer, Kaye, and Damien on the train to Lanzhou. Now all he had to do was arrange an itinerary for me. We said goodbye to Mary Pat and went to the China Travel Agency to figure out the best way to get to Lanzhou, which is in the middle of China. Lanzhou is more or less in central China, and relates to Beijing as Chicago relates to New York.

We were informed that there were no more direct trains from Beijing to Lanzhou for ten days, and the agent in the China Travel Agency decided that the best way for me to go was through Inner Mongolia. This was the schedule he worked out: leave Beijing at three in the afternoon on August 30, arrive in Hohot, Mongolia, at four-thirty a.m., August 31. The agent promised that an interpreter, who would meet me in Hohot, would have arranged a hotel room for me. Ticket agents in China project confidence; that's their job. He said that my interpreter would be my guide in Hohot during a short layover. I would tour around the city and leave Hohot at eleven-thirty p.m., August 31, arriving in Lanzhou at ten p.m., September 1. It sounded like a rugged forty-eight-hour journey through China, but I would have a chance to see the capital city of Inner Mongolia. I was given a piece of paper with all the information on it, except that I could not book a sleeper from Hohot to Lanzhou in advance. I had to do it in Hohot. Mr. Zhang argued forcefully, but the ticket agent was firm in his refusal.

Mr. Zhang had his orders from the Lanzhou Foreign Affairs Office that he was to show the foreign experts around Beijing, and he was determined to do that. So we toured Beijing for the next three days. We marched around Tianenmen Square in pouring rain, admiring the statues of heroic workers and Chairman Mao, and visited the various Halls of Harmony, Industry, and Martial Spirit. The exhibits were stunningly beautiful, and there was one intricate contrivance that I still remember. It was designed more than eight centuries ago to predict earthquakes. Surrounding it were statues of frogs, who are considered to be predictors of storms and floods, in addition to earthquakes. Then we wandered around the Imperial Gardens, which were impeccably maintained. The rain had stopped, and the stones steamed in the humid heat.

Walking around the buildings, the exhibit halls, the carefully maintained gardens, and realizing that millions of feet had trod those same stones gave me a sense of the glory and power of China. The Foreign Affairs officers knew what they were doing when they insisted that we foreign experts be exposed to the art, science, and grandeur of ancient as well as contemporary China. They are inextricably entwined in Beijing.

We stopped at a special noodle house that Mr. Zhang knew about and had a delicious dinner of noodles, buried eggs (called thousand-year eggs), rice, cabbage soup, and many rice wine toasts. I had the feeling that Mr. Zhang was thoroughly enjoying himself. Beijing was full of cyclists, pedicabs, rickshaws, buses, a few private cars, and people. The cyclists rode at a slow, steady pace, dodging in and around other vehicles.

They were especially careful of those pedaling with enormous loads on their backs, anchored with a strap around their foreheads.

On August 30, 1985, I arrived at the Beijing railway station at two, one hour before the train was scheduled to leave. Mr. Zhang had provided me with a special card that allowed me to use renminbi (Chinese money), and I made my way to the International First Class part of the station, walking past hundreds of second-and third-class passengers sitting, lying, sleeping on heaps of baggage. Some of them were playing cards, while others were eating or feeding children; hundreds of people, just patiently waiting.

The First Class area was a huge, empty area with special booking sections for Foreigners, Overseas Chinese, Hong Kong passengers, and International Travelers. The waiting room was high ceilinged, spacious, with crocheted antimacassars on the arms and backs of the capacious upholstered chairs. After getting my tickets, I made my way to the track, and found the proper coach to Hohot.

The narrow compartment held two levels of bunks, already made up for sleep at three p.m., so the four occupants (including me) sat on the lower bunks, drinking tea, smoking, and talking. The three men ignored me at first, until I kept opening the compartment door, coughing, and getting up to go outside the compartment for air. Then one of the men said something that sounded like "No smoke?" and I mimed choking, waving my hand around to brush away the smoke. They got the idea and all three stood up and went into the corridor to smoke.

I had put my coat and knapsack on the top bunk, since the other three bunks had coats and luggage on them. However, when the men came back in, the youngest of the men removed his baggage from one of the lower bunks, and gestured toward the now empty lower bunk. He gave a small bow, and I grinned my thanks. When dinner was announced, I was the only one who went to the dining car. My compartment mates opened their brown paper bag lunches and thermoses, and I went off to soup, noodles, and boiled vegetables. The view from the train window wasn't particularly interesting, and it became dark quite early, it seemed to me. *Time throughout China is set by*

Beijing, so throughout China the time is the same, even though China has a landmass larger than the United States. I tried to read by the faint, flickering light in the bunk, and finally fell asleep to the jolting, rocking rhythm of the train. There were several stops on the way, with much jerking of the car as it was coupled and uncoupled over and over again. I slept in my clothes and woke up about three a.m. After making my way to the toilet at the end of the car, I sat on my bunk, fully dressed, waiting for the train to arrive at Hohot. My compartment mates were snoring peacefully as I sat there.

Promptly at four-thirty a.m., the train pulled into the station, and I debarked. It was full moon, and the platform was empty. There were two other people who left the train when I did, and waiting cars quickly whisked them off. I looked around and spotted a female ticket-taker, and showed her my piece of paper. She shrugged and walked me over to the local taxi. It was a tin box mounted on a three-wheeled bicycle, and after nodding to the driver who was sitting astride the bicycle outside of the box, I climbed in over the back (sort of like climbing into the back of a truck), and sat down on one of the benches that ran along one side of the box.

I pulled my padded cotton Chinese coat around me (I called it my Marco Polo coat), as I settled down for the bumpy ride to wherever I was supposed to go. The full moon shone down on a ghostly landscape, mountains in the distance, the air cool and clear. The canvas top of the taxi fluttered in the breeze as we rolled along the deserted road. Bumping along, the wind whistling in my ears, I noticed two road sweepers, a man and a woman, methodically sweeping the road with long straw brooms. They worked rhythmically, sweeping an empty road under a full moon at four-thirty in the morning, never stopping or looking up as my taxi bicycled slowly past them.

We arrived at a dark, deserted compound, and the driver motioned to me to get out. I shook my head, and sat there, my hands in my sleeves. *No way was I going to get out onto that dark, deserted courtyard.* Suddenly a young man, pedaling furiously, came up behind us. It was my young guide, who jumped off his bike, apologizing profusely for having overslept. He had arrived at the station just in time to see us take off, he said, and had followed us all the way. He was very relieved to see me, but that was nothing compared to my relief at seeing *him!* The driver of the tin taxi had delivered me to the office of the China Travel Agency, now closed, but that's what my piece of paper said to do, and that's what he did! My interpreter, Mr. Lee, persuaded the driver to go around the corner to the Foreigners' Hotel in back of the office, and I got out. I paid the driver and the taxi tricycle took off. Mr. Lee rang the bell at the door of the hotel.

Mr. Lee also confessed that he had been unable to get a room with a bath for me, because the hotel was fully booked. The concierge shuffled out, in slippers and a robe, furious at being awakened, and grumblingly showed us into a dingy waiting room. She said we would have to wait until seven-thirty, and she wasn't sure there would be a room even then. Mr. Lee and I talked in whispers, and I found out that hotels like this one in Inner Mongolia make a lot of money on tours going to the grasslands to see pre-rehearsed rodeos. Tourists also get to eat Mongolian mutton with dressed-up Mongolian peasants, and a visit to a yurt.

At seven a.m., people began to stir, and I was ushered into another building and into another waiting room. A "server" came over to us and encouraged us to eat breakfast (now ready) while we waited for a room. After breakfast, I was shown to a room close to a shared toilet and shower. My room was narrow, with concrete walls and floor, and was furnished with a lumpy bed, nightstand, and lamp. The shower room was small, high ceilinged, with a tile floor, exposed plumbing, and clumsy grouting. There were two sinks in this room with the drainpipes hanging over a hole in the floor. A door led into an enclosed toilet area with a raised step. Stepping up and into this place, I found an oblong cover over a hole, and next to it were two foot-rests and a bar to hold onto. The flush mechanism worked.

Mr. Lee told me that the hotel had been completed about three years ago, but it looked as if it were at least fifty years old. I could only conclude that the Chinese, unlike the Aztecs, had not mastered the art of cement mixing, and yet they use cement for everything. The floors of the hotel were gray—they might just as well have been mud—they were the color of old mud and there was no finish on them. So no matter how much or how often they were washed, they always looked dirty. The walls were cracking, and I don't think the floors were ever really level. Telltale stains on the ceiling showed probable leaks during heavy rains.

I took a short nap on the lumpy bed in my room and met Mr. Lee in the lobby. We agreed that he would go to the train station and try to book a soft seat (sleeper) for me for the trip to Lanzhou. He asked me if I wanted to go on a short trek, about ninety kilometers from Hohot. I quickly figured that meant six hours on a tour bus—no thanks! I told him that I'd rather go touring just with him. He said he would try to book a car, and took off. I went into my room, lay down on my hard bed, put my head on the straw-filled pillow, and fell sound asleep again.

I can sleep deeply for short bursts of time and wake up refreshed, so when Mr. Lee returned from the train station about noon, I was ready for him. He had bad news for me; there was no compartment available, and the agent wouldn't even promise a "hard sleeper" which was six tiers in an open car. I had noticed many empty berths in compartments on the train from Beijing, but there was no point in applying Western logic to Chinese practice. Also, there was no car available until two-thirty in the afternoon.

Since the Chinese lunch hour was from noon to two-thirty, nothing much was open during that time. We had a short lunch and went out to walk around the town. The museum was closed, so Mr. Lee and I went to the Friendship Store to do some shopping. The government runs the Friendship Stores for tourists, and sets the prices in Foreign Exchange Certificates, not renminbi. That means that resident Chinese are mainly lookers, not buyers. We were quickly surrounded by curious Chinese, who followed us around the store, and when I stopped to admire a wonderful amethyst toad, I heard a murmur behind me.

"What are they saying?" I asked Mr. Lee. He said, "They are wondering why you want to buy something so ugly." I laughed, and decided I could never explain why that amethyst toad was so beautiful to me, *a toad that still lives on the shelf above my bed.* I asked Mr. Lee if I could take a photograph of the clerk, and the minute I lifted my Polaroid camera, the crowd around me immediately gathered itself together and grouped themselves for a photograph. Everyone in China, it seems, knew about the magic of Polaroids. I took a photo of the clerk with Mr. Lee, and then turned around and took a picture of my solemn-faced watchers. After I handed them the photo, I lifted my Minolta and pointed to my nose. That gesture meant that this photo was for me. Everybody nodded, and I proceeded to take a picture of the clerk and the group with the Minolta.

This was the pattern I used throughout my time in China, and when curious Chinese asked me why I was taking pictures of people I didn't know, I replied that I wanted to remember where I had been and who I had met. I am sure my answer didn't make sense to them, but it stopped the conversation.

In the car, Lee told me his life story. His full name was Lee Xi Min, and he wanted to be an interpreter as his main job. At the moment, he worked as a translator for an electrical company and volunteered for the job as my guide. He said he had had no chance to practice oral English for two years, and that he had gotten married recently, to an M.D. He confessed that his father had arranged the marriage, but he didn't feel ready for marriage. Lee's father was a professor, and they all lived together, along with his younger sister, in the father's small flat on the university compound. He said his wife felt superior to him, and hated it when he corrected her pronunciation of English. She read English well, he said, but she read mainly medical books written in English. Lee loved English literature, and said he had no one to share his thoughts with.

Xi Min said he wanted to transfer to the China Travel Service Unit, and that would give him more opportunities to meet foreigners, especially English speakers. I asked him if he wanted me to write a letter of commendation for him, and he said, "Yes. Just write that my language skills are good. That's all." Then I asked him if he wanted to write to me at Lanzhou, and he said, "There's strict discipline. Only certain personnel are allowed to write to foreigners." Then he shook his head for emphasis. *No.* The Chinese Communist government was suspicious of unsupervised contacts with foreigners, and Chinese had been imprisoned for what the government said were revelations of state secrets.

We went back to the hotel, and I asked Mr. Lee if he would like to join me for dinner. Again he refused, because of protocol, but said he would eat in a different part of the dining room, if I would be willing to pay for his dinner. I agreed, of course. I watched him walk to a table near the serving entrance, and sat down in the foreigners' section.

The meal was nothing special. Soup and cabbage, noodles with some kind of meat, probably pork, a boiled egg, and vegetables. After I paid for my meal and also Lee's, we stopped at the front desk of the hotel. One of the clerks handed me the reservation for the hard sleeper—the best they could do, she said, and added that I could try to negotiate for a soft sleeper or compartment on the train. I asked Lee if he would arrange for a car to take me to the train station at nine-thirty p.m. That would give me another few hours of sleep.

The platform was crowded when we arrived, with the largest crowd gathered near the steps to the hard sleeper car. The train was due to leave at ten p.m. Chinese travelers don't queue up, they push and shove to get closest to any gate, and then barricade themselves to hang on to that spot. There was one other non-Chinese traveler, a German who was arguing forcefully for a "soft seat"—that is, a sleeping bunk in a special car. He thought he was speaking Chinese, and managed to bully the conductor with his wild gestures and facial contortions.

Lee Xi Min helped me into the crowded car, and I settled myself onto a narrow sleeping slab in a middle tier of bunks. There were no curtains, and there was a lot of chatter and smoking. I asked Xi Min to write a polite letter in Chinese to the conductor, explaining my plight, and stating that I was an English professor at Lanzhou University.

I watched as Lee handed the letter to the conductor, and she looked over at me. Then Lee left. Before the train started, the conductor came back to me, and motioned that I was to follow her. I gathered my things, and left my heavy suitcase under the bottom bunk. Gesturing at my suitcase, I said, "Mingtian," which means "later," and she nodded. We went into the next car, where I gave the chief conductor the additional fare for a soft seat. My compartment was similar to the one I occupied on the trip from Beijing to Hohot, and I climbed into an upper bunk. The other three bunks were occupied by sleeping figures.

China, Part II:
Lanzhou University

⤺

W HEN I ARRIVED AT THE LANZHOU STATION, a small contingent
from the university was there to meet me. There was a representative
from the Foreign Affairs office, the librarian, and Chen Xi Long waiting for
me with a van. The Foreign Affairs officer assured me that my luggage would
arrive later as I climbed into the van. They wanted to know if I had had a
comfortable journey, and I found it easy to lie tactfully.

Xi Long informed me that there would be a welcoming ceremony at two
p.m. in the Teacher's Lounge, and I was respectfully expected to attend. As
I entered the room, I noticed that Chinese professors lined one side of the
room with foreign professors on the other side. I scanned the faces of the
Chinese professors, looking for Dr. Chiang, a professor of literature who had
sponsored my colleague, Tippy Schwabe. Chiang had lived in San Francisco
for one year, and I was looking forward to meeting him. Tippy had given me
a photo of the two of them, and I knew who I was looking for. But I didn't
see him.

The head of the Foreign Affairs office spoke first, and then other professors spoke words of welcome, according to age or seniority, or both. When it
came time for us to speak, Chen Xi Long motioned to me to speak first, since
I was the most senior of our group. In the course of my polite acceptance of
the honor of being invited to teach at such a prestigious university, I mentioned that I was looking forward to seeing Professor Chiang, since I had

personal words of greeting for him from colleagues in California. At the mention of Chiang's name, a sudden tense silence gripped the room. Then, after that awkward pause, someone in the English department said that Dr. Chiang wasn't feeling well, and that he wasn't teaching that semester.

I felt that I had made a faux pas of some sort, but didn't know what it was. Later I tracked Dr. Chiang down and in the course of my interview with him I found out that someone in the Communist Party at Lanzhou had decided that he had been "contaminated" by his year in California, and that he should be given a "rest" from teaching that year. My heart constricted as I realized that this setback involved a double humiliation. During the Mao years Chiang had been forced by the Lanzhou students to walk through the streets with a dunce cap on his head. He had been spared from going to the countryside to work in the fields because of his age, but he had not been allowed to do any teaching. After being reinstated after the Mao years, he had attended a conference in Beijing and had met one of my colleagues from San Francisco State who arranged his year in California. My heart went out to this courageous, gentle scholar who shrugged as he told me this story. He said, "This will pass. Perhaps I will teach Shakespeare again next year." His stoicism struck me as a true mark of a survivor.

After the greetings and salutations, I went over to the Residence Hall, which was a four-story concrete building with offices, a dining hall, a kitchen, sleeping rooms for staff, a large entry hall, and a reception desk on the first floor. Dormitory rooms and apartments were on the second, third, and fourth floors. As I entered the reception area with my small traveling bag and my two cameras, the male and female "servers" stood in a receiving line, smiling and bowing, obviously consumed with curiosity. I was the last foreign expert to arrive, and since I was the oldest, was considered the most prestigious. I felt as if I were entering a large English country house, with the staff lined up to greet me. We all bowed, and I walked across the stone floor to the steps leading to the upper floors. I flipped the switch at the bottom to illuminate the dark steps. My rooms were on the third floor, and as I moved from floor to floor, flipping switches as I went, a great sense of expectation and curiosity filled me. This was going to be my home for the next six months.

My apartment had three rooms, a bedroom, living room, and large bathroom. There was an unfurnished space for a kitchen, with nothing in it. The bathroom had a tile floor, a footed tub, a four-legged table that fit over the radiator, and a flush toilet. It was really luxurious by Chinese standards. I ended up using my bathroom for a kitchen, placing a board across the tub, and hooking up a two-burner hot plate on a stool near the sink.

I noticed with pleasure that the bedroom had a double bed, a small bedside table, desk and chair, and casement windows over a radiator. The sitting room was furnished with two overstuffed armchairs, a floor lamp, a glass-fronted bookcase, and another cupboard with sliding glass doors. The desk accommodated a gooseneck lamp, and there was also a small table which I used as a typing surface. The refrigerator and television set, covered with pleated green velvet, completed the furnishings that the people in the Foreign Affairs office had decided met the needs of their foreign experts. There was also a door leading out onto a balcony that ran along the length of the building. I walked out onto the balcony, and looked across our compound at the elementary school on the other side of the wall. The boys fought each other, kung fu style, while the girls jumped rope. *Boys fight and girls would rather jump rope, all over the world.*

Pleased with the spaciousness of my apartment, I went downstairs for dinner, not knowing what to expect. The dinner consisted of barely warm, watery soup, over-cooked tough chicken, and rice. *If that dinner was a sample of meals offered by the Chinese cooks at our dining hall, I decided I would cook as many meals by myself as I could.* As soon as I got back to my rooms, I rearranged the furniture, deciding to buy a rug and some paintings for the walls. On my list I added a two-burner hot plate, an electric wok, a heavy-duty plug for the grounded outlet in the bathroom, a teakettle, and a pot for soup, noodles or potatoes. I looked forward to shopping in the open market. This would give me a chance to get the feel of the city outside the walls of the campus.

Hot water was available from the tap, and I filled the long tub, easing myself into the steaming water with a grateful sigh. I thought about the people I would be working with, Bob and Samia from Southern California,

Jennifer from Australia, Hilary and John, a married couple, also from Australia, Celine from Canada, and Philip from Boston. We were not a team, carefully assembled for a specific purpose as in Korea; we were all separate teachers chosen by the head of the English department. I assumed that we all had been recommended by colleagues with connections in China, as I was. I didn't have any particular status, I just happened to be the oldest. Our classes were assigned to us by Professor Han, and I wondered if we would have any meetings to plan an organized curriculum. It wasn't up to me; I would have to wait and see.

As it turned out, I was the only one teaching postgraduate students. I had three classes: one in methodology for students learning to teach English, one in comparative American and British literature of the twentieth century, and one seminar for Chinese professors of English. I didn't expect anyone to show up for the seminar, since I had heard that once you became a professor, that was the end of your interest in the subject you were teaching, but five young professors showed up, one man and four women.

I had twenty-seven students in my literature class and twenty in the methodology class. Dr. Han had informed me that classes in the Foreign Language department were limited to twenty-five students, yet four of our teachers had forty or fifty students, and I saw classrooms jammed with eighty or more students. So reality did not match idealism.

We all met in the dining hall for breakfast, lunch, and dinner, and I always showed up for two or more meals. I discovered that my colleagues were not particularly interested in discussing ways of teaching, and that most of the conversation centered on personal and practical concerns. Jennifer wanted to buy a bicycle; Bob was interested in brushing up his Chinese; Celine was hoping to practice hers as well; and I wanted to talk about the caves at Dunhuang. I remembered the way teachers at the Berkeley Adult School, and even instructors at University of California Berkeley Extension, stayed pretty much to themselves, and didn't discuss ways of teaching or materials. However, I was hoping for more interaction within our group so that we could exchange better ways of teaching conversation in a class with thirty or more students, or how to improve reading comprehension and writing, but nobody seemed interested in that kind of discussion.

However, Hilary had studied Chinese politics and literature as well as the language itself, and I managed to have several in-depth conversations with her. I learned that *guanxi* (connections) is how all business is conducted in China. If you are the sixth cousin of a nephew twice removed, and you want to do business anywhere in China, you search out the relative connected to that particular business and contact him. Custom demands that he help you. However, if you don't have any personal connections, no matter how distant, you can forget it.

The other terms she gave me, which I remembered when I spoke with Dr. Chiang, were *hai gui* and *tu bie* which she defined as relating to Chinese who have been abroad and returned *(hai gui)* and Chinese with foreign connections *(tu bie)*. Hai gui people usually go through a period of readjustment, she said, because the foreign ideas and manners they have picked up from living abroad often create tension with the settled Chinese way of doing things. *I could see how that attitude applied to Dr. Chiang, especially in the cloistered atmosphere of a state-run university.*

I had shipped seven cartons of books to China by sea, and had been assured by the shipping company that they would be delivered to Lanzhou. However, they had not been delivered when I arrived, and it took a bit of digging to find out where they were. Apparently they were sitting onboard a ship in the harbor of Tianjin, and could not be released without a personal sign-off on necessary documents. Tianjin is in the northeastern part of China, north and east of Beijing, and that meant I had to make a long trip by train again. This time the Foreign Affairs officer made sure that Chen Xi Long and I would have soft seat compartments going and coming, and the trip was easier.

Arriving at the dock, we were shunted from office to office, until finally the chief of the department arrived. He was a tall, handsome, keen-eyed man who spoke excellent English and understood immediately that we wanted the seven boxes of books unloaded from the freighter and shipped to Lanzhou by mail. Chen signed a document stating that he accepted full responsibility for any subversive material that might be in the boxes. Then I produced the copy of the customs declaration I had filled out on the plane, which listed everything I was bringing in plus items being shipped. I hadn't realized that by listing the seven cartons of books on the declaration, I would have to take them back with me when I left China. The chief told me that I would have to fill out documents stating that the books were gifts and were to remain in China. Once the cartons arrived in Lanzhou, they would be held at the station, and then we would send the post office announcement of their arrival to the chief, who would add his documents to mine and send everything back to us in Lanzhou. Then I would be able to clear my customs declaration.

Living in Korea for two years had prepared me somewhat for accepting the unexpected, so I was happy to get a glimpse of one of the most internationally cosmopolitan cities in China. Tianjin had been occupied by the Russians, and it was still full of Russian architecture of the pre-Soviet period. It was also a port city, and as such, attracted foreigners from many lands, including sailors in various uniforms. I drank it all in, and accepted the bureaucratic rigmarole, reminding myself that all bureaucracies are equally burdensome, especially to foreigners.

When the seven cartons of books finally arrived at the university, I was there to help unpack them. I had previously canvassed the library and found mainly empty shelves.

"Where are all the books?" I asked the librarian.

"Oh, professors check them out and don't return them."

I asked about her system for keeping track of her books, and her answer didn't make any sense at all. Then I wanted to know where and how my books would be catalogued and when they would be put on the shelves. I had cleaned out my own library and had bought a wide selection of novels, plays, and poetry from secondhand bookstores in Berkeley. I wanted to make sure my students would have easy access to them.

Her reply to my question was to point to a glass-fronted locked bookcase in the library. I was horrified. "You mean they will be locked in that cabinet?" She nodded. "And you are the keeper of the key?" Again she nodded.

Recognizing the set of the mouth and stiffness of the shoulders as the immovable posture of a territory-defender, my own irresistible force gathered itself together and I marched out of the library to the department head's office. I had noticed an empty bookcase in an empty office near mine, and as

I mounted the stairs, I formed my plan.

Instead of attacking the librarian with the derogatory words boiling in my brain, I told the dean that I wanted the empty bookcase moved to my office first thing the next morning, and that I would be responsible for the books I had brought. They were my property, I informed him, until I formally turned them over to the university, and I intended to give my students access to them. I wouldn't have been able to get away with any of those demands if I hadn't had gray hair.

We both went back to the library, and I stood quietly while the dean explained the situation to the librarian in Chinese. She gave me a murderous look and then said that we would have to catalogue *all* of the books and if *any* of them was missing at the end of the semester, the same book would have to be replaced. I reminded her that the books were still my property and I would be responsible. I said I would select a student to do the cataloguing with her, and that we would double-check her count.

Classes had begun in September; it was now the middle of October, and I was anxious to get going with student presentations. I had selected three themes for comparing American and British literature of the twentieth century: economic, political and social. I intended to relate the literature of both countries to differences in the economic, political, and social conditions in both countries, and to demonstrate how conditions of life affect the writing that is produced. Up until now, I had relied on the sparse collection of books in the Lanzhou library: a copy of Dreiser's *Sister Carrie,* a copy of Jack London's *Martin Eden,* and a few books by Henry James. I had contacted friends at the British Cultural Affairs office in Beijing, and had ordered a collection of books from them, but they hadn't arrived either. I used E. M. Forster's book *Aspects of the Novel* as the basis of my lectures, and other historical material I had brought with me.

By this time, I had become well acquainted with my students, and one in particular, Chen Yu, became a lifelong friend. Yu was one of the most remarkable students I had ever had. His English was excellent, and he loved literature. He had translated the British mystery writer, Jeremy Archer, into Chinese, and he was interested in William Faulkner. Yu became my librarian. With his help, we transported my seven cartons of books to my office, created a Dewey decimal cataloguing system, issued library cards to my students, and I was finally able to implement my teaching plan.

I told my twenty-eight students that they were to choose one author and one work by that author for a presentation in class. Since this class met twice a week for two hours each time, I scheduled two student presentations for the first hour and my lecture for the second hour. In the second hour, I put the students' presentations into context, relating the author's work to the economic, political, and social conditions of her or his time. I recorded my lectures, in case the students wanted to listen to them before the exams.

None of the students had ever had this kind of challenge before. When the first student presented his report (it was on Sister Carrie), I noticed that many students put their heads down on their desks, and others began shuffling through their papers and books, preparing for the next class. I stopped my student, and told the class that they had better listen carefully, and take good notes, because the exam would be based on the presentations as well as on my lectures. You could hear the "snap!" as heads came up, and notebooks opened.

Then came a complaint. "We don't understand his English." These postgraduate students came from all over China, and Chinese speakers of English from Nanjing have a different way of pronouncing "n" than speakers from Shanghai, for example. I simply told them that it was their responsibility to ask the presenter for clarification or repetition. This was an English class, and they needed to make an effort to understand each other. If they wanted to speak Chinese, they had to leave the room. Inside my classroom the land and the space was for English speakers only.

I also had to establish basic social etiquette. For example, no spitting on the floor. I put two large boxes of Kleenex on my desk next to the wastebasket. I knew that Chinese thought it was barbaric to use a piece of paper or cloth to blow your nose into, and then put that paper or cloth in your pocket. As far as they were concerned, it was much more sanitary to blow into your fingers on the street, and snap your hands clean (or wipe them on your pants). But this was my classroom, and I established the rules.

The students presented reports on John Steinbeck with *The Grapes of Wrath*, Henry James's *The Turn of the Screw*, Willa Cather's *Sapphira and the Slave Girl,* Jack London's *Martin Eden,* Joseph Conrad's *Lord Jim,* John Osborne's *Look Back in Anger,* James Baldwin's *If Beale Street Could Talk,* Hemingway's, *Hills Like White Elephants,* Sherwood Anderson's, *Death in the Woods,* Theodore Dreiser's *Sister Carrie,* Kingsley Amis's *Lucky Jim,* to name a few. Those were some of the books students had chosen for their reports.

I had a lot of fun relating that diverse list of authors and topics to the economic, political, and social environments in which those books were written. I included a lecture on the importance of Freudian psychology, so popular and so influential in both Britain and the United States. The students were required to research available information on the authors, and since the Internet had not been invented in 1985, their main resource was the *Encyclopedia Britannica.* Their presentations included a brief background of their author, a description of the novel, and their own reaction to it. They were required to not only deliver their reports in person, but also to write an essay. I soon discovered that they simply copied the *Encyclopedia* material verbatim, without quotation marks as if it was their own writing. Also they often quoted whole passages from their chosen novels as if they were their own ideas.

I knew I had to create a strong spur to change an accepted pattern, since Chinese scholars consider it an honor to be quoted without attribution. So I told them that I was interested in their own writing, not in how well they copied the work of others. Therefore, I would give two points for every passage enclosed within quotation marks, with attribution cited, or footnotes, citing their sources. And, I would take off two points for every bit of copied information without attribution. The students accepted my dictum in silence, and after that, I was swamped with papers full of quotation marks and footnotes.

At the beginning of the course, I had told the students that all exams would be open. That is, they could bring their notes to class, and therefore I encouraged them to take good notes. When it came time for the midterm exam, I made sure that the questions would include material from their colleagues' presentations as well as from their own presentations. I asked them to choose any novel we had studied (other than the one they had presented), and select a thematic category into which the novel fit. They were to tell how the novel fit the theme; whether through the characters, the story, the plot, or a combination of all three. Out of twenty-eight students, sixteen chose *Martin Eden;* seven chose *Sister Carrie,* and five chose *Grapes of Wrath.* I found out later that both *Martin Eden* and *Sister Carrie* had been translated into Chinese and that both of those books were required reading during their freshman years. I also suspected, from some of the written comments on the test, that the *Grapes of Wrath* had also been translated.

All of the comments centered on the themes of the evils of capitalist society, and of how the individual is destroyed by the hopeless fight for individual success. They were very interesting papers, and there was no copying.

The students in my methodology courses were all teachers, and they were eager, enthusiastic students, anxious to discover different ways of teaching and learning English. They tested out everything on their own students and reported back. I used Spanish to teach each methodology, and it was fun to see how they reacted to learning the same language using different approaches. They liked using classical music with Suggestopedia, using a tape recorder with Counseling Learning/Community Language Learning, and commands with Total Physical Response. The Silent Way generated more enthusiasm than I expected, but they liked using wooden rods to teach grammar. I asked them to write papers on the adaptability or non-adaptability to using each method for teaching English to Chinese students. All of our discussions were in English, and they wrote all of their papers in English.

I felt as if my being in China was the culmination of my life; it offered a rationale, a meaning, a purpose for all of it. This final odyssey was a chance for me to see my life as a whole, and the experience had a lasting effect upon me. I found myself using all the knowledge I had accumulated thus far. I had time to reflect, and that made it possible for me to recall the books I had read in my teens and in my college years. Many of them were books that my students were studying in my literature class. The fifty-odd years between the time I had first read those authors and now seemed to vanish, and impassioned arguments and discussions came unbidden and easily to my mind. It was as if everything I had ever experienced in my life was surfacing, so that I could use it now with my Chinese students.

I could talk about and remember my experiences in Washington, D.C., in 1943–45, when I worked for the Office of War Information; I could freely associate my sense of fear and dread during the McCarthy era with the fear and dread expressed by my Chinese colleagues who had lived through the Cultural Revolution.

I found that my twelve years as a designer and manufacturer in San Francisco helped me understand the growing pains of young Chinese entrepreneurs, and their struggle to reconcile their socialist ideals with the excitement of owning and running their own businesses. I could understand the pride of a Chinese farmer on a wealthy commune, when he displayed his stereo radio equipment, his television set, and his refrigerator. He was aiming to buy a truck too, and was delighted to be a part of the new "free market."

The years I had spent as an ESL teacher in the Berkeley Adult School helped me understand the frustration of my young graduate students in methodology when they talked about the difficulty of motivating their science students. I could empathize with them, and offer insights I had acquired through sixteen years of classroom experience. My six years at the University of California, teaching teachers how to teach English as a second or foreign language gave me the knowledge and experience to help them with their own lesson planning, and to help them figure out ways of dealing with their own bureaucracies.

In China, as in Korea, I experienced the luxury of having time to just sit and reflect. This space created a kind of inner peace I didn't expect. I was more isolated in China, being older than any of the other teachers, but I wasn't an administrator in addition to being a teacher, and I didn't feel imprisoned. Rather, I felt lighter. I didn't have to be responsible for anyone but myself. I was able to devote my energies to my teaching, to thinking, to painting, to living in the deepest intellectual sense. External stimuli were negligible; television was not tempting, shortwave radio quickly became repetitious, and I found myself feeling more and more removed from the outside world. After all, I became deeply immersed in China and the way of life for its people. There was very little I could do about events in other parts of the world. I didn't have to feel guilty for not writing my congressperson about an upcoming vote; I was a spectator without responsibility.

I had a guaranteed income, people to clean my rooms and wash my clothes, and above all, a clear definition of my role in the society in which I was living. I was a professor, and I was supposed to teach three classes. How well or how poorly I did my job was up to me; no one would censor me, and no one would evaluate me, although if I were doing a very poor job, my students would complain.

Lives of elders, especially scholars, is revered and even envied in modern China, and since I was sixty-seven years old, the university personnel were worried about my health. They assigned Dr. Wang to look after me. He came to my rooms shortly after I arrived, and indicated, by sign language, that I was to come to his clinic for an evaluation. I enlisted the help of one of our staff who was bilingual, and we went to the hospital where he had his office. I went through a thorough physical examination, and he seemed worried by my irregular heart beat. I tried to reassure him, and established a connection between my Berkeley physician and Dr. Wang. I promised that Dr. Borson would write to him and would send him copies of recent publications of scientific journals. He looked as if I had promised him the moon.

From time to time, I noticed farmers lined up on the steps of the auditorium, and behind them sacks of rice or grain or apples or oranges or turnips or other kinds of produce. Students lined up in front of them with little paper chits or with money. Farmers with surplus produce could come to the university (with administrative approval) and sell their surplus produce at reduced prices. The rumor floating freely around the campus was that the peasants were rich, and if the commune I visited was any example, I could confirm that rumor. However, there still didn't seem to be any mad rush from the cities to the villages, no matter how attractive farm life was made out to be. My students knew that village work, centered on food production and farm life in general, was hard and never-ending; they knew that manual labor was tough. No one who had a choice between an educated life and farm life would choose farm life. Older students of mine who had spent part of their youth during the Cultural Revolution on farms certainly didn't want to go back.

I wondered about the resentment that the workers on the campus might feel toward the students, and I wondered if the workers in Lanzhou itself might feel the same way. One evening, while walking on the street outside the campus walls, I decided to try some of the lamb skewers being barbecued over open charcoal fires built in small tin boxes on stilts. Most of the people tending the open-air fast food stands were Uighur Moslems or Tibetans, in from the countryside, and they seasoned the lamb with lots of pepper. I tried to stop the "cooker" from sprinkling my chosen piece of lamb with pepper, but I was too late. I took a bite anyway, and choking and sputtering, rushed over to the stand selling orangeade. A young man, standing nearby, commiserated with me, using very good English.

"Oh," I said, after getting my breath back, "thank you for your concern. You speak very good English. Are you a student at Lanzhou University?"

"No," he said, "I'm a worker. I work at the post office." He emphasized the word "worker" in such a way as to convey pride in separating himself from "students." In replying to my question as to how he had learned his English, he said that he watched the BBC production, "Follow Me" every Sunday, and did all the exercises that the program advised.

Walking back to my rooms about nine that evening, I was thinking about the young man I had just met. I noticed that the lights were on in the Foreign Language Building, and the classrooms were full of students. I found out later that they were "continuing education" students—workers who hadn't passed qualifying examinations for entrance into universities or persons who hadn't graduated from high school for one reason or another. Many of my graduate students taught in those classes at night, and they described their students in much the same way as Adult School teachers in California described their students. "They're tired, since they come after work; it's hard to teach them. The groups are mixed; there is a spread of ages and abilities; but they are very earnest and they want to learn."

I thought about those eager students, attending classes in English, Russian, Japanese, mathematics, engineering, Chinese language and history. The fees were low, and my graduate students made extra money by teaching them. I also thought about the attitude of my Chinese students in general toward the learning of English, and of how they differed from students in Korea and Japan. The character for China means "center of the universe," and my Chinese students had a sense of pride and inner security I did not encounter in the other Asian countries. The South Koreans and the Japanese students were defensive; they seemed to operate from a sense of aggrieved inferiority; the Chinese had none of that. Secure in themselves, if they needed to learn French, they learned French; if they needed to learn Russian, they learned Russian. They knew how solidly Chinese they were; learning another language was simply another way to survive successfully.

Chen Yu, my librarian with a remarkable intellect, became the most important part of my life at Lanzhou. Whenever I had a problem of any kind, I turned to Chen. The time was October, and the weather was very cold, but the heat in the Residence Hall wouldn't be turned on until November 15, no matter what the temperature was. The weather was "unusual," I was told; it wasn't usually so cold in October. Nevertheless, since we had to sit bundled up in blankets and coats in our rooms, I decided I would try to buy a heater, and I asked Chen to help me go shopping that Saturday.

Heaters were expensive, and we went from shop to shop looking for one. We'd go into a store with a heater displayed on a shelf, and we would ask to see it. "That one," I would say, and Chen would translate. The clerk would shake her head.

"Why not?" I asked.

"It doesn't work," said Chen. I asked him why it was on display if it didn't work. He asked the clerk and then explained. "She says that if she took it off the shelf, the shelf would be empty, and it wouldn't look good."

In other stores we went into, the clerk simply said, "Mei yo," which simply means, "don't have," and is a polite way of saying no.

We finally found a heater that cost more than a month's salary for most Chinese, and cost me about one-quarter of my monthly salary. It had a fan, a humidifier, and an air purifier. I found an extension "box" with outlets, located wire for it, and came back to the campus just in time for dinner. Chen came back on Sunday and found an electrician on campus to wire the box for me. *I was so lucky to have Chen Yu as my interpreter, intermediary and all around good friend. I shudder to think what my existence in China would have been like without him.*

China, Part III:
Travels, 1985–86

⤺

O NE OF THE REASONS I WANTED TO GO TO LANZHOU was because of its proximity to the Dunhuang caves. Human imprint, as registered on the walls of ancient caves has always fascinated me; I had toured such places in Spain and France; now here was a chance to explore China. When I was in Japan and Korea, I observed how much of the art in the temples, and even of the design of the temples was connected to China; how the Chinese written language was the core of both Japanese and Korean literature, and I knew that somehow I had to go to China. China was the source of so much of Asian painting, poetry, architecture, and social structure that I felt an irresistible pull. I also knew about the influence of India on the practice of Taoism and Buddhism, but somehow the pull of China was stronger. When I was invited to teach at Lanzhou, thanks to the recommendation of my friend, Professor Tippy Schwabe, I jumped at the chance to visit the caves at Dunhuang.

At sixty-seven, I was full of curiosity, enthusiasm, and confidence. I was eager to go to what I considered the "source" of much of the Temple art I had seen in South Korea and Japan, even though I knew that much of Asian art and history came from India. One of the professors I had met in Korea had told me that "India will chew you up and spit you out," and somehow I felt that China would not do that.

Finally getting to the caves at Dunhuang, I came across empty spaces from which those artifacts and bits of sculpture had been taken, and I felt violated. The Chinese art I had looked at in so many museums had been ripped out of sections of caves at Dunhuang and Luoyang. I realized how monks had labored for years to carve the Buddhas and Bodhisattvas out of the limestone that forms the caves. *After I got home, I found it hard to go to the Asian Art Museum again and look at all the lovely statues, the hands and heads, seeing instead the empty spaces from which they came.*

In order to get to Dunhuang, Jennifer Nathan (one of the people from Australia) and I took a train from Lanzhou to Daheyon, where we visited the Altsana Graves tombs, and then traveled to Liuyuan, where we needed to transfer to a bus for Dunhuang. Sitting in the dusty waiting room of this town, I observed a group of Kazakh people who had just come off the desert. There were six people in that group: an old man, an old woman, a young man and woman, and two children, a boy and a girl.

The old man, his face and skin burned into leather, with a yellowed, gap-toothed mouth, looked like one of the corpses I had just seen in the Altsana Graves tombs. He was thin, the skin on his face clinging to the bony contours, and a thick kerchief covered most of his head. He looked at me, his eyes fixed upon my face, his jaws moving slightly, and I returned his gaze. It was almost as if we were trying to "read" each other.

The old woman, who could have been his wife, was swathed in cloth layers, her feet encased in tennis shoes. She sat impassively next to the old man, dozing from time to time. The daughter (or daughter-in-law) looked ill, worn, and sad. She lay on the bus station bench, her eyes vacant. The son (or son-in-law), wearing army boots, green army fatigues, and a bulky, padded green army jacket, paced up and down, smoking. He paid no attention to the others in the group, although occasionally he said something to the old man.

The children, a boy and girl, dressed in cast-off clothes which hung on them loosely, their hair matted with dirt, slouched on the floor near the old people. The girl's eyes were rheumy and watery, and she hung on to her grandmother's skirt, occasionally shoving her dirty fist into her mouth. The boy had a tubercular cough, and he was restless, getting up to run back and forth between his father and his grandfather. When he occasionally ventured as far as the door of the waiting room, his father barked at him, and he scurried back.

Their bundles included rugs, a saddle, and what looked like a wooden cistern cover. The saddle was beautiful. It had a carved silver pommel and silver decoration on the sides. I wondered if they were taking it to a market to sell, or if they had just acquired it. The cistern cover was obviously a very important possession. The boy would go over and pat it from time to time.

As I gazed at them, I couldn't resist creating this fantasy of their relationship, and I kept wondering where they came from and where they were going. In my mind's eye, I could see them plodding across the desert, on horseback, buffeted by the wind, whipped by sand and dust, just as their people had done for centuries. What was the story of the man in army fatigues? I drifted into a possible story during the long wait for the bus.

The morning sun filtered through the dusty haze that covered the area, and more and more Chinese travelers began to arrive. Jennifer and I were the only Westerners waiting to catch the bus to Dunhuang. Standing at the doorway of the waiting room, looking out, I noticed a group of people gathered around a man who was obviously selling something. He was demonstrating a homemade potato peeler! His gestures and spiel (although I couldn't understand a word he said) seemed to be the same as demonstrators of potato peelers in stores throughout the United States. I could hear the cadence of the seller's voice as he demonstrated how deftly and quickly he could peel potatoes, carrots, turnips and how he could also shred onions with his magical tool. I pushed my way through the crowd, and gesturing with my camera, asked if I could photograph him demonstrating his peeler. This was a traveling crowd; good-natured and obliging. First I bought a peeler, and then I photographed him.

My remarkable purchase was a piece of wood, about two and one-half inches long by one and one-half inches wide, with a thin strip of metal nailed to each end. The iron strip had been crudely cut and sharpened, and one end was bent at a slightly different angle from the other. I picked up a potato and tried to use it the way the seller had demonstrated. It worked! I was delighted, and so were several women who were clustered around me. They also bought one. *So I guess I became a kind of shill!* The seller beamed at me, and I beamed at him, and bought another one.

Jennifer thought I was quite mad, but when I got back to my rooms at Lanzhou, and showed everybody how ingenious my special tool was, I felt validated. For me, it was almost as if I had crossed a bridge across time. Here was an example of rural people adapting to the limitations of their lives, using whatever was available to solve a simple problem. It was another demonstration of human ingenuity and interaction through time. There will always be tool inventors, sellers, and buyers.

The bus arrived, and the Kazakh family piled their luggage, saddle, rugs, cistern cover on top of the bus, lovingly lashing it all down. The young father (as I thought of him), stayed on top to make doubly sure their stuff was safe. Several other passengers arrived with assorted bundles and baskets and pieces of furniture, all of which had to be loaded on top before we could leave.

The benches inside the bus were hard and the bus was full. I rolled up my Marco Polo coat and sat on it, but it didn't help much. The trip took three and a half hours on a road of coarsely ground gravel and cinders. Every time we hit a rough spot (and there were many) I bounced up to the top of the bus, and flopped down hard again. I began to brace myself as if I were on a horse, suspending my rear end slightly above the hard seat, and hanging on to the back of the s eat in front of me. It was hot, but when I opened the window, even slightly, I could feel the dust settling on my face and could taste it in my mouth.

We stumbled off the bus in front of the Dunhuang hotel gratefully, and were partly revived by a good dinner and a fairly good bed. We went out to the Magao caves the next morning. Dunhuang is on the old Silk Road to the Middle East; in fact, Lanzhou was an important stopping place on that route. Caravans leaving China traveled up the Gansu corridor to Dunhuang; the Yumen Pass (*Yu* = west, *men* = gate) was the starting point of the road which ran across the north of what is now Xinjiang province, of which Urumqi is the capital.

The Magao caves were the most exciting thing about Dunhuang, and they are one of the highlights of northwest China. It was a powerful experience for me, coming face to face with the living evidence of thousands of years of culture, dedication, as well as of plunder and destruction. I felt part of a continuum of humanity, of a connection between me and the artists who carved the sculptures and created the paintings on the walls of the caves. They reflected their world, as artists do. Here was additional evidence of my conviction that artists and poets are the true historians of human existence.

Several caves impressed me deeply. Cave 156 was created in the Tang dynasty (618–907 A.C.E). The wall mural in that cave showed a Tang army on the march. Only ten people at a time were allowed into the cave, and as I stood there in the cool quiet, I felt the wind whipping the flags, could hear the horses' hooves pounding the dirt, and was awed by the sharp, clear colors.

Another cave, created in the Northern Song dynasty (960-1127), was a landscape depicting the terrain, cities, towns, bridges, roads, temples, and travelers. They seemed to be traveling on a sacred Buddhist mountain, Wutai Shan. I looked at the mural closely, and took note of the loving detail with which the artist rendered the intricacies of the clothing, the shoes, the baggage, and the faces of the travelers. I seemed to fall into the landscape and could easily have been one of the travelers.

There was one other cave I will never forget. Meticulously rendered calligraphy describing different herbs and their uses for treatment of disease covered the walls and ceiling. I found out later that Japanese photographers had gotten permission to photograph those walls, and the reproductions filled twelve volumes. A library in Dunhuang contained the original photographs, although the Japanese were allowed to make copies to take back with them to Japan.

The trip back to Lanzhou, this time by plane, was predictably unpredictable. The public bus arrived on schedule, and since one of the passengers turned out to be an employee of CAAC, I was reasonably assured that it was the right bus, and that we would get to the airport on time. The plane was supposed to take off at three-thirty p.m. for the two-hour flight to Lanzhou. However, it didn't arrive until four p.m., and everyone queued up for the security check. The officials were extremely thorough. They opened everything and examined each bag diligently. They confiscated my trusty pocketknife, which was in my small backpack, and gave me a receipt for its retrieval at the other end. We finally took off at five-thirty, the time we were supposed to land at Lanzhou, and settled ourselves as comfortably as we could in the small, Russian-built plane.

Twenty minutes later, we touched down at Jiauguan, and all of the Westerners on board looked at each other in surprise. This was supposed to be a nonstop flight. The crew emerged from the cockpit, and the chief pilot, with a grin, rubbed his stomach, and said "Dinner."

The crew marched into the dining room, and we passengers sat down wearily in the waiting room. A uniformed Chinese woman appeared and waved us into a corner of the dining room, motioning us to a section separated from the crew. At first we thought we were being treated to dinner courtesy of Chinese Airlines, but it turned out that we were billed for a mediocre dinner as if we were at a first-class hotel in Beijing.

Arriving at Lanzhou at nine-thirty, we were relieved to see Chen Xi Long and Mrs. Song waiting for us with the van. *How little it takes to establish a feeling of home!*

We had plenty of opportunities to take short trips into the countryside around Lanzhou on the weekends, and I decided to take advantage of all of them. Jennifer, the one person from Australia with whom I felt comfortable, joined me on most of my trips. Jennifer came from Sydney, and although there was twenty years between us, we developed a kinship and close friendship that sustained me during the China experience.

Lanzhou is on the edge of the Gobi desert, and it is also the railroad station that is connected to Tibet. I had heard that Xining was an authentic Tibetan town even though it was in the province of Gansu within China. Jennifer, my colleague from Australia, wanted to visit this town with me. We were both interested in the ethnic minorities of China and we shared an interest in Chinese art and literature. She was studying calligraphy and Chinese. We found out that there was an ancient monastery in Xining, Ta'er, which offered overnight accommodations for foreign travelers. We decided to go, and prepared for a long weekend.

We prepared food for our six-hour train trip: hard boiled eggs, dried apricots, cookies, powdered soup, and noodles. Members of the Chinese staff at the compound were worried about us, clucking over us like anxious mothers. They assured us we would get boiled water to use for our soup and to drink, and they kept urging us to take more sweaters and extra socks.

The train to Xining was powered by steam, huffing and puffing its slow way, stopping at all the local stations, often pulling aside, breathing impatiently as it waited for faster trains to whiz by. It was the emptiest, most silent train I was in during the many train trips I took in China. Our car was peopled with train workers, train conductors, and three paying passengers—Jennifer, me, and one silent man who sat off by himself, staring out the dirty window. The padded seats were covered with dirty white covers, and the little fixed tables between the four seats, attached to the window ledge, were covered with greasy, spotted cloths.

As we plodded slowly through a dusty, sunless winter landscape, I fell into a dreamy reverie, as if I were in a surrealist film, especially because the train was warm and silent. We saw sharp, high, dry mountains rising from plowed fields full of cabbages, and at the base of many of the mountains we observed concrete lined irrigation ditches. Occasionally a donkey pulling a plow appeared, a few trucks on the dusty road running alongside the train tracks, but otherwise there was no traffic.

Since this was a coal-burning steam train, various workers with shovels and sooty gloves passed through our car, and we watched with amusement an interaction between two workmen. A worker in a blue uniform stretched himself out on the seat opposite us with his cap pulled down over his face. Another blue clad worker stopped next to him and poked him, argued with him, trying to thrust the shovel into his hands. Our recumbent neighbor refused to move, and shoved his cap farther down onto his face. Finally, the man with the shovel gave a disgusted shrug and left. Our relaxed worker sat up slowly, lit a cigarette, and threw the still lit match onto the floor. It seemed to us that he had successfully dodged his shift. *I puzzled over this display of independence.*

We got to Xining about three in the afternoon and immediately checked out the monastery. The monks were surprised to see us; there were no other foreign travelers at that time, but they agreed to rent us a room. We assured them that we had plenty of warm clothing with us, and they still looked dubious. *Ah! The self-assured delusion of novices! We had no idea what we were in for. And that was just as well.* We made arrangements for coal to be delivered to our room, for we had noticed a small stove in one corner. Our room contained six beds; we dumped our sleeping bags and clothes on two of the beds, and set out to explore the town.

As we walked down the hill, we noticed the faithful followers of the Tibetan religion, bowing before the pillared tombs of their priests, kissing the stone and touching their foreheads to it. I watched the women prostrating themselves in the dust, making their slow progress down the hillside to the place of the towers near the market-place. They took a step, threw themselves on the ground, prostrate, full length. Then they got up, took another step, and repeated the process.

What if I had been born into this society? Would I be doing that too? Or would I be one of the sellers in the booths, or a trader, or a stringer of beads? I think I would be a stringer of beads, or a carver of silver bracelets, and perhaps I would be a trader, selling my own work and that of others, bargaining in the market and shopping for materials for my craft. I wouldn't be an acolyte, my faithful face down in the dust.

In the bazaar, I stood in a shop, looking over a collection of coral and turquoise beads. As I hovered over the beads in the palm of my left hand, a bony finger pointed to several of the stones. I looked up and caught a smile, a knowing look on the face of one of the older women in a group of Tibetan women watching me. She nodded, and then to make sure I understood, reached over and pushed aside the beads she thought weren't very good. She was the elder of the group, which included several young women carrying babies on their hips, wrapped in shawls. I quickly scooped up another handful of beads, and held them out for her inspection. She was delighted to offer advice, and quickly sorted them for me. When I laid my chosen ones on the counter and began to bargain for them, she and the other women discreetly withdrew, in order not to jeopardize their standing with the seller. As soon as I left the stall, they all crowded around the counter again.

I met this woman again, later in the day, at another booth. This time I was looking at a variety of beads from all over the world—Italian cloisonné, Venetian glass, turquoise, bone, and coral. I was idly arranging them in a pattern, trying to see how I might string them myself. She settled herself comfortably next to me, looked at what I was doing, and reached over to rearrange my pattern. Her design was a vast improvement over mine. We grinned at each other in silent understanding—one bead-stringer to another. I pointed to her necklace; it was a work of art. I asked her, pointing to my camera, if I might take a photograph. She recognized the Polaroid, and as soon as I positioned it, five or six other people materialized behind her. After giving her the print, I motioned to my Minolta, and raised my eyebrows in a question. She nodded and I took a photograph of her for my collection.

The entire encounter was a warming experience. I had the lovely feeling of reaching across centuries and cultures, making a connection with a stranger on the basis of shared values when it came to beads and design and art.

After eating a rather strange meal (to us) of barbecued lamb, yak tea, and rice, we went back to the monastery compound. In our room, it was getting very, very cold, so we stripped the other beds of their mattresses and comforters, and piled them onto two of the beds closest to the stove. We crawled into the beds with most of our clothes on and yet the cold seeped in. So we bravely got up, put on another layer of clothes, our boots, heavy coats, and gloves, and set out to see the town under a full moon. But we couldn't get out of the compound. We wandered around, slipping and sliding on the icy ground, and made our way to the latrine. The silence was deafening. No wolves or dogs howling. No nothing. We found ourselves talking in whispers. So we made our way back to our room and climbed back into bed. It was only eight-thirty at night, and neither of us could sleep, so we played twenty questions until we fell asleep. Both of us slept with hats and gloves.

In the morning, we awoke with feet and hands thawed out, and we walked down to the town square where we boarded a bus that would take us back to the train station. We had bought "soft seats" on this train, which was destined for Shanghai, and we had a compartment to ourselves, so we were able to stretch out and relax. Jennifer had caught cold, and I was so stiff I could barely move.

After we got back to Lanzhou, my left hip was aching so badly that I hobbled over to the clinic, and Dr. Wang gave me an electronic treatment. I sat in a small room with other patients, all Chinese, holding metal gadgets on various parts of their bodies—hips, shoulders, knees, elbows. They all looked at me curiously, and Dr. Wang explained who I was. I noticed that all the patients had removed anything metallic; wristwatches, belts with metal buckles, for example, and I did the same. We clucked and nodded to each other. I positioned the curved metal device on my hip, and Dr. Wang turned the current on. I felt an electric current coursing through my hip, and the vibrations went through the hip and down my leg. Then Dr. Wang disconnected me, and I hobbled back to the dormitory.

When I went back for further treatments, I felt reassured that I was with a group in a clinic who were all in various degrees of pain, and I got over my initial panic. After two more days of treatment, by the fourth day, I was able to move without pain, and by the end of the week felt completely well. I thought this was pretty miraculous. Dr. Wang was very solicitous, and gave me massage, acupuncture, plus special thorns which he put in my ears. I was to press on those thorns when I felt pain in my hip. Everything worked.

Back at Lanzhou, Chen Yu, the most brilliant student in the class, told me he had won a scholarship from the British Broadcasting Corporation to come to London for a special six-week program, but the Chinese government had stalled and stalled over granting him a visa until the invitation expired. The grant had come with a stipend of three hundred pounds, to cover airplane travel via British Airways and miscellaneous expenses in London. All basic expenses would be paid by BBC once Chen got there.

Chen was distraught, and I decided to write to former Prime Minister Brian Heath about Chen Yu's case. I told him about Chen, about his translations of a famous British writer of detective fiction, and about what a remarkable person Chen was. I also said that I felt that somewhere in the United Kingdom, some person or persons ought to be able to come up with the three hundred pounds to get Chen to London.

Well! Brian Heath wrote back and said he was sending a letter of credit to the China Exchange Bank, so that Chen could take advantage of the scholarship offer, even though the time had expired. Unfortunately, the bank wouldn't release the money in Foreign Exchange Certificates, so Chen couldn't buy a ticket on British Airways. After a great deal of effort, and many trips to Beijing, he finally managed to get the money released, and he set off for London. He bought a ticket from Beijing to Moscow with renminbi, exchanged money in Moscow, and with rubles bought a ticket to Berlin, where he exchanged the rubles for marks, which he used to buy an airplane ticket to London! His persistence paid off, and he had a wonderful time in London.

Later, after I got back to the States, I helped Chen get a fellowship to the University of Washington, where he pursued a Master's Degree in English, writing his thesis on William Faulkner. Chen is now Mike Chen, an entrepreneur, with a cell phone, e-mail, and all the appurtenances of a big executive, and he is part of my extended family.

In China, Chen helped me plan my vacation time. My contract with Lanzhou was up in January 1986, and the Chinese government had awarded me a month's salary (in renminbi) to travel around China, and I took advantage of it. We arranged for me to travel to different parts of China where different students lived, and as I went from place to place, by train, bus, or ship, I was met by students and taken home with them. Each student sent a telegram to the next one with the words, "Curtis is coming!" and a small delegation met me on platforms, at bus stations or docks. It was a lovely experience. Each stop turned into a miniature teaching session, with elaborate dinners, and a variety of sleeping quarters.

I came back to Berkeley in February 1986 psychologically, spiritually, and emotionally enriched. When colleagues at conferences asked me, "How was China?" all I could say was, "It was interesting," while all sorts of images surged through my brain.

The Rocking Chair (1990)

Rhoda and Peter

Peter

Rhoda 2007

Chapter Forty:

Peter

⌒

ETURNING TO BERKELEY IN 1986, I was swallowed up in work. I found myself teaching several courses at UC Berkeley Extension in the Certificate TESOL program. I taught Methods and Materials, Cross Cultural Communication, Teaching Pronunciation, and the Practicum. Gradually we recruited enough qualified teachers so that I could let go of some of the classes. Many of the students in my classes went on to become stars in the world of TESOL. Some of them became administrators in various community college programs, and in later years, I found myself employed by one of them as a consultant. *What a sense of satisfaction I had! Imagine! Being employed by a former student! What a triumph of teaching.*

In the meantime, I was eager to share some of the insights I had gained teaching in Japan, Korea, and China, and busily wrote proposals for presentations at local and international conferences. Happily, most of them were successful, and for the next four years I bounced around the country doing presentations and teacher-training workshops. Then, in 1990, during a presentation at a TESOL conference in San Francisco, I made a connection with Peter Meilleur, and that changed my life again.

It all happened because of a meeting during that conference between Peter's son, Raoul, and me. I had known Raoul since 1980 through meetings at professional conferences. Raoul was a book publisher's representative when I first met him, and now he was head of the English department of a community college in Bellevue, Washington. He was a charming redhead with a lot of good stories to tell. We had an easygoing relationship, especially since I had bought classroom sets of many of the books he was selling. We had breakfast together on the last day of the conference.

"You're looking great, Rhoda," said Raoul. "Anything exciting going on in your life?"

"Not really," I replied. "I've just had my seventy-second birthday, and I'm tired of being alone. I'm thinking of putting an ad in the *Bay Guardian* or the *Jewish Bulletin* for a traveling companion, male, of course."

"Oh," said Raoul after a thoughtful pause. "You should meet my father. He's eighty-five and quite active. He likes to travel, and he likes women. My mother died about six years ago, and I think he would like a companion."

"That's good. I like men," I said. "Is he committed to anyone?" I had had it up to my eyebrows with married or unmarried men looking for a short-term fling.

"Well, he has a girlfriend in Paris who lives on a boat on the Seine, but they fight all the time." I figured Paris was far enough away, so I might as well give Raoul my card. "Here's my card," I said. "That's my sumi ink drawing of a frog on it."

"Oh," he said. "My father's a watercolor painter, and quite good, too."

Hmmm. Better and better. "Ask him to call me. I'll be back on Monday."

"Don't hold your breath," warned Raoul. "He doesn't like answering machines."

"That's all right," I replied as I got up to leave. "I won't hold you responsible either way."

When I returned to Berkeley on Monday, Peter's message was on the answering machine.

"This is Peter Meilleur. My son gave me your telephone number and suggested I call you. I live in Santa Rosa. My number is 707-527-7792. I like sevens."

I called him, and we set up our meeting. "How will I know you?" I asked.

"I have gray hair, and I wear my glasses around my neck. I'll be carrying a letter-size portfolio under my arm."

"Okay," I said, "I have gray hair and I wear my glasses on my face. I'll be wearing a bright embroidered jacket from Thailand. I'll be in Novato in the morning, doing an observation of a teacher. How about twelve-thirty at the Marin County Office Building?" Peter was eighty-five and I was seventy-two. I didn't know when I pulled into the County Office Building complex promptly at twelve-thirty that I was beginning one of the most companionable, sexually satisfying eight years of my life.

Standing on the steps of the Frank Lloyd Wright building, I saw a medium-sized, gray-haired man wearing a cashmere pullover, glasses hanging on a string around his neck, a letter-size portfolio under his arm, and an expectant look on his face. He was handsome, and his mouth turned up at the corners.

We went into the complex, joined the cafeteria line, and sat down at a quiet table for lunch. Peter began to talk. He opened his briefcase, pulled out some photographs, and began to tell me the story of his life. I was so fascinated that I didn't interrupt him, except for a few questions, for the next two and a half hours. It was easy to slip into a listening mode, a style I had developed over years of doing oral interviews and teaching. Peter had brought photographs of his family and himself, and told me the whole story of his family's emigration to the United States in 1908, three years after his birth. I realized that he was establishing who he was, in the French manner, letting me know his background, clarifying his status and his frames of reference.

"I have four nationalities," he said, his blue eyes twinkling. "I was born in Switzerland. Times were bad in Meribel, France, where my parents came from, and my father, who was a baker, moved my mother and my three brothers to a small town in Switzerland, just across the border from France. That's why I was named Peter Ludwig instead of Pierre Louis! So I have both French and Swiss citizenship. Then we came to the United States—to Plainsville, Kansas, from the Swiss Alps, when I was three years old. We lived in Plainsville for a few years, but not long enough for my parents to become citizens. Plainsville burned down and we moved to Vancouver, Canada, where my parents, and therefore I and my brothers, acquired Canadian citizenship!"

He paused, and I jumped in with a question. "You said you had four nationalities, and you've accounted for three of them. Did you stay in Vancouver?"

"Ah," said Peter. "That's the next part of the story. My father died at fifty, and all my brothers died by the age of forty. I didn't expect to live this long. I guess I inherited my mother's genes." He stopped, took a sip of his coffee, and continued. "My mother and I moved to Seattle, and I went to work for an advertising agency. The year was 1942, and I didn't think I would get drafted, since I was thirty-seven years old, but I remember thinking, *what if I do get drafted?* I remember standing on a street corner in Seattle. To my left, down the block, was the recruiting office for the Canadian army; to my right, was the office for the United States Army. I knew that if I went to the right, I would get instant citizenship in the United States, and I thought, that's a good idea, so I went to the right. It was a good decision; it changed my life."

I looked at my watch. It was almost three o'clock, and I knew I had to get on the freeway before four, or I would hit bumper-to-bumper traffic across the bridge to Berkeley. Peter saw me looking at my watch, and immediately leaped to his feet.

"Would you like to come to dinner tonight? I have a two-bedroom condominium in Santa Rosa, and each bedroom has its own separate bathroom. You could stay overnight." He was quite sincere, and I'm sure he wasn't aware of how his invitation sounded.

I laughed. "Sorry, Peter," I said. "I have to teach tonight. Maybe some weekend." As we walked out to the parking lot, he asked, "Do you play chess?"

"Yes," I answered, "but not very well."

He grinned, gave me a quick kiss on the cheek, and trotted off to his car. He almost kicked his heels in the air. I looked back at him and felt delight and warmth surge over me. It was odd. On one hand, I was pessimistic about meeting anyone exciting at my age, and on the other hand, I was still hopeful that companionship was possible. I went to Santa Rosa the following weekend, and on the drive up, kept trying to smother my excited anticipation.

As I walked into Peter's condominium, the first thing I noticed was an antique clock spread out in pieces on the coffee table in his combination dining and living room.

"I'm a collector of clocks," Peter said, "and I like to take them apart and repair them."

That was the understatement of the week. There were clocks all over the place—not just three-hundred-year-old chiming, pendulum clocks, but marble and onyx mantel clocks. Every kind of clock except cuckoo clocks. Peter had no use for cuckoo clocks...they were toys, he said.

There were also many very good paintings on the walls, and I discovered they were all Peter's watercolors. There were Mexican masks and pre-Columbian artifacts. As we walked around the room, Peter told me about the watercolors and the paintings. He was self-effacing about the paintings. He said they were "just sketches." They didn't look like sketches to me; they were full of movement and life.

He showed me the bedrooms and the bathrooms. There were paintings, sculpture, books, everywhere. I was entranced as one aspect of Peter's life after another unfolded; each one connecting to a period of my own. I too had spent a lot of time in Mexico and collected fabric as well as pottery; had made jewelry; had done some sketching; and I loved to read. I found echoes of my own taste in some of Peter's books, and felt more and more drawn to him.

Peter invited me to explore his garage, which was really his workroom. It was full of tools, two and maybe three of everything: hammers, files, pliers, clock parts, an acetylene tank, and even two bicycles hanging from the ceiling. There was a place for everything, and everything was in it.

I realized that Peter was really a serious collector. He loved garage sales and thrift stores, and he loved to fix things. He couldn't resist a bargain. We came back to his living room combination dining room, and I collapsed on his leather couch.

"Just relax," he said. "I've already prepared dinner. Chicken livers in wine, with rice and broccoli. I don't drink, but I like to use wine in cooking. How does that sound?"

"It sounds fantastic! Do I have to do anything?" *I couldn't believe my good luck. An intelligent, artistic man, who also liked to cook!*

"No, just relax," he said. "Dinner will be ready in about ten minutes."

Something strange was happening to my insides. A man who didn't drink, who liked to cook, who had an organized, positive outlook on life, who was not married, who seemed to be going out of his way to be hospitable—could this really be happening to me? I accepted the glass of wine he offered me, being careful to avoid the clock parts on the table in front of me.

Dinner was delicious, and we played Scrabble after dinner on the dining room table. I slept well in the guest bedroom, and in the morning, after breakfast, we decided to go to Bodega Bay for the art show celebrating Earth Day.

We examined the art pieces critically, and in the craft section, I spotted a handmade walnut rocker, so beautifully shaped and crafted that it looked like a human figure. I sat in it and sighed. It fit the curvature of my spine as if it had been made for me. I inquired about the price. It was thirty-five-hundred dollars. I swallowed, smiled, stroked the lovely curved arms of the rocker and turned away, regretfully.

I couldn't get that rocker out of my mind. When we got back to Santa Rosa, I mentioned to Peter how I yearned for that rocker.

"You should buy it," he said.

I protested that I couldn't, that I had just put a down payment on a trip to Russia, and that the cost of the trip was exactly the cost of the rocker. Peter gave me a long look, and said, "You can always go to Russia, and I'll go with you. Call him up and make him an offer."

How could I resist such a suggestion? I called the artist immediately and told him I'd fallen in love with his rocker. He was delighted, of course, and said that it was mine.

"Not so fast," I said. "How would it be if I gave you five hundred dollars down and one hundred dollars a month for three years? Would you accept that?"

The artist didn't hesitate a minute. He said yes, and offered to deliver it to Berkeley. I couldn't believe it. I hung up, and jumped up and down. "I did it! I did it!" I yelled, and threw my arms around Peter to give him a big hug. Peter grabbed me closer and gave me a big, open-mouth kiss, his tongue exploring my mouth. He moved his head back, and gave me a long look. "Let's go to bed," he said.

"Why not?" I said. It was only eleven a.m. We walked hand in hand into his bedroom. Peter's lovemaking was stunningly marvelous.

Later, as I walked around the apartment in a happy daze, I realized that Peter collected more things than electric irons, toaster ovens, and clocks. He also collected shoes and cashmere sweaters and well-made tweed jackets, all of them previously owned. At some point in our relationship I persuaded him to part with some of his collection of clothes to give to homeless people in San Francisco. I remember we covered his big double bed with shoes, sandals, and boots and there was still barely enough room in his closet for my shoes.

Peter liked to read before falling asleep, and I did too. I took a look at the books on his bedside table. In addition to books on travel and philosophy, there were also two books dealing with human sexuality. I asked him about them.

"I've always been interested in the why of everything," he said. "I want to know the difference between how men and women react to each other. This book on erotic zones of both women and men was fascinating. Did you know that our fingertips are extremely sensitive?" He picked up my hand and kissed each finger, lingering over each one.

We had a lovely day and night, and as I drove back to Berkeley the following day, I felt as if my car—and I—were floating three feet off the ground. We agreed that he would come to Berkeley the following weekend.

When I got home, I looked around my four-hundred-square-foot space; every corner economically used, and took a hard look at my narrow twin bed. *Oh, well, I have a large futon in the laundry room; maybe we can use that on my Chinese carpet.* I had created my living space on what had been the patio of my four-bedroom, two-bath Berkeley house when I first went to Korea. I rented the main house, and built the apartment for myself. It was designed as a solar greenhouse, with a wall of windows looking out onto the garden. The garden was long and deep, with a natural pond fed by four springs, and there was a thriving naval orange tree, a Meyer lemon tree, an apple tree, and blackberries. There was a waterfall, pouring over stones into the pond, which was filled with water lilies and Japanese koi. I looked upon the garden as my real living room.

My narrow rectangular space had two doors to the outside, one on the west side, opening onto a small patio, with steps up to the carport, and one on the east side, opening to more steps leading down to the garden. My desk was on the west side of the room, with bookshelves above it, and it contained my computer plus my telephone and miscellaneous penholders. Next to the desk, there was a small file cabinet, and next to that the handmade Korean chest/desk I had brought home from Seoul. Along the wall facing the windows was a couch, a small TV set, bookshelves, and paintings above the couch. I had a beautiful, handmade walnut coffee table in front of the couch. Scattered around the room were big, comfortable pillows and two armchairs.

The east side of the room had another door, and in the space next to the door, I had installed a Japanese rectangular wooden hot tub, complete with a small, thermostatically controlled hot water heater. It was a lovely arrangement. I could soak in my hot tub, and gaze at the full moon through my floor-to-ceiling windows while listening to symphonic music.

Three steps up from the main room led to a small, compact kitchen, about the size one would have on a boat or a trailer. It was enough for my needs. A small four-burner stove with oven, a counter with shelves underneath, and a full-size refrigerator. Two folding doors led to a compact dressing room with shower, toilet, and closet for my clothes. I also had built-in shelves for dishes. There were other built-in shelves over the sink in the kitchen area for glasses and spices.

The entire space was compact and efficient. I didn't have room to accumulate anything, even though I had what I called my "don't-know-where-else-to-put-this-stuff" room leading off the bathroom, into what had been part of the basement. That was where I stored the books and reference materials I used in teaching, the sewing machine I had used in my leather business, and clothes for different seasons. I wondered what Peter would make of my economical living space.

Peter arrived at the east door of my apartment, having parked on the street, and walked down the winding steps past the garbage cans to my door. His smiling face lit up the room as he put down his suitcase.

"So this is where you live," he said. "Well, it's certainly compact! Where do you sleep?"

I indicated the narrow twin bed, perpendicular to the couch. "But I have a double-bed-size futon in the basement," I hurried to add. "We can pull that out and sleep on the rug."

"Oh, no," said Peter. "That twin bed will do fine. I don't turn and toss when I sleep." He turned and went out into the garden. I watched him go and smiled. *This is going to be interesting!*

That was the beginning of eight deliriously wonderful years. Since Peter lived happily in Santa Rosa with his clocks and his collections of toaster ovens, electronic typewriters, and sewing machines, all in various stages of disrepair, and I lived happily in my spare four hundred square feet in the back of my big house in Berkeley, there really wasn't room in our separate abodes for both of us. Actually, I liked the fact that we had separate residences. We spent half the week in Santa Rosa, and half the week in Berkeley. We planted beans, corn, tomatoes, and lettuce in the garden; we went to Repertory Theater in Berkeley and in Santa Rosa. Peter painted, I wrote stories, we swam every day, and we made love deeply and often.

Peter was a wonderful traveling companion. He was interested in everything, as I was, and insisted on trying to interact with everybody. We went to visit Peter's son Brien in Hawaii and his son Raoul in Seattle in 1990, to Greece and Turkey in 1991, to Mexico in 1992, to Russia and Hungary in 1993, and then to France in 1995. We stayed with friends and former students of mine most of the places we went to, so our living conditions were comfortable. And we took long walks, swimming in local pools or lakes or rivers whenever we could.

Peter was the love of my life. Our lovemaking was so deep and so profound that he often said that he couldn't believe what was happening to him at this stage of his life. He often groaned in sheer agonized joy as he came to climax. His lovemaking was so gentle and complete that I managed to have an orgasm every time he did.

We were friends as well as lovers. We loved playing Scrabble, solving crossword puzzles, and talking about everything under the sun. There were no holds barred. Once, early on in our relationship, he made a remark about "your people," or "you people," meaning Jews, and I asked him, "Peter, did you imbibe anti-semitism with your mother's milk?" He thought for a moment, and then said, "Probably."

It was his openness and willingness to think deeply about his attitudes and prejudices that made me realize how important Peter was to me. He was the only man in my life who did not try to control me. He was the only man who appreciated me for who I was, with all my moods and extravagant ideas (which he tolerated with good humor), and who willingly took equal responsibility for the harmony of our life together.

Peter was quite determined, however, to stick to his physical regimen. He was used to getting up at six or six-thirty a.m., driving to the local swimming pool and swimming exactly eighteen laps in one-half hour, coming home, and eating breakfast. This was not my idea of how to start a day, any day, but I agreed to set the alarm and stagger off to the swimming pool with him. Returning home from our swim, and after breakfast, we went back to bed. Early morning sex and a good sleep afterward made up for that early morning rising.

Peter kept asking me if I wanted to get married during the eight years we spent together. I remember telling him my formula for marriage.

"There are three reasons for getting married, Peter," I told him, "and they all begin with the letter 'P.'" He looked at me quizzically, and I continued. "The first p is for Procreation, and it's too late for me—I don't know about you. The second p is for Property. I don't have any property; whatever I had belongs to my son and his wife, and I don't want any of yours. The third p is for Possession, and I have to tell you that I don't want to possess you, and if you try to possess me, you will choke on my dust."

I reached over, gave him a big kiss, and then I said, "However, I am committed to you for the rest of my life, and I hope you feel the same. Commitment is more important to me than marriage."

I have mentioned our extensive travels between 1990 and 1995, but I left out the details. The early trips to Seattle and Hawaii were designed to introduce me to Peter's family. I felt as if I were being presented for approval. Once the family visits were over, we began to travel for the love of it. In Mexico Peter got mixed up on zeroes—the difference between pesos and dollars, and went pale when a blouse he wanted to buy for me cost one hundred dollars instead of ten! After Mexico came Paris (working-class Paris and Peter's relatives), then Meribel, the French Alps, where his parents came from, and a pilgrimage to the Swiss town in which he was born. It was as if Peter wanted to share his life with me, rather than just tell me about it.

On another trip, we picked up Brien's Volvo in Meribel, and drove through Italy to Bari, where we took a ferry to Greece, then drove through the Greek Alps to Turkey, where I had friends. We celebrated Peter's eighty-sixth birthday on the ferry from Italy to Greece, where we were serenaded by the captain and crew. Peter was not the most careful driver in the world, and we got smashed on the Autostrada in Italy, bashing in the back of the Volvo. The car survived, so we continued our trip. We came back to Italy from Izmir by ferry, coming into Venice through an ancient waterway. What fun it was!

In 1993 we went to Russia, fulfilling Peter's promise to me the day we consummated our relationship in 1990. I did three teacher-training workshops at Moscow State University; we had ten days in St. Petersburg, spending several days at the Hermitage Museum, and then we went to Hungary, where I did a presentation at an International Conference for Teachers of English as a Foreign Language (IATEFL). Peter explained his presence to various people we met as the man who carries Rhoda's books.

Everywhere we went, Peter blended in with the locals. In Moscow, with his French beret, his green worker's coveralls with several pockets (which he'd bought at a flea market), and carrying a striped plastic shopping bag, he looked like a Muscovite. People would stop us and, looking at Peter, would ask him for directions. They looked betrayed when he shrugged and said, "Inglesi." He always lapsed into scrambled Italian or fluent French in foreign countries, while I fell into scrambled German or Spanish. None of it worked, of course, and especially not English.

After a long trip to France in 1995, where we stayed with friends in Fabrezan (near Carcassonne), we returned to our regular routine, swimming, walking, playing Scrabble. Our lives changed in February 1997, when I had a quadruple coronary bypass, and in August, when Peter had a small stroke. He was put on Coumadin, a blood thinner, and Peter's sons, Brien and Raoul, decided that Peter should move in with me permanently. They decided that Peter should sell the condo, and they also decided to sell his clock collection, along with his accumulation of tools and other equipment.

Suddenly Peter became dispossessed, stripped. On the day of the dispossession, Peter sat in the living room of his condo, his face gray, slumped in a chair, disconsolate over the loss of his beloved collections. Brien blithely tossed typewriters, toaster ovens, partially assembled coffee grinders, and other disabled mechanical devices into a truck, and drove off to the dump. The brothers argued over various pieces of antique furniture, while Peter and I sat silently, holding hands and mourned. We were both stunned, full of sorrow and disbelief.

Peter deteriorated rapidly after the move. Another stroke caused him to become blind on his left side, but he had become adjusted to the change in our lives. He never panicked, taking everything in stride, being mildly curious about what was happening. We tried to maintain a normal routine, but then Peter began to wander away while I was off teaching. He would go for a walk around our neighborhood and forget how to get back. We decided to move to an assisted living place in Oakland, called the *Altenheim*, in May 1998.

The *Altenheim*, meaning "old people's home," had been established by German Jewish families in the East Bay as a place for their parents to retire to. It was beautiful, resembling an elegant spa in Bavaria, and Peter kept asking me if we could afford to stay there, thinking we were on another of our European trips. I spent every evening and night with him, going off to Berkeley during the day, teaching my classes. We had two beautiful, light-filled rooms at the *Altenheim*, and I arranged to move Peter's bed, couch, and favorite antique chests to our rooms. We had his favorite Morbier chiming pendulum clock mounted on the wall, and we brought all his painting equipment. I'm sure that our practiced detachment was part of necessary denial for both of us. Peter's good nature and glass-is-half-full outlook on life didn't change.

One awful night at the end of June, he stood up from his chair and literally collapsed in my arms. I screamed and lowered him gently to the floor, then began pulling cords and pushing buttons in the room. The staff called 911, and when the paramedics arrived, they took him off to Alta Bates in a siren-shrieking ambulance while I followed in my car.

Against his wishes, Peter was put on life-support machines. He came out of his coma once, briefly, just to say goodbye. I couldn't do anything about the machines, because I was not his wife, and not legally connected to him. We had to wait until Raoul came from Seattle and gave the word to release him. Peter was finally allowed to die on July 2, 1998.

To Peter

We connected, you and I
from the first "Why Not?"
to the last "Hi, Sweetie,"
murmured through half-closed lips.

Then your eyes shut forever.

We gave each other love
and space to grow.
We gave each other love
and permission to change our minds about anything.

Laughter and shared sensuality
were the solid rocks of our relationship.

There is a hollow within me that memories cannot fill.

Epilogue, from 1998 to 2007

⤳

AFTER PETER DIED, I felt a piece of me had also died, and although I continued to teach my classes, I felt disconnected from the world around me. As I mentioned in the Introduction, I went to an intensive writing retreat in Oregon, called *The Flight of the Mind,* and there I took a class called "Landscape and Memory" with Judith Barrington. I learned to call myself a "writer."

I left the University of California Berkeley Extension TESOL Certificate Program in 2002, and went to Cal State University East Bay to design and conduct a TESOL workshop program, training foreign teachers to teach English in their own countries. Teaching invigorated me, and the drive to Hayward twice a week was an easy commute.

One evening in 2004, over dinner, a friend of long standing, David Eichorn, mentioned that he had been invited to show his handmade bread boards in a gallery in Berkeley. I had admired David's craftsmanship and artistry for many years, especially his weaving, his jewelry, and his photography. I decided immediately that viewers of his work at the gallery would be interested in how he made his beautiful boards, and therefore a video of him would be a good idea.

What I had in mind was an examination of "The Nature of the Creative Process," but I realized that would be an enormous endeavor, and yet a small examination of the procedure might satisfy me. We decided to call the video *The Making of a Cutting Board: From Process to Product*.

I wrote the storyboard and David and I planned the sequence of scenes we would shoot. We rented a digital camera from East Bay Media, and traveled around to the places David picked up his "found" wood. The men at Berkeley Mills, where David got a lot of his wood, were amused by his eighty-six-year-old Little-Old-Lady-in-tennis-shoes filmmaker. I filmed him in the studio and on location, and then we went to East Bay Media for editing. It was fun, and we emerged with a good twenty- minute video which he showed at the gallery opening in 2005.

I had been writing steadily by that time and much of the memoir was finished. I was ready for an editor, so I contacted Cathy Miller, the writing teacher I had first met in 1999. Cathy, a published writer and teacher of writing at San Jose State University, is also one of the founders of the Wild Writing Women. Cathy agreed to edit the manuscript.

I'm still teaching at California State University East Bay in Hayward. The book is finished, but I'm not. Now I can continue to work on other projects which were set aside; all the stories that were left out of the book; finish a play I started and set aside; rewrite a collection of poetry, self-published many years ago; sumi ink brush painting again. The future beckons, as always.

— Rhoda Curtis

Made in the USA
Lexington, KY
14 September 2011